REGULATION OF FINANCIAL INSTITUTIONS:

Selected Statutes, Regulations and Forms

By

Howell E. Jackson
Professor of Law
Harvard Law School

and

Edward L. Symons, Jr.
President, Dollins Symons Management, Inc.
(registered investment adviser)
Executive Vice President – Investments, Smithfield Trust Company
(state-chartered bank limited to trust powers)

AMERICAN CASEBOOK SERIES®

WEST GROUP

ST. PAUL, MINN., 1999

*TEXT IS PRINTED ON 10% POST
CONSUMER RECYCLED PAPER*

Preface

This volume of selected statutes and regulations is designed to supplement our casebook, REGULATION OF FINANCIAL INSTITUTIONS (1999). It includes selected statutes and regulations applicable to depository institutions, insurance companies, pension plans, securities firms, capital markets, investment advisers, and investment companies in the United States. The materials are generally current through September 1, 1998.

In compiling the volume, we faced considerable difficulties in determining which of many potentially relevant statutes to include. A truly comprehensive statutory and regulatory supplement for these fields would run to tens of thousands of pages. To keep the volume at a more manageable length, we have limited coverage to materials that are directly related to issues covered in our casebook. For depository institutions and, in particular, the commercial banking subsector, our casebook coverage is fairly extensive and so, too, is the selection of banking statutes and regulations included here (although even in this area, we have had to omit substantial areas of the law — for example, those governing payment systems and certain consumer protection statutes, such as the Truth in Lending Act and various other fair lending laws, as well as most international banking laws). For areas such as securities firms and trading markets, our casebook coverage is limited to selected topics that illustrate the characteristic regulatory strategies in these fields, and our selection of statutes and regulations for this volume is similarly limited. On occasion, the casebook covers a topic, such as the level pricing rules for money market mutual funds or CFTC regulation of futures trading, where applicable legal requirements are adequately described in the main text and are not reproduced here. In other areas, such as the new Federal Credit Union Act common-bond rules or the Federal Home Owners' Loan Act requirements for unitary thrift holding companies, we have included supplemental materials that are not discussed extensively in the casebook in anticipation that some professors may wish to cover these topical provisions in their courses.

Our decision to exclude from this volume substantial amounts of potentially relevant materials has been made easier by the knowledge that many readers will have access to the Internet and other on-line resources where substantial additional materials are available. To assist our readers in finding these on-line resources, we have developed a webpage, located at <http://cyber.harvard.edu/rfi/>, in connection with the preparation of our casebook and this statutory supplement. The webpage includes links to extensive statutory and regulatory sources related to financial institutions. In addition, the page provides access to various new materials, including financial modernization legislation and associated congressional reports from the 105th Congress, NAIC model insurance laws, and supplementary SEC materials regarding investment adviser and investment company regulation. Some professors many find it possible to use the webpage as an alternative to this statutory supplement, although in our experience most

students find it helpful to have paper copies of the essential statutes and regulations that this volume includes.

In preparing this supplement, we were greatly assisted by the word processing departments of the University of Pittsburgh School of Law and Harvard Law School as well as the diligent and reliable research assistance of Jim Davis, HLS '99.

We welcome comments about both this supplement and the additional materials available through our webpage. Please address your comments to Howell Jackson at Griswold 402, Harvard Law School, Cambridge, Massachusetts 02138, or by email to hjackson@law.harvard.edu.

HOWELL E. JACKSON
EDWARD L. SYMONS, JR.

November 1998

Summary of Contents

Table of Contents

PART II -- INSURANCE STATUTES

PART III -- SECURITIES INDUSTRY

PART IV — INVESTMENT MANAGEMENT

PART V — INTER-INDUSTRY COMPETITION

CHAPTER ONE

NATIONAL BANK ACT

§ 1. Office of Comptroller of the Currency

There shall be in the Department of the Treasury a bureau charged with the execution of all laws passed by Congress relating to the issue and regulation of a national currency secured by United States bonds and, under the general supervision of the Board of Governors of the Federal Reserve System, of all Federal Reserve notes, except for the cancellation and destruction, and accounting with respect to such cancellation and destruction, of Federal Reserve notes unfit for circulation, the chief officer of which bureau shall be called the Comptroller of the Currency, and shall perform his duties under the general directions of the Secretary of the Treasury. The Comptroller of the Currency shall have the same authority over matters within the jurisdiction of the Comptroller as the Director of the Office of Thrift Supervision has over matters within the Director's jurisdiction under section 1462a(b)(3) of this title. The Secretary of the Treasury may not delay or prevent the issuance of any rule or the promulgation of any regulation by the Comptroller of the Currency.

* * *

§ 21. Formation of national banking associations; incorporators; articles of association

Associations for carrying on the business of banking under this chapter may be formed by any number of natural persons, not less in any case than five. They shall enter into articles of association, which shall specify in general terms the object for which the association is formed, and may contain any other provisions, not inconsistent with law, which the association may see fit to adopt for the regulation of its business and the conduct of its affairs. These articles shall be signed by the persons uniting to form the association, and a copy of them shall be forwarded to the Comptroller of the Currency, to be filed and preserved in his office.

§ 22. Organization certificate

The persons uniting to form such an association shall, under their hands, make an organization certificate, which shall specifically state:

First. The name assumed by such association; which name shall include the word "national".

Second. The place where its operations of discount and deposit are to be carried on, designating the State, Territory, or District, and the particular county and city, town, or village.

Third. The amount of capital stock and the number of shares into which the same is to be divided.

Fourth. The names and places of residence of the shareholders and the number of shares held by each of them.

Fifth. The fact that the certificate is made to enable such persons to avail themselves of the advantages of this chapter.

* * *

§ 24. Corporate powers of associations

Upon duly making and filing articles of association and an organization certificate a national banking association shall become, as from the date of the execution of its organization certificate, a body corporate, and as such, and in the name designated in the organization certificate, it shall have power—

* * *

Seventh. To exercise by its board of directors or duly authorized officers or agents, subject to law, all such incidental powers as shall be necessary to carry on the business of banking; by discounting and negotiating promissory notes, drafts, bills of exchange, and other evidences of debt; by receiving deposits; by buying and selling exchange, coin, and bullion; by loaning money on personal security; and by obtaining, issuing, and circulating notes according to the provisions of title 62 of the Revised Statutes. The business of dealing in securities and stock by the association shall be limited to purchasing and selling such securities and stock without recourse, solely upon the order, and for the account of, customers, and in no case for its own account, and the association shall not underwrite any issue of securities or stock: Provided, That the association may purchase for its own account investment securities under such limitations and restrictions as the Comptroller of the Currency may by regulation prescribe. In no event shall the total amount of the investment securities of any one obligor or maker, held by the association for its own account, exceed at any time 10 per centum of its capital stock actually paid in and unimpaired and 10 per centum of its unimpaired surplus fund, except that this limitation shall not require any association to dispose of any securities lawfully held by it on August 23, 1935. As used in this section the term "investment securities" shall mean marketable obligations, evidencing indebtedness of any person, copartnership, association, or corporation in the form of bonds, notes and/or debentures commonly known as investment securities under such further definition of the term "investment securities" as may by regulation be prescribed by the Comptroller of the Currency. Except as herein after provided or otherwise permitted by law, nothing herein contained shall authorize the purchase by the association for its own account of any shares of stock

of any corporation. The limitations and restrictions herein contained as to dealing in, underwriting and purchasing for its own account, investment securities shall not apply to obligations of the United States, or general obligations of any State or of any political subdivision thereof, or obligations of the Washington Metropolitan Area Transit Authority which are guaranteed by the Secretary of Transportation under section 9 of the National Capital Transportation Act of 1969 [D.C. Code § 1-2458], or obligations issued under authority of the Federal Farm Loan Act, as amended, or issued by the thirteen banks for the cooperatives of any of them or the Federal Home Loan Banks, or obligations which are insured by the Secretary of Housing and Urban Development under title XI of the National Housing Act [12 U.S.C.A. § 1749aaa *et seq.*] or obligations which are insured by the Secretary of Housing and Urban Development * * * . Provided, That in carrying on the business commonly known as the safe-deposit business the association shall not invest in the capital stock of a corporation organized under the law of any State to conduct a safe- deposit business in an amount in excess of 15 per centum of the capital stock of the association actually paid in and unimpaired and 15 per centum of its unimpaired surplus. The limitations and restrictions herein, contained as to dealing in and underwriting investment securities shall not apply to obligations issued by the International Bank for Reconstruction and Development, the European Bank for Reconstruction and Development, the Inter-American Development Bank, the North American Development Bank, the Asian Development Bank, the African Development Bank, the Inter-American Investment Corporation, or the International Finance Corporation, or obligations issued by any State or political subdivision or any agency of a State or political subdivision for housing, university, or dormitory purposes, which are at the time eligible for purchase by a national bank for its own account, nor to bonds, notes and other obligations issued by the Tennessee Valley Authority or by the United States Postal Service: Provided, That no association shall hold obligations, issued by any of said organizations as a result of underwriting, dealing, or purchasing for its own account (and for this purpose obligations as to which it is under commitment shall be deemed to be held by it) in a total amount exceeding at any one time 10 per centum of its capital stock actually paid in and unimpaired and 10 per centum of its unimpaired surplus fund.

Tenth. To invest in tangible personal property, including without limitation, vehicles, manufactured homes, machinery, equipment, or furniture, for lease financing transactions on a net lease basis, but such investment may not exceed 10 percent of the assets of the association.

* * *

§ 29. Power to hold real property

A national banking association may purchase, hold, and convey real estate for the following purposes, and for no others:

First. Such as shall be necessary for its accommodation in the transaction of its business.

Second. Such as shall be mortgaged to it in good faith by way of security for debts previously contracted.

Third. Such as shall be conveyed to it in satisfaction of debts previously contracted in the course of its dealings.

Fourth. Such as it shall purchase at sales under judgments, decrees, or mortgages held by the association, or shall purchase to secure debts due to it.

But no such association shall hold the possession of any real estate under mortgage, or the title and possession of any real estate purchased to secure any debts due to it, for a longer period than five years except as otherwise provided in this section.

For real estate in the possession of a national banking association upon application by the association, the Comptroller of the Currency may approve the possession of any such real estate by such association for a period longer than five years, but not to exceed an additional five years, if (1) the association has made a good faith attempt to dispose of the real estate within the five- year period, or (2) disposal within the five-year period would be detrimental to the association. Upon notification by the association to the Comptroller of the Currency that such conditions exist that require the expenditure of funds for the development and improvement of such real estate, and subject to such conditions and limitations as the Comptroller of the Currency shall prescribe, the association may expend such funds as are needed to enable such association to recover its total investment.

* * *

§ 36. Branch banks

The conditions upon which a national banking association may retain or establish and operate a branch or branches are the following:

* * *

(c) New branches

A national banking association may, with the approval of the Comptroller of the Currency, establish and operate new branches: (1) Within the limits of the city, town or village in which said association is situated, if such establishment and operation are at the time expressly authorized to State banks by the law of the State in question; and (2) at any point within the State in which said association is situated, if such establishment and operation are at the time authorized to State banks by the statute law of the State in question by language specifically granting such authority affirmatively and not merely by implication or recognition,

and subject to the restrictions as to location imposed by the law of the State on State banks. * * *

(d) Branches resulting from interstate merger transactions

A national bank resulting from an interstate merger transaction (as defined in section 1831u(f)(6) of this title) may maintain and operate a branch in a State other than the home State (as defined in subsection (g)(3)(B) of this section) of such bank in accordance with section 1831u of this title.

(e) Exclusive authority for additional branches

(1) In general

Effective June 1, 1997, a national bank may not acquire, establish, or operate a branch in any State other than the bank's home State (as defined in subsection (g)(3)(B) of this section) or a State in which the bank already has a branch unless the acquisition, establishment, or operation of such branch in such State by such national bank is authorized under this section or section 1823(f), 1823(k), or 1831u of this title.

* * *

(f) Law applicable to interstate branching operations

(1) Law applicable to national bank branches

(A) In general

The laws of the host State regarding community reinvestment, consumer protection, fair lending, and establishment of intrastate branches shall apply to any branch in the host State of an out-of-State national bank to the same extent as such State laws apply to a branch of a bank chartered by that State, except–

(i) when Federal law preempts the application of such State laws to a national bank; or

(ii) when the Comptroller of the Currency determines that the application of such State laws would have a discriminatory effect on the branch in comparison with the effect the application of such State laws would have with respect to branches of a bank chartered by the host State.

(B) Enforcement of applicable State laws

The provisions of any State law to which a branch of a national bank is subject under this paragraph shall be enforced, with respect to such branch, by the Comptroller of the Currency.

(C) Review and Report on Actions by Comptroller

The Comptroller of the Currency shall conduct an annual review of the actions it has taken with regard to the applicability of State law to national banks (or their branches) during the preceding year, and shall include in its annual report required under section 333 of the Revised Statues (12 U.S.C. 14) the results of the review and the reasons for each such action. The first such review and report after the date of enactment of this subparagraph shall encompass all such actions taken on or after January 1, 1992.

(2) Treatment of branch as bank

All laws of a host State, other than the laws regarding community reinvestment, consumer protection, fair lending, establishment of intrastate branches, and the application or administration of any tax or method of taxation, shall apply to a branch (in such State) of an out-of-State national bank to the same extent as such laws would apply if the branch were a national bank the main office of which is in such State.

(3) Rule of construction

No provision of this subsection may be construed as affecting the legal standards for preemption of the application of State law to national banks.

(g) State "opt-in" election to permit interstate branching through de novo branches

(1) In general

Subject to paragraph (2), the Comptroller of the Currency may approve an application by a national bank to establish and operate a de novo branch in a State (other than the bank's home State) in which the bank does not maintain a branch if–

(A) there is in effect in the host State a law that–

    (i) applies equally to all banks; and

    (ii) expressly permits all out-of-State banks to establish de novo branches in such State; and

(B) the conditions established in, or made applicable to this paragraph by, paragraph (2) are met.

(2) Conditions on establishment and operation of interstate branch

(A) Establishment

An application by a national bank to establish and operate a de novo branch in a host State shall be subject to the same requirements and conditions to which an application for an

interstate merger transaction is subject under paragraphs (1), (3), and (4) of section 1831u(b) of this title.

(B) Operation

Subsections (c) and (d)(2) of section 1831u of this title shall apply with respect to each branch of a national bank which is established and operated pursuant to an application approved under this subsection in the same manner and to the same extent such provisions of such section 1831u of this title apply to a branch of a national bank which resulted from an interstate merger transaction approved pursuant to such section 1831u of this title.

* * *

(j) Branch defined

The term "branch" as used in this section shall be held to include any branch bank, branch office, branch agency, additional office, or any branch place of business located in any State or Territory of the United States or in the District of Columbia at which deposits are received, or checks paid, or money lent.

* * *

§ 43. Interpretations concerning preemption of certain State laws

(a) Notice and opportunity for comment required

Before issuing any opinion letter or interpretive rule, in response to a request or upon the agency's own motion, that concludes that Federal law preempts the application to a national bank of any State law regarding community reinvestment, consumer protection, fair lending, or the establishment of intrastate branches, or before making a determination under section 36(f)(1)(A)(ii) of this title the appropriate Federal banking agency (as defined in section 1813 of this title) shall–

(1) publish in the Federal Register notice of the preemption or discrimination issue that the agency is considering (including a description of each State law at issue);

(2) give interested parties not less than 30 days in which to submit written comments; and

(3) in developing the final opinion letter or interpretive rule issued by the agency, or making any determination under section 36(f)(1)(A)(ii) of this title, consider any comments received.

(b) Publication required

The appropriate Federal banking agency shall publish in the Federal Register–

(1)   any final opinion letter or interpretive rule concluding that Federal law preempts the application of any State law regarding community reinvestment, consumer protection, fair lending, or establishment of intrastate branches to a national bank; and

(2)   any determination under section 36(f)(1)(A)(ii) of this title.

(c)   Exceptions

(1)   No new issue or significant basis

This section shall not apply with respect to any opinion letter or interpretive rule that–

(A)   raises issues of Federal preemption of State law that are essentially identical to those previously resolved by the courts or on which the agency has previously issued an opinion letter or interpretive rule; or

(B)   responds to a request that contains no significant legal basis on which to make a preemption determination.

* * *

§ 81. Place of business

The general business of each national banking association shall be transacted in the place specified in its organization certificate and in the branch or branches, if any, established or maintained by it in accordance with the provisions of section 36 of this title.

* * *

§ 84. Lending limits

(a)   Total loans and extensions of credit

(1)   The total loans and extensions of credit by a national banking association to a person outstanding at one time and not fully secured, as determined in a manner consistent with paragraph (2) of this subsection, by collateral having a market value at least equal to the amount of the loan or extension of credit shall not exceed 15 per centum of the unimpaired capital and unimpaired surplus of the association.

(2)   The total loans and extensions of credit by a national banking association to a person outstanding at one time and fully secured by readily marketable collateral having a market value, as determined by reliable and continuously available price quotations, at least equal to the amount of the funds outstanding shall not exceed 10 per centum of the unimpaired capital and unimpaired surplus of the association.

This limitation shall be separate from and in addition to the limitation contained in paragraph (1) of this subsection.

(b) Definitions

For the purposes of this section–

(1) the term "loans and extensions of credit" shall include all direct or indirect advances of funds to a person made on the basis of any obligation of that person to repay the funds or repayable from specific property pledged by or on behalf of the person and, to the extent specified by the Comptroller of the Currency, such term shall also include any liability of a national banking association to advance funds to or on behalf of a person pursuant to a contractual commitment; and

(2) the term "person" shall include an individual, sole proprietorship, partnership, joint venture, association, trust, estate, business trust, corporation, sovereign government or agency, instrumentality, or political subdivision thereof, or any similar entity or organization.

(c) Exceptions

The limitations contained in subsection (a) of this section shall be subject to the following exceptions:

(1) Loans or extensions of credit arising from the discount of commercial or business paper evidencing an obligation to the person negotiating it with recourse shall not be subject to any limitation based on capital and surplus.

(2) The purchase of bankers' acceptances of the kind described in section 372 of this title and issued by other banks shall not be subject to any limitation based on capital and surplus.

(3) Loans and extensions of credit secured by bills of lading, warehouse receipts, or similar documents transferring or securing title to readily marketable staples shall be subject to a limitation of 35 per centum of capital and surplus in addition to the general limitations if the market value of the staples securing each additional loan or extension of credit at all times equals or exceeds 115 per centum of the outstanding amount of such loan or extension of credit. The staples shall be fully covered by insurance whenever it is customary to insure such staples.

(4) Loans or extensions of credit secured by bonds, notes, certificates of indebtedness, or Treasury bills of the United States or by other such obligations fully guaranteed as to principal and interest by the United States shall not be subject to any limitation based on capital and surplus.

(5)   Loans or extensions of credit to or secured by unconditional takeout commitments or guarantees of any department, agency, bureau, board, commission, or establishment of the United States or any corporation wholly owned directly or indirectly by the United States shall not be subject to any limitation based on capital and surplus.

(6)   Loans or extensions of credit secured by a segregated deposit account in the lending bank shall not be subject to any limitation based on capital and surplus.

(7)   Loans or extensions of credit to any financial institution or to any receiver, conservator, superintendent of banks, or other agent in charge of the business and property of such financial institution, when such loans or extensions of credit are approved by the Comptroller of the Currency, shall not be subject to any limitation based on capital and surplus.

(8)   (A)   Loans and extensions of credit arising from the discount of negotiable or nonnegotiable installment consumer paper which carries a full recourse endorsement or unconditional guarantee by the person transferring the paper shall be subject under this section to a maximum limitation equal to 25 per centum of such capital and surplus, notwithstanding the collateral requirements set forth in subsection (a)(2) of this section.

(B)   If the bank's files or the knowledge of its officers of the financial condition of each maker of such consumer paper is reasonably adequate, and an officer of the bank designated for that purpose by the board of directors of the bank certifies in writing that the bank is relying primarily upon the responsibility of each maker for payment of such loans or extensions of credit and not upon any full or partial recourse endorsement or guarantee by the transferor, the limitations of this section as to the loans or extensions of credit of each such maker shall be the sole applicable loan limitations.

(9)   (A)   Loans and extensions of credit secured by shipping documents or instruments transferring or securing title covering livestock or giving a lien on livestock when the market value of the livestock securing the obligation is not at any time less than 115 per centum of the face amount of the note covered, shall be subject under this section, notwithstanding the collateral requirements set forth in subsection (a)(2) of this section, to a maximum limitation equal to 25 per centum of such capital and surplus.

(B)   Loans and extensions of credit which arise from the discount by dealers in dairy cattle of paper given in payment for dairy cattle,

which paper carries a full recourse endorsement or unconditional guarantee of the seller, and which are secured by the cattle being sold, shall be subject under this section, notwithstanding the collateral requirements set forth in subsection (a)(2) of this section, to a limitation of 25 per centum of such capital and surplus.

(10) Loans or extensions of credit to the Student Loan Marketing Association shall not be subject to any limitation based on capital and surplus.

(d)   Authority of Comptroller of the Currency

(1)   The Comptroller of the Currency may prescribe rules and regulations to administer and carry out the purposes of this section including rules or regulations to define or further define terms used in this section and to establish limits or requirements other than those specified in this section for particular classes or categories of loans or extensions of credit.

(2)   The Comptroller of the Currency also shall have authority to determine when a loan putatively made to a person shall for purposes of this section be attributed to another person.

§ 85. Rate of interest on loans, discounts and purchases

Any association may take, receive, reserve, and charge on any loan or discount made, or upon any notes, bills of exchange, or other evidence of debt, interest at the rate allowed by the laws of the State, Territory, or District where the bank is located, or at a rate of 1 per centum in excess of the discount rate on ninety-day commercial paper in effect at the Federal reserve bank in the Federal reserve district where the bank is located, whichever may be the greater, and no more, except that where by the laws of any State a different rate is limited for banks organized under state laws, the rate so limited shall be allowed for associations organized or existing in any such State under this chapter. When no rate is fixed by the laws of the State, or Territory, or District, the bank may take, receive, reserve, or charge a rate not exceeding 7 per centum, or 1 per centum in excess of the discount rate on ninety-day commercial paper in effect at the Federal reserve bank in the Federal reserve district where the bank is located, whichever may be the greater, and such interest may be taken in advance, reckoning the days for which the note, bill, or other evidence of debt has to run. The maximum amount of interest or discount to be charged at a branch of an association located outside of the States of the United States and the District of Columbia shall be at the rate allowed by the laws of the country, territory, dependency, province, dominion, insular possession, or other political subdivision where the branch is located. And the purchase, discount, or sale of a bona fide bill of exchange, payable at another place than the place of such purchase, discount, or sale,

at not more than the current rate of exchange for sight drafts in addition to the interest, shall not be considered as taking or receiving a greater rate of interest.

* * *

§ 90. Depositaries of public moneys and financials agents

All national banking associations, designated for that purpose by the Secretary of the Treasury, shall be depositaries of public money, under such regulations as may be prescribed by the Secretary; and they may also be employed as financial agents of the Government; and they shall perform all such reasonable duties, as depositaries of public money and financial agents of the Government, as may be required of them. The Secretary of the Treasury shall require the associations thus designated to give satisfactory security, by the deposit of United States bonds and otherwise, for the safe-keeping and prompt payment of the public money deposited with them, and for the faithful performance of their duties as financial agents of the Government: Provided, That the Secretary shall, on or before the 1st of January of each year, make a public statement of the securities required during that year for such deposits. And every association so designated as receiver or depositary of the public money shall take and receive at par all of the national currency bills, by whatever association issued, which have been paid into the Government for internal revenue, or for loans or stocks: Provided, That the Secretary of the Treasury shall distribute the deposits herein provided for, as far as practicable, equitably between the different States and sections.

Any national banking association may, upon the deposit with it of any funds by any State or political subdivision thereof or any agency or other governmental instrumentality of one or more States or political subdivisions thereof, including any officer, employee, or agent thereof in his official capacity, give security for the safekeeping and prompt payment of the funds so deposited to the same extent and of the same kind as is authorized by the law of the State in which such association is located in the case of other banking institutions in the State.

Any national banking association may, upon the deposit with it of any funds by any federally recognized Indian tribe, or any officer, employee, or agent thereof in his or her official capacity, give security for the safekeeping and prompt payment of the funds so deposited by the deposit of United States bonds and otherwise as may be prescribed by the Secretary of the Treasury for public funds under the first paragraph of this section.

§ 91. Transfers by bank and other acts in contemplation of insolvency

All transfers of the notes, bonds, bills of exchange, or other evidences of debt owing to any national banking association, or of deposits to its credit; all assignments of mortgages, sureties on real estate, or of judgments or decrees in its favor; all

deposits of money, bullion, or other valuable thing for its use, or for the use of any of its shareholders or creditors; and all payments of money to either, made after the commission of an act of insolvency, or in contemplation thereof, made with a view to prevent the application of its assets in the manner prescribed by this chapter, or with a view to the preference of one creditor to another, except in payment of its circulating notes, shall be utterly null and void; and no attachment, injunction, or execution, shall be issued against such association or its property before final judgment in any suit, action, or proceeding, in any State, county, or municipal court.

§ 92. Acting as insurance agent or broker

In addition to the powers now vested by law in national banking associations organized under the laws of the United States any such association located and doing business in any place the population of which does not exceed five thousand inhabitants, as shown by the last preceding decennial census, may, under such rules and regulations as may be prescribed by the Comptroller of the Currency, act as the agent for any fire, life, or other insurance company authorized by the authorities of the State in which said bank is located to do business in said State, by soliciting and selling insurance and collecting premiums on policies issued by such company; and may receive for services so rendered such fees or commissions as may be agreed upon between the said association and the insurance company for which it may act as agent: Provided, however, That no such bank shall in any case assume or guarantee the payment of any premium on insurance policies issued through its agency by its principal: And provided further, That the bank shall not guarantee the truth of any statement made by an assured in filing his application for insurance.

§ 92a. Trust powers

(a) Authority of Comptroller of the Currency

The Comptroller of the Currency shall be authorized and empowered to grant by special permit to national banks applying therefor, when not in contravention of State or local law, the right to act as trustee, executor, administrator, registrar of stocks and bonds, guardian of estates, assignee, receiver, committee of estates of lunatics, or in any other fiduciary capacity in which State banks, trust companies, or other corporations which come into competition with national banks are permitted to act under the laws of the State in which the national bank is located.

* * *

(c) Segregation of fiduciary and general assets; separate books and records; access of State banking authorities to reports of examinations, books, records, and assets

National banks exercising any or all of the powers enumerated in this section shall segregate all assets held in any fiduciary capacity from the

general assets of the bank and shall keep a separate set of books and records showing in proper detail all transactions engaged in under authority of this section. The State banking authorities may have access to reports of examination made by the Comptroller of the Currency insofar as such reports relate to the trust department of such bank, but nothing in this section shall be construed as authorizing the State banking authorities to examine the books, records, and assets of such bank.

(d)   Prohibited operations; separate investment account; collateral for certain funds used in conduct of business

No national bank shall receive in its trust department deposits of current funds subject to check or the deposit of checks, drafts, bills of exchange, or other items for collection or exchange purposes. Funds deposited or held in trust by the bank awaiting investment shall be carried in a separate account and shall not be used by the bank in the conduct of its business unless it shall first set aside in the trust department United States bonds or other securities approved by the Comptroller of the Currency.

(e)   Lien and claim upon bank failure

In the event of the failure of such bank the owners of the funds held in trust for investment shall have a lien on the bonds or other securities so set apart in addition to their claim against the estate of the bank.

* * *

(h)   Loans of trust funds to officers and employees prohibited; penalties

It shall be unlawful for any national banking association to lend any officer, director, or employee any funds held in trust under the powers conferred by this section. Any officer, director, or employee making such loan, or to whom such loan is made, may be fined not more than $5,000, or imprisoned not more than five years, or may be both fined and imprisoned, in the discretion of the court.

* * *

§ 191. Appointment of Federal Deposit Insurance Corporation as receiver

The Comptroller of the Currency may, without prior notice or hearings, appoint a receiver for any national bank (and such receiver shall be the Federal Deposit Insurance Corporation if the national bank is an insured bank (as defined in section 1813(h) of this title)) if the Comptroller determines, in the Comptroller's discretion, that--

(1)   1 or more of the grounds specified in section 1821(c)(5) of this title exist; or

(2)   the association's board of directors consists of fewer than 5 members.

* * *

CHAPTER TWO

FEDERAL RESERVE ACT

---

* * *

§ 371. Real estate loans

(a) Authorization to make real estate loans; orders, rules, and regulations of Comptroller of the Currency

Any national banking association may make, arrange, purchase or sell loans or extensions of credit secured by liens on interests in real estate, subject to section 1828(o) of this title and such restrictions and requirements as the Comptroller of the Currency may prescribe by regulation or order.

* * *

§ 371c. Banking affiliates

(a) Restrictions on transactions with affiliates

(1) A member bank and its subsidiaries may engage in a covered transaction with an affiliate only if–

(A) in the case of any affiliate, the aggregate amount of covered transactions of the member bank and its subsidiaries will not exceed 10 per centum of the capital stock and surplus of the member bank; and

(B) in the case of all affiliates, the aggregate amount of covered transactions of the member bank and its subsidiaries will not exceed 20 per centum of the capital stock and surplus of the member bank.

(2) For the purpose of this section, any transaction by a member bank with any person shall be deemed to be a transaction with an affiliate to the extent that the proceeds of the transaction are used for the benefit of, or transferred to, that affiliate.

(3) A member bank and its subsidiaries may not purchase a low-quality asset from an affiliate unless the bank or such subsidiary, pursuant to an independent credit evaluation, committed itself to purchase such asset prior to the time such asset was acquired by the affiliate.

(4) Any covered transactions and any transactions exempt under subsection (d) of this section between a member bank and an affiliate

shall be on terms and conditions that are consistent with safe and sound banking practices.

(b) Definitions

For the purpose of this section–

(1) the term "affiliate" with respect to a member bank means–

    (A) any company that controls the member bank and any other company that is controlled by the company that controls the member bank;

    (B) a bank subsidiary of the member bank;

    (C) any company–

        (i) that is controlled directly or indirectly, by a trust or otherwise, by or for the benefit of shareholders who beneficially or otherwise control, directly or indirectly, by trust or otherwise, the member bank or any company that controls the member bank; or

        (ii) in which a majority of its directors or trustees constitute a majority of the persons holding any such office with the member bank or any company that controls the member bank;

    (D) (i) any company, including a real estate investment trust, that is sponsored and advised on a contractual basis by the member bank or any subsidiary or affiliate of the member bank; or

        (ii) any investment company with respect to which a member bank or any affiliate thereof is an investment advisor as defined in section 80a-2(a)(20) of Title 15; and

    (E) any company that the board determines by regulation or order to have a relationship with the member bank or any subsidiary or affiliate of the member bank, such that covered transactions by the member bank or its subsidiary with that company may be affected by the relationship to the detriment of the member bank or its subsidiary; and

(2) the following shall not be considered to be an affiliate:

    (A) any company, other than a bank, that is a subsidiary of a member bank, unless a determination is made under paragraph (1)(E) not to exclude such subsidiary company from the definition of affiliate;

    (B) any company engaged solely in holding the premises of the member bank;

(C) any company engaged solely in conducting a safe deposit business;

(D) any company engaged solely in holding obligations of the United States or its agencies or obligations fully guaranteed by the United States or its agencies as to principal and interest; and

(E) any company where control results from the exercise of rights arising out of a bona fide debt previously contracted, but only for the period of time specifically authorized under applicable State or Federal law or regulation or, in the absence of such law or regulation, for a period of two years from the date of the exercise of such rights or the effective date of this Act, whichever date is later, subject, upon application, to authorization by the Board for good cause shown of extensions of time for not more than one year at a time, but such extensions in the aggregate shall not exceed three years;

(3) (A) a company or shareholder shall be deemed to have control over another company if–

      (i) such company or shareholder, directly or indirectly, or acting through one or more other persons owns, controls, or has power to vote 25 per centum or more of any class of voting securities of the other company;

      (ii) such company or shareholder controls in any manner the election of a majority of the directors or trustees of the other company; or

      (iii) the Board determines, after notice and opportunity for hearing, that such company or shareholder, directly or indirectly, exercises a controlling influence over the management or policies of the other company; and

(B) notwithstanding any other provision of this section, no company shall be deemed to own or control another company by virtue of its ownership or control of shares in a fiduciary capacity, except as provided in paragraph (1)(C) of this subsection or if the company owning or controlling such shares is a business trust;

(4) the term "subsidiary" with respect to a specified company means a company that is controlled by such specified company;

(5) the term "bank" includes a State bank, national bank, banking association, and trust company;

(6) the term "company" means a corporation, partnership, business trust, association, or similar organization and, unless specifically excluded, the term "company" includes a "member bank" and a "bank";

(7)   the term "covered transaction" means with respect to an affiliate of a member bank–

(A)   a loan or extension of credit to the affiliate;

(B)   a purchase of or an investment in securities issued by the affiliate;

(C)   a purchase of assets, including assets subject to an agreement to repurchase, from the affiliate, except such purchase of real and personal property as may be specifically exempted by the Board by order or regulation;

(D)   the acceptance of securities issued by the affiliate as collateral security for a loan or extension of credit to any person or company; or

(E)   the issuance of a guarantee, acceptance, or letter of credit, including an endorsement or standby letter of credit, on behalf of an affiliate;

(8)   the term "aggregate amount of covered transactions" means the amount of the covered transactions about to be engaged in added to the current amount of all outstanding covered transactions;

(9)   the term "securities" means stocks, bonds, debentures, notes, or other similar obligations; and

(10)   the term "low-quality asset" means an asset that falls in any one or more of the following categories:

(A)   an asset classified as "substandard", "doubtful", or "loss" or treated as "other loans especially mentioned" in the most recent report of examination or inspection of an affiliate prepared by either a Federal or State supervisory agency;

(B)   an asset in a nonaccrual status;

(C)   an asset on which principal or interest payments are more than thirty days past due; or

(D)   an asset whose terms have been renegotiated or compromised due to the deteriorating financial condition of the obligor.

(c)   Collateral for certain transactions with affiliates

(1)   Each loan or extension of credit to, or guarantee, acceptance, or letter of credit issued on behalf of, an affiliate by a member bank or its subsidiary shall be secured at the time of the transaction by collateral having a market value equal to–

(A)   100 per centum of the amount of such loan or extension of credit, guarantee, acceptance, or letter of credit, if the collateral is composed of–

(i)   obligations of the United states or its agencies;

        (ii)   obligations fully guaranteed by the United States or its agencies as to principal and interest;

        (iii)   notes, drafts, bills of exchange or bankers' acceptances that are eligible for rediscount or purchase by a Federal Reserve Bank; or

        (iv)   a segregated, earmarked deposit account with the member bank;

   (B)   110 per centum of the amount of such loan or extension of credit, guarantee, acceptance, or letter of credit if the collateral is composed of obligations of any State or political subdivision of any State;

   (C)   120 per centum of the amount of such loan or extension of credit, guarantee, acceptance, or letter of credit if the collateral is composed of other debt instruments, including receivables; or

   (D)   130 per centum of the amount of such loan or extension of credit, guarantee, acceptance, or letter of credit if the collateral is composed of stock, leases, or other real or personal property.

(2)   Any such collateral that is subsequently retired or amortized shall be replaced by additional eligible collateral where needed to keep the percentage of the collateral value relative to the amount of the outstanding loan or extension of credit, guarantee, acceptance, or letter of credit equal to the minimum percentage required at the inception of the transaction.

(3)   A low-quality asset shall not be acceptable as collateral for a loan or extension of credit to, or guarantee, acceptance, or letter of credit issued on behalf of, an affiliate.

(4)   The securities issued by an affiliate of the member bank shall not be acceptable as collateral for a loan or extension of credit to, or guarantee, acceptance, or letter of credit issued on behalf of, that affiliate or any other affiliate of the member bank.

(5)   The collateral requirements of this paragraph shall not be applicable to an acceptance that is already fully secured either by attached documents or by other property having an ascertainable market value that is involved in the transaction.

(d) Exemptions

The provisions of this section, except paragraph (a)(4) of this section, shall not be applicable to–

(1)   any transaction, subject to the prohibition contained in subsection (a)(3) of this section, with a bank–

(A)   which controls 80 per centum or more of the voting shares of the member bank;

(B)   in which the member bank controls 80 per centum or more of the voting shares; or

(C)   in which 80 per centum or more of the voting shares are controlled by the company that controls 80 per centum or more of the voting shares of the member bank;

(2)   making deposits in an affiliated bank or affiliated foreign bank in the ordinary course of correspondent business, subject to any restrictions that the Board may prescribe by regulation or order;

(3)   giving immediate credit to an affiliate for uncollected items received in the ordinary course of business;

(4)   making a loan or extension of credit to, or issuing a guarantee, acceptance, or letter of credit on behalf of, an affiliate that is fully secured by–

(A)   obligations of the United States or its agencies;

(B)   obligations fully guaranteed by the United States or its agencies as to principal and interest; or

(C)   segregated, earmarked deposit account with the member bank;

(5)   purchasing securities issued by any company of the kinds described in section 1843(c)(1) of this title;

(6)   purchasing assets having a readily identifiable and publicly available market quotation and purchased at that market quotation or, subject to the prohibition contained in subsection (a)(3) of this section, purchasing loans on a nonrecourse basis from affiliated banks; and

(7)   purchasing from an affiliate a loan or extension of credit that was originated by the member bank and sold to the affiliate subject to a repurchase agreement or with recourse.

§ 371c-1. Restrictions on transactions with affiliates

(a)   In general

(1)   Terms

A member bank and its subsidiaries may engage in any of the transactions described in paragraph (2) only–

(A)   on terms and under circumstances, including credit standards, that are substantially the same, or at least as favorable to such bank or its subsidiary, as those prevailing at the time for comparable transactions with or involving other nonaffiliated companies, or

(B) in the absence of comparable transactions, on terms and under circumstances, including credit standards, that in good faith would be offered to, or would apply to, nonaffiliated companies.

(2) Transactions covered

Paragraph (1) applies to the following:

(A) Any covered transaction with an affiliate.

(B) The sale of securities or other assets to an affiliate, including assets subject to an agreement to repurchase.

(C) The payment of money or the furnishing of services to an affiliate under contract, lease, or otherwise.

(D) Any transaction in which an affiliate acts as an agent or broker or receives a fee for its services to the bank or to any other person.

(E) Any transaction or series of transactions with a third party–

    (i) if an affiliate has a financial interest in the third party, or

    (ii) if an affiliate is a participant in such transaction or series of transactions.

(3) Transactions that benefit an affiliate

For the purpose of this subsection, any transaction by a member bank or its subsidiary with any person shall be deemed to be a transaction with an affiliate of such bank if any of the proceeds of the transaction are used for the benefit of, or transferred to, such affiliate.

(b) Prohibited transactions

(1) In general

A member bank or its subsidiary–

(A) shall not purchase as fiduciary any securities or other assets from any affiliate unless such purchase is permitted–

    (i) under the instrument creating the fiduciary relationship,

    (ii) by court order, or

    (iii) by law of the jurisdiction governing the fiduciary relationship; and

(B) whether acting as principal or fiduciary, shall not knowingly purchase or otherwise acquire, during the existence of any underwriting or selling syndicate, any security if a principal underwriter of that security is an affiliate of such bank.

(2)   Exception

Subparagraph (B) of paragraph (1) shall not apply if the purchase or acquisition of such securities has been approved, before such securities are initially offered for sale to the public, by a majority of the directors of the bank who are not officers or employees of the bank or any affiliate thereof.

(3)   Definitions

For the purpose of this subsection—

(A)   the term "security" has the meaning given to such term in section 78c(a)(10) of Title 15; and

(B)   the term "principal underwriter" means any underwriter who, in connection with a primary distribution of securities—

(i)   is in privity of contract with the issuer or an affiliated person of the issuer;

(ii)   acting alone or in concert with one or more other persons, initiates or directs the formation of an underwriting syndicate; or

(iii) is allowed a rate of gross commission, spread, or other profit greater than the rate allowed another underwriter participating in the distribution.

(c)   Advertising restriction

A member bank or any subsidiary or affiliate of a member bank shall not publish any advertisement or enter into any agreement stating or suggesting that the bank shall in any way be responsible for the obligations of its affiliates.

(d)   Definitions

For the purpose of this section—

(1)   the term "affiliate" has the meaning given to such term in section 371c of this title (but does not include any company described in subsection (b)(2) of such section or any bank);

(2)   the terms "bank", "subsidiary", "person", and "security" (other than security as used in subsection (b) of this section) have the meanings given to such terms in section 371c of this title; and

(3)   the term "covered transaction" has the meaning given to such term in section 371c of this title (but does not include any transaction which is exempt from such definition under subsection (d) of such section).

§ 371d. Investment in bank premises or stock of corporation holding premises

(a) Conditions of Investment.—No national bank or State member bank shall invest in bank premises, or in the stock, bonds, debentures, or other such obligations of any corporation holding the premises of such bank, or make loans to or upon the security of any such corporation—

    (1) unless the bank receives the prior approval of the Comptroller of the Currency (with respect to a national bank) or the Board (with respect to a national bank) or the Board (with respect to a State member bank);

    (2) unless the aggregate of all such investments and loans, together with the amount of any indebtedness incurred by any such corporation that is an affiliate of the bank, is less than or equal to the amount of the capital stock of such bank; or

    (3) unless—

        (A) the aggregate of all such investments and loans, together with the amount of any indebtedness incurred by any such corporation that is an affiliate of the bank, is less than or equal to 150 percent of the capital and surplus of the bank; and;

        (B) the bank—

            (i) has a CAMEL composite rating of 1 or 2 under the Uniform Financial Institutions Rating System (or an equivalent rating under a comparable rating system) as of the most recent examination of such bank;

            (ii) is well capitalized and will continue to be well capitalized after the investment or loan; and

            (iii) provides notification to the Comptroller of the Currency (with respect to a national bank) or to the Board (with respect to a State member bank) not later than 30 days after making the investment or loan.

§ 372. Bankers' acceptances

(a) Institutions; drafts and bills of exchange; types

Any member bank and any Federal or State branch or agency of a foreign bank subject to reserve requirements under section 3105 of this title (hereinafter in this section referred to as "institutions"), may accept drafts or bills of exchange drawn upon it having not more than six months' sight to run, exclusive of days of grace—

    (i) which grow out of transactions involving the importation or exportation of goods;

(ii) which grow out of transactions involving the domestic shipment of goods; or

(iii) which are secured at the time of acceptance by a warehouse receipt or other such document conveying or securing title covering readily marketable staples.

(b) Ratio limit of bills to unimpaired capital stock and surplus

Except as provided in subsection (c) of this section, no institution shall accept such bills, or be obligated for a participation share in such bills, in an amount equal at any time in the aggregate to more than 150 per centum of its paid up and unimpaired capital stock and surplus or, in the case of a United States branch or agency of a foreign bank, its dollar equivalent as determined by the Board under subsection (h) of this section.

(c) Authorization for special ratio limit; foreign banks

The Board, under such conditions as it may prescribe, may authorize, by regulation or order, any institution to accept such bills, or be obligated for a participation share in such bills, in an amount not exceeding at any time in the aggregate 200 per centum of its paid up and unimpaired capital stock and surplus or, in the case of a United States branch or agency of a foreign bank, its dollar equivalent as determined by the Board under subsection (h) of this section.

(d) Ratio limit for domestic transactions

Notwithstanding subsections (b) and (c) of this section, with respect to any institution, the aggregate acceptances, including obligations for a participation share in such acceptances, growing out of domestic transactions shall not exceed 50 per centum of the aggregate of all acceptances, including obligations for a participation share in such acceptances, authorized for such institution under this section.

(e) Ratio limit for single entity; foreign banks; security

No institution shall accept bills, or be obligated for a participation share in such bills, whether in a foreign or domestic transaction, for any one person, partnership, corporation, association or other entity in an amount equal at any time in the aggregate to more than 10 per centum of its paid up and unimpaired capital stock and surplus, or, in the case of a United States branch or agency of a foreign bank, its dollar equivalent as determined by the Board under subsection (h) of this section, unless the institution is secured either by attached documents or by some other actual security growing out of the same transaction as the acceptance.

(f) Exception for participation agreements

With respect to an institution which issues an acceptance, the limitations contained in this section shall not apply to that portion of an acceptance which is issued by such institution and which is covered by a participation agreement sold to another institution.

* * *

§ 375a. Loans to executive officers of banks

(1) General prohibition; authorization for extension of credit; conditions for credit

Except as authorized under this section, no member bank may extend credit in any manner to any of its own executive officers. No executive officer of any member bank may become indebted to that member bank except by means of an extension of credit which the bank is authorized to make under this section. Any extension of credit under this section shall be promptly reported to the board of directors of the bank, and may be made only if–

(A) the bank would be authorized to make it to borrowers other than its officers;

(B) it is on terms not more favorable than those afforded other borrowers;

(C) the officer has submitted a detailed current financial statement; and

(D) it is on condition that it shall become due and payable on demand of the bank at any time when the officer is indebted to any other bank or banks on account of extensions of credit of any one of the three categories respectively referred to in paragraphs (2), (3), and (4) in an aggregate amount greater than the amount of credit of the same category that could be extended to him by the bank of which he is an officer.

(2) Mortgage loans

A member bank may make a loan to any executive officer of the bank if, at the time the loan is made–

(A) it is secured by a first lien on a dwelling which is expected, after the making of the loan, to be owned by the officer and used by him as his residence, and

(B) no other loan by the bank to the officer under authority of this paragraph is outstanding.

(3) Educational loans

A member bank may make extensions of credit to any executive officer of the bank to finance the education of the children of the officer.

(4) General limitation on amount of credit

A member bank may make extensions of credit not otherwise specifically authorized under this section to any executive officer of the bank, in an amount prescribed in a regulation of the member bank's appropriate Federal banking agency.

(5) Partnership loans

Except to the extent permitted under paragraph (4), a member bank may not extend credit to a partnership in which one or more of its executive officers are partners having either individually or together a majority interest. For the purposes of paragraph (4), the full amount of any credit so extended shall be considered to have been extended to each officer of the bank who is a member of the partnership.

(6) Report of date and amount of credit extensions, security, and uses of proceeds upon excessive extension of credit

Whenever an executive officer of a member bank becomes indebted to any bank or banks (other than the one of which he is an officer) on account of extensions of credit of any one of the three categories respectively referred to in paragraphs (2), (3), and (4) in an aggregate amount greater than the aggregate amount of credit of the same category that could lawfully be extended to him by the bank, he shall make a written report to the board of directors of the bank, stating the date and amount of each such extension of credit, the security therefor, and the purposes for which the proceeds have been or are to be used.

(7) Endorsement or guarantee of loans or assets; protective indebtedness

This section does not prohibit any executive officer of a member bank from endorsing or guaranteeing for the protection of the bank any loan or other asset previously acquired by the bank in good faith or from incurring any indebtedness to the bank for the purpose of protecting the bank against loss or giving financial assistance to it.

* * *

§ 375b. Extensions of credit to executive officers, directors, and principal shareholders of member banks

(1) In general

No member bank may extend credit to any of its executive officers, directors, or principal shareholders, or to any related interest of such a person, except to the extent permitted under paragraphs (2), (3), (4), (5), and (6).

(2) Preferential terms prohibited

A member bank may extend credit to its executive officers, directors, or principal shareholders, or to any related interest of such a person, only if the extension of credit—

(A) is made on substantially the same terms, including interest rates and collateral, as those prevailing at the time for comparable transactions by the bank with persons who are not executive officers, directors, principal shareholders, or employees of the bank;

(B) does not involve more than the normal risk of repayment or present other unfavorable features; and

(C) the bank follows credit underwriting procedures that are not less stringent than those applicable to comparable transactions by the bank with persons who are not executive officers, directors, principal shareholders, or employees of the bank.

(3) Prior approval required

A member bank may extend credit to a person described in paragraph (1) in an amount that, when aggregated with the amount of all other outstanding extensions of credit by that bank to each such person and that person's related interests, would exceed an amount prescribed by regulation of the appropriate Federal banking agency (as defined in section 1813 of this title) only if—

(A) the extension of credit has been approved in advance by a majority vote of that bank's entire board of directors; and

(B) the interested party has abstained from participating, directly or indirectly, in the deliberations or voting on the extension of credit.

(4) Aggregate limit on extensions of credit to any executive officer, director, or principal shareholder

A member bank may extend credit to any executive officer, director, or principal shareholder, or to any related interest of such a person, only if the extension of credit is in an amount that, when aggregated with the amount of all outstanding extensions of credit by that bank to that person and that person's related interests, would not exceed the limits on loans to a single borrower established by section 84 of this title. For purposes of this paragraph, section 84 of this title shall be deemed to apply to a State member bank as if the State member bank were a national banking association.

(5) Aggregate limit on extensions of credit to all executive officers, directors, and principal shareholders

(A) In general

A member bank may extend credit to any executive officer, director, or principal shareholder, or to any related interest of such a person, if the extension of credit is in an amount that, when aggregated with the amount of all outstanding extensions of credit by that bank to its executive officers, directors, principal shareholders, and those persons' related interests would not exceed the bank's unimpaired capital and unimpaired surplus.

(B) More stringent limit authorized

The Board may, by regulation, prescribe a limit that is more stringent than that contained in subparagraph (A).

(C) Board may make exceptions for certain banks

The Board may, by regulation, make exceptions to subparagraph (A) for member banks with less than $100,000,000 in deposits if the Board determines that the exceptions are important to avoid constricting the availability of credit in small communities or to attract directors to such banks. In no case may the aggregate amount of all outstanding extensions of credit to a bank's executive officers, directors, principal shareholders, and those persons' related interests be more than 2 times the bank's unimpaired capital and unimpaired surplus.

(6) Overdrafts by executive officers and directors prohibited

(A) In general

If any executive officer or director has an account at the member bank, the bank may not pay on behalf of that person an amount exceeding the funds on deposit in the account.

(B) Exceptions

Subparagraph (A) does not prohibit a member bank from paying funds in accordance with–

(i)   a written preauthorized, interest-bearing extension of credit specifying a method of repayment; or

(ii) a written preauthorized transfer of funds from another account of the executive officer or director at that bank.

(7) Prohibition on knowingly receiving unauthorized extension of credit

No executive officer, director, or principal shareholder shall knowingly receive (or knowingly permit any of that person's related interests to receive) from a member bank, directly or indirectly, any extension of credit not authorized under this section.

(8) Executive officer, director, or principal shareholder of certain affiliates treated as executive officer, director, or principal shareholder of member bank

(A) In general

For purposes of this section, any executive officer, director, or principal shareholder (as the case may be) of any company of which the member bank is a subsidiary, or of any other subsidiary of that company, shall be deemed to be an executive officer, director, or principal shareholder (as the case may be) of the member bank.

(B) Exception

The Board may, by regulation, make exceptions to subparagraph (A), except as that subparagraph makes applicable paragraph (2), for an executive officer or director of a subsidiary of a company that controls the member bank, if that executive officer or director does not have authority to participate, and does not participate, in major policymaking functions of the member bank.

(9) Definitions

For purposes of this section:

(A) Company

(i) In general

Except as provided in clause (ii), the term "company" means any corporation, partnership, business or other trust, association, joint venture, pool syndicate, sole proprietorship, unincorporated organization, or other business entity.

(ii) Exceptions

The term "company" does not include–

(I) an insured depository institution (as defined in section 1813 of this title); or

(II) a corporation the majority of the shares of which are owned by the United States or by any State.

(B) Control

A person controls a company or bank if that person, directly or indirectly, or acting through or in concert with 1 or more persons–

(i) owns, controls, or has the power to vote 25 percent or more of any class of the company's voting securities;

(ii) controls in any manner the election of a majority of the company's directors; or

(iii) has the power to exercise a controlling influence over the company's management or policies.

(C) Executive officer

> A person is an "executive officer" of a company or bank if that person participates or has authority to participate (other than as a director) in major policymaking functions of the company or bank.

(D) Extension of credit

> (i)   In general
>
>> A member bank extends credit by making or renewing any loan, granting a line of credit, or entering into any similar transaction as a result of which a person becomes obligated (directly or indirectly, or by any means whatsoever) to pay money or its equivalent to the bank.
>
> (ii)   Exceptions
>
>> The Board may, by regulation, make exceptions to clause (i) for transactions that the Board determines pose minimal risk.

(E) Member bank

> The term "member bank" includes any subsidiary of a member bank.

(F) Principal shareholder

> The term "principal shareholder"–
>
> (i)   means any person that directly or indirectly, or acting through or in concert with one or more persons, owns, controls, or has the power to vote more than 10 percent of any class of voting securities of a member bank or company; and
>
> (ii)   does not include a company of which a member bank is a subsidiary.

(G) Related interest

> A "related interest" of a person is–
>
> (i)   any company controlled by that person; and
>
> (ii)   any political or campaign committee that is controlled by that person or the funds or services of which will benefit that person.

(H) Subsidiary

> The term "subsidiary" has the same meaning as in section 1841 of this title.

* * *

CHAPTER THREE

HOME OWNERS' LOAN ACT

§ 1462. Definitions

For purposes of this Act—

    (1)   The term "Director" means the Director of the Office of Thrift Supervision.

* * *

    (3)   The term "savings association" means a savings association as defined in section 3 of the Federal Deposit Insurance Act [12 U.S.C.A. § 1813], the deposits of which are insured by the [Federal Deposit Insurance] Corporation.

* * *

§ 1467a Regulation of holding companies

(a) Definitions —

    (1)   **In General**

* * *

        (D)   Savings and Loan Holding Company. The term "savings and loan holding company" means any company which directly or indirectly controls a savings association or controls any other company which is a savings and loan holding company.

* * *

(c) Holding company activities

    (1)   **Prohibited activities**

Except as otherwise provided in this subsection, no savings and loan holding company and no subsidiary which is not a savings association shall--

        (A)   engage in any activity or render any service for or on behalf of a savings association subsidiary for the purpose or with

the effect of evading any law or regulation applicable to such savings association;

(B) commence any business activity, other than the activities described in paragraph (2); or

(C) continue any business activity, other than the activities described in paragraph (2), after the end of the 2-year period beginning on the date on which such company received approval under subsection (e) of this section to become a savings and loan holding company subject to the limitations contained in this subparagraph.

(2) Exempt activities

The prohibitions of subparagraphs (B) and (C) of paragraph (1) shall not apply to the following business activities of any savings and loan holding company or any subsidiary (of such company) which is not a savings association:

(A) Furnishing or performing management services for a savings association subsidiary of such company.

(B) Conducting an insurance agency or escrow business.

(C) Holding, managing, or liquidating assets owned or acquired from a savings association subsidiary of such company.

(D) Holding or managing properties used or occupied by a savings association subsidiary of such company.

(E) Acting as trustee under deed of trust.

(F) Any other activity--

(i) which the Board of Governors of the Federal Reserve System, by regulation, has determined to be permissible for bank holding companies under section 4(c) of the Bank Holding Company Act of 1956 [12 U.S.C.A. § 1843(c)], unless the Director, by regulation, prohibits or limits any such activity for savings and loan holding companies; or

(ii) in which multiple savings and loan holding companies were authorized (by regulation) to directly engage on March 5, 1987.

(G) In the case of a savings and loan holding company, purchasing, holding, or disposing of stock acquired in connection with a qualified stock issuance if the purchase

of such stock by such savings and loan holding company is approved by the Director pursuant to subsection (q)(1)(D) of this section.

(3) Certain limitations on activities not applicable to certain holding companies

Notwithstanding paragraphs (4) and (6) of this subsection, the limitations contained in subparagraphs (B) and (C) of paragraph (1) shall not apply to any savings and loan holding company (or any subsidiary of such company) which controls--

    (A)   only 1 savings association, if the savings association subsidiary of such company is a qualified thrift lender (as determined under subsection (m) of this section); or

    (B)   more than 1 savings association, if--

        (i)   all, or all but 1, of the savings association subsidiaries of such company were initially acquired by the company or by an individual who would be deemed to control such company if such individual were a company--

            (I)   pursuant to an acquisition under section 13(c) or 13(k) of the Federal Deposit Insurance Act [12 U.S.C.A. § 1823(c) or (k)] or section 408(m) of the National Housing Act [12 U.S.C.A. § 1730a(m)]; or

            (II)   pursuant to an acquisition in which assistance was continued to a savings association under section 13(i) of the Federal Deposit Insurance Act [12 U.S.C.A. § 1823(i)]; and

        (ii)   all of the savings association subsidiaries of such company are qualified thrift lenders (as determined under subsection (m) of this section).

(4) Prior approval of certain new activities required

    (A)   In general. No savings and loan holding company and no subsidiary which is not a savings association shall commence, either de novo or by an acquisition (in whole or in part) of a going concern, any activity described in paragraph (2)(F)(i) of this subsection without the prior approval of the Director.

(B) Factors to be considered by Director. In considering any application under subparagraph (A) by any savings and loan holding company or any subsidiary of any such company which is not a savings association, the Director shall consider--

    (i)   whether the performance of the activity described in such application by the company or the subsidiary can reasonably be expected to produce benefits to the public (such as greater convenience, increased competition, or gains in efficiency) that outweigh possible adverse effects of such activity (such as undue concentration of resources, decreased or unfair competition, conflicts of interest, or unsound financial practices);

    (ii)   the managerial resources of the companies involved; and

    (iii)   the adequacy of the financial resources, including capital, of the companies involved.

(C) Director may differentiate between new and ongoing activities. In prescribing any regulation or considering any application under this paragraph, the Director may differentiate between activities commenced de novo and activities commenced by the acquisition, in whole or in part, of a going concern.

(D) Approval or disapproval by order. The approval or disapproval of any application under this paragraph by the Director shall be made in an order issued by the Director containing the reasons for such approval or disapproval.

(5) Grace period to achieve compliance

If any savings association referred to in paragraph (3) fails to maintain the status of such association as a qualified thrift lender, the Director may allow, for good cause shown, any company that controls such association (or any subsidiary of such company which is not a savings association) up to 3 years to comply with the limitations contained in paragraph (1)(C).

(6) Special provisions relating to certain companies affected by 1987 amendments

(A) Exception to 2-year grace period for achieving compliance. Notwithstanding paragraph (1)(C), any company which received approval under subsection (e) of this section to acquire control of a savings association between March 5, 1987, and August 10, 1987, shall not continue any business activity other than an activity described in paragraph (2) after August 10, 1987.

(B) Exemption for activities lawfully engaged in before March 5, 1987. Notwithstanding paragraph (1)(C) and subject to subparagraphs (C) and (D), any savings and loan holding company which received approval, before March 5, 1987, under subsection (e) of this section to acquire control of a savings association may engage, directly or through any subsidiary (other than a savings association subsidiary of such company), in any activity in which such company or such subsidiary was lawfully engaged on such date.

(C) Termination of subparagraph (B) exemption. The exemption provided under subparagraph (B) for activities engaged in by any savings and loan holding company or a subsidiary of such company (which is not a savings association) which would otherwise be prohibited under paragraph (1)(C) shall terminate with respect to such activities of such company or subsidiary upon the occurrence (after August 10, 1987) of any of the following:

(i) The savings and loan holding company acquires control of a bank or an additional savings association (other than a savings association acquired pursuant to section 13(c) or 13(k) of the Federal Deposit Insurance Act [12 U.S.C.A. § 1823(c) or (k)] or section 406(f) or 408(m) of the National Housing Act [12 U.S.C.A. § 1729(f) or § 1730a(m)].

(ii) Any savings association subsidiary of the savings and loan holding company fails to qualify as a domestic building and loan association under section 7701(a)(19) of Title 26.

(iii) The savings and loan holding company engages in any business activity--

(I)   which is not described in paragraph (2); and

(II)   in which it was not engaged on March 5, 1987.

(iv) Any savings association subsidiary of the savings and loan holding company increases the number of locations from which such savings association conducts business after March 5, 1987 (other than an increase which occurs in connection with a transaction under section 13(c) or (k) of the Federal Deposit Insurance Act [12 U.S.C.A. § 1823(c) or (k)] or section 408(m) of the National Housing Act [12 U.S.C.A. § 1730a(m)].

(v)   Any savings association subsidiary of the savings and loan holding company permits any overdraft (including an intraday overdraft), or incurs any such overdraft in its account at a Federal Reserve bank, on behalf of an affiliate, unless such overdraft is the result of an inadvertent computer or accounting error that is beyond the control of both the savings association subsidiary and the affiliate.

(D) Order by Director to terminate subparagraph (B) activity. Any activity described in subparagraph (B) may also be terminated by the Director, after opportunity for hearing, if the Director determines, having due regard for the purposes of this title, that such action is necessary to prevent conflicts of interest or unsound practices or is in the public interest.

(7) Foreign savings and loan holding company

Notwithstanding any other provision of this section, any savings and loan holding company organized under the laws of a foreign country as of June 1, 1984 (including any subsidiary thereof which is not a savings association), which controls a single savings association on August 10, 1987, shall not be subject to this subsection with respect to any activities of such holding company which are conducted exclusively in a foreign country.

(8) Exemption for bank holding companies

Except for paragraph (1)(A), this subsection shall not apply to any company that is treated as a bank holding company for purposes of section 4 of the Bank Holding Company Act of 1956 [12 U.S.C.A. § 1843], or any of its subsidiaries.

* * *

(m) Qualified thrift lender test

(1) In general

Except as provided in paragraphs (2) and (7), any savings association is a qualified thrift lender if--

(A) the savings association qualifies as a domestic building and loan association, as such term is defined in section 7701(a)(19) of Title 26; or

(B) (i)   the savings association's qualified thrift investments equal or exceed 65 percent of the savings association's portfolio assets; and

(ii)   the savings association's qualified thrift investments continue to equal or exceed 65 percent of the savings association's portfolio assets on a monthly average basis in 9 out of every 12 months.

(2) Exceptions granted by Director

Notwithstanding paragraph (1), the Director may grant such temporary and limited exceptions from the minimum actual thrift investment percentage requirement contained in such paragraph as the Director deems necessary if--

(A) the Director determines that extraordinary circumstances exist, such as when the effects of high interest rates reduce mortgage demand to such a degree that an insufficient opportunity exists for a savings association to meet such investment requirements; or

(B) the Director determines that--

(i)   the grant of any such exception will significantly facilitate an acquisition under section 13(c) or 13(k) of the Federal Deposit Insurance Act [12 U.S.C.A. § 1823(c) or 1823(k)];

(ii)   the acquired association will comply with the transition requirements of paragraph (7)(B), as if the date of the exemption were the starting date for the transition period described in that paragraph; and

(iii)   the Director determines that the exemption will not have an undue adverse effect on competing savings associations in

the relevant market and will further the purposes of this subsection.

(3) Failure to become and remain a qualified thrift lender

(A) In general. A savings association that fails to become or remain a qualified thrift lender shall either become one or more banks (other than a savings bank) or be subject to subparagraph (B), except as provided in subparagraph (D).

(B) Restrictions applicable to savings associations that are not qualified thrift lenders

  (i) Restrictions effective immediately. The following restrictions shall apply to a savings association beginning on the date on which the savings association should have become or ceases to be a qualified thrift lender:

   (I) Activities. The savings association shall not make any new investment (including an investment in a subsidiary) or engage, directly or indirectly, in any other new activity unless that investment or activity would be permissible for the savings association if it were a national bank, and is also permissible for the savings association as a savings association.

   (II) Branching. The savings association shall not establish any new branch office at any location at which a national bank located in the savings association's home State may not establish a branch office. For purposes of this subclause, a savings association's home State is the State in which the savings association's total deposits were largest on the date on which the savings association should have become or ceased to be a qualified thrift lender.

   (III) Advances. The savings association shall not be eligible to obtain new advances from any Federal home loan bank.

   (IV) Dividends. The savings association shall be subject to all statutes and regulations governing the payment of dividends by a national bank in the same manner and to the same extent as if the savings association were a national bank.

       (ii) Additional restrictions effective after three years. The following additional restrictions shall apply to a savings association beginning 3 years after the date on which the savings association should have become or ceases to be a qualified thrift lender:

          (I) Activities. The savings association shall not retain any investment (including an investment in any subsidiary) or engage, directly or indirectly, in any activity unless that investment or activity would be permissible for the savings association if it were a national bank, and is also permissible for the savings association as a savings association.

          (II) Advances. The savings association shall repay any outstanding advances from any Federal home loan bank as promptly as can be prudently done consistent with the safe and sound operation of the savings association.

   (C) Holding company regulation. Any company that controls a savings association that is subject to any provision of subparagraph (B) shall, within one year after the date on which the savings association should have become or ceases to be a qualified thrift lender, register as and be deemed to be a bank holding company subject to all of the provisions of the Bank Holding Company Act of 1956 [12 U.S.C.A. § 1841 et seq.], section 8 of the Federal Deposit Insurance Act [12 U.S.C.A. § 1818], and other statutes applicable to bank holding companies, in the same manner and to the same extent as if the company were a bank holding company and the savings association were a bank, as those terms are defined in the Bank Holding Company Act of 1956 [12 U.S.C.A. § 1841 et seq.].

* * *

(4) Definitions

   For purposes of this subsection, the following definitions shall apply:

   (A) Actual thrift investment percentage. The term "actual thrift investment percentage" means the percentage determined by dividing --

      (i) the amount of a savings association's qualified thrift investments, by

      (ii) the amount of the savings association's portfolio assets.

(B) Portfolio assets. The term "portfolio assets" means, with respect to any savings association, the total assets of the savings association, minus the sum of--

(i)   goodwill and other intangible assets;

(ii)   the value of property used by the savings association to conduct its business; and

(iii) liquid assets of the type required to be maintained under section 1465 of this title, in an amount not exceeding the amount equal to 20 percent of the savings association's total assets.

(C) Qualified thrift investments.

(i)   In general. The term "qualified thrift investments" means, with respect to any savings association, the assets of the savings association that are described in clauses (ii) and (iii).

(ii)   Assets includible without limit. The following assets are described in this clause for purposes of clause (i):

(I)   The aggregate amount of loans held by the savings association that were made to purchase, refinance, construct, improve, or repair domestic residential housing or manufactured housing.

(II)   Home-equity loans.

(III) Securities backed by or representing an interest in mortgages on domestic residential housing or manufactured housing.

(IV) Existing obligations of deposit insurance agencies. Direct or indirect obligations of the Federal Deposit Insurance Corporation or the Federal Savings and Loan Insurance Corporation issued in accordance with the terms of agreements entered into prior to July 1, 1989, for the 10-year period beginning on the date of issuance of such obligations.

(V)   New obligations of deposit insurance agencies. Obligations of the Federal Deposit Insurance Corporation, the Federal Savings and Loan Insurance Corporation, the FSLIC Resolution Fund, and the Resolution Trust Corporation issued in accordance with the terms of agreements entered into on or after

July 1, 1989, for the 5-year period beginning on the date of issuance of such obligations.

(VI) Shares of stock issued by any Federal home loan bank.

(VII) Loans for educational purposes, loans to small businesses, and loans made through credit cards or credit card accounts.

(iii) Assets includible subject to percentage restriction. The following assets are described in this clause for purposes of clause (i):

(I)   50 percent of the dollar amount of the residential mortgage loans originated by such savings association and sold within 90 days of origination.

(II) Investments in the capital stock or obligations of, and any other security issued by, any service corporation if such service corporation derives at least 80 percent of its annual gross revenues from activities directly related to purchasing, refinancing, constructing, improving, or repairing domestic residential real estate or manufactured housing.

(III) 200 percent of the dollar amount of loans and investments made to acquire, develop, and construct 1- to 4-family residences the purchase price of which is or is guaranteed to be not greater than 60 percent of the median value of comparable newly constructed 1- to 4-family residences within the local community in which such real estate is located, except that not more than 25 percent of the amount included under this subclause may consist of commercial properties related to the development if those properties are directly related to providing services to residents of the development.

(IV) 200 percent of the dollar amount of loans for the acquisition or improvement of residential real property, churches, schools, and nursing homes located within, and loans for any other purpose

to any small businesses located within any area which has been identified by the Director, in connection with any review or examination of community reinvestment practices, as a geographic area or neighborhood in which the credit needs of the low- and moderate-income residents of such area or neighborhood are not being adequately met.

(V) Loans for the purchase or construction of churches, schools, nursing homes, and hospitals, other than those qualifying under clause (IV), and loans for the improvement and upkeep of such properties.

(VI) Loans for personal, family, or household purposes (other than loans for personal, family, or household purposes described in clause (ii)(VII)).

(VII) Shares of stock issued by the Federal Home Loan Mortgage Corporation or the Federal National Mortgage Association.

(iv) Percentage restriction applicable to certain assets. The aggregate amount of the assets described in clause (iii) which may be taken into account in determining the amount of the qualified thrift investments of any savings association shall not exceed the amount which is equal to 20 percent of a savings association's portfolio assets.

(v) The term "qualified thrift investments" excludes

(I)   except for home equity loans, that portion of any loan or investment that is used for any purpose other than those expressly qualifying under any subparagraph of clause (ii) or (iii); or

(II) goodwill or any other intangible asset.

* * *

CHAPTER FOUR

FEDERAL CREDIT UNION ACT

§ 1752. Definitions

As used in this chapter—

(1) the term "Federal credit union" means a cooperative association organized in accordance with the provisions of this chapter for the purpose of promoting thrift among its members and creating a source of credit for provident or productive purposes;

(2) the term "Chairman" means the Chairman of the National Credit Union Administration Board;

(3) the term "Administration" means the National Credit Union Administration;

(4) the term "Board" means the National Credit Union Administration Board;

* * *

§ 1759. Membership

(a) In General

Subject to subsection (b), Federal credit union membership shall consist of the incorporators and such other persons and incorporated and unincorporated organizations, to the extent permitted by rules and regulations prescribed by the Board, as may be elected to membership and as such shall each, subscribe to at least one share of its stock and pay the initial installment thereon and a uniform entrance fee if required by the board of directors. Shares may be issued in joint tenancy with right of survivorship with any persons designated by the credit union member, but no joint tenant shall be permitted to vote, obtain loans, or hold office, unless he is within the field of membership and is a qualified member.

(b) Membership Field

Subject to the other provisions of this section, the membership of any Federal credit union shall be limited to the membership described in one of the following categories:

(1)   Single Common-Bond Credit Union

One group that has a common bond of occupation or association.

(2)   Multiple Common-Bond Credit Union

More than one group —

(A)   each of which has (within the group) a common bond of occupation or association; and

(B)   the number of members, each of which (at the time the group is first included within the field of membership of a credit union described in this paragraph) does not exceed any numerical limitation applicable under subsection (d).

(3)   Community Credit Union — Persons or organizations within a well-defined local community, neighborhood, or rural district.

(c) Exceptions

(1)   Grandfathered Members and Groups

(A) In General

Notwithstanding subsection (b)--

(i)   any person or organization that is a member of any Federal credit union as of the date of enactment of the Credit Union Membership Access Act may remain a member of the credit union after that date of enactment; and

(ii)   a member of any group whose members constituted a portion of the membership of any Federal credit union as of that date of enactment shall continue to be eligible to become a member of that credit union, by virtue of membership in that group, after that date of enactment.

(B) Successors

If the common bond of any group referred to in subparagraph (A) is defined by any particular organization or business entity, subparagraph (A) shall continue to apply with respect to any successor to the organization or entity.

(2) Exception for Underserved Areas

Notwithstanding subsection (b), in the case of a Federal credit union, the field of membership category of which is described in subsection (b)(2), the Board may allow the membership of the credit union to include any person or organization within a local community, neighborhood, or rural district if--

(A)   the Board determines that the local community, neighborhood, or rural district--

   (i)   is an 'investment area', as defined in section 103(16) of the Community Development Banking and Financial Institutions Act of 1994 (12 U.S.C. 4703(16)), and meets such additional requirements as the Board may impose; and

   (ii)   is underserved, based on data of the Board and the Federal banking agencies (as defined in section 3 of the Federal Deposit Insurance Act), by other depository institutions (as defined in section 19(b)(1)(A) of the Federal Reserve Act); and

(B)   the credit union establishes and maintains an office or facility in the local community, neighborhood, or rural district at which credit union services are available.

(d) Multiple Common-Bond Credit Union Group Requirements.--

(1) Numerical Limitation

Except as provided in paragraph (2), only a group with fewer than 3,000 members shall be eligible to be included in the field of membership category of a credit union described in subsection (b)(2).

(2) Exceptions

In the case of any Federal credit union, the field of membership category of which is described in subsection (b)(2), the numerical limitation in paragraph (1) of this subsection shall not apply with respect to--

(A)   any group that the Board determines, in writing and in accordance with the guidelines and regulations issued under paragraph (3), could not feasibly or reasonably establish a new single common-bond credit union, the field of membership category of which is described in subsection (b)(1) because--

(i)   the group lacks sufficient volunteer and other resources to support the efficient and effective operation of a credit union;

(ii)   the group does not meet the criteria that the Board has determined to be important for the likelihood of success in establishing and managing a new credit union, including demographic characteristics such as geographical location of members, diversity of ages and income levels, and other factors that may affect the financial viability and stability of a credit union; or

(iii)   the group would be unlikely to operate a safe and sound credit union;

(B) any group transferred from another credit union--

(i) in connection with a merger or consolidation recommended by the Board or any appropriate State credit union supervisor based on safety and soundness concerns with respect to that other credit union; or

(ii) by the Board in the Board's capacity as conservator or liquidating agent with respect to that other credit union; or

(C) any group transferred in connection with a voluntary merger, having received conditional approval by the Administration of the merger application prior to October 25, 1996, but not having consummated the merger prior to October 25, 1996, if the merger is consummated not later than 180 days after the date of enactment of the Credit Union Membership Access Act.

(3) Regulations and Guidelines

The Board shall issue guidelines or regulations, after notice and opportunity for comment, setting forth the criteria that the Board will apply in determining under this subsection whether or not an additional group may be included within the field of membership category of an existing credit union described in subsection (b)(2).

(e) Additional Membership Eligibility Provisions.--

(1) Membership Eligibility Limited to Immediate Family or Household Members

No individual shall be eligible for membership in a credit union on the basis of the relationship of the individual to another person who is eligible for membership in the credit union, unless the individual is a

member of the immediate family or household (as those terms are defined by the Board, by regulation) of the other person.

(2) Retention of Membership

Except as provided in section 118, once a person becomes a member of a credit union in accordance with this title, that person or organization may remain a member of that credit union until the person or organization chooses to withdraw from the membership of the credit union.".

(f) Criteria for Approval of Expansion of Multiple Common-Bond Credit Unions

(1) In General

The Board shall—

(A) encourage the formation of separately chartered credit unions instead of approving an application to include an additional group within the field of membership of an existing credit union whenever practicable and consistent with reasonable standards for the safe and sound operation of the credit union; and

(B) if the formation of a separate credit union by the group is not practicable or consistent with the standards referred to in subparagraph (A), require the inclusion of the group in the field of membership of a credit union that is within reasonable proximity to the location of the group whenever practicable and consistent with reasonable standards for the safe and sound operation of the credit union.

(2) Approval Criteria

The Board may not approve any application by a Federal credit union, the field of membership category of which is described in subsection (b)(2) to include any additional group within the field of membership of the credit union (or an application by a Federal credit union described in subsection (b)(1) to include an additional group and become a credit union described in subsection (b)(2)), unless the Board determines, in writing, that —

(A) the credit union has not engaged in any unsafe or unsound practice (as defined in section 206(b)) that is material during the 1-year period preceding the date of filing of the application;

(B) the credit union is adequately capitalized;

(C)   the credit union has the administrative capability to serve the proposed membership group and the financial resources to meet the need for additional staff and assets to serve the new membership group;

(D)   any potential harm that the expansion of the field of membership of the credit union may have on any other insured credit union and its members is clearly outweighed in the public interest by the probable beneficial effect of the expansion in meeting the convenience and needs of the members of the group proposed to be included in the field of membership; and

(E)   the credit union has met such additional requirements as the Board may prescribe, by regulation."

(g) Regulations Required for Community Credit Unions

(1) Definition of Well-Defined Local Community, Neighborhood, or Rural District

The Board shall prescribe, by regulation, a definition for the term 'well-defined local community, neighborhood, or rural district' for purposes of —

(A)   making any determination with regard to the field of membership of a credit union described in subsection (b)(3); and

(B)   establishing the criteria applicable with respect to any such determination.

(2) Scope of Application

The definition prescribed by the Board under paragraph (1) shall apply with respect to any application to form a new credit union, or to alter or expand the field of membership of an existing credit union, that is filed with the Board after the date of enactment of the Credit Union Membership Access Act.".

* * *

FEDERAL DEPOSIT INSURANCE ACT

* * *

§ 1813. Definitions

As used in this chapter–

* * *

(l)   Deposit

The term "deposit" means–

(1)   the unpaid balance of money or its equivalent received or held by a bank or savings association in the usual course of business and for which it has given or is obligated to give credit, either conditionally or unconditionally, to a commercial, checking, savings, time, or thrift account, or which is evidenced by its certificate of deposit, thrift certificate, investment certificate, certificate of indebtedness, or other similar name, or a check or draft drawn against a deposit account and certified by the bank or savings association, or a letter of credit or a traveler's check on which the bank or savings association is primarily liable: Provided, That, without limiting the generality of the term "money or its equivalent", any such account or instrument must be regarded as evidencing the receipt of the equivalent of money when credited or issued in exchange for checks or drafts or for a promissory note upon which the person obtaining any such credit or instrument is primarily or secondarily liable, or for a charge against a deposit account, or in settlement of checks, drafts, or other instruments forwarded to such bank or savings association for collection.

* * *

(m) Insured deposit

(1)   In general

Subject to paragraph (2), the term "insured deposit" means the net amount due to any depositor for deposits in an insured depository institution as determined under sections 1817(i) and 1821(a) of this title.

* * *

(3) Uninsured deposits

The term "uninsured deposit" means the amount of any deposit of any depositor at any insured depository institution in excess of the amount of the insured deposits of such depositor (if any) at such depository institution.

(4) Preferred deposits

The term "preferred deposits" means deposits of any public unit (as defined in paragraph (1)) at any insured depository institution which are secured or collateralized as required under State law.

* * *

(p) Trust funds

The term "trust funds" means funds held by an insured depository institution in a fiduciary capacity and includes, without being limited to, funds held as trustee, executor, administrator, guardian, or agent.

(q) Appropriate Federal banking agency

The term "appropriate Federal banking agency" means–

(1) the Comptroller of the Currency, in the case of any national banking association, any District bank, or any Federal branch or agency of a foreign bank;

(2) the Board of Governors of the Federal Reserve System, in the case of–

(A) any State member insured bank (except a District bank),

* * *

(F) any bank holding company and any subsidiary of a bank holding company (other than a bank);

(3) the Federal Deposit Insurance Corporation in the case of a State nonmember insured bank (except a District bank), or a foreign bank having an insured branch; and

(4) the Director of the Office of Thrift Supervision in the case of any savings association or any savings and loan holding company.

Under the rule set forth in this subsection, more than one agency may be an appropriate Federal banking agency with respect to any given institution.

(r) State bank supervisor

(1) In general

The term "State bank supervisor" means any officer, agency, or other entity of any State which has primary regulatory authority over State banks or State savings associations in such State.

(2) Interstate application

The State bank supervisors of more than 1 State may be the appropriate State bank supervisor for any insured depository institution.

* * *

(u) Institution-affiliated party

The term "institution-affiliated party" means–

(1) any director, officer, employee, or controlling stockholder (other than a bank holding company) of, or agent for, an insured depository institution;

(2) any other person who has filed or is required to file a change-in-control notice with the appropriate Federal banking agency under section 1817(j) of this title;

(3) any shareholder (other than a bank holding company), consultant, joint venture partner, and any other person as determined by the appropriate Federal banking agency (by regulation or case-by-case) who participates in the conduct of the affairs of an insured depository institution; and

(4) any independent contractor (including any attorney, appraiser, or accountant) who knowingly or recklessly participates in–

(A) any violation of any law or regulation;

(B) any breach of fiduciary duty; or

(C) any unsafe or unsound practice, which caused or is likely to cause more than a minimal financial loss to, or a significant adverse effect on, the insured depository institution.

* * *

§ 1815. Deposit insurance

* * *

(e)   **Liability of commonly controlled depository institutions**

    (1)   **In general**

        (A)   Liability established

            Any insured depository institution shall be liable for any loss incurred by the Corporation, or any loss which the Corporation reasonably anticipates incurring, after August 9, 1989 in connection with–

            (i)   the default of a commonly controlled insured depository institution; or

            (ii)   any assistance provided by the Corporation to any commonly controlled insured depository institution in danger of default.

        (B)   Payment upon notice

            An insured depository institution shall pay the amount of any liability to the Corporation under subparagraph (A) upon receipt of written notice by the Corporation in accordance with this subsection.

        (C)   Notice required to be provided within 2 years of loss

            No insured depository institution shall be liable to the Corporation under subparagraph (A) if written notice with respect to such liability is not received by such institution before the end of the 2-year period beginning on the date the Corporation incurred the loss.

    (2)   **Amount of compensation; procedures**

        (A)   Use of estimates

            When an insured depository institution is in default or requires assistance to prevent default, the Corporation shall–

            (i)   in good faith, estimate the amount of the loss the Corporation will incur from such default or assistance;

            (ii)   if, with respect to such insured depository institution, there is more than 1 commonly controlled insured depository institution, estimate the amount of each such commonly controlled depository institution's share of such liability; and

(iii) advise each commonly controlled depository institution of the Corporation's estimate of the amount of such institution's liability for such losses.

(B) Procedures; immediate payment

The Corporation, after consultation with the appropriate Federal banking agency and the appropriate State chartering agency, shall–

(i) on a case-by-case basis, establish the procedures and schedule under which any insured depository institution shall reimburse the Corporation for such institution's liability under paragraph (1) in connection with any commonly controlled insured depository institution; or

(ii) require any insured depository institution to make immediate payment of the amount of such institution's liability under paragraph (1) in connection with any commonly controlled insured depository institution.

(C) Priority

The liability of any insured depository institution under this subsection shall have priority with respect to other obligations and liabilities as follows:

(i) Superiority

The liability shall be superior to the following obligations and liabilities of the depository institution:

(I) Any obligation to shareholders arising as a result of their status as shareholders (including any depository institution holding company or any shareholder or creditor of such company).

(II) Any obligation or liability owed to any affiliate of the depository institution (including any other insured depository institution) other than any secured obligation which was secured as of May 1, 1989.

(ii) Subordination

The liability shall be subordinate in right and payment to the following obligations and liabilities of the depository institution:

(I) Any deposit liability (which is not a liability described in clause (i)(II)).

(II)   Any secured obligation, other than any obligation owed to any affiliate of the depository institution (including any other insured depository institution) which was secured after May 1, 1989.

(III) Any other general or senior liability (which is not a liability described in clause (i)).

(IV) Any obligation subordinated to depositors or other general creditors (which is not an obligation described in clause (i)).

* * *

(4) Limitation on rights of private parties

To the extent the exercise of any right or power of any person would impair the ability of any insured depository institution to perform such institution's obligations under this subsection–

(A) the obligations of such insured depository institution shall supersede such right or power; and

(B) no court may give effect to such right or power with respect to such insured depository institution.

* * *

§ 1816. Factors to be considered

The factors that are required, under section 1814 of this title, to be considered in connection with, and enumerated in, any certificate issued pursuant to section 1814 of this title and that are required, under section 1815 of this title, to be considered by the Board of Directors in connection with any determination by such Board pursuant to section 1815 of this title are the following:

(1)   The financial history and condition of the depository institution.

(2)   The adequacy of the depository institution's capital structure.

(3)   The future earnings prospects of the depository institution.

(4)   The general character and fitness of the management of the depository institution.

(5)   The risk presented by such depository institution to the Bank Insurance Fund or the Savings Association Insurance fund.

(6)   The convenience and needs of the community to be served by such depository institution.

(7) Whether the depository institution's corporate powers are consistent with the purposes of this chapter.

§ 1817. Assessments

* * *

(b) Assessments

(1) Risk-based assessment system

(A) Risk-based assessment system required

The Board of Directors shall, by regulation, establish a risk-based assessment system for insured depository institutions.

* * *

(C) Risk-based assessment system defined

For purposes of this paragraph, the term "risk-based assessment system" means a system for calculating a depository institution's semiannual assessment based on–

(i) the probability that the deposit insurance fund will incur a loss with respect to the institution, taking into consideration the risks attributable to–

(I) different categories and concentrations of assets;

(II) different categories and concentrations of liabilities, both insured and uninsured, contingent and noncontingent; and

(III) any other factors the Corporation determines are relevant to assessing such probability;

(ii) the likely amount of any such loss; and

(iii) the revenue needs of the deposit insurance fund.

* * *

(i) Insurance of trust funds

(1) In general

Trust funds held on deposit by an insured depository institution in a fiduciary capacity as trustee pursuant to any irrevocable trust established pursuant to any statute or written trust agreement shall be insured in an amount not to exceed $100,000 for each trust estate.

* * *

§ 1818. Termination of status as insured depository institution

* * *

(b) Cease-and-desist proceedings

(1) If, in the opinion of the appropriate Federal banking agency, any insured depository institution, depository institution which has insured deposits, or any institution-affiliated party is engaging or has engaged, or the agency has reasonable cause to believe that the depository institution or any institution-affiliated party is about to engage, in an unsafe or unsound practice in conducting the business of such depository institution, or is violating or has violated, or the agency has reasonable cause to believe that the depository institution or any institution-affiliated party is about to violate, a law, rule, or regulation, or any condition imposed in writing by the agency in connection with the granting of any application or other request by the depository institution or any written agreement entered into with the agency, the agency may issue and serve upon the depository institution or such party a notice of charges in respect thereof. The notice shall contain a statement of the facts constituting the alleged violation or violations or the unsafe or unsound practice or practices, and shall fix a time and place at which a hearing will be held to determine whether an order to cease and desist therefrom should issue against the depository institution or the institution-affiliated party. Such hearing shall be fixed for a date not earlier than thirty days nor later than sixty days after service of such notice unless an earlier or a later date is set by the agency at the request of any party so served. Unless the party or parties so served shall appear at the hearing personally or by a duly authorized representative, they shall be deemed to have consented to the issuance of the cease-and-desist order. In the event of such consent, or if upon the record made at any such hearing, the agency shall find that any violation or unsafe or unsound practice specified in the notice of charges has been established, the agency may issue and serve upon the depository institution or the institution-affiliated party an order to cease and desist from any such violation or practice. Such order may, by provisions which may be mandatory or otherwise, require the depository institution or its institution-affiliated parties to cease and desist from the same, and, further, to take affirmative action to correct the conditions resulting from any such violation or practice.

(2) A cease-and-desist order shall become effective at the expiration of thirty days after the service of such order upon the depository

institution or other person concerned (except in the case of a cease-and-desist order issued upon consent, which shall become effective at the time specified therein), and shall remain effective and enforceable as provided therein, except to such extent as it is stayed, modified, terminated, or set aside by action of the agency or a reviewing court.

(3) This subsection and subsections (c) through (s) and subsection (u) of this section shall apply to any bank holding company, and to any subsidiary (other than a bank) of a bank holding company, as those terms are defined in the Bank Holding Company Act of 1956 [12 U.S.C.A. § 1841 *et seq.*], and to any organization organized and operated under section 25(a) of the Federal Reserve Act [12 U.S.C.A. § 611 *et seq.*] or operating under section 25 of the Federal Reserve Act [12 U.S.C.A. § 601 *et seq.*], in the same manner as they apply to a State member insured depository institution. Nothing in this subsection or in subsection (c) of this section shall authorize any Federal banking agency, other than the Board of Governors of the Federal Reserve System, to issue a notice of charges or cease-and-desist order against a bank holding company or any subsidiary thereof (other than a bank or subsidiary of that bank).

(4) This subsection and subsections (c) through (s) and subsection (u) of this section shall apply to any foreign bank or company to which subsection (a) of section 3106 of this title applies and to any subsidiary (other than a bank) of any such foreign bank or company in the same manner as they apply to a bank holding company and any subsidiary thereof (other than a bank) under paragraph (3) of this subsection. For the purposes of this paragraph, the term "subsidiary" shall have the meaning assigned it in section 2 of the Bank Holding Company Act of 1956 [12 U.S.C.A. § 1841].

(5) This section shall apply, in the same manner as it applies to any insured depository institution for which the appropriate Federal banking agency is the Comptroller of the Currency, to any national banking association chartered by the Comptroller of the Currency, including an uninsured association.

(6) Affirmative action to correct conditions resulting from violations or practices

The authority to issue an order under this subsection and subsection (c) of this section which requires an insured depository institution or any institution-affiliated party to take affirmative action to correct or remedy any conditions resulting from any violation or

practice with respect to which such order is issued includes the authority to require such depository institution or such party to–

(A) make restitution or provide reimbursement, indemnification, or guarantee against loss if–

  (i)   such depository institution or such party was unjustly enriched in connection with such violation or practice; or

  (ii) the violation or practice involved a reckless disregard for the law or any applicable regulations or prior order of the appropriate Federal banking agency;

(B) restrict the growth of the institution;

(C) dispose of any loan or asset involved;

(D) rescind agreements or contracts; and

(E) employ qualified officers or employees (who may be subject to approval by the appropriate Federal banking agency at the direction of such agency); and

(F) take such other action as the banking agency determines to be appropriate.

(7) Authority to limit activities

The authority to issue an order under this subsection or subsection (c) of this section includes the authority to place limitations on the activities or functions of an insured depository institution or any institution-affiliated party.

(8) Unsatisfactory asset quality, management, earnings, or liquidity as unsafe or unsound practice

If an insured depository institution receives, in its most recent report of examination, a less-than-satisfactory rating for asset quality, management, earnings, or liquidity, the appropriate Federal banking agency may (if the deficiency is not corrected) deem the institution to be engaging in an unsafe or unsound practice for purposes of this subsection.

* * *

(c) Temporary cease-and-desist orders

    (1) Whenever the appropriate Federal banking agency shall determine that the violation or threatened violation or the unsafe or unsound practice or practices, specified in the notice of charges served upon the depository institution or any institution-affiliated party pursuant to paragraph (1) of subsection (b) of this section, or the continuation thereof, is likely to cause insolvency or significant dissipation of assets or earnings of the depository institution, or is likely to weaken the condition of the depository institution or otherwise prejudice the interests of its depositors prior to the completion of the proceedings conducted pursuant to paragraph (1) of subsection (b) of this section, the agency may issue a temporary order requiring the depository institution or such party to cease and desist from any such violation or practice and to take affirmative action to prevent or remedy such insolvency, dissipation, condition, or prejudice pending completion of such proceedings. Such order may include any requirement authorized under subsection (b)(6) of this section. Such order shall become effective upon service upon the depository institution or such institution-affiliated party and, unless set aside, limited, or suspended by a court in proceedings authorized by paragraph (2) of this subsection, shall remain effective and enforceable pending the completion of the administrative proceedings pursuant to such notice and until such time as the agency shall dismiss the charges specified in such notice, or if a cease-and-desist order is issued against the depository institution or such party, until the effective date of such order.

    (2) Within ten days after the depository institution concerned or any institution-affiliated party has been served with a temporary cease-and-desist order, the depository institution or such party may apply to the United States district court for the judicial district in which the home office of the depository institution is located, or the United States District Court for the District of Columbia, for an injunction setting aside, limiting, or suspending the enforcement, operation, or effectiveness of such order pending the completion of the administrative proceedings pursuant to the notice of charges served upon the depository institution or such party under paragraph (1) of subsection (b) of this section, and such court shall have jurisdiction to issue such injunction.

    (3) Incomplete or inaccurate records

        (A) Temporary order

If a notice of charges served under subsection (b)(1) of this section specifies, on the basis of particular facts and circumstances, that an insured depository institution's books and records are so incomplete or inaccurate that the appropriate Federal banking agency is unable, through the normal supervisory process, to determine the financial condition of that depository institution or the details or purpose of any transaction or transactions that may have a material effect on the financial condition of that depository institution, the agency may issue a temporary order requiring–

(i)   the cessation of any activity or practice which gave rise, whether in whole or in part, to the incomplete or inaccurate state of the books or records; or

(ii)   affirmative action to restore such books or records to a complete and accurate state, until the completion of the proceedings under subsection (b)(1) of this section.

(B) Effective period

Any temporary order issued under subparagraph (A)–

(i)   shall become effective upon service; and

(ii)   unless set aside, limited, or suspended by a court in proceedings under paragraph (2), shall remain in effect and enforceable until the earlier of–

(I)   the completion of the proceeding initiated under subsection (b)(1) of this section in connection with the notice of charges; or

(II)   the date the appropriate Federal banking agency determines, by examination or otherwise, that the insured depository institution's books and records are accurate and reflect the financial condition of the depository institution.

(d)   Temporary cease-and-desist orders; enforcement

In the case of violation or threatened violation of, or failure to obey, a temporary cease-and-desist order issued pursuant to paragraph (1) of subsection (c) of this section, the appropriate Federal banking agency may apply to the United States district court, or the United States court of any territory, within the jurisdiction of which the home office of the depository institution is located, for an injunction to enforce such order, and, if the court shall determine that there has been such violation or threatened

violation or failure to obey, it shall be the duty of the court to issue such injunction.

(e) Removal and prohibition authority

(1)   Authority to issue order

Whenever the appropriate Federal banking agency determines that—

(A) any institution-affiliated party has, directly or indirectly—

(i)   violated—

(I)   any law or regulation;

(II)   any cease-and-desist order which has become final;

(III) any condition imposed in writing by the appropriate Federal banking agency in connection with the grant of any application or other request by such depository institution; or

(IV) any written agreement between such depository institution and   such agency;

(ii)   engaged or participated in any unsafe or unsound practice in connection with any insured depository institution or business institution; or

(iii) committed or engaged in any act, omission, or practice which constitutes a breach of such party's fiduciary duty;

(B) by reason of the violation, practice, or breach described in any clause of subparagraph (A)—

(i)   such insured depository institution or business institution has suffered or will probably suffer financial loss or other damage;

(ii)   the interests of the insured depository institution's depositors have been or could be prejudiced; or

(iii) such party has received financial gain or other benefit by reason of such violation, practice, or breach; and

(C) such violation, practice, or breach—

(i)   involves personal dishonesty on the part of such party; or

(ii)   demonstrates willful or continuing disregard by such party for the safety or soundness of such insured depository institution or business institution, the agency may serve

upon such party a written notice of the agency's intention to remove such party from office or to prohibit any further participation by such party, in any manner, in the conduct of the affairs of any insured depository institution.

(2) Specific violations

(A) In general

Whenever the appropriate Federal banking agency determines that–

(i) an institution-affiliated party has committed a violation of any provision of subchapter II of chapter 53 of Title 31 and such violation was not inadvertent or unintentional;

(ii) an officer or director of an insured depository institution has knowledge that an institution-affiliated party of the insured depository institution has violated any such provision or any provision of law referred to in subsection (g)(1)(A)(ii) of this section; or

(iii) an officer or director of an insured depository institution has committed any violation of the Depository Institution Management Interlocks Act [12 U.S.C.A. § 3201 *et seq.*], the agency may serve upon such party, officer, or director a written notice of the agency's intention to remove such party from office.

(B) Factors to be considered

In determining whether an officer or director should be removed as a result of the application of subparagraph (A)(ii), the agency shall consider whether the officer or director took appropriate action to stop, or to prevent the recurrence of, a violation described in such subparagraph.

(3) Suspension order

(A) Suspension or prohibition authorized

If the appropriate Federal banking agency serves written notice under paragraph (1) or (2) to any institution-affiliated party of such agency's intention to issue an order under such paragraph, the appropriate Federal banking agency may suspend such party from office or prohibit such party from further participation in any manner in the conduct of the affairs of the depository institution, if the agency–

(i)   determines that such action is necessary for the protection of the depository institution or the interests of the depository institution's depositors; and

(ii)   serves such party with written notice of the suspension order.

(B) Effective period

Any suspension order issued under subparagraph (A)–

(i)   shall become effective upon service; and

(ii)   unless a court issues a stay of such order under subsection (f) of this section, shall remain in effect and enforceable until–

(I)   the date the appropriate Federal banking agency dismisses the charges contained in the notice served under paragraph (1) or (2) with respect to such party; or

(II)   the effective date of an order issued by the agency to such party under paragraph (1) or (2).

(C) Copy of order

If an appropriate Federal banking agency issues a suspension order under subparagraph (A) to any institution-affiliated party, the agency shall serve a copy of such order on any insured depository institution with which such party is associated at the time such order is issued.

(4)   A notice of intention to remove an institution-affiliated party from office or to prohibit such party from participating in the conduct of the affairs of an insured depository institution, shall contain a statement of the facts constituting grounds therefor, and shall fix a time and place at which a hearing will be held thereon. Such hearing shall be fixed for a date not earlier than thirty days nor later than sixty days after the date of service of such notice, unless an earlier or a later date is set by the agency at the request of (A) such party, and for good cause shown, or (B) the Attorney General of the United States. Unless such party shall appear at the hearing in person or by a duly authorized representative, such party shall be deemed to have consented to the issuance of an order of such removal or prohibition. In the event of such consent, or if upon the record made at any such hearing the agency shall find that any of the grounds specified in such notice have been established, the agency may issue such orders of

suspension or removal from office, or prohibition from participation in the conduct of the affairs of the depository institution, as it may deem appropriate. In any action brought under this section by the Comptroller of the Currency in respect to any such party with respect to a national banking association or a District depository institution, the findings and conclusions of the Administrative Law Judge shall be certified to the Board of Governors of the Federal Reserve System for the determination of whether any order shall issue. Any such order shall become effective at the expiration of thirty days after service upon such depository institution and such party (except in the case of an order issued upon consent, which shall become effective at the time specified therein). Such order shall remain effective and enforceable except to such extent as it is stayed, modified, terminated, or set aside by action of the agency or a reviewing court.

* * *

(6) Prohibition of certain specific activities

Any person subject to an order issued under this subsection shall not–

(A) participate in any manner in the conduct of the affairs of any institution or agency specified in paragraph (7)(A);

(B) solicit, procure, transfer, attempt to transfer, vote, or attempt to vote any proxy, consent, or authorization with respect to any voting rights in any institution described in subparagraph (A);

(C) violate any voting agreement previously approved by the appropriate Federal banking agency; or

(D) vote for a director, or serve or act as an institution-affiliated party.

(7) Industrywide prohibition

(A) In general

Except as provided in subparagraph (B), any person who, pursuant to an order issued under this subsection or subsection (g) of this section, has been removed or suspended from office in an insured depository institution or prohibited from participating in the conduct of the affairs of an insured depository institution may not, while such order is in effect, continue or commence to hold any office in, or participate in any manner in the conduct of the affairs of–

(i)   any insured depository institution;

* * *

(B) Exception if agency provides written consent

If, on or after the date an order is issued under this subsection which removes or suspends from office any institution-affiliated party or prohibits such party from participating in the conduct of the affairs of an insured depository institution, such party receives the written consent of–

(i)   the agency that issued such order; and

(ii) the appropriate Federal financial institutions regulatory agency of the institution described in any clause of subparagraph (A) with respect to which such party proposes to become an institution-affiliated party, subparagraph (A) shall, to the extent of such consent, cease to apply to such party with respect to the institution described in each written consent. Any agency that grants such a written consent shall report such action to the Corporation and publicly disclose such consent.

(C) Violation of paragraph treated as violation of order

Any violation of subparagraph (A) by any person who is subject to an order described in such subparagraph shall be treated as a violation of the order.

* * *

(f)   Stay of suspension and/or prohibition of institution-affiliated party

Within ten days after any institution-affiliated party has been suspended from office and/or prohibited from participation in the conduct of the affairs of an insured depository institution under subsection (e)(3) of this section, such party may apply to the United States district court for the judicial district in which the home office of the depository institution is located, or the United States District Court for the District of Columbia, for a stay of such suspension and/or prohibition pending the completion of the administrative proceedings pursuant to the notice served upon such party under subsection (e)(1) or (e)(2) of this section, and such court shall have jurisdiction to stay such suspension and/or prohibition.

(g) **Suspension or removal of institution-affiliated party charged with felony**

(1) **Suspension or prohibition**

(A) **In general**

Whenever any institution-affiliated party is charged in any information, indictment, or complaint, with the commission of or participation in–

(i)   a crime involving dishonesty or breach of trust which is punishable by imprisonment for a term exceeding one year under State or Federal law, or

(ii) a criminal violation of section 1956, 1957, or 1960 of Title 18 or section 5322 or 5324 of Title 31, the appropriate Federal banking agency may, if continued service or participation by such party may pose a threat to the interests of the depository institution's depositors or may threaten to impair public confidence in the depository institution, by written notice served upon such party, suspend such party from office or prohibit such party from further participation in any manner in the conduct of the affairs of the depository institution.

(B) **Provisions applicable to notice**

(i)   Copy

A copy of any notice under subparagraph (A) shall also be served upon the depository institution.

(ii) Effective period

A suspension or prohibition under subparagraph (A) shall remain in effect until the information, indictment, or complaint referred to in such subparagraph is finally disposed of or until terminated by the agency.

(C) **Removal or prohibition**

(i)   In general

If a judgment of conviction or an agreement to enter a pretrial diversion or other similar program is entered against an institution-affiliated party in connection with a crime described in subparagraph (A)(i), at such time as such judgment is not subject to further appellate review, the appropriate Federal banking agency may, if continued

service or participation by such party may pose a threat to the interests of the depository institution's depositors or may threaten to impair public confidence in the depository institution, issue and serve upon such party an order removing such party from office or prohibiting such party from further participation in any manner in the conduct of the affairs of the depository institution without the prior written consent of the appropriate agency.

* * *

(D) Provisions applicable to order

* * *

(ii) Effect of acquittal

A finding of not guilty or other disposition of the charge shall not preclude the agency from instituting proceedings after such finding or disposition to remove such party from office or to prohibit further participation in depository institution affairs, pursuant to paragraph (1), (2), or (3) of subsection (e) of this section.

* * *

(3) Within thirty days from service of any notice of suspension or order of removal issued pursuant to paragraph (1) of this subsection, the institution-affiliated party concerned may request in writing an opportunity to appear before the agency to show that the continued service to or participation in the conduct of the affairs of the depository institution by such party does not, or is not likely to, pose a threat to the interests of the depository institution's depositors or threaten to impair public confidence in the depository institution. Upon receipt of any such request, the appropriate Federal banking agency shall fix a time (not more than thirty days after receipt of such request, unless extended at the request of such party) and place at which such party may appear, personally or through counsel, before one or more members of the agency or designated employees of the agency to submit written materials (or, at the discretion of the agency, oral testimony) and oral argument. Within sixty days of such hearing, the agency shall notify such party whether the suspension or prohibition from participation in any manner in the conduct of the affairs of the depository institution will be continued, terminated, or otherwise modified, or whether the order removing such party from office or prohibiting such party from further participation in any

manner in the conduct of the affairs of the depository institution will be rescinded or otherwise modified. Such notification shall contain a statement of the basis for the agency's decision, if adverse to such party. The Federal banking agencies are authorized to prescribe such rules as may be necessary to effectuate the purposes of this subsection.

(h) Hearings and judicial review

(1) Any hearing provided for in this section (other than the hearing provided for in subsection (g)(3) of this section) shall be held in the Federal judicial district or in the territory in which the home office of the depository institution is located unless the party afforded the hearing consents to another place, and shall be conducted in accordance with the provisions of chapter 5 of Title 5. After such hearing, and within ninety days after the appropriate Federal banking agency or Board of Governors of the Federal Reserve System has notified the parties that the case has been submitted to it for final decision, it shall render its decision (which shall include findings of fact upon which its decision is predicated) and shall issue and serve upon each party to the proceeding an order or orders consistent with the provisions of this section. Judicial review of any such order shall be exclusively as provided in this subsection (h) of this section. Unless a petition for review is timely filed in a court of appeals of the United States, as hereinafter provided in paragraph (2) of this subsection, and thereafter until the record in the proceeding has been filed as so provided, the issuing agency may at any time, upon such notice and in such manner as it shall deem proper, modify, terminate, or set aside any such order. Upon such filing of the record, the agency may modify, terminate, or set aside any such order with permission of the court.

(2) Any party to any proceeding under paragraph (1) may obtain a review of any order served pursuant to paragraph (1) of this subsection (other than an order issued with the consent of the depository institution or the institution-affiliated party concerned, or an order issued under paragraph (1) of subsection (g) of this section) by the filing in the court of appeals of the United States for the circuit in which the home office of the depository institution is located, or in the United States Court of Appeals for the District of Columbia Circuit, within thirty days after the date of service of such order, a written petition praying that the order of the agency be modified, terminated, or set aside. A copy of such petition shall be forthwith transmitted by the clerk of the court to the agency, and thereupon the agency shall

file in the court the record in the proceeding, as provided in section 2112 of Title 28. Upon the filing of such petition, such court shall have jurisdiction, which upon the filing of the record shall except as provided in the last sentence of said paragraph (1) be exclusive, to affirm, modify, terminate, or set aside, in whole or in part, the order of the agency. Review of such proceedings shall be had as provided in chapter 7 of Title 5. The judgment and decree of the court shall be final, except that the same shall be subject to review by the Supreme Court upon certiorari, as provided in section 1254 of Title 28.

(3) The commencement of proceedings for judicial review under paragraph (2) of this subsection shall not, unless specifically ordered by the court, operate as a stay of any order issued by the agency.

(i) Jurisdiction and enforcement; civil money penalty

(1) The appropriate Federal banking agency may in its discretion apply to the United States district court, or the United States court of any territory, within the jurisdiction of which the home office of the depository institution is located, for the enforcement of any effective and outstanding notice or order issued under this section or under section 1831o or 1831p-1 of this title, and such courts shall have jurisdiction and power to order and require compliance herewith; but except as otherwise provided in this section or under section 1831o or 1831p-1 of this title no court shall have jurisdiction to affect by injunction or otherwise the issuance or enforcement of any notice or order under any such section, or to review, modify, suspend, terminate, or set aside any such notice or order.

(2) Civil money penalty

(A) First tier

Any insured depository institution which, and any institution-affiliated party who–

(i) violates any law or regulation;

(ii) violates any final order or temporary order issued pursuant to subsection (b), (c), (e), (g), or (s) of this section or any final order under section 1831o or 1831p-1 of this title;

(iii) violates any condition imposed in writing by the appropriate Federal banking agency in connection with the grant of any application or other request by such depository institution; or

(iv) violates any written agreement between such depository institution and such agency, shall forfeit and pay a civil penalty of not more than $5,000 for each day during which such violation continues.

(B) Second tier

Notwithstanding subparagraph (A), any insured depository institution which, and any institution-affiliated party who–

(i) (I) commits any violation described in any clause of subparagraph (A);

(II) recklessly engages in an unsafe or unsound practice in conducting the affairs of such insured depository institution; or

(III) breaches any fiduciary duty;

(ii) which violation, practice, or breach–

(I) is part of a pattern of misconduct;

(II) causes or is likely to cause more than a minimal loss to such depository institution; or

(III) results in pecuniary gain or other benefit to such party, shall forfeit and pay a civil penalty of not more than $25,000 for each day during which such violation, practice, or breach continues.

(C) Third tier

Notwithstanding subparagraphs (A) and (B), any insured depository institution which, and any institution-affiliated party who–

(i) knowingly–

(I) commits any violation described in any clause of subparagraph (A);

(II) engages in any unsafe or unsound practice in conducting the affairs of such depository institution; or

(III) breaches any fiduciary duty; and

(ii) knowingly or recklessly causes a substantial loss to such depository institution or a substantial pecuniary gain or other benefit to such party by reason of such violation, practice, or breach, shall forfeit and pay a civil penalty in an

amount not to exceed the applicable maximum amount determined under subparagraph (D) for each day during which such violation, practice, or breach continues.

(D) Maximum amounts of penalties for any violation described in subparagraph (c)

The maximum daily amount of any civil penalty which may be assessed pursuant to subparagraph (C) for any violation, practice, or breach described in such subparagraph is–

(i)   in the case of any person other than an insured depository institution, an amount to not exceed $1,000,000; and

(ii)   in the case of any insured depository institution, an amount not to exceed the lesser of–

(I) $1,000,000; or

(II)   1 percent of the total assets of such institution.

(E) Assessment

(i)   Written notice

Any penalty imposed under subparagraph (A), (B), or (C) may be assessed and collected by the appropriate Federal banking agency by written notice.

(ii)   Finality of assessment

If, with respect to any assessment under clause (i), a hearing is not requested pursuant to subparagraph (H) within the period of time allowed under such subparagraph, the assessment shall constitute a final and unappealable order.

(F) Authority to modify or remit penalty

Any appropriate Federal banking agency may compromise, modify, or remit any penalty which such agency may assess or had already assessed under subparagraph (A), (B), or (C).

(G) Mitigating factors

In determining the amount of any penalty imposed under subparagraph (A), (B), or (C), the appropriate agency shall take into account the appropriateness of the penalty with respect to–

(i)   the size of financial resources and good faith of the insured depository institution or other person charged;

(ii)   the gravity of the violation;

    (iii) the history of previous violations; and

    (iv) such other matters as justice may require.

(H) Hearing

The insured depository institution or other person against whom any penalty is assessed under this paragraph shall be afforded an agency hearing if such institution or person submits a request for such hearing within 20 days after the issuance of the notice of assessment.

* * *

(3) Notice under this section after separation from service

The resignation, termination of employment or participation, or separation of an institution-affiliated party (including a separation caused by the closing of an insured depository institution) shall not affect the jurisdiction and authority of the appropriate Federal banking agency to issue any notice and proceed under this section against any such party, if such notice is served before the end of the 6-year period beginning on the date such party ceased to be such a party with respect to such depository institution (whether such date occurs before, on, or after August 9, 1989).

(4) Prejudgment attachment

(A) In general

In any action brought by an appropriate Federal banking agency (excluding the Corporation when acting in a manner described in section 1821(d)(18) of this title) pursuant to this section, or in actions brought in aid of, or to enforce an order in, any administrative or other civil action for money damages, restitution, or civil money penalties brought by such agency, the court may, upon application of the agency, issue a restraining order that—

    (i) prohibits any person subject to the proceeding from withdrawing, transferring, removing, dissipating, or disposing of any funds, assets or other property; and

    (ii) appoints a temporary receiver to administer the restraining order.

* * *

(n)   Ancillary provisions; subpena power, etc.

In the course of or in connection with any proceeding under this section, or in connection with any claim for insured deposits or any examination or investigation under section 1820(c) of this title, the agency conducting the proceeding, examination, or investigation or considering the claim for insured deposits, or any member or designated representative thereof, including any person designated to conduct any hearing under this section, shall have the power to administer oaths and affirmations, to take or cause to be taken depositions, and to issue, revoke, quash, or modify subpoenas and subpoenas duces tecum; and such agency is empowered to make rules and regulations with respect to any such proceedings, claims, examinations, or investigations. The attendance of witnesses and the production of documents provided for in this subsection may be required from any place in any State or in any territory or other place subject to the jurisdiction of the United States at any designated place where such proceeding is being conducted. Any such agency or any party to proceedings under this section may apply to the United States District Court for the District of Columbia, or the United States district court for the judicial district or the United States court in any territory in which such proceeding is being conducted, or where the witness resides or carries on business, for enforcement of any subpena or subpena duces tecum issued pursuant to this subsection, and such courts shall have jurisdiction and power to order and require compliance therewith. Witnesses subpoenaed under this subsection shall be paid the same fees and mileage that are paid witnesses in the district courts of the United States. Any court having jurisdiction of any proceeding instituted under this section by an insured depository institution or a director or officer thereof, may allow to any such party such reasonable expenses and attorneys' fees as it deems just and proper; and such expenses and fees shall be paid by the depository institution or from its assets. Any person who willfully shall fail or refuse to attend and testify or to answer any lawful inquiry or to produce books, papers, correspondence, memoranda, contracts, agreements, or other records, if in such person's power so to do, in obedience to the subpoena of the appropriate Federal banking agency, shall be guilty of a misdemeanor and, upon conviction, shall be subject to a fine of not more than $1,000 or to imprisonment for a term of not more than one year or both.

* * *

(u) Public disclosures of final orders and agreements

(1) In general

The appropriate Federal banking agency shall publish and make available to the public on a monthly basis–

(A) any written agreement or other written statement for which a violation may be enforced by the appropriate Federal banking agency, unless the appropriate Federal banking agency, in its discretion, determines that publication would be contrary to the public interest;

(B) any final order issued with respect to any administrative enforcement proceeding initiated by such agency under this section or any other law; and

(C) any modification to or termination of any order or agreement made public pursuant to this paragraph.

* * *

§ 1819. Corporate powers

* * *

(b) Agency Authority

* * *

(2) Federal court jurisdiction

(A) In general

Except as provided in subparagraph (D), all suits of a civil nature at common law or in equity to which the Corporation, in any capacity, is a party shall be deemed to arise under the laws of the United States.

(B) Removal

Except as provided in subparagraph (D), the Corporation may, without bond or security, remove any action, suit, or proceeding from a State court to the appropriate United States district court before the end of the 90-day period beginning on the date the action, suit, or proceeding is filed against the Corporation or the Corporation is substituted as a party.

(C) Appeal of remand

The Corporation may appeal any order of remand entered by any United States district court.

(D) State actions

Except as provided in subparagraph (E), any action–

(i)   to which the Corporation, in the Corporation's capacity as receiver of a State insured depository institution by the exclusive appointment by State authorities, is a party other than as a plaintiff;

(ii) which involves only the preclosing rights against the State insured depository institution, or obligations owing to, depositors, creditors, or stockholders by the State insured depository institution; and

(iii) in which only the interpretation of the law of such State is necessary, shall not be deemed to arise under the laws of the United States.

(E) Rule of construction

Subparagraph (D) shall not be construed as limiting the right of the Corporation to invoke the jurisdiction of any United States district court in any action described in such subparagraph if the institution of which the Corporation has been appointed receiver could have invoked the jurisdiction of such court.

* * *

§ 1820. Administration of corporation

* * *

(b) Examinations

(1) Appointment of examiners and claims agents

The Board of Directors shall appoint examiners and claims agents.

(2)   Regular examinations

Any examiner appointed under paragraph (1) shall have power, on behalf of the Corporation, to examine–

(A)   any insured State nonmember bank (except a District bank) or insured State branch of any foreign bank;

(B)   any depository institution which files an application with the Corporation to become an insured depository institution; and

(C)   any insured depository institution in default, whenever the Board of Directors determines an examination of any such depository institution is necessary.

(3)   Special examination of any insured depository institution

In addition to the examinations authorized under paragraph (2), any examiner appointed under paragraph (1) shall have power, on behalf of the Corporation, to make any special examination of any insured depository institution whenever the Board of Directors determines a special examination of any such depository institution is necessary to determine the condition of such depository institution for insurance purposes.

(4)   Examination of affiliates

(A)   In general

In making any examination under paragraph (2) or (3), any examiner appointed under paragraph (1) shall have power, on behalf of the Corporation, to make such examinations of the affairs of any affiliate of any depository institution as may be necessary to disclose fully–

(i)   the relationship between such depository institution and any such affiliate; and

(ii)   the effect of such relationship on the depository institution.

* * *

(6)   Power and duty of examiners

Each examiner appointed under paragraph (1) shall–

(A)   have power to make a thorough examination of any insured depository institution or affiliate under paragraph (2), (3), (4), or (5); and

(B)   shall make a full and detailed report of condition of any insured depository institution or affiliate examined to the Corporation.

* * *

(d)   **Annual on-site examinations of all insured depository institutions required**

(1)   **In general**

The appropriate Federal banking agency shall, not less than once during each 12-month period, conduct a full-scope, on-site examination of each insured depository institution.

(2)   **Examinations by corporation**

Paragraph (1) shall not apply during any 12-month period in which the Corporation has conducted a full-scope, on-site examination of the insured depository institution.

(3)   **State examinations acceptable**

The examinations required by paragraph (1) may be conducted in alternate 12-month periods, as appropriate, if the appropriate Federal banking agency determines that an examination of the insured depository institution conducted by the State during the intervening 12-month period carries out the purpose of this subsection.

(4)   **18-month rule for certain small institutions**

Paragraphs (1), (2), and (3) shall apply with "18-month" substituted for "12-month" if–

(A)   the insured depository institution has total assets of less than $250,000,000;

(B)   the institution is well capitalized, as defined in section 1831o of this title;

(C)   when the institution was most recently examined, it was found to be well managed, and its composite condition–

(i)   was found to be outstanding; or

(ii)   was found to be outstanding or good, in the case of an insured depository institution that has total assets of not more than $100,000,000;

(D)   the insured institution is not currently subject to a formal enforcement proceeding or order by the Corporation or the appropriate Federal banking agency; and

(E)   no person acquired control of the institution during the 12-month period in which a full-scope, on-site examination would be required but for this paragraph.

* * *

§ 1821. Insurance funds; conservatorship and receivership powers of Corporation

(a) **Deposit insurance**

   (1) **Insured amounts payable**

* * *

      (C) **Aggregation of deposits**

For the purpose of determining the net amount due to any depositor under subparagraph (B), the Corporation shall aggregate the amounts of all deposits in the insured depository institution which are maintained by a depositor in the same capacity and the same right for the benefit of the depositor either in the name of the depositor or in the name of any other person, other than any amount in a trust fund described in paragraph (1) or (2) of section 1817(i) of this title or any funds described in section 1817(i)(3) of this title.

* * *

(c) **Appointment of Corporation as conservator or receiver**

   (1) **In general**

Notwithstanding any other provision of Federal law, the law of any State, or the constitution of any State, the Corporation may accept appointment and act as conservator or receiver for any insured depository institution upon appointment in the manner provided in paragraph (2) or (3).

   (2) **Federal depository institutions**

      (A) **Appointment**

         (i) **Conservator**

The Corporation may, at the discretion of the supervisory authority, be appointed conservator of any insured Federal depository institution or District bank and the Corporation may accept such appointment.

         (ii) **Receiver**

The Corporation shall be appointed receiver, and shall accept such appointment, whenever a receiver is appointed for the purpose of liquidation or winding up the affairs of an insured

Federal depository institution or District bank by the appropriate Federal banking agency, notwithstanding any other provision of Federal law (other than section 1441a of this title) or the code of law for the District of Columbia.

(B)   Additional powers

In addition to and not in derogation of the powers conferred and the duties imposed by this section on the Corporation as conservator or receiver, the Corporation, to the extent not inconsistent with such powers and duties, shall have any other power conferred on or any duty (which is related to the exercise of such power) imposed on a conservator or receiver for any Federal depository institution under any other provision of law.

(C)   Corporation not subject to any other agency

When acting as conservator or receiver pursuant to an appointment described in subparagraph (A), the Corporation shall not be subject to the direction or supervision of any other agency or department of the United States or any State in the exercise of the Corporation's rights, powers, and privileges.

(D)   Depository institution in conservatorship subject to banking agency supervision

Notwithstanding subparagraph (C), any Federal depository institution for which the Corporation has been appointed conservator shall remain subject to the supervision of the appropriate Federal banking agency.

(3)   Insured State depository institutions

(A)   Appointment by appropriate State supervisor

Whenever the authority having supervision of any insured State depository institution (other than a District depository institution) appoints a conservator or receiver for such institution and tenders appointment to the Corporation, the Corporation may accept such appointment.

(B) Additional powers

In addition to the powers conferred and the duties related to the exercise of such powers imposed by State law on any conservator or receiver appointed under the law of such State for an insured State depository institution, the Corporation, as conservator or receiver pursuant to an appointment described in subparagraph (A), shall have the powers conferred and the duties imposed by this section on the Corporation as conservator or receiver.

(C) Corporation not subject to any other agency

When acting as conservator or receiver pursuant to an appointment described in subparagraph (A), the Corporation shall not be subject to the direction or supervision of any other agency or department of the United States or any State in the exercise of its rights, powers, and privileges.

(D) Depository institution in conservatorship subject to banking agency supervision

Notwithstanding subparagraph (C), any insured State depository institution for which the Corporation has been appointed conservator shall remain subject to the supervision of the appropriate State bank or savings association supervisor.

(4) Appointment of Corporation by the Corporation

Except as otherwise provided in section 1441a of this title and notwithstanding any other provision of Federal law, the law of any State, or the constitution of any State, the Corporation may appoint itself as sole conservator or receiver of any insured State depository institution if–

(A) the Corporation determines–

(i)   that–

(I)   a conservator, receiver, or other legal custodian has been appointed for such institution;

(II)   such institution has been subject to the appointment of any such conservator, receiver, or custodian for a period of at least 15 consecutive days; and

(III) 1 or more of the depositors in such institution is unable to withdraw any amount of any insured deposit; or

         (ii)   that such institution has been closed by or under the laws of any State; and

     (B) **the Corporation determines that 1 or more of the grounds specified in paragraph (5)—**

         (i)   existed with respect to such institution at the time—

            (I)   the conservator, receiver, or other legal custodian was appointed; or

            (II)   such institution was closed; or

         (ii)   exist at any time—

            (I)   during the appointment of the conservator, receiver, or other legal custodian; or

            (II)   while such institution is closed.

(5) Grounds for appointing conservator or receiver

The grounds for appointing a conservator or receiver (which may be the Corporation) for any insured depository institution are as follows:

(A) Assets insufficient for obligations

The institution's assets are less than the institution's obligations to its creditors and others, including members of the institution.

(B) Substantial dissipation

Substantial dissipation of assets or earnings due to—

     (i)   any violation of any statute or regulation; or

     (ii)   any unsafe or unsound practice.

(C) Unsafe or unsound condition

An unsafe or unsound condition to transact business.

(D) Cease and desist orders

Any willful violation of a cease-and-desist order which has become final.

(E) Concealment

Any concealment of the institution's books, papers, records, or assets, or any refusal to submit the institution's books, papers, records, or affairs for inspection to any examiner or to any lawful agent of the appropriate Federal banking agency or State bank or savings association supervisor.

(F) Inability to meet obligations

The institution is likely to be unable to pay its obligations or meet its depositors' demands in the normal course of business.

(G) Losses

The institution has incurred or is likely to incur losses that will deplete all or substantially all of its capital, and there is no reasonable prospect for the institution to become adequately capitalized (as defined in section 1831o(b) of this title) without Federal assistance.

(H) Violations of law

Any violation of any law or regulation, or any unsafe or unsound practice or condition that is likely to–

(i)   cause insolvency or substantial dissipation of assets or earnings;

(ii)   weaken the institution's condition; or

(iii) otherwise seriously prejudice the interests of the institution's depositors or the deposit insurance fund.

(I) Consent

The institution, by resolution of its board of directors or its shareholders or members, consents to the appointment.

(J) Cessation of insured status

The institution ceases to be an insured institution.

(K) Undercapitalization

The institution is undercapitalized (as defined in section 1831o(b) of this title), and–

(i)   has no reasonable prospect of becoming adequately capitalized (as defined in that section);

(ii)   fails to become adequately capitalized when required to do so under section 1831o(f)(2)(A) of this title;

(iii) fails to submit a capital restoration plan acceptable to that agency within the time prescribed under section 1831o(e)(2)(D) of this title; or

(iv) materially fails to implement a capital restoration plan submitted and accepted under section 1831o(e)(2) of this title.

(L) The institution

(i) is critically undercapitalized, as defined in section 1831o(b) of this title; or

(ii) otherwise has substantially insufficient capital.

(M) Money laundering offense

The Attorney General notifies the appropriate Federal banking agency or the Corporation in writing that the insured depository institution has been found guilty of a criminal offense under section 1956 or 1957 of Title 18 or section 5322 or 5324 of Title 31.

* * *

(7) Judicial review

If the Corporation appoints itself as conservator or receiver under paragraph (4), the insured State depository institution may, within 30 days thereafter, bring an action in the United States district court for the judicial district in which the home office of such institution is located, or in the United States District Court for the District of Columbia, for an order requiring the Corporation to remove itself as such conservator or receiver, and the court shall, upon the merits, dismiss such action or direct the Corporation to remove itself as such conservator or receiver.

* * *

(d) Powers and duties of Corporation as conservator or receiver

(1) Rulemaking authority of Corporation

The Corporation may prescribe such regulations as the Corporation determines to be appropriate regarding the conduct of conservatorships or receiverships.

(2) General powers

(A) Successor to institution

The Corporation shall, as conservator or receiver, and by operation of law, succeed to–

(i)   all rights, titles, powers, and privileges of the insured depository institution, and of any stockholder, member, account holder, depositor, officer, or director of such institution with respect to the institution and the assets of the institution; and

(ii)   title to the books, records, and assets of any previous conservator or other legal custodian of such institution.

(B) Operate the institution

The Corporation may (subject to the provisions of section 1831q of this title), as conservator or receiver–

(i)   take over the assets of and operate the insured depository institution with all the powers of the members or shareholders, the directors, and the officers of the institution and conduct all business of the institution;

(ii)   collect all obligations and money due the institution;

(iii) perform all functions of the institution in the name of the institution which are consistent with the appointment as conservator or receiver; and

(iv)   preserve and conserve the assets and property of such institution.

(C) Functions of institution's officers, directors, and shareholders

The Corporation may, by regulation or order, provide for the exercise of any function by any member or stockholder, director, or officer of any insured depository institution for which the Corporation has been appointed conservator or receiver.

* * *

(3) Authority of receiver to determine claims

(A) In general

The Corporation may, as receiver, determine claims in accordance with the requirements of this subsection and regulations prescribed under paragraph (4).

(B) Notice requirements

The receiver, in any case involving the liquidation or winding up of the affairs of a closed depository institution, shall—

(i) promptly publish a notice to the depository institution's creditors to present their claims, together with proof, to the receiver by a date specified in the notice which shall be not less than 90 days after the publication of such notice; and

(ii) republish such notice approximately 1 month and 2 months, respectively, after the publication under clause (i).

(C) Mailing required

The receiver shall mail a notice similar to the notice published under subparagraph (B)(i) at the time of such publication to any creditor shown on the institution's books—

(i) at the creditor's last address appearing in such books; or

(ii) upon discovery of the name and address of a claimant not appearing on the institution's books within 30 days after the discovery of such name and address.

* * *

(5) Procedures for determination of claims

(A) Determination period

(i) In general

Before the end of the 180-day period beginning on the date any claim against a depository institution is filed with the Corporation as receiver, the Corporation shall determine whether to allow or disallow the claim and shall notify the claimant of any determination with respect to such claim.

(ii)   Extension of time

The period described in clause (i) may be extended by a written agreement between the claimant and the Corporation.

(iii) Mailing of notice sufficient

The requirements of clause (i) shall be deemed to be satisfied if the notice of any determination with respect to any claim is mailed to the last address of the claimant which appears–

(I)   on the depository institution's books;

(II)   in the claim filed by the claimant; or

(III) in documents submitted in proof of the claim.

(iv)   Contents of notice of disallowance

If any claim filed under clause (i) is disallowed, the notice to the claimant shall contain–

(I)   a statement of each reason for the disallowance; and

(II)   the procedures available for obtaining agency review of the determination to disallow the claim or judicial determination of the claim.

(B) Allowance of proven claims

The receiver shall allow any claim received on or before the date specified in the notice published under paragraph (3)(B)(i) by the receiver from any claimant which is proved to the satisfaction of the receiver.

(C) Disallowance of claims filed after end of filing period

(i)   In general

Except as provided in clause (ii), claims filed after the date specified in the notice published under paragraph (3)(B)(i) shall be disallowed and such disallowance shall be final.

(ii)   Certain exceptions

Clause (i) shall not apply with respect to any claim filed by any claimant after the date specified in the notice published under paragraph (3)(B)(i) and such claim may be considered by the receiver if–

(I)   the claimant did not receive notice of the appointment of the receiver in time to file such claim before such date; and

(II)   such claim is filed in time to permit payment of such claim.

(D)   Authority to disallow claims

(i)   In general

The receiver may disallow any portion of any claim by a creditor or claim of security, preference, or priority which is not proved to the satisfaction of the receiver.

(ii)   Payments to less than fully secured creditors

In the case of a claim of a creditor against an insured depository institution which is secured by any property or other asset of such institution, any receiver appointed for any insured depository institution–

(I)   may treat the portion of such claim which exceeds an amount equal to the fair market value of such property or other asset as an unsecured claim against the institution; and

(II)   may not make any payment with respect to such unsecured portion of the claim other than in connection with the disposition of all claims of unsecured creditors of the institution.

* * *

(E)   No judicial review of determination pursuant to subparagraph (d)

No court may review the Corporation's determination pursuant to subparagraph (D) to disallow a claim.

(F)   Legal effect of filing

(i)   Statute of limitation tolled

For purposes of any applicable statute of limitations, the filing of a claim with the receiver shall constitute a commencement of an action.

(ii) No prejudice to other actions

Subject to paragraph (12), the filing of a claim with the receiver shall not prejudice any right of the claimant to continue any action which was filed before the appointment of the receiver.

(6) Provision for agency review or judicial determination of claims

(A) In general

Before the end of the 60-day period beginning on the earlier of–

(i)   the end of the period described in paragraph (5)(A)(i) with respect to any claim against a depository institution for which the Corporation is receiver; or

(ii)   the date of any notice of disallowance of such claim pursuant to paragraph (5)(A)(i), the claimant may request administrative review of the claim in accordance with subparagraph (A) or (B) of paragraph (7) or file suit on such claim (or continue an action commenced before the appointment of the receiver) in the district or territorial court of the United States for the district within which the depository institution's principal place of business is located or the United States District Court for the District of Columbia (and such court shall have jurisdiction to hear such claim).

(B) Statute of limitations

If any claimant fails to–

(i)   request administrative review of any claim in accordance with subparagraph (A) or (B) of paragraph (7); or

(ii)   file suit on such claim (or continue an action commenced before the appointment of the receiver), before the end of the 60-day period described in subparagraph (A), the claim shall be deemed to be disallowed (other than any portion of such claim which was allowed by the receiver) as of the end of such period, such disallowance shall be final, and the claimant shall have no further rights or remedies with respect to such claim.

(7)   Review of claims

(A)   Administrative hearing

If any claimant requests review under this subparagraph in lieu of filing or continuing any action under paragraph (6) and the Corporation agrees to such request, the Corporation shall consider the claim after opportunity for a hearing on the record. The final determination of the Corporation with respect to such claim shall be subject to judicial review under chapter 7 of Title 5.

(B)   Other review procedures

(i)   In general

The Corporation shall also establish such alternative dispute resolution processes as may be appropriate for the resolution of claims filed under paragraph (5)(A)(i).

* * *

(9)   Agreement as basis of claim

(A)   Requirements

Except as provided in subparagraph (B), any agreement which does not meet the requirements set forth in section 1823(e) of this title shall not form the basis of, or substantially comprise, a claim against the receiver or the Corporation.

(B)   Exception to contemporaneous execution requirement

Notwithstanding section 1823(e)(2) of this title, any agreement relating to an extension of credit between a Federal home loan bank or Federal Reserve bank and any insured depository institution which was executed before the extension of credit by such bank to such institution shall be treated as having been executed contemporaneously with such extension of credit for purposes of subparagraph (A).

(10)   Payment of claims

(A)   In general

The receiver may, in the receiver's discretion and to the extent funds are available, pay creditor claims which are allowed by the receiver, approved by the Corporation pursuant to a final determination pursuant to paragraph (7) or (8), or determined by the final judgment of any court of competent jurisdiction in such manner and amounts as are authorized under this chapter.

(B) Payment of dividends on claims

The receiver may, in the receiver's sole discretion, pay dividends on proved claims at any time, and no liability shall attach to the Corporation (in such Corporation's corporate capacity or as receiver), by reason of any such payment, for failure to pay dividends to a claimant whose claim is not proved at the time of any such payment.

(11)   Depositor preference

(A) In general

Subject to section 1815(e)(2)(C) of this title, amounts realized from the liquidation or other resolution of any insured depository institution by any receiver appointed for such institution shall be distributed to pay claims (other than secured claims to the extent of any such security) in the following order of priority:

(i)   Administrative expenses of the receiver.

(ii)   Any deposit liability of the institution.

(iii)   Any other general or senior liability of the institution (which is not a liability described in clause (iv) or (v)).

(iv)   Any obligation subordinated to depositors or general creditors (which is not an obligation described in clause (v)).

(v)   Any obligation to shareholders or members arising as a result of their status as shareholders or members (including any depository institution holding company or any shareholder or creditor of such company).

* * *

(12)   Suspension of legal actions

(A) In general

After the appointment of a conservator or receiver for an insured depository institution, the conservator or receiver may request a stay for a period not to exceed–

(i)   45 days, in the case of any conservator; and

(ii)   90 days, in the case of any receiver, in any judicial action or proceeding to which such institution is or becomes a party.

(B) Grant of stay by all courts required

Upon receipt of a request by any conservator or receiver pursuant to subparagraph (A) for a stay of any judicial action or proceeding in any court with jurisdiction of such action or proceeding, the court shall grant such stay as to all parties.

(13) Additional rights and duties

(A) Prior final adjudication

The Corporation shall abide by any final unappealable judgment of any court of competent jurisdiction which was rendered before the appointment of the Corporation as conservator or receiver.

(B) Rights and remedies of conservator or receiver

In the event of any appealable judgment, the Corporation as conservator or receiver shall–

(i) have all the rights and remedies available to the insured depository institution (before the appointment of such conservator or receiver) and the Corporation in its corporate capacity, including removal to Federal court and all appellate rights; and

(ii) not be required to post any bond in order to pursue such remedies.

(C) No attachment or execution

No attachment or execution may issue by any court upon assets in the possession of the receiver.

(D) Limitation on judicial review

Except as otherwise provided in this subsection, no court shall have jurisdiction over–

(i) any claim or action for payment from, or any action seeking a determination of rights with respect to, the assets of any depository institution for which the Corporation has been appointed receiver, including assets which the Corporation may acquire from itself as such receiver; or

(ii) any claim relating to any act or omission of such institution or the Corporation as receiver.

* * *

(14)   Statute of limitations for actions brought by conservator or receiver

(A) In general

Notwithstanding any provision of any contract, the applicable statute of limitations with regard to any action brought by the Corporation as conservator or receiver shall be–

(i)   in the case of any contract claim, the longer of–

(I)   the 6-year period beginning on the date the claim accrues; or

(II)   the period applicable under State law; and

(ii)   in the case of any tort claim (other than a claim which is subject to section 1441a(b)(14) of this title), the longer of–

(I)   the 3-year period beginning on the date the claim accrues; or

(II)   the period applicable under State law.

(B) Determination of the date on which a claim accrues

For purposes of subparagraph (A), the date on which the statute of limitations begins to run on any claim described in such subparagraph shall be the later of–

(i)   the date of the appointment of the Corporation as conservator or receiver; or

(ii)   the date on which the cause of action accrues.

(C) Revival of expired State causes of action

(i)   In general

In the case of any tort claim described in clause (ii) for which the statute of limitation applicable under State law with respect to such claim has expired not more than 5 years before the appointment of the Corporation as conservator or receiver, the Corporation may bring an action as conservator or receiver on such claim without regard to the expiration of the statute of limitation applicable under State law.

(ii)   Claims described

A tort claim referred to in clause (i) is a claim arising from fraud, intentional misconduct resulting in unjust enrichment, or intentional misconduct resulting in substantial loss to the institution.

* * *

(17)   Fraudulent transfers

(A) In general

The Corporation, as conservator or receiver for any insured depository institution, and any conservator appointed by the Comptroller of the Currency or the Director of the Office of Thrift Supervision may avoid a transfer of any interest of an institution-affiliated party, or any person who the Corporation or conservator determines is a debtor of the institution, in property, or any obligation incurred by such party or person, that was made within 5 years of the date on which the Corporation or conservator was appointed conservator or receiver if such party or person voluntarily or involuntarily made such transfer or incurred such liability with the intent to hinder, delay, or defraud the insured depository institution, the Corporation or other conservator, or any other appropriate Federal banking agency.

(B) Right of recovery

To the extent a transfer is avoided under subparagraph (A), the Corporation or any conservator described in such subparagraph may recover, for the benefit of the insured depository institution, the property transferred, or, if a court so orders, the value of such property (at the time of such transfer) from–

(i)   the initial transferee of such transfer or the institution-affiliated party or person for whose benefit such transfer was made; or

(ii)   any immediate or mediate transferee of any such initial transferee.

(C) Rights of transferee or obligee

The Corporation or any conservator described in subparagraph (A) may not recover under subparagraph (B) from–

(i)   any transferee that takes for value, including satisfaction or securing of a present or antecedent debt, in good faith; or

(ii)   any immediate or mediate good faith transferee of such transferee.

(D) Rights under this paragraph

The rights under this paragraph of the Corporation and any conservator described in subparagraph (A) shall be superior to any rights of a trustee or any other party (other than any party which is a Federal agency) under Title 11.

* * *

(20) Treatment of claims arising from breach of contracts executed by the receiver or conservator.—Notwithstanding any other provision of this subsection, any final and unappealable judgment for monetary damages entered against a receiver or conservator after the date of its appointment shall be paid as an administrative expense of the receiver or conservator. Nothing in this paragraph shall be construed to limit the power of a receiver or conservator to exercise any rights under contract or law, including to terminate, breach, cancel, or otherwise discontinue such agreement.

(e) Provisions relating to contracts entered into before appointment of conservator or receiver

(1) Authority to repudiate contracts

In addition to any other rights a conservator or receiver may have, the conservator or receiver for any insured depository institution may disaffirm or repudiate any contract or lease–

(A)   to which such institution is a party;

(B)   the performance of which the conservator or receiver, in the conservator's or receiver's discretion, determines to be burdensome; and

    (C) the disaffirmance or repudiation of which the conservator or receiver determines, in the conservator's or receiver's discretion, will promote the orderly administration of the institution's affairs.

(2) Timing of repudiation

    The conservator or receiver appointed for any insured depository institution in accordance with subsection (c) of this section shall determine whether or not to exercise the rights of repudiation under this subsection within a reasonable period following such appointment.

(3) Claims for damages for repudiation

(A) In general

    Except as otherwise provided in subparagraph (C) and paragraphs (4), (5), and (6), the liability of the conservator or receiver for the disaffirmance or repudiation of any contract pursuant to paragraph (1) shall be–

    (i) limited to actual direct compensatory damages; and

    (ii) determined as of–

        (I) the date of the appointment of the conservator or receiver; or

        (II) in the case of any contract or agreement referred to in paragraph (8), the date of the disaffirmance or repudiation of such contract or agreement.

(B) No liability for other damages

    For purposes of subparagraph (A), the term "actual direct compensatory damages" does not include–

    (i) punitive or exemplary damages;

    (ii) damages for lost profits or opportunity; or

    (iii) damages for pain and suffering.

(C) Measure of damages for repudiation of financial contracts

    In the case of any qualified financial contract or agreement to which paragraph (8) applies, compensatory damages shall be–

    (i) deemed to include normal and reasonable costs of cover or other reasonable measures of damages utilized in the industries for such contract and agreement claims; and

(ii)   paid in accordance with this subsection and subsection (i) of this section except as otherwise specifically provided in this section.

* * *

(7)   Provisions applicable to service contracts

(A)   Services performed before appointment

In the case of any contract for services between any person and any insured depository institution for which the Corporation has been appointed conservator or receiver, any claim of such person for services performed before the appointment of the conservator or the receiver shall be–

(i)   a claim to be paid in accordance with subsections (d) and (i) of this section; and

(ii)   deemed to have arisen as of the date the conservator or receiver was appointed.

(B)   Services performed after appointment and prior to repudiation

If, in the case of any contract for services described in subparagraph (A), the conservator or receiver accepts performance by the other person before the conservator or receiver makes any determination to exercise the right of repudiation of such contract under this section–

(i)   the other party shall be paid under the terms of the contract for the services performed; and

(ii)   the amount of such payment shall be treated as an administrative expense of the conservatorship or receivership.

(C)   Acceptance of performance no bar to subsequent repudiation

The acceptance by any conservator or receiver of services referred to in subparagraph (B) in connection with a contract described in such subparagraph shall not affect the right of the conservator or receiver to repudiate such contract under this section at any time after such performance.

(8) Certain qualified financial contracts

(A) Rights of parties to contracts

Subject to paragraph (10) of this subsection and notwithstanding any other provision of this chapter (other than subsection (d)(9) of this section and section 1823(e) of this title), any other Federal law, or the law of any State, no person shall be stayed or prohibited from exercising–

(i) any right to cause the termination or liquidation of any qualified financial contract with an insured depository institution which arises upon the appointment of the Corporation as receiver for such institution at any time after such appointment;

(ii) any right under any security arrangement relating to any contract or agreement described in clause (i); or

(iii) any right to offset or net out any termination value, payment amount, or other transfer obligation arising under or in connection with 1 or more contracts and agreements described in clause (i), including any master agreement for such contracts or agreements.

(B) Applicability of other provisions

Subsection (d)(12) of this section shall apply in the case of any judicial action or proceeding brought against any receiver referred to in subparagraph (A), or the insured depository institution for which such receiver was appointed, by any party to a contract or agreement described in subparagraph (A)(i) with such institution.

(C) Certain transfers not avoidable

(i) In general

Notwithstanding paragraph (11), the Corporation, whether acting as such or as conservator or receiver of an insured depository institution, may not avoid any transfer of money or other property in connection with any qualified financial contract with an insured depository institution.

* * *

(D) Certain contracts and agreements defined

For purposes of this subsection–

(i)   Qualified financial contract

The term "qualified financial contract" means any securities contract, commodity contract, forward contract, repurchase agreement, swap agreement, and any similar agreement that the Corporation determines by regulation to be a qualified financial contract for purposes of this paragraph.

(ii)   Securities contract

The term "securities contract"–

(I)   has the meaning given to such term in section 741 of Title 11 except that the term "security" (as used in such section) shall be deemed to include any mortgage loan, any mortgage-related security (as defined in section 78c(a)(41) of Title 15), and any interest in any mortgage loan or mortgage-related security; and

(II)   does not include any participation in a commercial mortgage loan unless the Corporation determines by regulation, resolution, or order to include any such participation within the meaning of such term.

(iii)   Commodity contract

The term "commodity contract" has the meaning given to such term in section 761 of Title 11.

(iv)   Forward contract

The term "forward contract" has the meaning given to such term in section 101 of Title 11.

(v)   Repurchase agreement

The term "repurchase agreement"–

(I)   has the meaning given to such term in section 101 of Title 11, except that the items (as described in such section) which may be subject to any such agreement shall be deemed to include mortgage-related securities (as such term is defined in section 78c(a)(41) of Title 15), any mortgage loan, and any interest in any mortgage loan; and

(II) does not include any participation in a commercial mortgage loan unless the Corporation determines by regulation, resolution, or order to include any such participation within the meaning of such term.

(vi) Swap agreement

The term "swap agreement"–

(I) means any agreement, including the terms and conditions incorporated by reference in any such agreement, which is a rate swap agreement, basis swap, commodity swap, forward rate agreement, interest rate future, interest rate option purchased, forward foreign exchange agreement, rate cap agreement, rate floor agreement, rate collar agreement, currency swap agreement, cross-currency rate swap agreement, currency future, or currency option purchased or any other similar agreement, and

(II) includes any combination of such agreements and any option to enter into any such agreement.

(vii) Treatment of master agreement as 1 swap agreement

Any master agreement for any agreements described in clause (vi)(I) together with all supplements to such master agreement shall be treated as 1 swap agreement.

(viii) Transfer

The term "transfer" has the meaning given to such term in section 101 of Title 11.

(E) Certain protections in event of appointment of conservator

Notwithstanding any other provision of this chapter (other than paragraph (12) of this subsection, subsection (d)(9) of this section, and section 1823(e) of this title), any other Federal law, or the law of any State, no person shall be stayed or prohibited from exercising–

(i) any right such person has to cause the termination, liquidation, or acceleration of any qualified financial contract with a depository institution in a conservatorship based upon a default under such financial contract which is enforceable under applicable noninsolvency law;

(ii) any right under any security arrangement relating to such qualified financial contracts; or

(iii)   any right to offset or net out any termination values, payment amounts, or other transfer obligations arising under or in connection with such qualified financial contracts.

(9)   Transfer of qualified financial contracts

In making any transfer of assets or liabilities of a depository institution in default which includes any qualified financial contract, the conservator or receiver for such depository institution shall either–

(A)   transfer to 1 depository institution (other than a depository institution in default)–

(i)   ..ll qualified financial contracts between–

(I)   any person or any affiliate of such person; and

(II)   the depository institution in default;

(ii)   all claims of such person or any affiliate of such person against such depository institution under any such contract (other than any claim which, under the terms of any such contract, is subordinated to the claims of general unsecured creditors of such institution);

(iii)   all claims of such depository institution against such person or any affiliate of such person under any such contract; and

(iv)   all property securing any claim described in clause (ii) or (iii) under any such contract; or

(B)   transfer none of the financial contracts, claims, or property referred to in subparagraph (A) (with respect to such person and any affiliate of such person).

(10)   Notification of transfer

(A)   In general

If–

(i)   the conservator or receiver for an insured depository institution in default makes any transfer of the assets and liabilities of such institution; and

(ii)   the transfer includes any qualified financial contract, the conservator or receiver shall use such conservator's or receiver's best efforts to notify any person who is a party to any such contract of such transfer by 12:00, noon (local time) on the business day following such transfer.

(B) Business day defined

For purposes of this paragraph, the term "business day" means any day other than any Saturday, Sunday, or any day on which either the New York Stock Exchange or the Federal Reserve Bank of New York is closed.

(11)   Certain security interests not avoidable

No provision of this subsection shall be construed as permitting the avoidance of any legally enforceable or perfected security interest in any of the assets of any depository institution except where such an interest is taken in contemplation of the institution's insolvency or with the intent to hinder, delay, or defraud the institution or the creditors of such institution.

(12)   Authority to enforce contracts

(A)   In general

The conservator or receiver may enforce any contract, other than a director's or officer's liability insurance contract or a depository institution bond, entered into by the depository institution notwithstanding any provision of the contract providing for termination, default, acceleration, or exercise of rights upon, or solely by reason of, insolvency or the appointment of a conservator or receiver.

(B)   Certain rights not affected

No provision of this paragraph may be construed as impairing or affecting any right of the conservator or receiver to enforce or recover under a director's or officer's liability insurance contract or depository institution bond under other applicable law.

(13)   Exception for federal reserve and federal home loan banks

No provision of this subsection shall apply with respect to—

(A)   any extension of credit from any Federal home loan bank or Federal Reserve bank to any insured depository institution; or

(B)   any security interest in the assets of the institution securing any such extension of credit.

* * *

(f)   Payment of insured deposits

(1)   In general

In case of the liquidation of, or other closing or winding up of the affairs of, any insured depository institution, payment of the insured deposits in such institution shall be made by the Corporation as soon as possible, subject to the provisions of subsection (g) of this section, either by cash or by making available to each depositor a transferred deposit in a new insured depository institution in the same community or in another insured depository institution in an amount equal to the insured deposit of such depositor, except that–

(A)   all payments made pursuant to this section on account of a closed Bank Insurance Fund member shall be made only from the Bank Insurance Fund, and

(B)   all payments made pursuant to this section on account of a closed Savings Association Insurance Fund member shall be made only from the Savings Association Insurance Fund.

(2)   Proof of claims

The Corporation, in its discretion, may require proof of claims to be filed and may approve or reject such claims for insured deposits.

(3)   Resolution of disputes

(A)   Resolutions in accordance with Corporation regulations

In the case of any disputed claim relating to any insured deposit or any determination of insurance coverage with respect to any deposit, the Corporation may resolve such disputed claim in accordance with regulations prescribed by the Corporation establishing procedures for resolving such claims.

(B)   Adjudication of claims

If the Corporation has not prescribed regulations establishing procedures for resolving disputed claims, the Corporation may require the final determination of a court of competent jurisdiction before paying any such claim.

(4)   Review of corporation's determination

Final determination made by the Corporation shall be reviewable in accordance with chapter 7 of Title 5 by the United States Court of Appeals for the District of Columbia or the court of appeals for the Federal judicial circuit where the principal place of business of the depository institution is located.

(5) Statute of limitations

Any request for review of a final determination by the Corporation shall be filed with the appropriate circuit court of appeals not later than 60 days after such determination is ordered.

(g) Subrogation of Corporation

(1) In general

Notwithstanding any other provision of Federal law, the law of any State, or the constitution of any State, the Corporation, upon the payment to any depositor as provided in subsection (f) of this section in connection with any insured depository institution or insured branch described in such subsection or the assumption of any deposit in such institution or branch by another insured depository institution pursuant to this section or section 1823 of this title, shall be subrogated to all rights of the depositor against such institution or branch to the extent of such payment or assumption.

(2) Dividends on subrogated amounts

The subrogation of the Corporation under paragraph (1) with respect to any insured depository institution shall include the right on the part of the Corporation to receive the same dividends from the proceeds of the assets of such institution and recoveries on account of stockholders' liability as would have been payable to the depositor on a claim for the insured deposit, but such depositor shall retain such claim for any uninsured or unassumed portion of the deposit.

(3) Waiver of certain claims

With respect to any bank which closes after May 25, 1938, the Corporation shall waive, in favor only of any person against whom stockholders' individual liability may be asserted, any claim on account of such liability in excess of the liability, if any, to the bank or its creditors, for the amount unpaid upon such stock in such bank; but any such waiver shall be effected in such manner and on such terms and conditions as will not increase recoveries or dividends on account of claims to which the Corporation is not subrogated.

(4)   Applicability of State law

Subject to subsection (d)(11) of this section, if the Corporation is appointed pursuant to subsection (c)(3) of this section, or determines not to invoke the authority conferred in subsection (c)(4) of this section, the rights of depositors and other creditors of any State depository institution shall be determined in accordance with the applicable provisions of State law.

* * *

(i)   Valuation of claims in default

(1)   In general

Notwithstanding any other provision of Federal law or the law of any State and regardless of the method which the Corporation determines to utilize with respect to an insured depository institution in default or in danger of default, including transactions authorized under subsection (n) of this section and section 1823(c) of this title, this subsection shall govern the rights of the creditors (other than insured depositors) of such institution.

(2)   Maximum liability

The maximum liability of the Corporation, acting as receiver or in any other capacity, to any person having a claim against the receiver or the insured depository institution for which such receiver is appointed shall equal the amount such claimant would have received if the Corporation had liquidated the assets and liabilities of such institution without exercising the Corporation's authority under subsection (n) of this section or section 1823 of this title.

(3)   Additional payments authorized

(A) In general

The Corporation may, in its discretion and in the interests of minimizing its losses, use its own resources to make additional payments or credit additional amounts to or with respect to or for the account of any claimant or category of claimants. Notwithstanding any other provision of Federal or State law, or the constitution of any State, the Corporation shall not be obligated, as a result of having made any such payment or credited any such amount to or with respect to or for the account of any claimant or category of claimants, to make payments to any other claimant or category of claimants.

(B) Source of funds

If the depository institution in default is a Bank Insurance Fund member, the Corporation may only make such payments out of funds held in the Bank Insurance Fund. If the depository institution in default is a Savings Association Insurance Fund member, the Corporation may only make such payments out of funds held in the Savings Association Insurance Fund.

(C) Manner of payment

The Corporation may make the payments or credit the amounts specified in subparagraphs (A) and (B) directly to the claimants or may make such payments or credit such amounts to an open insured depository institution to induce such institution to accept liability for such claims.

(j) Limitation on court action

Except as provided in this section, no court may take any action, except at the request of the Board of Directors by regulation or order, to restrain or affect the exercise of powers or functions of the Corporation as a conservator or a receiver.

(k) Liability of directors and officers

A director or officer of an insured depository institution may be held personally liable for monetary damages in any civil action by, on behalf of, or at the request or direction of the Corporation, which action is prosecuted wholly or partially for the benefit of the Corporation–

(1) acting as conservator or receiver of such institution,

(2) acting based upon a suit, claim, or cause of action purchased from, assigned by, or otherwise conveyed by such receiver or conservator, or

(3) acting based upon a suit, claim, or cause of action purchased from, assigned by, or otherwise conveyed in whole or in part by an insured depository institution or its affiliate in connection with assistance provided under section 1823 of this title, for gross negligence, including any similar conduct or conduct that demonstrates a greater disregard of a duty of care (than gross negligence) including intentional tortious conduct, as such terms are defined and determined under applicable State law. Nothing in this paragraph shall impair or affect any right of the Corporation under other applicable law.

(l)   Damages

In any proceeding related to any claim against an insured depository institution's director, officer, employee, agent, attorney, accountant, appraiser, or any other party employed by or providing services to an insured depository institution, recoverable damages determined to result from the improvident or otherwise improper use or investment of any insured depository institution's assets shall include principal losses and appropriate interest.

* * *

§ 1822. Corporation as receiver

* * *

(b)   Payment of insured deposit as discharge from liability

Payment of an insured deposit to any person by the Corporation shall discharge the Corporation, and payment of a transferred deposit to any person by the new bank or by an insured depository institution in which a transferred deposit has been made available shall discharge the Corporation and such new bank or other insured depository institution, to the same extent that payment to such person by the depository institution in default would have discharged it from liability for the insured deposit.

(c)   Recognition of claimant not on bank records

Except as otherwise prescribed by the Board of Directors, neither the Corporation nor such new bank or other insured depository institution shall be required to recognize as the owner of any portion of a deposit appearing on the records of the depository institution in default under a name other than that of the claimant, any person whose name or interest as such owner is not disclosed on the records of such depository institution in default as part owner of said deposit, if such recognition would increase the aggregate amount of the insured deposits in such depository institution in default.

(d)   Withholding payments to meet liability to depository institution

The Corporation may withhold payment of such portion of the insured deposit of any depositor in a depository institution in default as may be required to provide for the payment of any liability of such depositor to the depository institution in default or its receiver, which is not offset against a claim due from such depository institution, pending the determination and payment of such liability by such depositor or any other person liable therefor.

* * *

§ 1823. Corporation monies

* * *

(c) Assistance to insured depository institutions

    (1) The Corporation is authorized, in its sole discretion and upon such terms and conditions as the Board of Directors may prescribe, to make loans to, to make deposits in, to purchase the assets or securities of, to assume the liabilities of, or to make contributions to, any insured depository institution–

        (A) if such action is taken to prevent the default of such insured depository institution;

        (B) if, with respect to an insured bank in default, such action is taken to restore such insured bank to normal operation; or

        (C) if, when severe financial conditions exist which threaten the stability of a significant number of insured depository institutions or of insured depository institutions possessing significant financial resources, such action is taken in order to lessen the risk to the Corporation posed by such insured depository institution under such threat of instability.

    (2) (A) In order to facilitate a merger or consolidation of an insured depository institution described in subparagraph (B) with another insured depository institution or the sale of any or all of the assets of such insured depository institution or the assumption of any or all of such insured depository institution's liabilities by another insured depository institution, or the acquisition of the stock of such insured depository institution, the Corporation is authorized, in its sole discretion and upon such terms and conditions as the Board of Directors may prescribe–

        (i) to purchase any such assets or assume any such liabilities;

        (ii) to make loans or contributions to, or deposits in, or purchase the securities of, such other insured depository institution or the company which controls or will acquire control of such other insured depository institution;

        (iii) to guarantee such other insured depository institution or the company which controls or will acquire control of such

other insured depository institution against loss by reason of such insured institution's merging or consolidating with or assuming the liabilities and purchasing the assets of such insured depository institution or by reason of such company acquiring control of such insured depository institution; or

(iv)   to take any combination of the actions referred to in subparagraphs (i) through (iii).

(B)   For the purpose of subparagraph (A), the insured depository institution must be an insured depository institution–

(i)   which is in default;

(ii)   which, in the judgment of the Board of Directors, is in danger of default; or

(iii) which, when severe financial conditions exist which threaten the stability of a significant number of insured depository institutions or of insured depository institutions possessing significant financial resources, is determined by the Corporation, in its sole discretion, to require assistance under subparagraph (A) in order to lessen the risk to the Corporation posed by such insured depository institution under such threat of instability.

(C)   Any action to which the Corporation is or becomes a party by acquiring any asset or exercising any other authority set forth in this section shall be stayed for a period of 60 days at the request of the Corporation.

(3)   The Corporation may provide any person acquiring control of, merging with, consolidating with or acquiring the assets of an insured depository institution under subsection (f) or (k) of this section with such financial assistance as it could provide an insured institution under this subsection.

(4)   Least-cost resolution required

(A)   In general

Notwithstanding any other provision of this chapter, the Corporation may not exercise any authority under this subsection or subsection (d), (f), (h), (i), or (k) of this section with respect to any insured depository institution unless–

(i)   the Corporation determines that the exercise of such authority is necessary to meet the obligation of the

Corporation to provide insurance coverage for the insured deposits in such institution; and

(ii) the total amount of the expenditures by the Corporation and obligations incurred by the Corporation (including any immediate and long-term obligation of the Corporation and any direct or contingent liability for future payment by the Corporation) in connection with the exercise of any such authority with respect to such institution is the least costly to the deposit insurance fund of all possible methods for meeting the Corporation's obligation under this section.

(B) Determining least costly approach

In determining how to satisfy the Corporation's obligations to an institution's insured depositors at the least possible cost to the deposit insurance fund, the Corporation shall comply with the following provisions:

(i) Present-value analysis; documentation required

The Corporation shall–

(I) evaluate alternatives on a present-value basis, using a realistic discount rate;

(II) document that evaluation and the assumptions on which the evaluation is based, including any assumptions with regard to interest rates, asset recovery rates, asset holding costs, and payment of contingent liabilities; and

(III) retain the documentation for not less than 5 years.

(ii) Foregone tax revenues

Federal tax revenues that the Government would forego as the result of a proposed transaction, to the extent reasonably ascertainable, shall be treated as if they were revenues foregone by the deposit insurance fund.

(C) **Time of determination**

(i) General rule

For purposes of this subsection, the determination of the costs of providing any assistance under paragraph (1) or (2) or any other provision of this section with respect to any depository institution shall be made as of the date on

which the Corporation makes the determination to provide such assistance to the institution under this section.

(ii)   Rule for liquidations

For purposes of this subsection, the determination of the costs of liquidation of any depository institution shall be made as of the earliest of–

(I)   the date on which a conservator is appointed for such institution;

(II)   the date on which a receiver is appointed for such institution; or

(III)   the date on which the Corporation makes any determination to provide any assistance under this section with respect to such institution.

(D)   Liquidation costs

In determining the cost of liquidating any depository institution for the purpose of comparing the costs under subparagraph (A) (with respect to such institution), the amount of such cost may not exceed the amount which is equal to the sum of the insured deposits of such institution as of the earliest of the dates described in subparagraph (C), minus the present value of the total net amount the Corporation reasonably expects to receive from the disposition of the assets of such institution in connection with such liquidation.

(E)   Deposit insurance funds available for intended purpose only

(i)   In general

After December 31, 1994, or at such earlier time as the Corporation determines to be appropriate, the Corporation may not take any action, directly or indirectly, with respect to any insured depository institution that would have the effect of increasing losses to any insurance fund by protecting–

(I)   depositors for more than the insured portion of deposits (determined without regard to whether such institution is liquidated); or

(II)   creditors other than depositors.

    (ii)   Deadline for regulations

        The Corporation shall prescribe regulations to implement clause (i) not later than January 1, 1994, and the regulations shall take effect not later than January 1, 1995.

    (iii) Purchase and assumption transactions

        No provision of this subparagraph shall be construed as prohibiting the Corporation from allowing any person who acquires any assets or assumes any liabilities of any insured depository institution for which the Corporation has been appointed conservator or receiver to acquire uninsured deposit liabilities of such institution so long as the insurance fund does not incur any loss with respect to such deposit liabilities in an amount greater than the loss which would have been incurred with respect to such liabilities if the institution had been liquidated.

(F) Discretionary determinations

    Any determination which the Corporation may make under this paragraph shall be made in the sole discretion of the Corporation.

(G) Systemic risk

    (i)   Emergency determination by Secretary of the Treasury

        Notwithstanding subparagraphs (A) and (E), if, upon the written recommendation of the Board of Directors (upon a vote of not less than two-thirds of the members of the Board of Directors) and the Board of Governors of the Federal Reserve System (upon a vote of not less than two-thirds of the members of such Board), the Secretary of the Treasury (in consultation with the President) determines that—

        (I)   the Corporation's compliance with subparagraphs (A) and (E) with respect to an insured depository institution would have serious adverse effects on economic conditions or financial stability; and

        (II) any action or assistance under this subparagraph would avoid or mitigate such adverse effects, the Corporation may take other action or provide assistance under this section as necessary to avoid or mitigate such effects.

(ii)   Repayment of loss

The Corporation shall recover the loss to the appropriate insurance fund arising from any action taken or assistance provided with respect to an insured depository institution under clause (i) expeditiously from 1 or more emergency special assessments on the members of the insurance fund (of which such institution is a member) equal to the product of–

(I)   an assessment rate established by the Corporation; and

(II)   the amount of each member's average total assets during the semiannual period, minus the sum of the amount of the member's average total tangible equity and the amount of the member's average total subordinated debt.

(iii)   Documentation required

The Secretary of the Treasury shall–

(I)   document any determination under clause (i); and

(II)   retain the documentation for review under clause (iv).

(iv)   GAO review

The Comptroller General of the United States shall review and report to the Congress on any determination under clause (i), including–

(I)   the basis for the determination;

(II)   the purpose for which any action was taken pursuant to such clause; and

(III)   the likely effect of the determination and such action on the incentives and conduct of insured depository institutions and uninsured depositors.

(v)   Notice

(I)   In general

The Secretary of the Treasury shall provide written notice of any determination under clause (i) to the Committee on Banking, Housing, and Urban Affairs of the Senate and the Committee on Banking, Finance and Urban Affairs of the House of Representatives.

(II) Description of basis of determination

The notice under subclause (I) shall include a description of the basis for any determination under clause (i).

(H) Rule of construction

No provision of law shall be construed as permitting the Corporation to take any action prohibited by paragraph (4) unless such provision expressly provides, by direct reference to this paragraph, that this paragraph shall not apply with respect to such action.

(5) The Corporation may not use its authority under this subsection to purchase the voting or common stock of an insured depository institution. Nothing in the preceding sentence shall be construed to limit the ability of the Corporation to enter into and enforce covenants and agreements that it determines to be necessary to protect its financial interest.

(6) (A) During any period in which an insured depository institution has received assistance under this subsection and such assistance is still outstanding, such insured depository institution may defer the payment of any State or local tax which is determined on the basis of the deposits held by such insured depository institution or of the interest or dividends paid on such deposits.

(B) When such insured depository institution no longer has any outstanding assistance, such insured depository institution shall pay all taxes which were deferred under subparagraph (A). Such payments shall be made in accordance with a payment plan established by the Corporation, after consultation with the applicable State and local taxing authorities.

(7) The transfer of any assets or liabilities associated with any trust business of an insured depository institution in default under subparagraph (2)(A) shall be effective without any State or Federal approval, assignment, or consent with respect thereto.

(8) Assistance before appointment of conservator or receiver

(A) In general

Subject to the least-cost provisions of paragraph (4), the Corporation shall consider providing direct financial assistance under this section for depository institutions before the appointment of a conservator or receiver for such institution only under the following circumstances:

(i)   Troubled condition criteria

The Corporation determines–

(I)   grounds for the appointment of a conservator or receiver exist or likely will exist in the future unless the depository institution's capital levels are increased; and

(II)   it is unlikely that the institution can meet all currently applicable capital standards without assistance.

(ii)   Other criteria

The depository institution meets the following criteria:

(I)   The appropriate Federal banking agency and the Corporation have determined that, during such period of time preceding the date of such determination as the agency or the Corporation considers to be relevant, the institution's management has been competent and has complied with applicable laws, rules, and supervisory directives and orders.

(II)   The institution's management did not engage in any insider dealing, speculative practice, or other abusive activity.

(B) Public disclosure

Any determination under this paragraph to provide assistance under this section shall be made in writing and published in the Federal Register.

(9)   Any assistance provided under this subsection may be in subordination to the rights of depositors and other creditors.

(10) In its annual report to the Congress, the Corporation shall report the total amount it has saved, or estimates it has saved, by exercising the authority provided in this subsection.

(11) Payments made under this subsection shall be made

    (A) from the Bank Insurance Fund in the case of payments to or on behalf of a member of such Fund; or

    (B) from the Savings Association Insurance Fund or from funds made available by the Resolution Trust Corporation in the case of payments to or on behalf of any Savings Association Insurance Fund member.

(d) Sale of assets to Corporation

  (1) In general

    Any conservator, receiver, or liquidator appointed for any insured depository institution in default, including the Corporation acting in such capacity, shall be entitled to offer the assets of such depository institutions for sale to the Corporation or as security for loans from the Corporation.

  (2) Proceeds

    The proceeds of every sale or loan of assets to the Corporation shall be utilized for the same purposes and in the same manner as other funds realized from the liquidation of the assets of such depository institutions.

* * *

(e) Agreements against interests of Corporation

  (1) In general

    No agreement which tends to diminish or defeat the interest of the Corporation in any asset acquired by it under this section or section 1821 of this title, either as security for a loan or by purchase or as receiver of any insured depository institution, shall be valid against the Corporation unless such agreement–

    (A) is in writing,

    (B) was executed by the depository institution and any person claiming an adverse interest thereunder, including the obligor, contemporaneously with the acquisition of the asset by the depository institution,

    (C) was approved by the board of directors of the depository institution or its loan committee, which approval shall be reflected in the minutes of said board or committee, and

    (D) has been, continuously, from the time of its execution, an official record of the depository institution.

(2) Public deposits

   An agreement to provide for the lawful collateralization of deposits of a Federal, State, or local governmental entity or of any depositor referred to in section 1821(a)(2) of this title shall not be deemed to be invalid pursuant to paragraph (1)(B) solely because such agreement was not executed contemporaneously with the acquisition of the collateral or with any changes in the collateral made in accordance with such agreement.

* * *

§ 1828. Regulations governing insured depository institutions

* * *

(c) Merger transactions; consent of banking agencies; emergency approval; notice; uniform standards; antitrust actions; review de novo; limitations; report to Congress; applicability

   (1) Except with the prior written approval of the responsible agency, which shall in every case referred to in this paragraph be the Corporation, no insured depository institution shall–

      (A) merge or consolidate with any noninsured bank or institution;

* * *

   (5) The responsible agency shall not approve–

      (A) any proposed merger transaction which would result in a monopoly, or which would be in furtherance of any combination or conspiracy to monopolize or to attempt to monopolize the business of banking in any part of the United States, or

      (B) any other proposed merger transaction whose effect in any section of the country may be substantially to lessen competition, or to tend to create a monopoly, or which in any other manner would be in restraint of trade, unless it finds that the anticompetitive effects of the proposed transaction are clearly outweighed in the public interest by the probable effect of the transaction in meeting the convenience and needs of the community to be served.

In every case, the responsible agency shall take into consideration the financial and managerial resources and future prospects of the existing and proposed institutions, and the convenience and needs of the community to be served.

* * *

(7) (A) Any action brought under the antitrust laws arising out of a merger transaction shall be commenced prior to the earliest time under paragraph (6) at which a merger transaction approved under paragraph (5) might be consummated. The commencement of such an action shall stay the effectiveness of the agency's approval unless the court shall otherwise specifically order. In any such action, the court shall review de novo the issues presented.

(B) In any judicial proceeding attacking a merger transaction approved under paragraph (5) on the ground that the merger transaction alone and of itself constituted a violation of any antitrust laws other than section 2 of Title 15, the standards applied by the court shall be identical with those that the banking agencies are directed to apply under paragraph (5).

(C) Upon the consummation of a merger transaction in compliance with this subsection and after the termination of any antitrust litigation commenced within the period prescribed in this paragraph, or upon the termination of such period if no such litigation is commenced therein, the transaction may not thereafter be attacked in any judicial proceeding on the ground that it alone and of itself constituted a violation of any antitrust laws other than section 2 of Title 15, but nothing in this subsection shall exempt any bank or savings association resulting from a merger transaction from complying with the antitrust laws after the consummation of such transaction.

* * *

(f) Publication of reports

Whenever any insured depository institution (except a national bank or a District bank), after written notice of the recommendations of the Corporation based on a report of examination of such insured depository institution by an examiner of the Corporation, shall fail to comply with such recommendations within one hundred and twenty days after such notice, the Corporation shall have the power, and is authorized, to publish only such part of such report of examination as relates to any recommendation not complied with: Provided, That notice of intention to make such publication shall be given to the insured depository institution at least ninety days before such publication is made.

* * *

(j)   Restrictions on transactions with affiliates and insiders

(1)   Transactions with affiliates

(A)   In general

Sections 371c and 371c-1 of this title shall apply with respect to every nonmember insured bank in the same manner and to the same extent as if the nonmember insured bank were a member bank.

(B)   Affiliate defined

For the purpose of subparagraph (A), any company that would be an affiliate (as defined in sections 371c and 371c-1 of this title) of a nonmember insured bank if the nonmember insured bank were a member bank shall be deemed to be an affiliate of that nonmember insured bank.

(2)   Extensions of credit to officers, directors, and principal shareholders

Sections 375a and 375b of this title shall apply with respect to every nonmember insured bank in the same manner and to the same extent as if the nonmember insured bank were a member bank.

* * *

(r)   Subsidiary depository institutions as agents for certain affiliates

(1)   In general

Any bank subsidiary of a bank holding company may receive deposits, renew time deposits, close loans, service loans, and receive payments on loans and other obligations as an agent for a depository institution affiliate.

(2)   Bank acting as agent is not a branch

Notwithstanding any other provision of law, a bank acting as an agent in accordance with paragraph (1) for a depository institution affiliate shall not be considered to be a branch of the affiliate.

(3)   Prohibitions on activities

A depository institution may not–

(A)   conduct any activity as an agent under paragraph (1) or (6) which such institution is prohibited from conducting as a principal under any applicable Federal or State law; or

(B) as a principal, have an agent conduct any activity under paragraph (1) or (6) which the institution is prohibited from conducting under any applicable Federal or State law.

(4) Existing authority not affected

No provision of this subsection shall be construed as affecting–

(A) the authority of any depository institution to act as an agent on behalf of any other depository institution under any other provision of law; or

(B) whether a depository institution which conducts any activity as an agent on behalf of any other depository institution under any other provision of law shall be considered to be a branch of such other institution.

(5) Agency relationship required to be consistent with safe and sound banking practices

An agency relationship between depository institutions under paragraph (1) or (6) shall be on terms that are consistent with safe and sound banking practices and all applicable regulations of any appropriate Federal banking agency.

* * *

§ 1831a. Activities of insured State banks

(a) Permissible Activities

(1) In general

After the end of the 1-year period beginning on December 19, 1991, an insured State bank may not engage as principal in any type of activity that is not permissible for a national bank unless–

(A) the Corporation has determined that the activity would pose no significant risk to the appropriate deposit insurance fund; and

(B) the State bank is, and continues to be, in compliance with applicable capital standards prescribed by the appropriate Federal banking agency.

* * *

(b)   Insurance underwriting

(1)   In general

Notwithstanding subsection (a) of this section, an insured State bank may not engage in insurance underwriting except to the extent that activity is permissible for national banks.

* * *

(c)   Equity Investments by insured State banks

(1)   In general

An insured State bank may not, directly or indirectly, acquire or retain any equity investment of a type that is not permissible for a national bank.

(2)   Exception for certain subsidiaries

Paragraph (1) shall not prohibit an insured State bank from acquiring or retaining an equity investment in a subsidiary of which the insured State bank is a majority owner.

* * *

(d)   Subsidiaries of insured State banks

(1)   In general

After the end of the 1-year period beginning on December 19, 1991, a subsidiary of an insured State bank may not engage as principal in any type of activity that is not permissible for a subsidiary of a national bank unless–

(A)   the Corporation has determined that the activity poses no significant risk to the appropriate deposit insurance fund; and

(B)   the bank is, and continues to be, in compliance with applicable capital standards prescribed by the appropriate Federal banking agency.

(2)   Insurance underwriting prohibited

(A)   Prohibition

Notwithstanding paragraph (1), no subsidiary of an insured State bank may engage in insurance underwriting except to the extent such activities are permissible for national banks.

(B) Continuation of existing activities

Notwithstanding subparagraph (A), a well-capitalized insured State bank or any of its subsidiaries that was lawfully providing insurance as principal in a State on November 21, 1991, may continue to provide, as principal, insurance of the same type to residents of the State (including companies or partnerships incorporated in, organized under the laws of, licensed to do business in, or having an office in the State, but only on behalf of their employees resident in or property located in the State), individuals employed in the State, and any other person to whom the bank or subsidiary has provided insurance as principal, without interruption, since such person resided in or was employed in such State.

* * *

(f) Common and preferred stock investment

(1) In general

An insured State bank shall not acquire or retain, directly or indirectly, any equity investment of a type or in an amount that is not permissible for a national bank or is not otherwise permitted under this section.

(2) Exception for banks in certain states

Notwithstanding paragraph (1), an insured State bank may, to the extent permitted by the Corporation, acquire and retain ownership of securities described in paragraph (1) to the extent the aggregate amount of such investment does not exceed an amount equal to 100 percent of the bank's capital if such bank–

(A) is located in a State that permitted, as of September 30, 1991, investment in common or preferred stock listed on a national securities exchange or shares of an investment company registered under the Investment Company Act of 1940 [15 U.S.C.A. § 80a-1 *et seq.*]; and

(B) made or maintained an investment in such securities during the period beginning on September 30, 1990, and ending on November 26, 1991.

* * *

(g)   Activities of branches of out-of-State banks

(1)   In general

The laws of a host State, including laws regarding community reinvestment, consumer protection, fair lending, and establishment of intrastate branches, shall apply to any branch in the host State of an out-of-State State bank to the same extent as such State laws apply to a branch of a bank chartered by that State.

(2)   Activities of branches

An insured State bank that established a branch in a host State may not conduct any activity at such branch that is not permissible for a bank chartered by that host State.

(3)   Definitions

The terms "host State" "interstate merger transaction", and "out-of-State bank" have the same meanings as in section 1831u of this title.

§ 1831d. State-chartered insured depository institutions and insured branches of foreign banks

(a)   Interest rates

In order to prevent discrimination against State-chartered insured depository institutions, including insured savings banks, or insured branches of foreign banks with respect to interest rates, if the applicable rate prescribed in this subsection exceeds the rate such State bank or insured branch of a foreign bank would be permitted to charge in the absence of this subsection, such State bank or such insured branch of a foreign bank may, notwithstanding any State constitution or statute which is hereby preempted for the purposes of this section, take, receive, reserve, and charge on any loan or discount made, or upon any note, bill of exchange, or other evidence of debt, interest at a rate of not more than 1 per centum in excess of the discount rate on ninety-day commercial paper in effect at the Federal Reserve bank in the Federal Reserve district where such State bank or such insured branch of a foreign bank is located or at the rate allowed by the laws of the State, territory, or district where the bank is located, whichever may be greater.

* * *

§ 1831f. Brokered deposits

(a) In general

An insured depository institution that is not well capitalized may not accept funds obtained, directly or indirectly, by or through any deposit broker for deposit into 1 or more deposit accounts.

* * *

(c) Waiver authority

The Corporation may, on a case-by-case basis and upon application by an insured depository institution which is adequately capitalized (but not well capitalized), waive the applicability of subsection (a) of this section upon a finding that the acceptance of such deposits does not constitute an unsafe or unsound practice with respect to such institution.

* * *

(e) Restriction on interest rate paid

Any insured depository institution which, under subsection (c) or (d) of this section, accepts funds obtained, directly or indirectly, by or through a deposit broker, may not pay a rate of interest on such funds which, at the time that such funds are accepted, significantly exceeds–

(1) the rate paid on deposits of similar maturity in such institution's normal market area for deposits accepted in the institution's normal market area; or

(2) the national rate paid on deposits of comparable maturity, as established by the Corporation, for deposits accepted outside the institution's normal market area.

* * *

(h) Deposit solicitation restricted

An insured depository institution that is undercapitalized, as defined in section 1831o of this title, shall not solicit deposits by offering rates of interest that are significantly higher than the prevailing rates of interest on insured deposits–

(1) in such institution's normal market areas; or

(2) in the market area in which such deposits would otherwise be accepted.

§ 1831g. Contracts between depository institutions and persons providing goods, products, or services

(a)   In general

An insured depository institution may not enter into a written or oral contract with any person to provide goods, products, or services to or for the benefit of such depository institution if the performance of such contract would adversely affect the safety or soundness of the institution.

(b)   Rulemaking

The Corporation shall prescribe such regulations and issue such orders, including definitions consistent with this section, as may be necessary to administer and carry out the purposes of, and prevent evasions of, this section.

(c)   Enforcement

Any action taken by any appropriate Federal banking agency under section 1818 of this title to enforce compliance on the part of any insured depository institution with the requirements of this section may include a requirement that such institution properly reflect the transaction on its books and records.

(d)   No private right of action

This section may not be construed as creating any private right of action.

* * *

§ 1831o. Prompt corrective action

(a)   Resolving problems to protect deposit insurance funds

(1)   Purpose

The purpose of this section is to resolve the problems of insured depository institutions at the least possible long-term loss to the deposit insurance fund.

(2) Prompt corrective action required

Each appropriate Federal banking agency and the Corporation (acting in the Corporation's capacity as the insurer of depository institutions under this chapter) shall carry out the purpose of this section by taking prompt corrective action to resolve the problems of insured depository institutions.

(b) Definitions

For purposes of this section:

(1) Capital categories

(A) Well capitalized

An insured depository institution is "well capitalized" if it significantly exceeds the required minimum level for each relevant capital measure.

(B) Adequately capitalized

An insured depository institution is "adequately capitalized" if it meets the required minimum level for each relevant capital measure.

(C) Undercapitalized

An insured depository institution is "undercapitalized" if it fails to meet the required minimum level for any relevant capital measure.

(D) Significantly undercapitalized

An insured depository institution is "significantly undercapitalized" if it is significantly below the required minimum level for any relevant capital measure.

(E) Critically undercapitalized

An insured depository institution is "critically undercapitalized" if it fails to meet any level specified under subsection (c)(3)(A) of this section.

* * *

(c)   Capital standards

(1)   Relevant capital measures

(A)   In general

Except as provided in subparagraph (B)(ii), the capital standards prescribed by each appropriate Federal banking agency shall include–

(i)   a leverage limit; and

(ii)   a risk-based capital requirement.

* * *

(2)   Capital categories generally

Each appropriate Federal banking agency shall, by regulation, specify for each relevant capital measure the levels at which an insured depository institution is well capitalized, adequately capitalized, undercapitalized, and significantly undercapitalized.

(3) Critical capital

(A)   Agency to specify level

(i)   Leverage limit

Each appropriate Federal banking agency shall, by regulation, in consultation with the Corporation, specify the ratio of tangible equity to total assets at which an insured depository institution is critically undercapitalized.

(ii)   Other relevant capital measures

The agency may, by regulation, specify for 1 or more other relevant capital measures, the level at which an insured depository institution is critically undercapitalized.

(B)   Leverage limit range

The level specified under subparagraph (A)(i) shall require tangible equity in an amount–

(i)   not less than 2 percent of total assets; and

(ii)   except as provided in clause (i), not more than 65 percent of the required minimum level of capital under the leverage limit.

(C) FDIC's concurrence required

The appropriate Federal banking agency shall not, without the concurrence of the Corporation, specify a level under subparagraph (A)(i) lower than that specified by the Corporation for State nonmember insured banks.

(d) Provisions applicable to all institutions

(1) Capital distributions restricted

(A) In general

An insured depository institution shall make no capital distribution if, after making the distribution, the institution would be undercapitalized.

* * *

(2) Management fees restricted

An insured depository institution shall pay no management fee to any person having control of that institution if, after making the payment, the institution would be undercapitalized.

(e) Provisions applicable to undercapitalized institutions

(1) Monitoring required

Each appropriate Federal banking agency shall–

(A) closely monitor the condition of any undercapitalized insured depository institution;

(B) closely monitor compliance with capital restoration plans, restrictions, and requirements imposed under this section; and

(C) periodically review the plan, restrictions, and requirements applicable to any undercapitalized insured depository institution to determine whether the plan, restrictions, and requirements are achieving the purpose of this section.

(2) Capital restoration plan required

(A) In general

Any undercapitalized insured depository institution shall submit an acceptable capital restoration plan to the appropriate Federal banking agency within the time allowed by the agency under subparagraph (D).

(B)   Contents of plan

The capital restoration plan shall–

(i)   specify–

   (I)   the steps the insured depository institution will take to become adequately capitalized;

   (II)   the levels of capital to be attained during each year in which the plan will be in effect;

   (III)   how the institution will comply with the restrictions or requirements then in effect under this section; and

   (IV)   the types and levels of activities in which the institution will engage; and

(ii)   contain such other information as the appropriate Federal banking agency may require.

(C)   Criteria for accepting plan

The appropriate Federal banking agency shall not accept a capital restoration plan unless the agency determines that–

(i)   the plan–

   (I)   complies with subparagraph (B);

   (II)   is based on realistic assumptions, and is likely to succeed in restoring the institution's capital; and

   (III)   would not appreciably increase the risk (including credit risk, interest-rate risk, and other types of risk) to which the institution is exposed; and

(ii)   if the insured depository institution is undercapitalized, each company having control of the institution has–

   (I)   guaranteed that the institution will comply with the plan until the institution has been adequately capitalized on average during each of 4 consecutive calendar quarters; and

   (II)   provided appropriate assurances of performance.

(D) Deadlines for submission and review of plans

The appropriate Federal banking agency shall by regulation establish deadlines that–

(i) provide insured depository institutions with reasonable time to submit capital restoration plans, and generally require an institution to submit a plan not later than 45 days after the institution becomes undercapitalized;

(ii) require the agency to act on capital restoration plans expeditiously, and generally not later than 60 days after the plan is submitted; and

(iii) require the agency to submit a copy of any plan approved by the agency to the Corporation before the end of the 45-day period beginning on the date such approval is granted.

(E) Guarantee liability limited

(i) In general

The aggregate liability under subparagraph (C)(ii) of all companies having control of an insured depository institution shall be the lesser of–

(I) an amount equal to 5 percent of the institution's total assets at the time the institution became undercapitalized; or

(II) the amount which is necessary (or would have been necessary) to bring the institution into compliance with all capital standards applicable with respect to such institution as of the time the institution fails to comply with a plan under this subsection.

(ii) Certain affiliates not affected

This paragraph may not be construed as–

(I) requiring any company not having control of an undercapitalized insured depository institution to guarantee, or otherwise be liable on, a capital restoration plan;

(II) requiring any person other than an insured depository institution to submit a capital restoration plan; or

(III) affecting compliance by brokers, dealers, government securities brokers, and government securities dealers

with the financial responsibility requirements of the Securities Exchange Act of 1934 [15 U.S.C.A. § 78a *et seq.*] and regulations and orders thereunder.

(3)   Asset growth restricted

An undercapitalized insured depository institution shall not permit its average total assets during any calendar quarter to exceed its average total assets during the preceding calendar quarter unless–

(A)   the appropriate Federal banking agency has accepted the institution's capital restoration plan;

(B)   any increase in total assets is consistent with the plan; and

(C)   the institution's ratio of tangible equity to assets increases during the calendar quarter at a rate sufficient to enable the institution to become adequately capitalized within a reasonable time.

(4)   Prior approval required for acquisitions, branching, and new lines of business

An undercapitalized insured depository institution shall not, directly or indirectly, acquire any interest in any company or insured depository institution, establish or acquire any additional branch office, or engage in any new line of business unless–

(A)   the appropriate Federal banking agency has accepted the insured depository institution's capital restoration plan, the institution is implementing the plan, and the agency determines that the proposed action is consistent with and will further the achievement of the plan; or

(B)   the Board of Directors determines that the proposed action will further the purpose of this section.

(5)   Discretionary safeguards

The appropriate Federal banking agency may, with respect to any undercapitalized insured depository institution, take actions described in any subparagraph of subsection (f)(2) of this section if the agency determines that those actions are necessary to carry out the purpose of this section.

(f) Provisions applicable to significantly undercapitalized institutions and undercapitalized institutions that fail to submit and implement capital restoration plans

(1) In general

This subsection shall apply with respect to any insured depository institution that–

(A) is significantly undercapitalized; or

(B) is undercapitalized and–

    (i) fails to submit an acceptable capital restoration plan within the time allowed by the appropriate Federal banking agency under subsection (e)(2)(D) of this section; or

    (ii) fails in any material respect to implement a plan accepted by the agency.

(2) Specific actions authorized

The appropriate Federal banking agency shall carry out this section by taking 1 or more of the following actions:

(A) Requiring recapitalization

Doing 1 or more of the following:

    (i) Requiring the institution to sell enough shares or obligations of the institution so that the institution will be adequately capitalized after the sale.

    (ii) Further requiring that instruments sold under clause (i) be voting shares.

    (iii) Requiring the institution to be acquired by a depository institution holding company, or to combine with another insured depository institution, if 1 or more grounds exist for appointing a conservator or receiver for the institution.

(B) Restricting transactions with affiliates

    (i) Requiring the institution to comply with section 371c of this title as if subsection (d)(1) of that section (exempting transactions with certain affiliated institutions) did not apply.

    (ii) Further restricting the institution's transactions with affiliates.

(C) Restricting interest rates paid

(i)   In general

Restricting the interest rates that the institution pays on deposits to the prevailing rates of interest on deposits of comparable amounts and maturities in the region where the institution is located, as determined by the agency.

(ii) Retroactive restrictions prohibited

This subparagraph does not authorize the agency to restrict interest rates paid on time deposits made before (and not renewed or renegotiated after) the agency acted under this subparagraph.

(D) Restricting asset growth

Restricting the institution's asset growth more stringently than subsection (e)(3) of this section, or requiring the institution to reduce its total assets.

(E) Restricting activities

Requiring the institution or any of its subsidiaries to alter, reduce, or terminate any activity that the agency determines poses excessive risk to the institution.

(F) Improving management

Doing 1 or more of the following:

(i)   New election of directors

Ordering a new election for the institution's board of directors.

(ii) Dismissing directors or senior executive officers

Requiring the institution to dismiss from office any director or senior executive officer who had held office for more than 180 days immediately before the institution became undercapitalized. Dismissal under this clause shall not be construed to be a removal under section 1818 of this title.

(iii) Employing qualified senior executive officers

Requiring the institution to employ qualified senior executive officers (who, if the agency so specifies, shall be subject to approval by the agency).

(G) Prohibiting deposits from correspondent banks

Prohibiting the acceptance by the institution of deposits from correspondent depository institutions, including renewals and rollovers of prior deposits.

(H) Requiring prior approval for capital distributions by bank holding company

Prohibiting any bank holding company having control of the insured depository institution from making any capital distribution without the prior approval of the Board of Governors of the Federal Reserve System.

(I) Requiring divestiture

Doing one or more of the following:

(i) Divestiture by the institution

Requiring the institution to divest itself of or liquidate any subsidiary if the agency determines that the subsidiary is in danger of becoming insolvent and poses a significant risk to the institution, or is likely to cause a significant dissipation of the institution's assets or earnings.

(ii) Divestiture by parent company of nondepository affiliate

Requiring any company having control of the institution to divest itself of or liquidate any affiliate other than an insured depository institution if the appropriate Federal banking agency for that company determines that the affiliate is in danger of becoming insolvent and poses a significant risk to the institution, or is likely to cause a significant dissipation of the institution's assets or earnings.

(iii) Divestiture of institution

Requiring any company having control of the institution to divest itself of the institution if the appropriate Federal banking agency for that company determines that divestiture would improve the institution's financial condition and future prospects.

(J) Requiring other action

Requiring the institution to take any other action that the agency determines will better carry out the purpose of this section than any of the actions described in this paragraph.

(3) Presumption in favor of certain actions

In complying with paragraph (2), the agency shall take the following actions, unless the agency determines that the actions would not further the purpose of this section:

(A) The action described in clause (i) or (iii) of paragraph (2)(A) (relating to requiring the sale of shares or obligations, or requiring the institution to be acquired by or combine with another institution).

(B) The action described in paragraph (2)(B)(i) (relating to restricting transactions with affiliates).

(C) The action described in paragraph (2)(C) (relating to restricting interest rates).

(4) Senior executive officers' compensation restricted

(A) In general

The insured depository institution shall not do any of the following without the prior written approval of the appropriate Federal banking agency:

(i) Pay any bonus to any senior executive officer.

(ii) Provide compensation to any senior executive officer at a rate exceeding that officer's average rate of compensation (excluding bonuses, stock options, and profit-sharing) during the 12 calendar months preceding the calendar month in which the institution became undercapitalized.

(B) Failing to submit plan

The appropriate Federal banking agency shall not grant any approval under subparagraph (A) with respect to an institution that has failed to submit an acceptable capital restoration plan.

(5) Discretion to impose certain additional restrictions

The agency may impose 1 or more of the restrictions prescribed by regulation under subsection (i) of this section if the agency determines that those restrictions are necessary to carry out the purpose of this section.

(6) Consultation with other regulators

Before the agency or Corporation makes a determination under paragraph (2)(I) with respect to an affiliate that is a broker, dealer, government securities broker, government securities dealer, investment company, or investment adviser, the agency or Corporation shall consult with the Securities and Exchange Commission and, in the case of any other affiliate which is subject to any financial responsibility or capital requirement, any other appropriate regulator of such affiliate with respect to the proposed determination of the agency or the Corporation and actions pursuant to such determination.

(g) More stringent treatment based on other supervisory criteria

(1) In general

If the appropriate Federal banking agency determines (after notice and an opportunity for hearing) that an insured depository institution is in an unsafe or unsound condition or, pursuant to section 1818(b)(8) of this title, deems the institution to be engaging in an unsafe or unsound practice, the agency may–

(A) if the institution is well capitalized, reclassify the institution as adequately capitalized;

(B) if the institution is adequately capitalized (but not well capitalized), require the institution to comply with 1 or more provisions of subsections (d) and (e) of this section, as if the institution were undercapitalized; or

(C) if the institution is undercapitalized, take any 1 or more actions authorized under subsection (f)(2) of this section as if the institution were significantly undercapitalized.

(2) Contents of plan

Any plan required under paragraph (1) shall specify the steps that the insured depository institution will take to correct the unsafe or unsound condition or practice. Capital restoration plans shall not be required under paragraph (1)(B).

(h) Provisions applicable to critically undercapitalized institutions

(1) Activities restricted

Any critically undercapitalized insured depository institution shall comply with restrictions prescribed by the Corporation under subsection (i) of this section.

(2) Payments on subordinated debt prohibited

(A) In general

A critically undercapitalized insured depository institution shall not, beginning 60 days after becoming critically undercapitalized, make any payment of principal or interest on the institution's subordinated debt.

(B) Exceptions

The Corporation may make exceptions to subparagraph (A) if–

(i)   the appropriate Federal banking agency has taken action with respect to the insured depository institution under paragraph (3)(A)(ii); and

(ii)   the Corporation determines that the exception would further the purpose of this section.

(C) Limited exemption for certain subordinated debt

Until July 15, 1996, subparagraph (A) shall not apply with respect to any subordinated debt outstanding on July 15, 1991, and not extended or otherwise renegotiated after July 15, 1991.

(D) Accrual of interest

Subparagraph (A) does not prevent unpaid interest from accruing on subordinated debt under the terms of that debt, to the extent otherwise permitted by law.

(3) Conservatorship, receivership, or other action required

(A) In general

The appropriate Federal banking agency shall, not later than 90 days after an insured depository institution becomes critically undercapitalized–

(i) appoint a receiver (or, with the concurrence of the Corporation, a conservator) for the institution; or

(ii) take such other action as the agency determines, with the concurrence of the Corporation, would better achieve the purpose of this section, after documenting why the action would better achieve that purpose.

(B) Periodic redeterminations required

Any determination by an appropriate Federal banking agency under subparagraph (A)(ii) to take any action with respect to an insured depository institution in lieu of appointing a conservator or receiver shall cease to be effective not later than the end of the 90-day period beginning on the date that the determination is made and a conservator or receiver shall be appointed for that institution under subparagraph (A)(i) unless the agency makes a new determination under subparagraph (A)(ii) at the end of the effective period of the prior determination.

(C) Appointment of receiver required if other action fails to restore capital

(i) In general

Notwithstanding subparagraphs (A) and (B), the appropriate Federal banking agency shall appoint a receiver for the insured depository institution if the institution is critically undercapitalized on average during the calendar quarter beginning 270 days after the date on which the institution became critically undercapitalized.

(ii) Exception

Notwithstanding clause (i), the appropriate Federal banking agency may continue to take such other action as the agency determines to be appropriate in lieu of such appointment if–

(I) the agency determines, with the concurrence of the Corporation, that (aa) the insured depository

institution has positive net worth, (bb) the insured depository institution has been in substantial compliance with an approved capital restoration plan which requires consistent improvement in the institution's capital since the date of the approval of the plan, (cc) the insured depository institution is profitable or has an upward trend in earnings the agency projects as sustainable, and (dd) the insured depository institution is reducing the ratio of nonperforming loans to total loans; and

(II) the head of the appropriate Federal banking agency and the Chairperson of the Board of Directors both certify that the institution is viable and not expected to fail.

(i) Restricting activities of critically undercapitalized institutions

To carry out the purpose of this section, the Corporation shall, by regulation or order–

(1) restrict the activities of any critically undercapitalized insured depository institution; and

(2) at a minimum, prohibit any such institution from doing any of the following without the Corporation's prior written approval:

(A) Entering into any material transaction other than in the usual course of business, including any investment, expansion, acquisition, sale of assets, or other similar action with respect to which the depository institution is required to provide notice to the appropriate Federal banking agency.

(B) Extending credit for any highly leveraged transaction.

(C) Amending the institution's charter or bylaws, except to the extent necessary to carry out any other requirement of any law, regulation, or order.

(D) Making any material change in accounting methods.

(E) Engaging in any covered transaction (as defined in section 371c(b) of this title).

(F) Paying excessive compensation or bonuses.

(G) Paying interest on new or renewed liabilities at a rate that would increase the institution's weighted average cost of funds to a level significantly exceeding the prevailing rates of interest on insured deposits in the institution's normal market areas.

* * *

(n) Administrative review of dismissal orders

(1) Timely petition required

A director or senior executive officer dismissed pursuant to an order under subsection (f)(2)(F)(ii) of this section may obtain review of that order by filing a written petition for reinstatement with the appropriate Federal banking agency not later than 10 days after receiving notice of the dismissal.

(2) Procedure

(A) Hearing required

The agency shall give the petitioner an opportunity to–

(i) submit written materials in support of the petition; and

(ii) appear, personally or through counsel, before 1 or more members of the agency or designated employees of the agency.

(B) Deadline for hearing

The agency shall–

(i) schedule the hearing referred to in subparagraph (A)(ii) promptly after the petition is filed; and

(ii) hold the hearing not later than 30 days after the petition is filed, unless the petitioner requests that the hearing be held at a later time.

(C) Deadline for decision

Not later than 60 days after the date of the hearing, the agency shall–

(i) by order, grant or deny the petition;

(ii) if the order is adverse to the petitioner, set forth the basis for the order; and

(iii) notify the petitioner of the order.

(3)   Standard for review of dismissal orders

The petitioner shall bear the burden of proving that the petitioner's continued employment would materially strengthen the insured depository institution's ability–

(A)   to become adequately capitalized, to the extent that the order is based on the institution's capital level or failure to submit or implement a capital restoration plan; and

(B)   to correct the unsafe or unsound condition or unsafe or unsound practice, to the extent that the order is based on subsection (g)(1) of this section.

* * *

§ 1831p-1. Standards for safety and soundness

(a)   Operational and managerial standards

Each appropriate Federal banking agency shall, for all insured depository institutions, prescribe–

(1)   standards relating to–

(A)   internal controls, information systems, and internal audit systems, in accordance with section 1831m of this title;

(B)   loan documentation;

(C)   credit underwriting;

(D)   interest rate exposure;

(E)   asset growth; and

(F)   compensation, fees, and benefits, in accordance with subsection (c) of this section; and

(2)   such other operational and managerial standards as the agency determines to be appropriate.

(b)   Asset quality, earnings, and stock valuation standards

Each appropriate Federal banking agency shall prescribe standards, by regulation or guideline, for all insured depository institutions relating to asset quality, earnings, and stock valuation that the agency determines to be appropriate.

(c)   Compensation standards

Each appropriate Federal banking agency shall, for all insured depository institutions, prescribe–

(1) standards prohibiting as an unsafe and unsound practice any employment contract, compensation or benefit agreement, fee arrangement, perquisite, stock option plan, postemployment benefit, or other compensatory arrangement that–

   (A) would provide any executive officer, employee, director, or principal shareholder of the institution with excessive compensation, fees or benefits; or

   (B) could lead to material financial loss to the institution;

(2) standards specifying when compensation, fees, or benefits referred to in paragraph (1) are excessive, which shall require the agency to determine whether the amounts are unreasonable or disproportionate to the services actually performed by the individual by considering–

   (A) the combined value of all cash and noncash benefits provided to the individual;

   (B) the compensation history of the individual and other individuals with comparable expertise at the institution;

   (C) the financial condition of the institution;

   (D) comparable compensation practices at comparable institutions, based upon such factors as asset size, geographic location, and the complexity of the loan portfolio or other assets;

   (E) for postemployment benefits, the projected total cost and benefit to the institution;

   (F) any connection between the individual and any fraudulent act or omission, breach of trust or fiduciary duty, or insider abuse with regard to the institution; and

   (G) other factors that the agency determines to be relevant; and

(3) such other standards relating to compensation, fees, and benefits as the agency determines to be appropriate.

(d) Standards to be prescribed

(1) In general

Standards under subsections (a), (b), and (c) of this section shall be prescribed by regulation or guideline. Such regulations or guidelines may not prescribe standards that set a specific level or range of compensation for directors, officers, or employees of insured depository institutions.

(2) Applicability of other laws

Paragraph (1) shall not affect the authority of any appropriate Federal banking agency to restrict the level of compensation, including golden parachute payments (as defined in section 1828(k)(4) of this title), paid to any director, officer, or employee of an insured depository institution under any other provision of law.

(3) Senior executive officers at undercapitalized institutions

Paragraph (1) shall not affect the authority of any appropriate Federal banking agency to restrict compensation paid to any senior executive officer of an undercapitalized insured depository institution pursuant to section 1831o of this title.

(4) Safety and soundness or enforcement actions

Paragraph (1) shall not be construed as affecting the authority of any appropriate Federal banking agency under any provision of this chapter other than this section, or under any other provision of law, to prescribe a specific level or range of compensation for any director, officer, or employee of an insured depository institution–

(A) to preserve the safety and soundness of the institution; or

(B) in connection with any action under section 1818 of this title or any order issued by the agency, any agreement between the agency and the institution, or any condition imposed by the agency in connection with the agency's approval of an application or other request by the institution, which is enforceable under section 1818 of this title.

* * *

§ 1831u. Interstate bank mergers

(a) Approval of interstate merger transactions authorized

(1) In general

Beginning on June 1, 1997, the responsible agency may approve a merger transaction under section 1828(c) of this title between insured banks with different home States, without regard to whether such transaction is prohibited under the law of any State.

(2) State election to prohibit interstate merger transactions

(A) In general

Notwithstanding paragraph (1), a merger transaction may not be approved pursuant to paragraph (1) if the transaction involves a bank the home State of which has enacted a law after September 29, 1994, and before June 1, 1997, that–

(i) applies equally to all out-of-State banks; and

(ii) expressly prohibits merger transactions involving out-of-State banks.

(B) No effect on prior approvals of merger transactions

A law enacted by a State pursuant to subparagraph (A) shall have no effect on merger transactions that were approved before the effective date of such law.

(3) State election to permit early interstate merger transactions

(A) In general

A merger transaction may be approved pursuant to paragraph (1) before June 1, 1997, if the home State of each bank involved in the transaction has in effect, as of the date of the approval of such transaction, a law that–

(i) applies equally to all out-of-State banks; and

(ii) expressly permits interstate merger transactions with all out-of-State banks.

(B) Certain conditions allowed

A host State may impose conditions on a branch within such State of a bank resulting from an interstate merger transaction if–

(i) the conditions do not have the effect of discriminating against out-of-State banks, out-of-State bank holding companies, or any subsidiary of such bank or company (other than on the basis of a nationwide reciprocal treatment requirement);

(ii) the imposition of the conditions is not preempted by Federal law; and

(iii) the conditions do not apply or require performance after May 31, 1997.

(4) Interstate merger transactions involving acquisitions of branches

(A) In general

An interstate merger transaction may involve the acquisition of a branch of an insured bank without the acquisition of the bank only if the law of the State in which the branch is located permits out-of-State banks to acquire a branch of a bank in such State without acquiring the bank.

(B) Treatment of branch for purposes of this section

In the case of an interstate merger transaction which involves the acquisition of a branch of an insured bank without the acquisition of the bank, the branch shall be treated, for purposes of this section, as an insured bank the home State of which is the State in which the branch is located.

(5) Preservation of State age laws

(A) In general

The responsible agency may not approve an application pursuant to paragraph (1) that would have the effect of permitting an out-of-State bank or out-of-State bank holding company to acquire a bank in a host State that has not been in existence for the minimum period of time, if any, specified in the statutory law of the host State.

(B) Special rule for State age laws specifying a period of more than 5 years

Notwithstanding subparagraph (A), the responsible agency may approve a merger transaction pursuant to paragraph (1) involving the acquisition of a bank that has been in existence at least 5 years without regard to any longer minimum period of time specified in a statutory law of the host State.

(6) Shell banks

For purposes of this subsection, a bank that has been chartered solely for the purpose of, and does not open for business prior to, acquiring control of, or acquiring all or substantially all of the assets of, an existing bank or branch shall be deemed to have been in existence for the same period of time as the bank or branch to be acquired.

(b) Provisions relating to application and approval process

* * *

(2) Concentration limits

(A) Nationwide concentration limits

The responsible agency may not approve an application for an interstate merger transaction if the resulting bank (including all insured depository institutions which are affiliates of the resulting bank), upon consummation of the transaction, would control more than 10 percent of the total amount of deposits of insured depository institutions in the United States.

(B) Statewide concentration limits other than with respect to initial entries

The responsible agency may not approve an application for an interstate merger transaction if–

(i) any bank involved in the transaction (including all insured depository institutions which are affiliates of any such bank) has a branch in any State in which any other bank involved in the transaction has a branch; and

(ii) the resulting bank (including all insured depository institutions which would be affiliates of the resulting bank), upon consummation of the transaction, would control 30 percent or more of the total amount of deposits of insured depository institutions in any such State.

(C) Effectiveness of State deposit caps

No provision of this subsection shall be construed as affecting the authority of any State to limit, by statute, regulation, or order, the percentage of the total amount of deposits of insured depository institutions in the State which may be held or controlled by any bank or bank holding company (including all insured depository institutions which are affiliates of the bank or bank holding company) to the extent the application of such limitation does not discriminate against out-of-State banks, out-of-State bank holding companies, or subsidiaries of such banks or holding companies.

* * *

(j)   Activities of branches of out-of-State banks.

(1)   Application of host State law.

The laws of a host State, including laws regarding community reinvestment, consumer protection, fair lending, and establishment of intrastate branches, shall apply to any branch in the host State of an out-of-State bank to the same extent as such State laws apply to an branch in the host State of an out-of-State national bank. To the extent host State law is inapplicable to a branch of an out-of-State State bank in such host State pursuant to the preceding sentence, home State law shall apply to such branch.

(2)   Activities of branches.

An insured State bank that established a branch in a host State may conduct any activity at such branch that is permissible under the laws of the home State of such bank, to the extent such activity is permissible either for a bank chartered by the host State (subject to the restrictions in this section) or for a branch in the host State of an out-of-State of an out-of-State national bank.

* * *

CHAPTER SIX

BANK HOLDING COMPANY ACT

§ 1841. Definitions

(a) (1) Except as provided in paragraph (5) of this subsection, "bank holding company" means any company which has control over any bank or over any company that is or becomes a bank holding company by virtue of this chapter.

      (2) Any company has control over a bank or over any company if–

        (A) the company directly or indirectly or acting through one or more other persons owns, controls, or has power to vote 25 per centum or more of any class of voting securities of the bank or company;

        (B) the company controls in any manner the election of a majority of the directors or trustees of the bank or company; or

        (C) the Board determines, after notice and opportunity for hearing, that the company directly or indirectly exercises a controlling influence over the management or policies of the bank or company.

      (3) For the purposes of any proceeding under paragraph (2)(C) of this subsection, there is a presumption that any company which directly or indirectly owns, controls, or has power to vote less than 5 per centum of any class of voting securities of a given bank or company does not have control over that bank or company.

      (4) In any administrative or judicial proceeding under this chapter, other than a proceeding under paragraph (2)(C) of this subsection, a company may not be held to have had control over any given bank or company at any given time unless that company, at the time in question, directly or indirectly owned, controlled, or had power to vote 5 per centum or more of any class of voting securities of the bank or company, or had already been found to have control in a proceeding under paragraph (2)(C).

      (5) Notwithstanding any other provision of this subsection–

        (A) No bank and no company owning or controlling voting shares of a bank is a bank holding company by virtue of its ownership or control of shares in a fiduciary capacity, except as provided in paragraphs (2) and (3) of subsection (g) of this section. For the purpose of the preceding sentence, bank shares shall not be deemed to have been acquired in a fiduciary capacity if the acquiring bank or company has sole discretionary authority to exercise voting rights with respect thereto; . . .

(B)   No company is a bank holding company by virtue of its ownership or control of shares acquired by it in connection with its underwriting of securities if such shares are held only for such period of time as will permit the sale thereof on a reasonable basis.

(C)   No company formed for the sole purpose of participating in a proxy solicitation is a bank holding company by virtue of its control of voting rights of shares acquired in the course of such solicitation.

(D)   No company is a bank holding company by virtue of its ownership or control of shares acquired in securing or collecting a debt previously contracted in good faith, until two years after the date of acquisition. The Board is authorized upon application by a company to extend, from time to time for not more than one year at a time, the two-year period referred to herein for disposing of any shares acquired by a company in the regular course of securing or collecting a debt previously contracted in good faith, if, in the Board's judgment, such an extension would not be detrimental to the public interest, but no such extension shall in the aggregate exceed three years.

* * *

(b)   "Company" means any corporation, partnership, business trust, association, or similar organization, or any other trust unless by its terms it must terminate within twenty-five years or not later than twenty-one years and ten months after the death of individuals living on the effective date of the trust but shall not include any corporation the majority of the shares of which are owned by the United States or by any State, and shall not include a qualified family partnership. . . .

(c)   **Bank defined**

For purposes of this chapter–

(1)   In general: Except as provided in paragraph (2), the term "bank" means any of the following:

(A)   An insured bank as defined in section 3(h) of the Federal Deposit Insurance Act [12 U.S.C.A. § 1813(h)].

(B)   An institution organized under the laws of the United States, any State of the United States, the District of Columbia, any territory of the United States, Puerto Rico, Guam, American Samoa, or the Virgin Islands which both--

(i)   accepts demand deposits or deposits that the depositor may withdraw by check or similar means for payment to third parties or others; and

(ii)   is engaged in the business of making commercial loans.

(2) Exceptions: The term "bank" does not include any of the following:

(A) A foreign bank which would be a bank within the meaning of paragraph (1) solely because such bank has an insured or uninsured branch in the United States.

(B) An insured institution (as defined in subsection (j) of this section).

(C) An organization that does not do business in the United States except as an incident to its activities outside the United States.

(D) An institution that functions solely in a trust or fiduciary capacity, if--

(i) all or substantially all of the deposits of such institution are in trust funds and are received in a bona fide fiduciary capacity;

(ii) no deposits of such institution which are insured by the Federal Deposit Insurance Corporation are offered or marketed by or through an affiliate of such institution;

(iii) such institution does not accept demand deposits or deposits that the depositor may withdraw by check or similar means for payment to third parties or others or make commercial loans; and

(iv) such institution does not--

(I) obtain payment or payment related services from any Federal Reserve bank, including any service referred to in section 11A of the Federal Reserve Act [12 U.S.C.A. § 248a]; or

(II) exercise discount or borrowing privileges pursuant to section 19(b)(7) of the Federal Reserve Act [12 U.S.C.A. § 461(b)(7)].

(E) A credit union (as described in section 19(b)(1)(A)(iv) of the Federal Reserve Act [12 U.S.C.A. § 461(b)(1)(A)(iv)]).

(F) An institution, including an institution that accepts collateral for extensions of credit by holding deposits under $100,000, and by other means which--

(i) engages only in credit card operations;

(ii) does not accept demand deposits or deposits that the depositor may withdraw by check or similar means for payment to third parties or others;

(iii) does not accept any savings or time deposit of less than $100,000;

(iv) maintains only one office that accepts deposits; and

      (v)   does not engage in the business of making commercial loans.

* * *

(d)   "Subsidiary", with respect to a specified bank holding company, means (1) any company 25 per centum or more of whose voting shares (excluding shares owned by the United States or by any company wholly owned by the United States) is directly or indirectly owned or controlled by such bank holding company, or is held by it with power to vote; (2) any company the election of a majority of whose directors is controlled in any manner by such bank holding company; or (3) any company with respect to the management of policies of which such bank holding company has the power, directly or indirectly, to exercise a controlling influence, as determined by the Board, after notice and opportunity for hearing.

* * *

(g)   For the purposes of this chapter-

(1)   shares owned or controlled by any subsidiary of a bank holding company shall be deemed to be indirectly owned or controlled by such bank holding company;

(2)   shares held or controlled directly or indirectly by trustees for the benefit of (A) a company, (B) the shareholders or members of a company, or (C) the employees (whether exclusively or not) of a company, shall be deemed to be controlled by such company; and

(3)   shares transferred after January 1, 1966, by any bank holding company (or by any company which, but for such transfer, would be a bank holding company) directly or indirectly to any transferee that is indebted to the transferor, or has one or more officers, directors, trustees, or beneficiaries in common with or subject to control by the transferor, shall be deemed to be indirectly owned or controlled by the transferor unless the Board, after opportunity for hearing, determines that the transferor is not in fact capable of controlling the transferee.

* * *

(k) Affiliate

For purposes of this chapter, the term "affiliate" means any company that controls, is controlled by, or is under common control with another company.

* * *

§ 1842. Acquisition of bank shares or assets

(a) Prior approval of Board as necessary; exceptions; disposition, time extension; subsequent approval or disposition upon disapproval

It shall be unlawful, except with the prior approval of the Board, (1) for any action to be taken that causes any company to become a bank

holding company; (2) for any action to be taken that causes a bank to become a subsidiary of a bank holding company; (3) for any bank holding company to acquire direct or indirect ownership or control of any voting shares of any bank if, after such acquisition, such company will directly or indirectly own or control more than 5 per centum of the voting shares of such bank; (4) for any bank holding company or subsidiary thereof, other than a bank, to acquire all or substantially all of the assets of a bank; or (5) for any bank holding company to merge or consolidate with any other bank holding company.

* * *

(c)   Factors for consideration by Board

(1)   Competitive factors

The Board shall not approve–

(A)   any acquisition or merger or consolidation under this section which would result in a monopoly, or which would be in furtherance of any combination or conspiracy to monopolize or to attempt to monopolize the business of banking in any part of the United States, or

(B)   any other proposed acquisition or merger or consolidation under this section whose effect in any section of the country may be substantially to lessen competition, or to tend to create a monopoly, or which in any other manner would be in restraint of trade, unless it finds that the anticompetitive effects of the proposed transaction are clearly outweighed in the public interest by the probable effect of the transaction in meeting the convenience and needs of the community to be served.

(2)   Banking and community factors

In every case, the Board shall take into consideration the financial and managerial resources and future prospects of the company or companies and the banks concerned, and the convenience and needs of the community to be served.

(3)   Supervisory factors

The Board shall disapprove any application under this section by any company if–

(A)   the company fails to provide the Board with adequate assurances that the company will make available to the Board such information on the operations or activities of the company, and any affiliate of the company, as the Board determines to be appropriate to determine and enforce compliance with this chapter; or

(B)   in the case of an application involving a foreign bank, the foreign bank is not subject to comprehensive supervision or regulation

on a consolidated basis by the appropriate authorities in the
bank's home country.

* * *

(d)   Interstate banking

(1)   Approvals authorized

(A)   Acquisition of banks

The Board may approve an application under this section
by a bank holding company that is adequately capitalized and
adequately managed to acquire control of, or acquire all or
substantially all of the assets of, a bank located in a State other
than the home State of such bank holding company, without
regard to whether such transaction is prohibited under the law of
any State.

(B)   Preservation of State age laws

(i)   In general

Notwithstanding subparagraph (A), the Board may not
approve an application pursuant to such subparagraph that
would have the effect of permitting an out-of-State bank
holding company to acquire a bank in a host State that has
not been in existence for the minimum period of time, if
any, specified in the statutory law of the host State.

(ii)   Special rule for State age laws specifying a period of more
than 5 years

Notwithstanding clause (i), the Board may approve,
pursuant to subparagraph (A), the acquisition of a bank that
has been in existence for at least 5 years without regard to
any longer minimum period of time specified in a statutory
law of the host State.

(C)   Shell banks

For purposes of this subsection, a bank that has been
chartered solely for the purpose of, and does not open for
business prior to, acquiring control of, or acquiring all or
substantially all of the assets of, an existing bank shall be deemed
to have been in existence for the same period of time as the bank
to be acquired.

(D)   Effect on State contingency laws

No provision of this subsection shall be construed as
affecting the applicability of a State law that makes an acquisition
of a bank contingent upon a requirement to hold a portion of
such bank's assets available for call by a State-sponsored housing
entity established pursuant to State law, if–

(i)   the State law does not have the effect of discriminating against out-of-State banks, out-of-State bank holding companies, or subsidiaries of such banks or bank holding companies;

(ii) that State law was in effect as of September 29, 1994;

(iii) the Federal Deposit Insurance Corporation has not determined that compliance with such State law would result in an unacceptable risk to the appropriate deposit insurance fund; and

(iv) the appropriate Federal banking agency for such bank has not found that compliance with such State law would place the bank in an unsafe or unsound condition.

(2) Concentration limits

(A) Nationwide concentration limits

The Board may not approve an application pursuant to paragraph (1)(A) if the applicant (including all insured depository institutions which are affiliates of the applicant) controls, or upon consummation of the acquisition for which such application is filed would control, more than 10 percent of the total amount of deposits of insured depository institutions in the United States.

(B) Statewide concentration limits other than with respect to initial entries

The Board may not approve an application pursuant to paragraph (1)(A) if–

(i)   immediately before the consummation of the acquisition for which such application is filed, the applicant (including any insured depository institution affiliate of the applicant) controls any insured depository institution or any branch of an insured depository institution in the home State of any bank to be acquired or in any host State in which any such bank maintains a branch; and

(ii) the applicant (including all insured depository institutions which are affiliates of the applicant), upon consummation of the acquisition, would control 30 percent or more of the total amount of deposits of insured depository institutions in any such State.

(C) Effectiveness of State deposit caps

No provision of this subsection shall be construed as affecting the authority of any State to limit, by statute, regulation, or order, the percentage of the total amount of deposits of insured

depository institutions in the State which may be held or
controlled by any bank or bank holding company (including all
insured depository institutions which are affiliates of the bank or
bank holding company) to the extent the application of such
limitation does not discriminate against out-of-State banks,
out-of-State bank holding companies, or subsidiaries of such
banks or holding companies.

* * *

§ 1843. Interests in nonbanking organizations

(a)   **Ownership or control of voting shares of any company not a bank;
engagement in activities other than banking**

Except as otherwise provided in this chapter, no bank holding company
shall–

(1)   after May 9, 1956, acquire direct or indirect ownership or control of
any voting shares of any company which is not a bank, or

(2)   after two years from the date as of which it becomes a bank holding
company, * * * retain direct or indirect ownership or control of any
voting shares of any company which is not a bank or bank holding
company or engage in any activities other than (A) those of banking or
of managing or controlling banks and other subsidiaries authorized
under this chapter or of furnishing services to or performing services
for its subsidiaries, and (B) those permitted under paragraph (8) of
subsection (c) of this section subject to all the conditions specified in
such paragraph or in any order or regulation issued by the Board under
such paragraph:

* * *

(c)   **Exemptions**

The prohibitions in this section shall not apply to– * * *

(1)   shares of any company engaged or to be engaged solely in one or more
of the following activities: (A) holding or operating properties used
wholly or substantially by any banking subsidiary of such bank
holding company in the operations of such banking subsidiary or
acquired for such future use; or (B) conducting a safe deposit business;
or (C) furnishing services to or performing services for such bank
holding company or its banking subsidiaries; * * *

(2)   shares acquired by a bank holding company or any of its subsidiaries
in satisfaction of a debt previously contracted in good faith, but such
shares shall be disposed of within a period of two years from the date
on which they were acquired, except that the Board is authorized upon
application by such bank holding company to extend such period of
two years from time to time as to such holding company for not more
than one year at a time if, in its judgment, such an extension would not

be detrimental to the public interest, but no such extensions shall extend beyond a date five years after the date on which such shares were acquired;

(3) shares acquired by such bank holding company from any of its subsidiaries which subsidiary has been requested to dispose of such shares by any Federal or State authority having statutory power to examine such subsidiary, but such bank holding company shall dispose of such shares within a period of two years from the date on which they were acquired;

(4) shares held or acquired by a bank in good faith in a fiduciary capacity, except where such shares are held under a trust that constitutes a company as defined in section 1841(b) of this title and except as provided in paragraphs (2) and (3) of section 1841(g) of this title;

(5) shares which are of the kinds and amounts eligible for investment by national banking associations under the provisions of section 24 of this title;

(6) shares of any company which do not include more than 5 per centum of the outstanding voting shares of such company;

(7) shares of an investment company which is not a bank holding company and which is not engaged in any business other than investing in securities, which securities do not include more than 5 per centum of the outstanding voting shares of any company;

(8) shares of any company the activities of which the Board after due notice (and opportunity for hearing in the case of an acquisition of a savings association) has determined (by order or regulation) to be so closely related to banking or managing or controlling banks as to be a proper incident thereto, but for purposes of this subsection it is not closely related to banking or managing or controlling banks for a bank holding company to provide insurance as a principal, agent, or broker except (A) where the insurance is limited to assuring repayment of the outstanding balance due on a specific extension of credit by a bank holding company or its subsidiary in the event of the death, disability, or involuntary unemployment of the debtor; (B) in the case of a finance company which is a subsidiary of a bank holding company, where the insurance is also limited to assuring repayment of the outstanding balance on an extension of credit in the event of loss or damage to any property used as collateral on such extension of credit and, during the period beginning October 15, 1982, and ending on December 31, 1982, such extension of credit is not more than $10,000 ($25,000 in the case of an extension of credit which is made to finance the purchase of a residential manufactured home and which is secured by such residential manufactured home) and for any given year after 1982, such extension of credit is not more than an amount equal to

$10,000 ($25,000 in the case of an extension of credit which is made to finance the purchase of a residential manufactured home and which is secured by such residential manufactured home) increased by the percentage increase in the Consumer Price Index for Urban Wage Earners and Clerical Workers published monthly by the Bureau of Labor Statistics for the period beginning on January 1, 1982, and ending on December 31 of the year preceding the year in which such extension of credit is made; (C) any insurance agency activity in a place that (i) has a population not exceeding five thousand (as shown by the last preceding decennial census), or (ii) the bank holding company, after notice and opportunity for a hearing, demonstrates has inadequate insurance agency facilities; (D) any insurance agency activity which was engaged in by the bank holding company or any of its subsidiaries on May 1, 1982, or which the Board approved for such company or any of its subsidiaries on or before May 1, 1982, including (i) sales of insurance at new locations of the same bank holding company or the same subsidiary or subsidiaries with respect to which insurance was sold on May 1, 1982, or approved to be sold on or before May 1, 1982, if such new locations are confined to the State in which the principal place of business of the bank holding company is located, any State or States immediately adjacent to such State, and any State or States in which insurance activities were conducted by the bank holding company or any of its subsidiaries on May 1, 1982, or were approved to be conducted by the bank holding company or any of its subsidiaries on or before May 1, 1982, and (ii) sales of insurance coverages which may become available after May 1, 1982, so long as those coverages insure against the same types of risks, as, or are otherwise functionally equivalent to, coverages sold on May 1, 1982, or approved to be sold on or before May 1, 1982 (for purposes of this subparagraph, activities engaged in or approved by the Board on May 1, 1982, shall include activities carried on subsequent to that date as the result of an application to engage in such activities pending on May 1, 1982, and approved subsequent to that date or of the acquisition by such company pursuant to a binding written contract entered into on or before May 1, 1982, of another company engaged in such activities at the time of the acquisition); (E) any insurance activity where the activity is limited solely to supervising on behalf of insurance underwriters the activities of retail insurance agents who sell (i) fidelity insurance and property and casualty insurance on the real and personal property used in the operations of the bank holding company or any of its subsidiaries, and (ii) group insurance that protects the employees of the bank holding company or any of its subsidiaries; (F) any insurance agency activity engaged in by a bank holding company, or any of its subsidiaries, which bank holding

company has total assets of $50,000,000 or less: Provided, however, That such a bank holding company and its subsidiaries may not engage in the sale of life insurance or annuities except as provided in subparagraph (A), (B), or (C); or (G) where the activity is performed, or shares of the company involved are owned, directly or indirectly, by a bank holding company which is registered with the Board of Governors of the Federal Reserve System and which, prior to January 1, 1971, was engaged, directly or indirectly, in insurance agency activities as a consequence of approval by the Board prior to January 1, 1971. In determining whether a particular activity is a proper incident to banking or managing or controlling banks the Board shall consider whether its performance by an affiliate of a holding company can reasonably be expected to produce benefits to the public, such as greater convenience, increased competition, or gains in efficiency, that outweigh possible adverse effects, such as undue concentration of resources, decreased or unfair competition, conflicts of interests, or unsound banking practices. In orders and regulations under this subsection, the Board may differentiate between activities commenced de novo and activities commenced by the acquisition, in whole or in part, of a going concern. Notwithstanding any other provision of this chapter, if the Board finds that an emergency exists which requires the Board to act immediately on any application under this subsection involving a thrift institution, and the primary Federal regulator of such institution concurs in such finding, the Board may dispense with the notice and hearing requirement of this subsection and the Board may approve or deny any such application without notice or hearing. If an application is filed under this paragraph in connection with an application to make an acquisition pursuant to section 13(f) of the Federal Deposit Insurance Act [12 U.S.C.A. § 1823(f)], the Board may dispense with the notice and hearing requirement of this paragraph and the Board may approve or deny the application under this paragraph without notice or hearing. If an application described in the preceding sentence is approved, the Board shall publish in the Federal Register, not later than 7 days after such approval is granted, the order approving the application and a description of the nonbanking activities involved in the acquisition;

* * *

§ 1844. Administration

(a) Registration of bank holding company

Within one hundred and eighty days after May 9, 1956, or within one hundred and eighty days after becoming a bank holding company, whichever is later, each bank holding company shall register with the Board on forms prescribed by the Board, which shall include such information

with respect to the financial condition and operations, management, and intercompany relationships of the bank holding company and its subsidiaries, and related matters, as the Board may deem necessary or appropriate to carry out the purposes of this chapter. The Board may, in its discretion, extend the time within which a bank holding company shall register and file the requisite information.

(b)   Regulations and orders

The Board is authorized to issue such regulations and orders as may be necessary to enable it to administer and carry out the purposes of this chapter and prevent evasions thereof.

(c)   Reports required by Board; examinations; cost of examination

The Board from time to time may require reports under oath to keep it informed as to whether the provisions of this chapter and such regulations and orders issued thereunder have been complied with; and the Board may make examinations of each bank holding company and each subsidiary thereof, the cost of which shall be assessed against, and paid by, such holding company. The Board shall, as far as possible, use the report of examinations made by the Comptroller of the Currency, the Federal Deposit Insurance Corporation, or the appropriate State bank supervisory authority for the purposes of this section.

* * *

(e)   Termination of activities or ownership or control of nonbank subsidiaries constituting serious risk

(1)   Notwithstanding any other provision of this chapter, the Board may, whenever it has reasonable cause to believe that the continuation by a bank holding company of any activity or of ownership or control of any of its nonbank subsidiaries, other than a nonbank subsidiary of a bank, constitutes a serious risk to the financial safety, soundness, or stability of a bank holding company subsidiary bank and is inconsistent with sound banking principles or with the purposes of this chapter or with the Financial Institutions Supervisory Act of 1966, order the bank holding company or any such nonbank subsidiaries, after due notice and opportunity for hearing, and after considering the views of the bank's primary supervisor, which shall be the Comptroller of the Currency in the case of a national bank or the Federal Deposit Insurance Corporation and the appropriate State supervisory authority in the case of an insured nonmember bank, to terminate such activities or to terminate (within one hundred and twenty days or such longer period as the Board may direct in unusual circumstances) its ownership or control of any such subsidiary either by sale or by distribution of the shares of the subsidiary to the shareholders of the bank holding company. Such distribution shall be pro rata with respect to all of the shareholders of the distributing bank holding

company, and the holding company shall not make any charge to its shareholders arising out of such a distribution.

(2)   The Board may in its discretion apply to the United States district court within the jurisdiction of which the principal office of the holding company is located, for the enforcement of any effective and outstanding order issued under this section, and such court shall have jurisdiction and power to order and require compliance therewith, but except as provided in section 1848 of this title, no court shall have jurisdiction to affect by injunction or otherwise the issuance or enforcement of any notice or order under this section, or to review, modify, suspend, terminate, or set aside any such notice or order.

(f)   Powers of Board respecting applications, examinations, or other proceedings

In the course of or in connection with an application, examination, investigation or other proceeding under this chapter, the Board, or any member or designated representative thereof, including any person designated to conduct any hearing under this chapter, shall have the power to administer oaths and affirmations, to take or cause to be taken depositions, and to issue, revoke, quash, or modify subpenas and subpenas duces tecum; and the Board is empowered to make rules and regulations to effectuate the purposes of this subsection. The attendance of witnesses and the production of documents provided for in this subsection may be required from any place in any State or in any territory or other place subject to the jurisdiction of the United States at any designated place where such proceeding is being conducted. Any party to proceedings under this chapter may apply to the United States District Court for the District of Columbia, or the United States district court for the judicial district or the United States court in any territory in which such proceeding is being conducted or where the witness resides or carries on business, for the enforcement of any subpena or subpena duces tecum issued pursuant to this subsection, and such courts shall have jurisdiction and power to order and require compliance therewith. Witnesses subpenaed under this subsection shall be paid the same fees and mileage that are paid witnesses in the district courts of the United States.   Any service required under this subsection may be made by registered mail, or in such other manner reasonably calculated to give actual notice as the Board may by regulation or otherwise provide. Any court having jurisdiction of any proceeding instituted under this subsection may allow to any such party such reasonable expenses and attorneys' fees as it deems just and proper. Any person who willfully shall fail or refuse to attend and testify or to answer any lawful inquiry or to produce books, papers, correspondence, memoranda, contracts, agreements, or other records, if in such person's power so to do, in obedience to the subpena of the Board, shall be guilty of a misdemeanor and, upon conviction, shall be subject to a fine of not more

than $1,000 or to imprisonment for a term of not more than one year or both.

* * *

§ 1846. Reservation of rights to States

(a)   In general

No provision of this chapter shall be construed as preventing any State from exercising such powers and jurisdiction which it now has or may hereafter have with respect to companies, banks, bank holding companies, and subsidiaries thereof.

* * *

§ 1972. Certain tying arrangements prohibited; correspondent accounts

(1)   A bank shall not in any manner extend credit, lease or sell property of any kind, or furnish any service, or fix or vary the consideration for any of the foregoing, on the condition or requirement–

(A)   that the customer shall obtain some additional credit, property, or service from such bank other than a loan, discount, deposit, or trust service;

(B)   that the customer shall obtain some additional credit, property, or service from a bank holding company of such bank, or from any other subsidiary of such bank holding company;

(C)   that the customer provide some additional credit, property, or service to such bank, other than those related to and usually provided in connection with a loan, discount, deposit, or trust service;

(D)   that the customer provide some additional credit, property, or service to a bank holding company of such bank, or to any other subsidiary of such bank holding company; or

(E)   that the customer shall not obtain some other credit, property, or service from a competitor of such bank, a bank holding company of such bank, or any subsidiary of such bank holding company, other than a condition or requirement that such bank shall reasonably impose in a credit transaction to assure the soundness of the credit.

The Board may by regulation or order permit such exceptions to the foregoing prohibition * * * as it considers will not be contrary to the purposes of this chapter.

* * *

CHAPTER SEVEN

COMMUNITY REINVESTMENT ACT

§ 2901. Congressional findings and statement of purpose

(a) The Congress finds that–

   (1) regulated financial institutions are required by law to demonstrate that their deposit facilities serve the convenience and needs of the communities in which they are chartered to do business;

   (2) the convenience and needs of communities include the need for credit services as well as deposit services; and

   (3) regulated financial institutions have continuing and affirmative obligation to help meet the credit needs of the local communities in which they are chartered.

(b) It is the purpose of this chapter to require each appropriate Federal financial supervisory agency to use its authority when examining financial institutions, to encourage such institutions to help meet the credit needs of the local communities in which they are chartered consistent with the safe and sound operation of such institutions.

* * *

§ 2903. Financial institutions; evaluation

(a) In general

In connection with its examination of a financial institution, the appropriate Federal financial supervisory agency shall–

   (1) assess the institution's record of meeting the credit needs of its entire community, including low-and moderate-income neighborhoods, consistent with the safe and sound operation of such institution; and

   (2) take such record into account in its evaluation of an application for a deposit facility by such institution.

(b) Majority-owned institutions

In assessing and taking into account, under subsection (a) of this section, the record of a nonminority-owned and nonwomen-owned financial institution, the appropriate Federal financial supervisory agency may consider as a factor capital investment, loan participation, and other ventures undertaken by the institution in cooperation with minority-and women-owned financial institutions and low-income credit unions provided that these activities help meet the credit needs of local communities in which such institutions and credit unions are chartered.

§ 2906. Written evaluations

(a) Required

(1) In general

Upon the conclusion of each examination of an insured depository institution under section 2903 of this title, the appropriate Federal financial supervisory agency shall prepare a written evaluation of the institution's record of meeting the credit needs of its entire community, including low and moderate-income neighborhoods.

(2) Public and confidential sections

Each written evaluation required under paragraph (1) shall have a public section and a confidential section.

(b) Public section of report

(1) Findings and conclusions

(A) Contents of written evaluation

The public section of the written evaluation shall–

(i)   state the appropriate Federal financial supervisory agency's conclusions for each assessment factor identified in the regulations prescribed by the Federal financial supervisory agencies to implement this chapter;

(ii)   discuss the facts and data supporting such conclusions; and

(iii) contain the institution's rating and a statement describing the basis for the rating.

(B) Metropolitan area distinctions

The information required by clauses (i) and (ii) of subparagraph (A) shall be presented separately for each metropolitan area in which a regulated depository institution maintains one or more domestic branch offices.

(2) Assigned rating

The institution's rating referred to in paragraph (1)(C) shall be 1 of the following:

(A) "Outstanding record of meeting community credit needs".

(B) "Satisfactory record of meeting community credit needs".

(C) "Needs to improve record of meeting community credit needs".

(D) "Substantial noncompliance in meeting community credit needs".

Such ratings shall be disclosed to the public on and after July 1, 1990.

(c) Confidential section of report

(1) Privacy of named individuals

The confidential section of the written evaluation shall contain all references that identify any customer of the institution, any employee or officer of the institution, or any person or organization that has provided information in confidence to a Federal or State financial supervisory agency.

(2) Topics not suitable for disclosure

The confidential section shall also contain any statements obtained or made by the appropriate Federal financial supervisory agency in the course of an examination which, in the judgment of the agency, are too sensitive or speculative in nature to disclose to the institution or the public.

(3) Disclosure to depository institution

The confidential section may be disclosed, in whole or part, to the institution, if the appropriate Federal financial supervisory agency determines that such disclosure will promote the objectives of this chapter. However, disclosure under this paragraph shall not identify a person or organization that has provided information in confidence to a Federal or State financial supervisory agency.

(d) Institutions with interstate branches

(1) State-by-State evaluation

In the case of a regulated financial institution that maintains domestic branches in 2 or more States, the appropriate Federal financial supervisory agency shall prepare–

(A) a written evaluation of the entire institution's record of performance under this chapter, as required by subsections (a), (b), and (c) of this section; and

(B) for each State in which the institution maintains 1 or more domestic branches, a separate written evaluation of the institution's record of performance within such State under this chapter, as required by subsections (a), (b), and (c) of this section.

(2) Multistate metropolitan areas

In the case of a regulated financial institution that maintains domestic branches in 2 or more States within a multistate metropolitan area, the appropriate Federal financial supervisory agency shall prepare a separate written evaluation of the institution's record of performance within such metropolitan area under this chapter, as required by subsections (a), (b), and (c) of this section. If the agency prepares a written evaluation pursuant to this paragraph, the scope of the written evaluation required under paragraph (1)(B) shall be adjusted accordingly.

(3) Content of State level evaluation

A written evaluation prepared pursuant to paragraph (1)(B) shall–

(A) present the information required by subparagraphs (A) and (B) of subsection (b)(1) of this section separately for each metropolitan area in which the institution maintains 1 or more domestic branch offices and separately for the remainder of the nonmetropolitan area of the State if the institution maintains 1 or more domestic branch offices in such nonmetropolitan area; and

(B) describe how the Federal financial supervisory agency has performed the examination of the institution, including a list of the individual branches examined.

* * *

CHAPTER EIGHT

INTERNATIONAL LENDING SUPERVISION ACT OF 1983

§ 3907. Capital adequacy

(a) (1) Each appropriate Federal banking agency shall cause banking institutions to achieve and maintain adequate capital by establishing minimum levels of capital for such banking institutions and by using such other methods as the appropriate Federal banking agency deems appropriate.

(2) Each appropriate Federal banking agency shall have the authority to establish such minimum level of capital for a banking institution as the appropriate Federal banking agency, in its discretion, deems to be necessary or appropriate in light of the particular circumstances of the banking institution.

(b) (1) Failure of a banking institution to maintain capital at or above its minimum level as established pursuant to subsection (a) of this section may be deemed by the appropriate Federal banking agency, in its discretion, to constitute an unsafe and unsound practice within the meaning of section 1818 of this title.

(2) (A) In addition to, or in lieu of, any other action authorized by law, including paragraph (1), the appropriate Federal banking agency may issue a directive to a banking institution that fails to maintain capital at or above its required level as established pursuant to subsection (a) of this section.

(B) (i) Such directive may require the banking institution to submit and adhere to a plan acceptable to the appropriate Federal banking agency describing the means and timing by which the banking institution shall achieve its required capital level.

(ii) Any such directive issued pursuant to this paragraph, including plans submitted pursuant thereto, shall be enforceable under the provisions of section 1818(i) of this title to the same extent as an effective and outstanding

order issued pursuant to section 1818(b) of this title which has become final.

(3) (A) Each appropriate Federal banking agency may consider such banking institution's progress in adhering to any plan required under this subsection whenever such banking institution, or an affiliate thereof, or the holding company which controls such banking institution, seeks the requisite approval of such appropriate Federal banking agency for any proposal which would divert earnings, diminish capital, or otherwise impede such banking institution's progress in achieving its minimum capital level.

(B) Such appropriate Federal banking agency may deny such approval where it determines that such proposal would adversely affect the ability of the banking institution to comply with such plan.

(C) The Chairman of the Board of Governors of the Federal Reserve System and the Secretary of the Treasury shall encourage governments, central banks, and regulatory authorities of other major banking countries to work toward maintaining and, where appropriate, strengthening the capital bases of banking institutions involved in international lending.

CHAPTER NINE

SELECTED BANKING REGULATIONS

CODE OF FEDERAL REGULATIONS
TITLE 12–BANKS AND BANKING

CHAPTER I–COMPTROLLER OF THE CURRENCY, DEPARTMENT OF THE TREASURY

PART 1–INVESTMENT SECURITIES

---

§ 1.2 Definitions.

* * *

(b) General obligation of a State or political subdivision means:

    (1) An obligation supported by the full faith and credit of an obliger possessing general powers of taxation, including property taxation; or

    (2) An obligation payable from a special fund or by an obliger not possessing general powers of taxation, when an obliger possessing general powers of taxation, including property taxation, has unconditionally promised to make payments into the fund or otherwise provide funds to cover all required payments on the obligation.

(c) Investment company means an investment company, including a mutual fund, registered under section 8 of the Investment Company Act of 1940, 15 U.S.C. § 80a-8.

(d)   Investment grade means a security that is rated in one of the four highest rating categories by:

    (1)   Two or more NRSROs; or

    (2)   One NRSRO if the security has been rated by only one NRSRO.

(e)   Investment security means a marketable debt obligation that is not predominantly speculative in nature. A security is not predominantly speculative in nature if it is rated investment grade. When a security is not rated, the security must be the credit equivalent of a security rated investment grade.

(f)   Marketable means that the security:

    (1)   Is registered under the Securities Act of 1933, 15 U.S.C. 77a et seq.;

    (2)   Is a municipal revenue bond exempt from registration under the Securities Act of 1933, 15 U.S.C. 77c(a)(2);

    (3)   Is offered and sold pursuant to Securities and Exchange Commission Rule 144A, 17 CFR 230.144A, and rated investment grade or is the credit equivalent of investment grade; or

    (4)   Can be sold with reasonable promptness at a price that corresponds reasonably to its fair value.

(g)   NRSRO means a nationally recognized statistical rating organization.

(h)   Political subdivision means a county, city, town, or other municipal corporation, a public authority, and generally any publicly-owned entity that is an instrumentality of a State or of a municipal corporation.

(i)   Type I security means:

    (1)   Obligations of the United States;

    (2)   Obligations issued, insured, or guaranteed by a department or an agency of the United States Government, if the obligation, insurance, or guarantee commits the full faith and credit of the United States for the repayment of the obligation;

    (3)   Obligations issued by a department or agency of the United States, or an agency or political subdivision of a State of the United States, that represent an interest in a loan or a pool of loans made to third parties, if the full faith and credit of the United States has been validly pledged for the full and timely payment of interest on, and principal of, the loans in the event of non- payment by the third party obligor(s);

    (4)   General obligations of a State of the United States or any political subdivision;

bank's own account, including qualified Canadian government obligations; and

(6) Other securities the OCC determines to be eligible as Type I securities under 12 U.S.C. 24 (Seventh).

(j) Type II security means an investment security that represents:

(1) Obligations issued by a State, or a political subdivision or agency of a State, for housing, university, or dormitory purposes;

(2) Obligations of international and multilateral development banks and organizations listed in 12 U.S.C. 24 (Seventh);

(3) Other obligations listed in 12 U.S.C. 24 (Seventh) as permissible for a bank to deal in, underwrite, purchase, and sell for the bank's own account, subject to a limitation per obliger of 10 percent of the bank's capital and surplus; and

(4) Other securities the OCC determines to be eligible as Type II securities under 12 U.S.C. 24 (Seventh).

(k) Type III security means an investment security that does not qualify as a Type I, II, IV, or V security, such as corporate bonds and municipal revenue bonds.

(1) Type IV security means:

(1) A small business-related security as defined in section 3(a)(53)(A) of the Securities Exchange Act of 1934, 15 U.S.C. 78c(a)(53)(A), that is rated investment grade or is the credit equivalent thereof, that is fully secured by interests in a pool of loans to numerous obligers.

(2) A commercial mortgage-related security that is offered or sold pursuant to section 4(5) of the Securities Act of 1933, 15 U.S.C. 77d(5), that is rated investment grade or is the credit equivalent thereof, or a commercial mortgage-related security as described in section 3(a)(41) of the Securities Exchange Act of 1934, 15 U.S.C. 78c(a)(41), that is rated investment grade in one of the two highest investment grade rating categories, and that represents ownership of a promissory note or certificate of interest or participation that is directly secured by a first lien on one or more parcels of real estate upon which one or more commercial structures are located and that is fully secured by interests in a pool of loans to numerous obligers.

(3) A residential mortgage-related security that is offered and sold pursuant to section 4(5) of the Securities Act of 1933, 15 U.S.C. 77d(5), that is rated investment grade or is the credit equivalent thereof, or a residential mortgage-related security as described in

77d(5), that is rated investment grade or is the credit equivalent thereof, or a residential mortgage-related security as described in section 3(a)(41) of the Securities Exchange Act of 1934, 15 U.S.C. 78c(a)(41)), that is rated investment grade in one of the two highest investment grade rating categories, and that does not otherwise qualify as a Type I security.

(m) Type V security means a security that is:

(1) Rated investment grade;

(2) Marketable;

(3) Not a Type IV security; and

(4) Fully secured by interests in a pool of loans to numerous obligers and in which a national bank could invest directly.

§ 1.3 Limitations on dealing in, underwriting, and purchase and sale of securities.

(a) Type I securities. A national bank may deal in, underwrite, purchase, and sell Type I securities for its own account. The amount of Type I securities that the bank may deal in, underwrite, purchase, and sell is not limited to a specified percentage of the bank's capital and surplus.

(b) Type II securities. A national bank may deal in, underwrite, purchase, and sell Type II securities for its own account, provided the aggregate par value of Type II securities issued by any one obliger held by the bank does not exceed 10 percent of the bank's capital and surplus. In applying this limitation, a national bank shall take account of Type II securities that the bank is legally committed to purchase or to see in addition to the bank's existing holdings.

(c) Type III securities. A national bank may purchase and sell Type III securities for its own account, provided the aggregate par value of Type III securities issued by any one obliger held by the bank does not exceed 10 percent of the bank's capital and surplus. In applying this limitation, a national bank shall take account of Type III securities that the bank is legally committed to purchase or to sell in addition to the bank's existing holdings.

(d) Type III and m securities; other investment securities limitations. A national bank may not hold Type II and III securities issued by any one obliger with an aggregate par value exceeding 10 percent of the bank's capital and

industrial tenants, and if each issue is payable solely from and secured by a first lien on the revenues to be derived from rentals paid by the lessee under net noncancellable leases, the bank may apply the 10 percent investment limitation separately to each issue of a single obliger.

(e) Type IV securities—-

    (1) General. A national bank may purchase and sell Type IV securities for its own account. A national bank may deal in Type IV securities that are fully secured by Type I securities. Except as described in paragraph (e)(2) of this section, the amount of the Type IV securities that a bank may purchase and sell is not limited to a specified percentage of the bank's capital and surplus.

    (2) Limitation on small business-related securities rated in the third and fourth highest rating categories by an NRSRO. A national bank may hold small busuness-related securities, as defined in section 3(a)(53)(A) of the Securities Exchange Act of 1934, 15 U.S.C. 78c(a)(53)(A), of any one issuer with an aggregate par value not exceeding 25 percent of the bank's capital and surplus if those securities are rated investment grade in the third or fourth highest investment grade rating categories. In applying this limitation, a national bank shall take account of securities that the bank is legally committed to purchase or to sell in addition to the bank's existing holdings. No percentage of capital and surplus limit applies to small business related securities rated investment grade in the highest two investment grade rating categories.

(f) Type V securities. A national bank may purchase and sell Type V securities for its own account provided that the aggregate par value of Type V securities issued by any one issuer held by the bank does not exceed 25 percent of the bank's capital and surplus. In applying this limitation, a national bank shall take account of Type V securities that the bank is legally committed to purchase or to sell in addition to the bank's existing holdings.

(g) Securitization. A national bank may securitize and sell assets that it holds, as a part of its banking business. The amount of securitized loans and obligations that a bank may sell is not limited to a specified percentage of the bank's capital and surplus.

(h) Investment company shares--

    (1) General. A national bank may purchase and sell for its own account investment company shares provided that:

(i)   The portfolio of the investment company consists exclusively of assets that the national bank may purchase and sell for its own account under this part; and

(ii)   The bank's holdings of investment company shares do not exceed the limitations in s 1.4(e).

(2)   Other issuers. The OCC may determine that a national bank may invest in an entity that is exempt from registration as an investment company under section 3(c)(1) of the Investment Company Act of 1940, provided that the portfolio of the entity consists exclusively of assets that a national bank may purchase and sell for its own account under this part.

(i)   Securities held based on estimates of obligor's performance.

(1)   Notwithstanding ss 1.2(d) and (e), a national bank may treat a debt security as an investment security for purposes of this part if the bank concludes, on the basis of estimates that the bank reasonably believes are reliable, that the obliger will be able to satisfy its obligations under that security, and the bank believes that the security may be sold with reasonable promptness at a price that corresponds reasonably to its fair value.

(2)   The aggregate par value of securities treated as investment securities under paragraph (i)(l) of this section may not exceed 5 percent of the bank's capital and surplus.

§ 1.4 Calculation of limits.

* * *

(d)   Calculation of Type III and Type V securities holdings-

(1)   General. In calculating the amount of its investment in Type III or Type V securities issued by any one obliger, a bank shall aggregate:

(i)   Obligations issued by obligers that are related directly or indirectly through common control; and

(ii)   Securities that are credit enhanced by the same entity.

(2)   Aggregation by type. The aggregation requirement in paragraph (d)(l) of this section applies separately to the Type III and Type V securities held by a bank.

(e)   Limit on investment company holdings—

(1)   General. In calculating the amount of its investment in investment company shares under this part, a bank shall use reasonable efforts to

calculate and combine its pro rata share of a particular security in the portfolio of each investment company with the bank's direct holdings of that security. The bank's direct holdings of the particular security and the bank's pro rata interest in the same security in the investment company's portfolio may not, in the aggregate, exceed the investment limitation that would apply to that security.

(2) Alternate limit for diversified investment companies. A national bank may elect not to combine its pro rata interest in a particular security in an investment company with the bank's direct holdings of that security if:

(i) The investment company's holdings of the securities of any one issuer do not exceed 5 percent of its total portfolio; and

(ii) The bank's total holdings of the investment company's shares do not exceed the most stringent investment limitation that would apply to any of the securities in the company's portfolio if those securities were purchased directly by the bank.

§ 1.5 Safe and sound banking practices; credit information required.

(a) A national bank shall adhere to safe and sound banking practices and the specific requirements of this part in conducting the activities described in s 1.3. The bank shall consider, as appropriate, the interest rate, credit, liquidity, price, foreign exchange, transaction, compliance, strategic, and reputation risks presented by a proposed activity, and the particular activities undertaken by the bank must be appropriate for that bank.

(b) In conducting these activities, the bank shall determine that there is adequate evidence that an obliger possesses resources sufficient to provide for an required payments on its obligations, or, in the case of securities deemed to be investment securities on the basis of reliable estimates of an obligor's performance, that the bank reasonably believes that the obliger will be able to satisfy the obligation.

(c) Each bank shall maintain records available for examination purposes adequate to demonstrate that it meets the requirements of this part. The bank may store the information in any manner that can be readily retrieved and reproduced in a readable form.

* * *

PART 3–MINIMUM CAPITAL RATIOS; ISSUANCE OF DIRECTIVES

* * *

SUBPART B–MINIMUM CAPITAL RATIOS

* * *

§ 3.6. Minimum capital ratios.

(a)   Risk-weighted assets ratio. All national banks must have and maintain the minimum ratios of Tier 1 and total capital to risk-weighted assets as set forth in appendix A of this part.

(b)   Total assets leverage ratio. All national banks must have and maintain Tier 1 capital in an amount equal to at least 3.0 percent of adjusted total assets.

(c)   Additional leverage ratio requirements. An institution operating at or near the level in subsection (b) above is expected to have well-diversified risks, including no undue interest rate risk exposure; excellent control systems; good earnings; high asset quality; high liquidity; and well managed on- and off-balance sheet activities; and in general be considered a strong banking organization, rated composite 1 under the CAMEL rating system of banks. For all but the most highly-rated banks meeting the conditions set forth above, the minimum Tier 1 leverage ratio is to be 3 percent plus an additional cushion of at least 100 to 200 basis points. In all cases, banking institutions should hold capital commensurate with the level and nature of all risks.

SUBPART C–ESTABLISHMENT OF MINIMUM CAPITAL RATIOS FOR N INDIVIDUAL BANK

* * *

§ 3.12. Procedures.

(a)   Notice. When the OCC determines that minimum capital ratios above those set forth in § 3.6 or other legal authority are necessary or appropriate for a particular bank, the OCC will notify the bank in writing of the proposed minimum capital ratios and the date by which they should be reached (if applicable) and will provide an explanation of why the ratios proposed are considered necessary or appropriate for the bank.

(b)   Response.

(1)   The bank may respond to any or all of the items in the notice. The response should include any matters which the bank would have the

Office consider in deciding whether individual minimum capital ratios should be established for the bank, what those capital ratios should be, and, if applicable, when they should be achieved. The response must be in writing and delivered to the designated OCC official within 30 days after the date on which the bank received the notice. The Office may shorten the time period when, in the opinion of the Office, the condition of the bank so requires, provided that the bank is informed promptly of the new time period, or with the consent of the bank. In its discretion, the Office may extend the time period for good cause.

(2) Failure to respond within 30 days or such other time period as may be specified by the Office shall constitute a waiver of any objections to the proposed minimum capital ratios or the deadline for their achievement.

(c) Decision. After the close of the bank's response period, the Office will decide, based on a review of the bank's response and other information concerning the bank, whether individual minimum capital ratios should be established for the bank and, if so, the ratios and the date the requirements will become effective. The bank will be notified of the decision in writing. The notice will include an explanation of the decision, except for a decision not to establish individual minimum capital requirements for the bank.

(d) Submission of plan. The decision may require the bank to develop and submit to the Office, within a time period specified, an acceptable plan to reach the minimum capital ratios established for the bank by the date required.

(e) Change in circumstances. If, after the Office's decision in paragraph (c) of this section, there is a change in the circumstances affecting the bank's capital adequacy or its ability to reach the required minimum capital ratios by the specified date, either the bank or the Office may propose to the other a change in the minimum capital ratios for the bank, the date when the minimums must be achieved, or the bank's plan (if applicable). The Office may decline to consider proposals that are not based on a significant change in circumstances or are repetitive or frivolous. Pending a decision on reconsideration, the Office's original decision and any plan required under that decision shall continue in full force and effect.

SUBPART D–ENFORCEMENT

§ 3.14. Remedies.

A bank that does not have or maintain the minimum capital ratios applicable to it, whether required in subpart B of this part, in a decision pursuant to subpart C of this part, in a written agreement or temporary or final order under 12 U.S.C. 1818(b) or (c), or in a condition for approval of an application, or a bank that has failed to submit or comply with an acceptable plan to attain those ratios, will be subject to such administrative action or sanctions as the OCC considers appropriate. These sanctions may include the issuance of a Directive pursuant to subpart E of this part or other enforcement action, assessment of civil money penalties, and/or the denial, conditioning, or revocation of applications. A national bank's failure to achieve or maintain minimum capital ratios in § 3.6 (a) or (b) may also be the basis for an action by the Federal Deposit Insurance Corporation to terminate federal deposit insurance. See 12 CFR 325.4.

SUBPART E–ISSUANCE OF A DIRECTIVE

§ 3.15. Purpose and scope.

This subpart is applicable to proceedings by the Office to issue a directive under 12 U.S.C. 3907(b)(2). A directive is an order issued to a bank that does not have or maintain capital at or above the minimum ratios set forth in § 3.6, or established for the bank under subpart C, by a written agreement under 12 U.S.C. 1818(b), or as a condition for approval of an application. A directive may order the bank to:

(a) Achieve the minimum capital ratios applicable to it by a specified date;

(b) Adhere to a previously submitted plan to achieve the applicable capital ratios;

(c) Submit and adhere to a plan acceptable to the Office describing the means and time schedule by which the bank shall achieve the applicable capital ratios;

(d) Take other action, such as reduction of assets or the rate of growth of assets, or restrictions on the payment of dividends, to achieve the applicable capital ratios; or

(e) A combination of any of these or similar actions.

A directive issued under this rule, including a plan submitted under a directive, is enforceable in the same manner and to the same extent as an effective and outstanding cease and desist order which has become final as

defined in 12 U.S.C. 1818(k). Violation of a directive may result in assessment of civil money penalties in accordance with 12 U.S.C. 3909(d).

§ 3.16. Notice of intent to issue a directive.

The Office will notify a bank in writing of its intention to issue a directive. The notice will state:

(a) Reasons for issuance of the directive; and

(b) The proposed contents of the directive.

§ 3.17. Response to notice.

(a) A bank may respond to the notice by stating why a directive should not be issued and/or by proposing alternative contents for the directive. The response should include any matters which the bank would have the Office consider in deciding whether to issue a directive and/or what the contents of the directive should be. The response may include a plan for achieving the minimum capital ratios applicable to the bank. The response must be in writing and delivered to the designated OCC official within 30 days after the date on which the bank received the notice. The Office may shorten the 30-day time period:

   (1) When, in the opinion of the Office, the condition of the bank so requires, provided that the bank shall be informed promptly of the new time period;

   (2) With the consent of the bank; or

   (3) When the bank already has advised the Office that it cannot or will not achieve its applicable minimum capital ratios. In its discretion, the Office may extend the time period for good cause.

(b) Failure to respond within 30 days or such other time period as may be specified by the Office shall constitute a waiver of any objections to the proposed directive.

§ 3.18. Decision.

After the closing date of the bank's response period, or receipt of the bank's response, if earlier, the Office will consider the bank's response, and may seek additional information or clarification of the response. Thereafter, the Office will determine whether or not to issue a directive, and if one is to be issued, whether it should be as originally proposed or in modified form.

§ 3.19. Issuance of a directive.

(a)   A directive will be served by delivery to the bank. It will include or be accompanied by a statement of reasons for its issuance.

(b)   A directive is effective immediately upon its receipt by the bank, or upon such later date as may be specified therein, and shall remain effective and enforceable until it is stayed, modified, or terminated by the Office.

* * *

APPENDIX A TO PART 3–RISK-BASED CAPITAL GUIDELINES
* * *

§ 2. Components of Capital.

A national bank's qualifying capital base consists of two types of capital–core (Tier 1) and supplementary (Tier 2).

(a)   Tier 1 Capital. The following elements comprise a national bank's Tier 1 capital:

(1)   Common stockholders' equity;

(2)   Noncumulative perpetual preferred stock and related surplus; and

(3)   Minority interests in the equity accounts of consolidated subsidiaries.

(b)   Tier 2 Capital. The following elements comprise a national bank's Tier 2 capital:

(1)   Allowance for loan and lease losses, up to a maximum of 1.25% of risk-weighted assets, * * * .

(2)   Cumulative perpetual preferred stock, long-term preferred stock, convertible preferred stock, and any related surplus, without limit, if the issuing national bank has the option to defer payment of dividends on these instruments. For long-term preferred stock, the amount that is eligible to be included as Tier 2 capital is reduced by 20% of the

original amount of the instrument (net of redemptions) at the beginning of each of the last five years of the life of the instrument;

(3) Hybrid capital instruments, without limit. Hybrid capital instruments are those instruments that combine certain characteristics of debt and equity, such as perpetual debt. To be included as Tier 2 capital, these instruments must meet the following criteria:

(i) The instrument must be unsecured, subordinated to the claims of depositors and general creditors, and fully paid-up;

(ii) The instrument must not be redeemable at the option of the holder prior to maturity, except with the prior approval of the OCC;

(iii) The instrument must be available to participate in losses while the issuer is operating as a going concern (in this regard, the instrument must automatically convert to common stock or perpetual preferred stock, if the sum of the retained earnings and capital surplus accounts of the issuer shows a negative balance); and

(iv) The instrument must provide the option for the issuer to defer principal and interest payments, if

(A) The issuer does not report a net profit for the most recent combined four quarters, and

(B) The issuer eliminates cash dividends on its common and preferred stock.

(4) Term subordinated debt instruments, and intermediate-term preferred stock and related surplus are included in Tier 2 capital, but only to a maximum of 50% of Tier 1 capital as calculated after deductions pursuant to section 2(c) of this appendix. * * * Also, at the beginning of each of the last five years of the life of either type of instrument, the amount that is eligible to be included as Tier 2 capital is reduced by 20% of the original amount of that instrument (net of redemptions).

* * *

§ 3. Risk Categories/Weights for On-Balance Sheet Assets and Off-Balance Sheet Items

The denominator of the risk-based capital ratio, i.e., a national bank's risk-weighted assets, is derived by assigning that bank's assets and off-balance sheet items to one of the four risk categories detailed in section 3(a) of this Appendix A. Each category has a specific risk weight. Before an off-balance sheet item is assigned a risk weight, it is converted to an on-balance sheet credit equivalent amount in accordance with section 3(b) of this Appendix A. The risk weight assigned to a particular asset or on-balance sheet credit equivalent amount determines the percentage of that asset/credit equivalent that is included in the denominator of the bank's risk-based capital ratio. Any asset deducted from a bank's capital in computing the numerator of the risk-based capital ratio is not included as part of the bank's risk-weighted assets.

* * *

(a)   On-Balance Sheet Assets. The following are the risk categories/weights for on-balance sheet assets.

   (1)   Zero percent risk weight.

      (i)   Cash, including domestic and foreign currency owned and held in all offices of a national bank or in transit. Any foreign currency held by a national bank should be converted into U.S. dollar equivalents.

      (ii)   Deposit reserves and other balances at Federal Reserve Banks.

      (iii)   Securities issued by, and other direct claims on, the United States Government or its agencies, or the central government of an OECD country.

      (iv)   That portion of assets directly and unconditionally guaranteed by the United States Government or its agencies, or the central government of an OECD country.

      (v)   That portion of local currency claims on or unconditionally guaranteed by central governments of non-OECD countries, to the extent the bank has local currency liabilities in that country. Any amount of such claims that exceeds the amount of the bank's local currency liabilities is assigned to the 100% risk category of section 3(a)(4) of this appendix.

      (vi)   Gold bullion held in the bank's own vaults or in another bank's vaults on an allocated basis, to the extent it is backed by gold bullion liabilities.

      (vii)   The book value of paid-in Federal Reserve Bank stock.

(viii)   That portion of assets and off-balance sheet transactions collateralized by cash or securities issued or directly and unconditionally guaranteed by the United States Government or its agencies, or the central government of an OECD country,   * * *

(2) 20 percent risk weight.

(i)   All claims on depository institutions incorporated in an OECD country, and all assets backed by the full faith and credit of depository institutions incorporated in an OECD country. This includes the credit equivalent amount of participations in commitments and standby letters of credit sold to other depository institutions incorporated in an OECD country, but only if the originating bank remains liable to the customer or beneficiary for the full amount of the commitment or standby letter of credit. Also included in this category are the credit equivalent amounts of risk participations in bankers' acceptances conveyed to other depository institutions incorporated in an OECD country. However, bank-issued securities that qualify as capital of the issuing bank are not included in this risk category, but are assigned to the 100% risk category of section 3(a)(4) of this appendix A.

(ii)   Claims on, or guaranteed by depository institutions, other than the central bank, incorporated in a non-OECD country, with a residual maturity of one year or less.

(iii) Cash items in the process of collection.

(iv) That portion of assets collateralized by cash or by securities issued or directly and unconditionally guaranteed by the United States Government or its agencies, or the central government of an OECD country, that does not qualify for the zero percent risk-weight category.

(v)   That portion of assets conditionally guaranteed by the United States Government or its agencies, or the central government of an OECD country.

(vi)   Securities issued by, or other direct claims on, United States Government-sponsored agencies.

(vii) That portion of assets guaranteed by United States Government-sponsored agencies.

    (viii)   That portion of assets collateralized by the current market value of securities issued or guaranteed by United States Government-sponsored agencies.

    (ix)   Claims representing general obligations of any public-sector entity in an OECD country, and that portion of any claims guaranteed by any such public-sector entity. In the U.S., these obligations must meet the requirements of 12 CFR 1.3(g).

    (x)   Claims on, or guaranteed by, official multilateral lending institutions or regional development institutions in which the United States Government is a shareholder or contributing member.

* * *

(3)   50 percent risk weight.

    (i)   Revenue obligations of any public-sector entity in an OECD country for which the underlying obligor is the public-sector entity, but which are repayable solely from the revenues generated by the project financed through the issuance of the obligations.

* * *

    (iii)   Loans secured by first mortgages on one-to-four family residential properties, either owner-occupied or rented, provided that such loans are not otherwise 90 days or more past due, or on nonaccrual or restructured. It is presumed that such loans will meet prudent underwriting standards. Furthermore, residential property loans that are made for the purpose of construction financing are assigned to the 100% risk category of section 3(a)(4) of this Appendix A; however, this exclusion from the 50% risk category does not apply to loans to individual purchasers for the construction of their own homes.

    (iv)   Loans to residential real estate builders for one-to-four family residential property construction, if the bank obtains, prior to the making of the construction loan, sufficient documentation demonstrating that the buyer of the home intends to purchase the home (i.e., a legally binding written sales contract) and has the ability to obtain a mortgage loan sufficient to purchase the home (i.e., a firm written commitment for permanent financing of the home upon completion), subject to the following additional criteria:

* * *

(v) Loans secured by a first mortgage on multifamily residential properties:

* * *

(4) 100 percent risk weight. All other assets not specified above, including, but not limited to: * * *

(b) Off-Balance Sheet Activities. The risk weight assigned to an off-balance sheet item is determined by a two-step process. First, the face amount of the off-balance sheet item is multiplied by the appropriate credit conversion factor specified in this section. This calculation translates the face amount of an off-balance sheet item into an on-balance sheet credit equivalent amount. Second, the resulting credit equivalent amount is then assigned to the proper risk category using the criteria regarding obligors, guarantors, and collateral listed in section 3(a) of this appendix A. Collateral and guarantees are applied to the face amount of an off-balance sheet item; however, with respect to derivative contracts under section 3(b)(5) of this appendix A, collateral and guarantees are applied to the credit equivalent amounts of such derivative contracts. The following are the credit conversion factors and the off-balance sheet items to which they apply.

(1) 100 percent credit conversion factor.

(i) Direct credit substitutes, including financial guarantee-type standby letters of credit that support financial claims on the account party. The face amount of a direct credit substitute is netted against the amount of any participations sold in that item. The amount not sold is converted to an on-balance sheet credit equivalent and assigned to the proper risk category using the criteria regarding obligors, guarantors and collateral listed in section 3(a) of this appendix A. Participations are treated as follows:

(A) If the originating bank remains liable to the beneficiary for the full amount of the standby letter of credit, in the event the participant fails to perform under its participation agreement, the amount of participations sold are converted to an on-balance sheet credit equivalent using a credit conversion factor of 100%, with that amount then being assigned to the risk category appropriate for the purchaser of the participation.

(B) If the participations are such that each participant is responsible only for its pro rata share of the risk, and there is no recourse to the originating bank, the full amount of the

participations sold is excluded from the originating bank's risk-weighted assets;

(ii)   Risk participations purchased in bankers' acceptances and participations purchased in direct credit substitutes;

(iii) Assets sold under an agreement to repurchase and assets sold with recourse, to the extent that these assets are not reported on a national bank's statement of condition (this includes loan strips sold without direct recourse, where the maturity of the participation is shorter than the maturity of the underlying loan); and

* * *

(2)   50 percent credit conversion factor.

(i)   Transaction-related contingencies including, among other things, performance bonds and performance-based standby letters of credit related to a particular transaction. To the extent permitted by law or regulation, performance-based standby letters of credit include such things as arrangements backing subcontractors' and suppliers' performance, labor and materials contracts, and construction bids;

(ii)   Unused portion of commitments, including home equity lines of credit, with an original maturity exceeding one year; and

(iii) Revolving underwriting facilities, note issuance facilities, and similar arrangements pursuant to which the bank's customer can issue short-term debt obligations in its own name, but for which the bank has a legally binding commitment to either:

(A)   Purchase the obligations the customer is unable to sell by a stated date; or

(B)   Advance funds to its customer, if the obligations cannot be sold.

(3)   20 percent credit conversion factor.

(i)   Trade-related contingencies. These are short-term self-liquidating instruments used to finance the movement of goods and are collateralized by the underlying shipment. A commercial letter of credit is an example of such an instrument.

(4)   Zero percent credit conversion factor.

(i)   Unused portion of commitments with an original maturing of one year or less;

      (ii) Unused portion of commitments with an original maturity of greater than one year, if they are unconditionally cancelable at any time at the option of the bank and the bank has the contractual right to make, and in fact does make, either–

          (A) A separate credit decision based upon the borrower's current financial condition, before each drawing under the lending facility; or

          (B) An annual (or more frequent) credit review based upon the borrower's current financial condition to determine whether or not the lending facility should be continued; and

      (iii) The unused portion of retail credit card lines or other related plans that are unconditionally cancelable by the bank in accordance with applicable law.

    (5) Derivative contracts. (i) Calculation of credit equivalent amounts. The credit equivalent amount of a derivative contract equals the sum of the current credit exposure and the potential future credit exposure of the derivative contract. The calculation of credit equivalent amounts must be measured in U.S. dollars, regardless of the currency or currencies specified in the derivative contract.

* * *

§ 4. Implementation, Transition Rules, and Target Ratios

    (b) On December 31, 1992.

      (1) All national banks are expected to maintain a minimum ratio of total capital (after deductions) to risk-weighted assets of 8.0%.

      (2) Tier 2 capital elements qualify as part of a national bank's total capital base up to a maximum of 100% of that bank's Tier 1 capital.

      (3) In addition to the standards established by these risk-based capital guidelines, all national banks must maintain a minimum capital-to-total assets ratio in accordance with the provisions of 12 CFR part. 3.

PART 5–RULES, POLICIES, AND PROCEDURES FOR CORPORATE ACTIVITIES

SUBPART B–INITIAL ACTIVITIES

§ 5.20 Organizing a bank.

* * *

(f)   Policy—

    (1)   General. The marketplace is normally the best regulator of economic activity, and competition within the marketplace promotes efficiency and better customer service. Accordingly, it is the OCC's policy to approve proposals to establish national banks, including minority-owned institutions, that have a reasonable chance of success and that will be operated in a safe and sound manner. It is not the OCC's policy to ensure that a proposal to establish a national bank is without risk to the organizers or to protect existing institutions from healthy competition from a new national bank.

    (2)   Policy considerations.

        (i)   in evaluating an application to establish a national bank, the OCC considers whether the proposed bank:

            (A)   Has organizers who are familiar with national banking laws and regulations;

            (B)   Has competent management, including a board of directors, with ability and experience relevant to the types of services to be provided;

            (C)   Has capital that is sufficient to support the projected volume and type of business;

            (D)   Can reasonably be expected to achieve and maintain profitability, and

            (E)   Will be operated in a safe and sound manner.

        (ii)   The OCC may also consider additional factors listed in section 6 of the Federal Deposit Insurance Act, 12 U.S.C. 1816, including the risk to the Federal deposit insurance fund, and whether the proposed bank's corporate powers are consistent with the purposes of the Federal Deposit Insurance Act and the National Bank Act.

    (3)   OCC evaluation.

        The OCC evaluates a proposed national bank's organizing group and its operating plan together. The OCC's judgment concerning one may affect the evaluation of the other. An organizing group and its

operating plan must be stronger in markets where economic conditions are marginal or competition is intense.

(g) Organizing group—

    (i) General. Strong organizing groups generally include diverse business and financial interests and community involvement. An organizing group must have the experience, competence, willingness, and ability to be active in directing the proposed national bank's affairs in a safe and sound manner. The bank's initial board of directors generally is comprised of many, if not all, of the organizers. The operating plan and other information supplied in the application must demonstrate an organizing group's collective ability to establish and operate a successful bank in the economic and competitive conditions of the market to be served. Each organizer should be knowledgeable about the Operating plan. A poor operating plan reflects adversely on the organizing group's ability, and the OCC generally denies applications with poor operating plans.

(h) Operating plan—

    (1) General.

        (i) Organizers of a proposed national bank shall submit an operating plan that adequately addresses the statutory and policy considerations set forth in paragraphs (e) and (f)(2) of this section. The plan must reflect sound banking principles and demonstrate realistic assessments of risk in light of economic and competitive conditions in the market to be served.

        (ii) The OCC may offset deficiencies in one factor by strengths in one or more other factors. However, deficiencies in some factors, such as unrealistic earnings prospects, may have a negative influence on the evaluation of other factors, such as capital adequacy, or may be serious enough by themselves to result in denial. The OCC considers inadequacies in an operating plan to reflect negatively on the organizing group's ability to operate a successful bank.

    (2) Earnings prospects. The organizing group shall submit pro forma balance sheets and income statements as part of the operating plan. The OCC reviews all projections for reasonableness of assumptions and consistency with the operating plan.

    (3) Management.

        (i) The organizing group shall include in the operating plan information sufficient to permit the OCC to evaluate the overall

management ability of the organizing group. If the organizing group has limited banking experience or community involvement, the senior executive officers must be able to compensate for such deficiencies.

(ii)   The organizing group may not hire an officer or elect or appoint a director if the OCC objects to that person at any time prior to the date the bank commences business.

(4)   Capital. A proposed bank must have sufficient initial capital, net of any organizational expenses that will be charged to the bank's capital after it begins operations, to support the bank's projected volume and type of business.

(5)   Community service.

(i)   The operating plan must indicate the organizing group's knowledge of and plans for serving the community. The organizing group shall evaluate the banking needs of the community, including its consumer, business, nonprofit, and government sectors. The operating plan must demonstrate how the proposed bank responds to those needs consistent with the safe and sound operation of the bank. The provisions of this paragraph may not apply to an application to organize a bank for a special purpose.

(ii)   As part of its operating plan, the organizing group shall submit a statement that demonstrates its plans to achieve CRA objectives.

(iii)   Because community support is important to the long-term success of a bank, the organizing group shall include plans for attracting and maintaining community support.

* * *

§ 5.34 Operating subsidiaries

(a)   Authority. 12 U.S.C. 24(Seventh) and 93a.

(b)   Licensing requirements. A national bank generally shall submit an application and obtain prior OCC approval to establish or commence new activities in an operating subsidiary. In certain circumstances, a national bank need only notify the OCC after it has established or commenced specified activities in an operating subsidiary.

(c)   Scope. This section sets forth authorized activities and application and notice procedures for the establishment and operation of an operating subsidiary by a national bank.

(d)   Standards and requirements—

(1) Authorized activities. A national bank may establish or acquire an operating subsidiary to conduct, or may conduct in an existing operating subsidiary, activities that are part of or incidental to the business of banking, as determined by the Comptroller of the Currency pursuant to 12 U.S.C. 24(Seventh), and other activities permissible for national banks or their subsidiaries under other statutory authority.

* * *

(e) Procedures—

* * *

(2) Notice process for certain activities—

* * *

(ii) Activities eligible for notice. The following activities qualify for the preapproved notice procedures:

(A) Holding property, such as real estate, personal property, securities, or other assets, acquired by the bank through foreclosure or otherwise in good faith to compromise a doubtful claim, or in the ordinary course of collecting a debt previously contracted

(B) Business services for the bank or its affiliates. Furnishing services for the internal operations of the bank or its affiliates, including: accounting, auditing, appraising, advertising and public relations, data processing and data transmission services, databases, or facilities;

(C) Financial advice and consulting for the bank or its affiliates

(D) Selling money orders, savings bonds, or travelers checks

(E) Management consulting, operational advice, and specialized services for other depository institutions;

(F) Courier services between financial institutions

(G) Providing check guaranty and verification services

(H) Data processing and warehousing products, services, and related activities, including associated equipment and technology, for the operating subsidiary, its parent bank, and their affiliates;

(I) Acting as investment or financial adviser, (not involving the exercise of investment discretion), or providing financial counseling, including:

(1) Serving as the advisory company for a mortgage or real estate investment trust;

(2) Furnishing general economic information and advice, general: economic statistical forecasting services, and industry studies;

(3) Providing financial advice to state or local governments or foreign governments with respect to issuance of securities;

(4) Providing tax planning and preparation; and

(5) Providing consumer financial counseling;

(J) Providing financial and transactional advice to customers and assisting customers in structuring, arranging, and executing various financial transactions (provided that the bank and its affiliates do not participate as a principal), including:.

(1) Mergers, acquisitions, divestitures, joint ventures, leveraged buyouts, recapitalizations, capital structurings, and financial transactions (including private and public financings and loan syndications); and conducting financial feasibility studies; and

(2) Arranging commercial real estate equity financing;

(K) Investment advice, (not involving the exercise of investment discretion), on futures and options on futures;

(L) Making, purchasing, selling, servicing, or warehousing loans or other extensions of credit, or interests therein, for the subsidiary's account, or for the account of others, including consumer loans, credit cards loans, commercial loans, residential mortgage loans, and commercial mortgage loans. The notice procedure is not available under this paragraph, however, if the notice involves the direct or indirect acquisition by the bank of any low-quality asset from an affiliate in connection with a transaction subject to this section. For purposes of this paragraph (e)(2)(ii)(L), the terms "low-quality asset" and "affiliate" have the same meaning as provided in section 23A of the Federal Reserve Act, 12 U.S.C. 371c;

(M) Leasing of personal property, including:

(1) Leases in which the bank may invest pursuant to 12 U.S.C. 24(Seventh);

(2) Leases in which the bank may invest pursuant to 12 U.S.C. 24(Tenth); and

(3) Acting as agent, broker, or adviser in leases for others. The notice process for any leasing activity under this paragraph is not available, however, if the notice involves the direct or indirect acquisition by the bank of any low-quality asset from an affiliate in connection with a transaction subject to this section. For purposes of this paragraph (M), the terms "low-quality asset" and "affiliate" have the same meaning as provided in section 23A of the Federal Reserve Act, 12 U.S.C. 371c; or

(N) Owning, holding, and managing all or part of the parent bank's investment securities portfolio.

(3) Expedited review—

(i) General. An eligible bank may acquire or establish an operating subsidiary to engage in the activities listed in paragraph (e)(3)(ii) of this section, or may perform such activities in an existing operating subsidiary, by submitting an application to the appropriate district office and receiving approval thereof. Such an application is deemed approved by the OCC 30 days after the filing is received by the OCC, unless the OCC notifies the bank prior to that date that the filing is not eligible for expedited review under §5.13(a)(2); The application must include a complete description of the bank's investment in the subsidiary and of the activity to be conducted and a representation and undertaking that the activity will be conducted in accordance with the OCC policies contained in guidance issued by the OCC regarding the activity. All approvals are subject to the condition that the subsidiary conduct the activity in a manner consistent with OCC policies contained in the published guidance. The OCC also may impose additional conditions in connection with any approval under this section.

(ii) Activities eligible for expedited review. The following activities qualify for expedited review:

(A) Providing securities brokerage, related securities credit, and related activities, including investment advice;

(B)   Underwriting and dealing in securities permissible for a national bank under 12 U.S.C. 24(Seventh) and 12 CFR part 1;

(C)   Acting as futures commission merchant

(D)   Serving as an investment adviser for investment companies under the Investment Company Act of 1940, 15 U.S.C. 80a-1 *et seq.*

(E)   Providing financial and transactional advice to customers and assisting customers in structuring, arranging, and executing various financial transactions relating to swaps and other derivatives and foreign exchange, coin and bullion, and related transactions;

(F)   Data processing and warehousing products, services, and related activities, including associated equipment and technology permissible under 12 U.S.C. 24(Seventh) and 12 CFR 7.1019; or

(G)   Real estate appraisal services for the subsidiary, parent bank or other financial institution.

* * *

(5)   Fiduciary powers. If an operating subsidiary proposes to exercise investment discretion on behalf of customers or provide investment advice for a fee, the national bank must have prior OCC approval to exercise fiduciary powers pursuant to § 5.26 and the subsidiary shall be subject to the requirements of 12 CFR part 9, unless:

(i)   The subsidiary is registered under the Investment Advisers Act of 1940, 15 U.S.C. 80b-1 *et seq.*; or

(ii)   The subsidiary is registered, or has filed a notice, under the applicable provisions of sections 15, 15B or 15C of the Securities Exchange Act of 1934, 15 U.S.C. 780, 780-4, or 780-5, as a broker, dealer, municipal securities dealer, government securities broker or government securities dealer; and the subsidiary's performance of investment advisory services as described in 15 U.S.C. 80b-2(a)(11) is solely incidental to the conduct of its business as broker or dealer and there is no special compensation to the subsidiary for those advisory services.

(f)   Additional requirements for certain permissible activities. A national bank may acquire or establish an operating subsidiary to engage in an activity authorized under § 5.34(d) for the subsidiary but different from that permissible for the parent national bank or may perform such activities in an

existing operating subsidiary, subject to the following additional requirements:

(1) Notice and comment. If the OCC has not previously approved the proposed activity, the OCC will provide public notice and opportunity for comment on the application by publishing notice of the application in the Federal Register. For subsequent applications to conduct the activity, the OCC may also publish notice of the application in the Federal Register and provide an opportunity for public comment.

(2) Corporate requirements. The following corporate requirements apply:

(i) The subsidiary shall be physically separate and distinct in its operations from the parent bank, including ensuring that the employees of the subsidiary are compensated by the subsidiary. However, this requirement shall not be construed to prohibit the parent bank and the subsidiary from sharing the same facility, provided that any area in which the subsidiary conducts business with the public is distinguishable, to the extent practicable, from the area in which customers of the bank conduct business with the bank;

(ii) The subsidiary shall be held out as a separate and distinct entity from the bank in its written material and direct contact with outside parties. All written marketing material shall clearly state that the subsidiary is a separate entity from the bank and the obligations of the subsidiary are not obligations of the bank;

(iii) The subsidiary's name shall not be the same name as its parent bank, and a subsidiary that has a name similar to its parent bank shall take appropriate steps to minimize the risk of customer confusion, including with respect to the separate character of the two entities and the extent to which their respective obligations are insured or not insured by the Federal Deposit Insurance Corporation;

(iv) The subsidiary shall be adequately capitalized according to relevant industry measures and shall maintain capital adequate to support its activities and to cover reasonably expected expenses and losses;

(v) The subsidiary shall maintain separate accounting and corporate records;

(vi) The subsidiary shall conduct its operations pursuant to independent policies and procedures that are also intended to

inform customers that the subsidiary is an organization separate from the bank;

(vii)   Contracts between the subsidiary and the bank for any services shall be on terms and conditions substantially, comparable to those 'available to or from independent entities,

(viii)   The subsidiary shall observe appropriate separate corporate formalities, such as separate board of directors' meetings

(ix)   The subsidiary shall maintain a board of directors at least one-third of whom shall not be directors of the bank and shall have relevant expertise capable of overseeing the subsidiary's activities; and

(x)   The subsidiary and the parent bank shall have internal controls appropriate to manage the financial and operational risks associated with the subsidiary.

(3)   Supervisory requirements. When the subsidiary will conduct an activity described in this paragraph (f) as principal, the following additional requirements apply.

(i)   The bank's capital and total assets shall each be reduced by an amount equal to the bank's equity investment in the subsidiary (for purposes of risk-based capital this deduction shall be made equally from Tier 1 and Tier 2 capital), and the subsidiary's assets and liabilities shall not be consolidated with those of the bank. The OCC may, however, require the bank to calculate its capital on a consolidated basis for purposes of determining whether the bank is adequately capitalized under 12 CFR part 6;

(ii)   The standards of sections 23A an 23B of the Federal Reserve Act (12 U.S.C. 371c and 371c-1) shall apply to and shall be enforced and applied by the OCC with respect to transactions between the bank and the subsidiary; and

(iii)   The bank must qualify as an eligible bank under the criteria set forth at § 5.3(g), both prior to commencement of the activity, and thereafter, taking into account the capital deduction required by paragraph (f)(3)(i) of this section. If the bank ceases to be well capitalized for two consecutive quarters it shall submit to the OCC, within the period specified by the OCC, an acceptable plan to become well capitalized.

* * *

PART 6–PROMPT CORRECTIVE ACTION

SUBPART A–CAPITAL CATEGORIES

§ 6.2. Definitions.

For purposes of section 38 and this part, the definitions related to capital in part 3 of this chapter shall apply. In addition, except as modified in this section or unless the context otherwise requires, the terms used in this subpart have the same meanings as set forth in section 38 and section 3 of the FDI Act.

* * *

(d) Leverage ratio means the ratio of Tier 1 capital to adjusted total assets, as calculated in accordance with the OCC's Minimum Capital Ratios in part 3 of this chapter.

(e) Management fee means any payment of money or provision of any other thing of value to a company or individual for the provision of management services or advice to the bank or related overhead expenses, including payments related to supervisory, executive, managerial, or policymaking functions, other than compensation to an individual in the individual's capacity as an officer or employee of the bank.

(f) Risk-weighted assets means total risk weighted assets, as calculated in accordance with the OCC's Minimum Capital Ratios in part 3 of this chapter.

(g) Tangible equity means the amount of Tier 1 capital elements in the OCC's Risk-Based Capital Guidelines (appendix A to part 3 of this chapter) plus the amount of outstanding cumulative perpetual preferred stock (including related surplus) minus all intangible assets except mortgage servicing rights to the extent permitted in Tier 1 capital under section 2(c) in appendix A to part 3 of this chapter.

(h) Tier 1 capital means the amount of Tier 1 capital as defined in the OCC's Minimum Capital Ratios in part 3 of this chapter.

(i) Tier 1 risk-based capital ratio means the ratio of Tier 1 capital to risk weighted assets, as calculated in accordance with the OCC's Minimum Capital Ratios in part 3 of this chapter.

(j) Total assets means quarterly average total assets as reported in a bank's Consolidated Reports of Condition and Income (Call Report), minus

intangible assets as provided in the definition of tangible equity. The OCC reserves the right to require a bank to compute and maintain its capital ratios on the basis of actual, rather than average, total assets when computing tangible equity.

(k)   Total risk-based capital ratio means the ratio of qualifying total capital to risk-weighted assets, as calculated in accordance with the OCC's Minimum Capital Ratios in part 3 of this chapter.

PART 7–INTERPRETIVE RULINGS

SUBPART A–BANK POWERS

§ 7.1006. Loan agreement providing for a share in profits, income, or earnings or for stock warrants.

A national bank may take as consideration for a loan a share in the profit, income, or earnings from a business enterprise of a borrower. A national bank also may take as consideration for a loan a stock warrant issued by a business enterprise of a borrower, provided that the bank does not exercise the warrant. The share or stock warrant may be taken in addition to, or in lieu of, interest. The borrower's obligation to repay principal, however, may not be conditioned upon the value of the profit, income, or earnings of the business enterprise or upon the value of the warrant received.

§ 7.1012. Messenger service.

(a)   Definition. For purposes of this section, a "messenger service" means any service, such as a courier service or armored car service, used by a national bank and its customers to pick up from, and deliver to, specific customers at locations such as their homes or offices, items relating to transactions between the bank and those customers.

(b)   Pick-up and delivery of items constituting nonbranching activities. Pursuant to 12 U.S.C. 24 (Seventh), a national bank may establish and operate a messenger service, or use, with its customers, a third party messenger service. The bank may use the messenger service to transport items relevant to the bank's transactions with its customers without regard to the branching limitations set forth in 12 U.S.C. 36, provided the service does not engage in branching functions within the meaning of 12 U.S.C. 36(j).

In establishing or using such a facility, the national bank may establish terms, conditions, and limitations consistent with this section and appropriate to assure compliance with safe and sound banking practices.

(c)   Pick-up and delivery of items constituting branching functions by a messenger service established by a third party.

   (1)   Pursuant to 12 U.S.C. 24 (Seventh), a national bank and its customers may use a messenger service to pick up from, and deliver to, customers items that relate to branching functions within the meaning of 12 U.S.C. 36(j) without regard to the branching limitations set forth in 12 U.S.C. 36, provided the messenger service is established and operated by a third party. In using such a facility, a national bank may establish terms, conditions, and limitations, consistent with this section and appropriate to assure compliance with safe and sound banking practices.

* * *

§ 7.1019. Furnishing of products and services by electronic means and facilities.

A national bank may perform, provide, or deliver through electronic means and facilities any activity, function, product, or service that it is otherwise authorized to perform, provide, or deliver. A national bank may also, in order to optimize the use of the bank's resources, market and sell to third parties electronic capacities acquired or developed by the bank in good faith for banking purposes.

§ 7.3001. Sharing space and employees.

(a)   Sharing space. A national bank may:

   (1)   Lease excess space on bank premises to one or more other businesses (including other banks and financial institutions);

   (2)   Share space jointly held with one or more other businesses; or

   (3)   Offer its services in space owned or leased to other businesses.

(b)   Sharing employees. When sharing space with other businesses as described in paragraph (a) of this section, a national bank may provide, under one or more written agreements among the bank, the other businesses, and their employees, that:

   (1)   A bank employee may act as agent for the other business; or

   (2)   An employee of the other business may act as agent for the bank.

(c)   Supervisory conditions. When a national bank engages in arrangements of the types listed in paragraphs (a) and (b) of this section, the bank shall ensure that:

    (1)   The other business is conspicuously, accurately, and separately identified;

    (2)   Shared employees clearly and fully disclose the nature of their agency relationship to customers of the bank and of the other businesses so that customers will know the identity of the bank or business that is providing the product or service;

* * *

§ 7.4001. Charging interest at rates permitted competing institutions; charging interest to corporate borrowers.

(a)   Definition. The term "interest" as used in 12 U.S.C. 85 includes any payment compensating a creditor or prospective creditor for an extension of credit, making available of a line of credit, or any default or breach by a borrower of a condition upon which credit was extended. It includes, among other things, the following fees connected with credit extension or availability: numerical periodic rates, late fees, not sufficient funds (NSF) fees, overlimit fees, annual fees, cash advance fees, and membership fees. It does not ordinarily include appraisal fees, premiums and commissions attributable to insurance guaranteeing repayment of any extension of credit, finders' fees, fees for document preparation or notarization, or fees incurred to obtain credit reports.

(b)   Authority. A national bank located in a state may charge interest at the maximum rate permitted to any state-chartered or licensed lending institution by the law of that state. If state law permits different interest charges on specified classes of loans, a national bank making such loans is subject only to the provisions of state law relating to that class of loans that are material to the determination of the permitted interest. For example, a national bank may lawfully charge the highest rate permitted to be charged by a state-licensed small loan company, without being so licensed, but subject to state law limitations on the size of loans made by small loan companies.

(c)   Effect on state definitions of interest. The Federal definition of the term "interest" in paragraph (a) of this section does not change how interest is defined by the individual states (nor how the state definition of interest is used) solely for purposes of state law. For example, if late fees are not "interest" under state law where a national bank is located but state law

permits its most favored lender to charge late fees, then a national bank located in that state may charge late fees to its intrastate customers. The national bank may also charge late fees to its interstate customers because the fees are interest under the Federal definition of interest and an allowable charge under state law where the national bank is located. However, the late fees would not be treated as interest for purposes of evaluating compliance with state usury limitations because state law excludes late fees when calculating the maximum interest that lending institutions may charge under those limitations.

(d) Usury. A national bank located in a state the law of which denies the defense of usury to a corporate borrower may charge a corporate borrower any rate of interest agreed upon by a corporate borrower.

PART 9–FIDUCIARY ACTIVITIES OF NATIONAL BANKS

---

§ 9.2 Definitions

(b) Applicable law means the law of a state or other jurisdiction governing a national bank's fiduciary relationships, any applicable Federal law governing those relationships, the terms of the instrument governing a fiduciary relationship, or any court order pertaining to the relationship.

* * *

(e) Fiduciary capacity menas: trustee, executor, administrator, registrar of stocks and bonds, transfer agent, guardian, assignee, receiver, or custodian under a uniform gifts to minors act; investment advisor, if the bank recieves a fee for its investment advice; any capacity in which the bank possesses investment discretion on behalf of another; or any other similar capacity that the OCC authorizes pursuant to 12 U.S.C. 92a.

* * *

(g) Fiduciary powers means the authority the OCC permits a national bank to exercise pursuant to 12 U.S.C. 92a. The extent of fiduciary powers is the same for out-of-state national banks as for in-state national banks, and that extent depends upon what powers the state grants to the fiduciaries in in the state with which national banks compete.

* * *

(i)   Investment discretion means, with respect to an account, the osle or shared authority (whether or not that authority is exercisd) to determine what securities or other assets to purchase or sell on behalf of the account. A bank that delegates its authority over investments and a bank that receives delegated authority over investments are both deemed to have investment discretion.

* * *

§ 9.10 Fiduciary Funds awaiting Investment or distribution.

(a)   In general. With respect to a fiduciary account for which a national bank has investment discretion or discretion over distributions, the bank may not allow funds awaiting investment or distribution to remain uninvested and undistributed any longer than is reasonable for the proper management of the account and consistent with applicable law. With respect to a fiduciary account for which a national bank has investment discretion, the bank shall obtain for funds awaiting investment or distribution a rate of return that is consistent with applicable law.

(b)   Self-deposits—(1) In general. A national bank may deposit funds of a fiduciary account that are awaiting investment or distribution in the commercial, savings, or another department of the bank unless prohibited by applicable law. To the extent that the funds ark not insured by the Federal Deposit Insurance Corporation, the bank shall set aside collateral as security, under the control of appropriate fiduciary officers and employees, in accordance with paragraph (b)(2) of this section. The market value of the collateral set aside must at an times equal or exceed the amount of the uninsured fiduciary funds.

* * *

§ 9.12 Self-dealing and convicts of Interest.

(a)   Investments for fiduciary accounts—

(1)   In general. Unless authorized by applicable law, a national bank may not invest funds of a fiduciary account for which a national bank has investment discretion in the stock or obligations of, or in assets acquired from: the bank or any of its directors, officers, or employees; affiliates of the bank or any of their directors, officers, or employees; or individuals or organizations with whom there exists an interest that might affect the exercise of the best judgment of the bank.

(2) Additional securities investments. If retention of stock or obligations of the bank or its affiliates in a fiduciary account is consistent with applicable law, the bank may:

    (i) Exercise rights to purchase additional stock (or securities convertible into additional stock) when offered pro rata to stockholders; and

    (ii) Purchase fractional shares to complement fractional shares acquired through the exercise of rights or the receipt of a stock dividend resulting in fractional share holdings.

(b) Loans, sales, or other transfers from fiduciary accounts—

    (1) In general A national bank may not lend, sell, or otherwise transfer assets of a fiduciary account for which a national bank has investment discretion to the bank or any of its directors, officers, or employees, or to affiliates of the bank or any of their directors, officers, or employees, or to individuals or organizations with whom there exists an interest that might affect the exercise of the best judgment of the bank, unless:

        (i) The transaction is authorized by applicable law;

        (ii) Legal counsel advises the bank in writing that the bank has incurred, in its fiduciary capacity, a contingent or potential liability, in which case the bank, upon the sale or transfer of assets, shall reimburse the fiduciary account in cash at the greater of book or market value of the assets

        (iii) As provided in § 9.18(b)(8)(iii) for defaulted investments; or

        (iv) Required in writing by the OCC.

    (2) Loans of funds held as trustee. Notwithstanding paragraph (b)(1) of this section, a national bank may not lend to any of its directors, officers, or employees any funds held in trust, except with respect to employee benefit plans in accordance with the exemptions found in section 408 of the Employee Retirement Income Security Act of 1974 (29 U.S.C. 1108).

(c) Loans to fiduciary accounts. A national bank may make a loan to a fiduciary account and may hold a security interest in assets of the account if the transaction is fair to the account and is not prohibited by applicable law.

(d) Sales between fiduciary accounts. A national bank may sell assets between any of its fiduciary accounts if the transaction is fair to both accounts and is not prohibited by applicable law.

(e)   Loans between fiduciary accounts. A national bank may make a loan between any of its fiduciary accounts if the transaction is fair to both accounts and is not prohibited by applicable law.

§ 9.15 Fiduciary compensation.

(a)   Compensation of bank. If the amount of a national bank's compensation for acting in a fiduciary capacity is not set or governed by applicable law, the bank may charge a reasonable fee for its services.

(b)   Compensation of co-fiduciary officers and employees. A national bank may not permit any officer or employee to retain any compensation for acting as a co-fiduciary with the bank in the administration of a fiduciary account, except with the specific approval of the bank's board of directors.

* * *

§ 9.18 Collective Investment funds.

(a)   In general. Where consistent with applicable law, a national bank may invest assets that it holds as fiduciary in the following collective investment funds:[1]

(1)   A fund maintained by the bank, or by one or more affiliated banks,[2] exclusively for the collective investment and reinvestment of money contributed to the fund by the bank, or by one or more affiliated banks, in its capacity as trustee, executor, administrator, guardian, or custodian-under a uniform gifts to minors act.

(2)   A fund consisting solely of assets of retirement, pension, profit sharing, stock bonus or other trusts that are exempt from Federal income tax.

---

[1]   In determining whether investing fiduciary assets in a collective investment fund is proper, the bank may consider the fund as a whole and. for example. shall not be prohibited from making that investment because any particular asset is nonincome producing.

[2]   A fund established pursuant to this paragraph (a)(1) that includes money contributed by entitiesthat are affiliates under 12 U.S.C. 221a(b), but are not members of the same affiliated group, as defined at 26 U.S.C. 1504, may fail to qualify for tax-exempt status under the Internal Revenue Code. See 26 U.S.C. 584.

(i) A national bank may invest assets of retirement, pension, profit sharing, stock bonus, or other trusts exempt from Federal income tax and that the bank holds in its capacity as trustee in a collective investment fund established under paragraph (a)(l) or (a)(2) of this section.

(ii) A national bank may invest assets of retirement, pension, profit sharing, stock bonus, or other employee benefit trusts exempt from Federal income tax and that the bank holds in any capacity(including agent), in a collective investment fund established under this paragraph (a)(2) if the fund itself qualifies for exemption from Federal income tax.

(b) Requirements. A national bank administering a collective investment fund authorized under paragraph (a) of this section shall comply with the following requirements:

* * *

(7) Advertising restriction. A bank may not advertise or publicize any fund authorized under paragraph (a)(l) of this section, except in connection with the advertisement of the general fiduciary services of the bank.

(8) Self-dealing and conflicts of interest. A national bank administering a collective investment fund must comply with the following (in addition to § 9.12):

(i) Bank interests. A bank administering a collective investment fund may not have an interest in that fund other than in its fiduciary capacity. If, because of a creditor relationship or otherwise, the bank acquires an interest in a participating account, the participating account must he withdrawn on the next withdrawal date. However, a bank may invest assets that it holds as fiduciary for its own employees in a collective investment fund.

(ii) Loans to participating accounts. A bank administering a collective investment fund may not make any loan on the security of a parlicipant's interest in the fund. An unsecured advance to a fiduciary account participating in the fund until the time of the next valuation date does not constitute the acquisition of an interest in a participating account by the bank.

* * *

(9) Management fees. A bank administering a collective investment fund may charge a reasonable fund management fee only if:

(i)   The fee is permitted under applicable law (and complies with fee disclosure requirements, if any) in the state in which the bank maintains the fund; and

(ii) The amount of the fee does not exceed an amount commensurate with the value of legitimate services of tangible benefit to the participating fiduciary accounts that would not have been provided to the accounts were they not invested in the fund.

(10)   Expenses. A bank administering a collective investment fund may charge reasonable expenses incurred in operating the collective investment fund, to the extent not prohibited byapplicable law in the state in which the bank maintains the fund. However, a bank shall absorb the expenses of establishing or reorganizing a collective investment fund.

* * *

§ 9.100 Acting as indenture trustee and creditor.

With respect to a debt securities issuance, a national bank may act both as indenture trustee and as creditor until 90days after deault, if the bank maintains adequate controls to manage the potnetial conflicts of interest.

Any institution that must comply with this section in order to receive favorable tax treatment under 26 U.S.C. 584 (namely, any corporate fiduciary) may seek OCC approval of special exemption funds in accordance with this paragraph (c)(5).

PART 23–LEASING

SUBPART A—GENERAL PROVISIONS

§ 23.1 Authority, purpose, and scope.

(a)   Authority. A national bank may engage in personal property lease financing transactions pursuant to 12 U.S.C. 24(Seventh) or 12 U.S.C. 24(Tenth).

(b)   Purpose. The purpose of this part is to set forth standards for personal property lease financing transaction authorized for national banks.

(c) Scope. This part applies to the acquisition of personal property by a national bank for the purpose of, or in connection with, the leasing of that property.

§ 23.2 Definitions.

* * *

(c) CEBA Lease means a personal property lease authorized under 12 U.S.C. 24(Tenth).

(d) Conforming lease means:

(1) A CEBA Lease that conforms with the requirements of subparts A and B of this part; or

(2) A Section 24(Seventh) Lease that conforms with the requirements of subparts A and C of this part.

(e) Full-payout lease means a lease in which the national bank reasonably expects to realize the return of its full investment in the leased property, plus the estimated cost of financing the property over the term of the lease, from:

(1) Rentals;

(2) Estimated tax benefits; and

(3) The estimated residual value of the property at the expiration of the lease term.

(f) Net lease means a lease under which the national bank will not, directly or indirectly, provide or be obligated to provide for:

(1) Servicing repair, or maintenance of the leased property during the lease term;

(2) Parts or accessories for the leased property;

(3) Loan of replacement or substitute property while the leased property is being serviced;

(4) Payment of insurance for the lessee, except where the lessee has failed on its contractual obligation to purchase or maintain required insurance; or

(5) Renewal of any license or registration for the property unless renewal by the bank is necessary to protect its interest as owner or financier of the property.

(g)   Off-lease property means property that reverts to a national bank's possession or control upon the expiration of lease or upon the default of the lessee.

(h)   Section 24(Seventh) Lease means a personal property lease authorized under 12 U.S.C. 24(Seventh).

§ 23.3 Lease requirements.

(a)   General requirements. A national bank may acquire personal property for the purpose of, or in connection with leasing that property, and may engage in activities incidental thereto, if the lease qualifies as a full-payout lease and a net lease.

(b)   Exceptions—

    (1)   Change in condition. If, in good faith, a national bank believes that there has been a change in condition that threatens its financial position by increasing its exposure to loss, then the bank may:

        (i)   Take reasonable and appropriate action, including the actions specified in s 23.2(f), to salvage or protect the value of the leased property or its interests arising under the lease; and

        (ii)   Acquire or perfect title to the leased property pursuant to any existing rights.

    (2)   Provisions to protect the bank's interests. A national bank may include any provision in a lease, or make any additional agreement, to protect its financial position or investment in the event of a change in conditions that would increase its exposure to loss.

    (3)   Arranging for services by a third party. A national bank may arrange for a third party to provide any of the services enumerated in s 23.2(f) to the lessee at the expense of the lessee.

§ 23.4 Investment in personal property.

(a)   General rule. A national bank may acquire specific property to be leased only after the bank has entered into:

    (1)   A conforming lease;

    (2)   A legally binding written agreement that indemnifies the bank against loss in connection with its acquisition of the property; or

    (3)   A legally binding written commitment to enter into a conforming lease.

(b) Exception. A national bank may acquire property to be leased without complying with the requirements of paragraph (a) of this section, if:

    (1) The acquisition of the property is consistent with the leasing business then conducted by the bank or is consistent with a business plan for expansion of the bank's existing leasing business or for entry into the leasing business; and

    (2) The bank's aggregate investment in property held pursuant to this paragraph (b) does not exceed 15 percent of the bank's capital and surplus.

(c) Holding period. At the expiration of the lease (including any renewals or extensions with the same lessee), or in the event of a default on a lease agreement prior to the expiration of the lease term, a national bank shall either liquidate the off-lease property or re-lease it under a conforming lease as soon as practicable. Liquidation or re-lease must occur not later than five years from the date that the bank acquires the legal right to possession or control of the property, except the OCC may extend the period for up to an additional five years, if the bank provides a clearly convincing demonstration why any additional holding period is necessary. The bank must value off-lease property at the lower of current fair market value or book value promptly after the property becomes off-lease property.

(d) Bridge or interim leases. During the holding period allowed by paragraph (c) of this section, a national bank may enter into a short-term bridge or interim lease pending the liquidation of off-lease property or the re-lease of the property under a conforming lease. A short-term bridge or interim lease must be a net lease, but need not comply with any requirement of subpart B or C of this part.

§ 23.6 Application of lending limits; restrictions on transactions with affiliates.

A lease entered into pursuant to this part is subject to the lending limits prescribed by 12 U.S.C. 84 or, if the lessee is an affiliate of the bank, to the restrictions on transactions with affiliates prescribed by 12 U.S.C. 371c and 371c-1. The OCC may also determine that other limits or restrictions apply. The term affiliate means an affiliate as defined in 12 U.S.C. 371c or 371c-1, as applicable. For the purpose of measuring compliance with the lending limits prescribed by 12 U.S.C. 84, a national bank records the investment in a lease net of any nonrecourse debt the bank has incurred to finance the acquisition of the leased asset.

SUBPART B—CEBA LEASES

§ 23.10 General rule.

Pursuant to 12 U.S.C. 24(Tenth) a national bank may invest in tangible personal property, including vehicles, manufactured homes, machinery, equipment, or furniture, for the purpose of, or in connection with leasing that property, if the aggregate book value of the property does not exceed 10 percent of the bank's consolidated assets and the related lease is a conforming lease. For the purpose of measuring compliance with the 10 percent limit prescribed by this section, a national bank records the investment in a lease entered into pursuant to this subpart net of any nonrecourse debt the bank has incurred to finance the acquisition of the leased asset.

§ 23.11 Lease term.

A CEBA Lease must have an initial term of not less than 90 days. A national bank may acquire property subject to an existing lease with a remaining maturity of less than 90 days if, at its inception, the lease was a conforming lease.

SUBPART C—SECTION 24(SEVENTH) LEASES

* * *

§ 23.20 General rule.

Pursuant to 12 U.S.C. 24(Seventh) a national bank may invest in tangible or intangible personal property, including vehicles, manufactured homes, machinery, equipment, furniture, patents, copyrights, and other intellectual property, for the purpose of, or in connection with leasing that property, if the related lease is a conforming lease representing a noncancelable obligation of the lessee (notwithstanding the possible early termination of that lease).

§ 23.21 Estimated residual value.

(a)   Recovery of investment and costs. A national bank's estimate of the residual value of the property that the bank relies upon to satisfy the requirements of a full-payout lease, for purposes of this subpart:

(1)   Must be reasonable in light of the nature of the leased property and all circumstances relevant to the transaction; and

(2)   Any unguaranteed amount must not exceed 25 percent of the original cost of the property to the bank.

(b) *Estimated residual value subject to guarantee.* The amount of any estimated residual value guaranteed by the manufacturer, the lessee, or other third party may exceed 25 percent of the original cost of the property if the bank determines, and demonstrates by appropriate documentation, that the guarantor has the resources to meet the guarantee and the guarantor is not an affiliate of the bank.

(c) *Leases to government entities.* A bank's calculations of estimated residual value in connection with leases of personal property to Federal, State, or local governmental entities may be based on future transactions or renewals that the bank reasonably anticipates will occur.

PART 25–COMMUNITY REINVESTMENT ACT REGULATIONS

§ 25.21. Performance tests, standards, and ratings, in general.

(a) *Performance tests and standards.* The OCC assesses the CRA performance of a bank in an examination as follows:

(1) *Lending, investment, and service tests.* The OCC applies the lending, investment, and service tests, as provided in §§ 25.22 through 25.24, in evaluating the performance of a bank, except as provided in paragraphs (a)(2), (a)(3), and (a)(4) of this section.

(2) *Community development test for wholesale or limited purpose banks.* The OCC applies the community development test for a wholesale or limited purpose bank, as provided in § 25.25, except as provided in paragraph (a)(4) of this section.

(3) *Small bank performance standards.* The OCC applies the small bank performance standards as provided in § 25.26 in evaluating the performance of a small bank or a bank that was a small bank during the prior calendar year, unless the bank elects to be assessed as provided in paragraphs (a)(1), (a)(2), or (a)(4) of this section. The bank may elect to be assessed as provided in paragraph (a)(1) of this section only if it collects and reports the data required for other banks under § 25.42.

(4) *Strategic plan.* The OCC evaluates the performance of a bank under a strategic plan if the bank submits, and the OCC approves, a strategic plan as provided in § 25.27.

(b)   Performance context. The OCC applies the tests and standards in paragraph (a) of this section and also considers whether to approve a proposed strategic plan in the context of:

(1)   Demographic data on median income levels, distribution of household income, nature of housing stock, housing costs, and other relevant data pertaining to a bank's assessment area(s);

(2)   Any information about lending, investment, and service opportunities in the bank's assessment area(s) maintained by the bank or obtained from community organizations, state, local, and tribal governments, economic development agencies, or other sources;

(3)   The bank's product offerings and business strategy as determined from data provided by the bank;

(4)   Institutional capacity and constraints, including the size and financial condition of the bank, the economic climate (national, regional, and local), safety and soundness limitations, and any other factors that significantly affect the bank's ability to provide lending, investments, or services in its assessment area(s);

(5)   The bank's past performance and the performance of similarly situated lenders;

(6)   The bank's public file, as described in § 25.43, and any written comments about the bank's CRA performance submitted to the bank or the OCC; and

(7)   Any other information deemed relevant by the OCC.

(c)   Assigned ratings. The OCC assigns to a bank one of the following four ratings pursuant to § 25.28 and Appendix A of this part: "outstanding"; "satisfactory"; "needs to improve"; or "substantial noncompliance" as provided in 12 U.S.C. 2906(b)(2). The rating assigned by the OCC reflects the bank's record of helping to meet the credit needs of its entire community, including low- and moderate-income neighborhoods, consistent with the safe and sound operation of the bank.

(d)   Safe and sound operations. This part and the CRA do not require a bank to make loans or investments or to provide services that are inconsistent with safe and sound operations. To the contrary, the OCC anticipates banks can meet the standards of this part with safe and sound loans, investments, and services on which the banks expect to make a profit. Banks are permitted and encouraged to develop and apply flexible underwriting standards for loans that benefit low- or moderate-income geographies or individuals, only if consistent with safe and sound operations.

SUBPART B–STANDARDS FOR ASSESSING PERFORMANCE

§ 25.22. Lending test.

(a) Scope of test.

    (1) The lending test evaluates a bank's record of helping to meet the credit needs of its assessment area(s) through its lending activities by considering a bank's home mortgage, small business, small farm, and community development lending. If consumer lending constitutes a substantial majority of a bank's business, the OCC will evaluate the bank's consumer lending in one or more of the following categories: motor vehicle, credit card, home equity, other secured, and other unsecured loans. In addition, at a bank's option, the OCC will evaluate one or more categories of consumer lending, if the bank has collected and maintained, as required in § 25.42(c)(1), the data for each category that the bank elects to have the OCC evaluate.

* * *

(b) Performance criteria. The OCC evaluates a bank's lending performance pursuant to the following criteria:

    (1) Lending activity. The number and amount of the bank's home mortgage, small business, small farm, and consumer loans, if applicable, in the bank's assessment area(s);

    (2) Geographic distribution. The geographic distribution of the bank's home mortgage, small business, small farm, and consumer loans, if applicable, based on the loan location, including:

        (i) The proportion of the bank's lending in the bank's assessment area(s);

        (ii) The dispersion of lending in the bank's assessment area(s); and

        (iii) The number and amount of loans in low-, moderate-, middle-, and upper-income geographies in the bank's assessment area(s);

    (3) Borrower characteristics. The distribution, particularly in the bank's assessment area(s), of the bank's home mortgage, small business, small farm, and consumer loans, if applicable, based on borrower characteristics, including the number and amount of:

        (i) Home mortgage loans to low-, moderate-, middle-, and upper-income individuals;

      (ii)   Small business and small farm loans to businesses and farms with gross annual revenues of $1 million or less;

      (iii) Small business and small farm loans by loan amount at origination; and

      (iv) Consumer loans, if applicable, to low-, moderate-, middle-, and upper-income individuals;

  (4) Community development lending. The bank's community development lending, including the number and amount of community development loans, and their complexity and innovativeness; and

  (5) Innovative or flexible lending practices. The bank's use of innovative or flexible lending practices in a safe and sound manner to address the credit needs of low- or moderate-income individuals or geographies.

* * *

(d) Lending by a consortium or a third party. Community development loans originated or purchased by a consortium in which the bank participates or by a third party in which the bank has invested:

  (1) Will be considered, at the bank's option, if the bank reports the data pertaining to these loans under § 25.42(b)(2); and

  (2) May be allocated among participants or investors, as they choose, for purposes of the lending test, * * * .

§ 25.23. Investment test.

(a) Scope of test. The investment test evaluates a bank's record of helping to meet the credit needs of its assessment area(s) through qualified investments that benefit its assessment area(s) or a broader statewide or regional area that includes the bank's assessment area(s).

* * *

(d) Disposition of branch premises. Donating, selling on favorable terms, or making available on a rent-free basis a branch of the bank that is located in a predominantly minority neighborhood to a minority depository institution or women's depository institution (as these terms are defined in 12 U.S.C. 2907(b)) will be considered as a qualified investment.

(e) Performance criteria. The OCC evaluates the investment performance of a bank pursuant to the following criteria:

  (1) The dollar amount of qualified investments;

  (2) The innovativeness or complexity of qualified investments;

    (3)   The responsiveness of qualified investments to credit and community development needs; and

    (4)   The degree to which the qualified investments are not routinely provided by private investors.

(f)   Investment performance rating. The OCC rates a bank's investment performance as provided in Appendix A of this part.

§ 25.24. Service test.

(a)   Scope of test. The service test evaluates a bank's record of helping to meet the credit needs of its assessment area(s) by analyzing both the availability and effectiveness of a bank's systems for delivering retail banking services and the extent and innovativeness of its community development services.

(b)   Area(s) benefitted. Community development services must benefit a bank's assessment area(s) or a broader statewide or regional area that includes the bank's assessment area(s).

* * *

(d)   Performance criteria–retail banking services. The OCC evaluates the availability and effectiveness of a bank's systems for delivering retail banking services, pursuant to the following criteria:

    (1)   The current distribution of the bank's branches among low-, moderate-, middle-, and upper-income geographies;

    (2)   In the context of its current distribution of the bank's branches, the bank's record of opening and closing branches, particularly branches located in low- or moderate-income geographies or primarily serving low- or moderate-income individuals;

    (3)   The availability and effectiveness of alternative systems for delivering retail banking services (e.g., ATMs, ATMs not owned or operated by or exclusively for the bank, banking by telephone or computer, loan production offices, and bank-at-work or bank-by-mail programs) in low- and moderate-income geographies and to low- and moderate-income individuals; and

    (4)   The range of services provided in low-, moderate-, middle-, and upper-income geographies and the degree to which the services are tailored to meet the needs of those geographies.

(e)   Performance criteria–community development services. The OCC
      evaluates community development services pursuant to the following
      criteria:

      (1)   The extent to which the bank provides community development
            services; and

      (2)   The innovativeness and responsiveness of community development
            services.

* * *

§ 25.25. Community development test for wholesale or limited purpose banks.

(a)   Scope of test. The OCC assesses a wholesale or limited purpose bank's
      record of helping to meet the credit needs of its assessment area(s) under
      the community development test through its community development
      lending, qualified investments, or community development services.

(b)   Designation as a wholesale or limited purpose bank. In order to receive a
      designation as a wholesale or limited purpose bank, a bank shall file a
      request, in writing, with the OCC, at least three months prior to the
      proposed effective date of the designation. If the OCC approves the
      designation, it remains in effect until the bank requests revocation of the
      designation or until one year after the OCC notifies the bank that the OCC
      has revoked the designation on its own initiative.

(c)   Performance criteria. The OCC evaluates the community development
      performance of a wholesale or limited purpose bank pursuant to the
      following criteria:

      (1)   The number and amount of community development loans (including
            originations and purchases of loans and other community
            development loan data provided by the bank, such as data on loans
            outstanding, commitments, and letters of credit), qualified
            investments, or community development services;

      (2)   The use of innovative or complex qualified investments, community
            development loans, or community development services and the
            extent to which the investments are not routinely provided by private
            investors; and

      (3)   The bank's responsiveness to credit and community development
            needs.

(d) Indirect activities. At a bank's option, the OCC will consider in its community development performance assessment:

    (1) Qualified investments or community development services provided by an affiliate of the bank, if the investments or services are not claimed by any other institution; and

    (2) Community development lending by affiliates, consortia and third parties, subject to the requirements and limitations in § 25.22(c) and (d).

(e) Benefit to assessment area(s)–

    (1) Benefit inside assessment area(s). The OCC considers all qualified investments, community development loans, and community development services that benefit areas within the bank's assessment area(s) or a broader statewide or regional area that includes the bank's assessment area(s).

    (2) Benefit outside assessment area(s). The OCC considers the qualified investments, community development loans, and community development services that benefit areas outside the bank's assessment area(s), if the bank has adequately addressed the needs of its assessment area(s).

* * *

§ 25.26. Small bank performance standards.

(a) Performance criteria. The OCC evaluates the record of a small bank, or a bank that was a small bank during the prior calendar year, of helping to meet the credit needs of its assessment area(s) pursuant to the following criteria:

    (1) The bank's loan-to-deposit ratio, adjusted for seasonal variation and, as appropriate, other lending-related activities, such as loan originations for sale to the secondary markets, community development loans, or qualified investments;

    (2) The percentage of loans and, as appropriate, other lending-related activities located in the bank's assessment area(s);

    (3) The bank's record of lending to and, as appropriate, engaging in other lending-related activities for borrowers of different income levels and businesses and farms of different sizes;

    (4) The geographic distribution of the bank's loans; and

(5) The bank's record of taking action, if warranted, in response to written complaints about its performance in helping to meet credit needs in its assessment area(s).

(b) Small bank performance rating. The OCC rates the performance of a bank evaluated under this section as provided in Appendix A of this part.

§ 25.27. Strategic plan.

(a) Alternative election. The OCC will assess a bank's record of helping to meet the credit needs of its assessment area(s) under a strategic plan if:

(1) The bank has submitted the plan to the OCC as provided for in this section;

(2) The OCC has approved the plan;

(3) The plan is in effect; and

(4) The bank has been operating under an approved plan for at least one year.

(b) Data reporting. The OCC's approval of a plan does not affect the bank's obligation, if any, to report data as required by § 25.42.

(c) Plans in general.–

(1) Term. A plan may have a term of no more than five years, and any multi-year plan must include annual interim measurable goals under which the OCC will evaluate the bank's performance.

(2) Multiple assessment areas. A bank with more than one assessment area may prepare a single plan for all of its assessment areas or one or more plans for one or more of its assessment areas.

(3) Treatment of affiliates. Affiliated institutions may prepare a joint plan if the plan provides measurable goals for each institution. Activities may be allocated among institutions at the institutions' option, provided that the same activities are not considered for more than one institution.

(d) Public participation in plan development. Before submitting a plan to the OCC for approval, a bank shall:

(1) Informally seek suggestions from members of the public in its assessment area(s) covered by the plan while developing the plan;

(2) Once the bank has developed a plan, formally solicit public comment on the plan for at least 30 days by publishing notice in at least one

newspaper of general circulation in each assessment area covered by the plan; and

(3) During the period of formal public comment, make copies of the plan available for review by the public at no cost at all offices of the bank in any assessment area covered by the plan and provide copies of the plan upon request for a reasonable fee to cover copying and mailing, if applicable.

(e) Submission of plan. The bank shall submit its plan to the OCC at least three months prior to the proposed effective date of the plan. The bank shall also submit with its plan a description of its informal efforts to seek suggestions from members of the public, any written public comment received, and, if the plan was revised in light of the comment received, the initial plan as released for public comment.

(f) Plan content.–

(1) Measurable goals.

   (i) A bank shall specify in its plan measurable goals for helping to meet the credit needs of each assessment area covered by the plan, particularly the needs of low- and moderate-income geographies and low- and moderate-income individuals, through lending, investment, and services, as appropriate.

   (ii) A bank shall address in its plan all three performance categories and, unless the bank has been designated as a wholesale or limited purpose bank, shall emphasize lending and lending-related activities. Nevertheless, a different emphasis, including a focus on one or more performance categories, may be appropriate if responsive to the characteristics and credit needs of its assessment area(s), considering public comment and the bank's capacity and constraints, product offerings, and business strategy.

* * *

(3) Satisfactory and outstanding goals. A bank shall specify in its plan measurable goals that constitute "satisfactory" performance. A plan may specify measurable goals that constitute "outstanding" performance. If a bank submits, and the OCC approves, both "satisfactory" and "outstanding" performance goals, the OCC will consider the bank eligible for an "outstanding" performance rating.

(4) Election if satisfactory goals not substantially met. A bank may elect in its plan that, if the bank fails to meet substantially its plan goals for

a satisfactory rating, the OCC will evaluate the bank's performance under the lending, investment, and service tests, the community development test, or the small bank performance standards, as appropriate.

* * *

§ 25.28 Assigned ratings

(a) Ratings in general. Subject to pargraphs (b) and (c) of this section, the OCC assigns to a bank a rating of "outstanding" "satisfactory," "needs to improve," or "substantial non-compliance" based on the bank's performance under the lending, investment and service tests, the community development test, the small bank performance standards, or an approved strategic plan, as applicable.

(b) Lending, investment, and service tests. The OCC assigns a rating for a bank assessed under the lending, investment, and service tests in accordance with the following principles:

   (1) A bank that receives an "outstanding" rating on the lending test receives an assigned rating of at least "satisfactory";

   (2) A bank that receives an "outstanding" rating on both the service test and the investment test and a rating of at least "high satsifactory" on the lending test receives an assigned rating of "outstanding"; and

   (3) No bank may receive an assigned rating of "satisfactory" or higher unless it receives a rating of at least "low satisfactory" on the lending test.

* * *

SUBPART C–RECORDS, REPORTING, AND DISCLOSURE REQUIREMENTS

§ 25.41. Assessment area delineation.

(a) In general. A bank shall delineate one or more assessment areas within which the OCC evaluates the bank's record of helping to meet the credit needs of its community. The OCC does not evaluate the bank's delineation of its assessment area(s) as a separate performance criterion, but the OCC

reviews the delineation for compliance with the requirements of this section.

(b) Geographic area(s) for wholesale or limited purpose banks. The assessment area(s) for a wholesale or limited purpose bank must consist generally of one or more MSAs (using the MSA boundaries that were in effect as of January 1 of the calendar year in which the delineation is made) or one or more contiguous political subdivisions, such as counties, cities, or towns, in which the bank has its main office, branches, and deposit-taking ATMs.

(c) Geographic area(s) for other banks. The assessment area(s) for a bank other than a wholesale or limited purpose bank must:

(1) Consist generally of one or more MSAs (using the MSA boundaries that were in effect as of January 1 of the calendar year in which the delineation is made) or one or more contiguous political subdivisions, such as counties, cities, or towns; and

(2) Include the geographies in which the bank has its main office, its branches, and its deposit-taking ATMs, as well as the surrounding geographies in which the bank has originated or purchased a substantial portion of its loans (including home mortgage loans, small business and small farm loans, and any other loans the bank chooses, such as those consumer loans on which the bank elects to have its performance assessed).

(d) Adjustments to geographic area(s). A bank may adjust the boundaries of its assessment area(s) to include only the portion of a political subdivision that it reasonably can be expected to serve. An adjustment is particularly appropriate in the case of an assessment area that otherwise would be extremely large, of unusual configuration, or divided by significant geographic barriers.

(e) Limitations on the delineation of an assessment area. Each bank's assessment area(s):

(1) Must consist only of whole geographies;

(2) May not reflect illegal discrimination;

(3) May not arbitrarily exclude low- or moderate-income geographies, taking into account the bank's size and financial condition; and

(4) May not extend substantially beyond a CMSA boundary or beyond a state boundary unless the assessment area is located in a multistate MSA. If a bank serves a geographic area that extends substantially beyond a state boundary, the bank shall delineate separate assessment

areas for the areas in each state. If a bank serves a geographic area that extends substantially beyond a CMSA boundary, the bank shall delineate separate assessment areas for the areas inside and outside the CMSA.

* * *

§ 25.42. Data collection, reporting, and disclosure.

(a) Loan information required to be collected and maintained. A bank, except a small bank, shall collect, and maintain in machine readable form (as prescribed by the OCC) until the completion of its next CRA examination, the following data for each small business or small farm loan originated or purchased by the bank:

    (1) A unique number or alpha-numeric symbol that can be used to identify the relevant loan file;

    (2) The loan amount at origination;

    (3) The loan location; and

    (4) An indicator whether the loan was to a business or farm with gross annual revenues of $1 million or less.

(b) Loan information required to be reported. A bank, except a small bank or a bank that was a small bank during the prior calendar year, shall report annually by March 1 to the OCC in machine readable form (as prescribed by the OCC) the following data for the prior calendar year:

    (1) Small business and small farm loan data. For each geography in which the bank originated or purchased a small business or small farm loan, the aggregate number and amount of loans:

        (i) With an amount at origination of $100,000 or less;

        (ii) With amount at origination of more than $100,000 but less than or equal to $250,000;

        (iii) With an amount at origination of more than $250,000; and

        (iv) To businesses and farms with gross annual revenues of $1 million or less (using the revenues that the bank considered in making its credit decision);

    (2) Community development loan data. The aggregate number and aggregate amount of community development loans originated or purchased; and

(3) Home mortgage loans. If the bank is subject to reporting under part 203 of this title, the location of each home mortgage loan application, origination, or purchase outside the MSAs in which the bank has a home or branch office (or outside any MSA) in accordance with the requirements of part 203 of this title.

(c) Optional data collection and maintenance.–

(1) Consumer loans. A bank may collect and maintain in machine readable form (as prescribed by the OCC) data for consumer loans originated or purchased by the bank for consideration under the lending test. A bank may maintain data for one or more of the following categories of consumer loans: motor vehicle, credit card, home equity, other secured, and other unsecured. If the bank maintains data for loans in a certain category, it shall maintain data for all loans originated or purchased within that category. The bank shall maintain data separately for each category, including for each loan:

(i) A unique number or alpha-numeric symbol that can be used to identify the relevant loan file;

(ii) The loan amount at origination or purchase;

(iii) The loan location; and

(iv) The gross annual income of the borrower that the bank considered in making its credit decision.

(2) Other loan data. At its option, a bank may provide other information concerning its lending performance, including additional loan distribution data.

* * *

(g) Assessment area data. A bank, except a small bank or a bank that was a small bank during the prior calendar year, shall collect and report to the OCC by March 1 of each year a list for each assessment area showing the geographies within the area.

(h) CRA Disclosure Statement. The OCC prepares annually for each bank that reports data pursuant to this section a CRA Disclosure Statement that contains, on a state-by-state basis:

(1) For each county (and for each assessment area smaller than a county) with a population of 500,000 persons or fewer in which the bank reported a small business or small farm loan:

(i)   The number and amount of small business and small farm loans reported as originated or purchased located in low-, moderate-, middle-, and upper-income geographies;

(ii)   A list grouping each geography according to whether the geography is low-, moderate-, middle-, or upper-income;

(iii)   A list showing each geography in which the bank reported a small business or small farm loan; and

(iv)   The number and amount of small business and small farm loans to businesses and farms with gross annual revenues of $1 million or less;

(2)   For each county (and for each assessment area smaller than a county) with a population in excess of 500,000 persons in which the bank reported a small business or small farm loan:

(i)   The number and amount of small business and small farm loans reported as originated or purchased located in geographies with median income relative to the area median income of less than 10 percent, 10 or more but less than 20 percent, 20 or more but less than 30 percent, 30 or more but less than 40 percent, 40 or more but less than 50 percent, 50 or more but less than 60 percent, 60 or more but less than 70 percent, 70 or more but less than 80 percent, 80 or more but less than 90 percent, 90 or more but less than 100 percent, 100 or more but less than 110 percent, 110 or more but less than 120 percent, and 120 percent or more;

(ii)   A list grouping each geography in the county or assessment area according to whether the median income in the geography relative to the area median income is less than 10 percent, 10 or more but less than 20 percent, 20 or more but less than 30 percent, 30 or more but less than 40 percent, 40 or more but less than 50 percent, 50 or more but less than 60 percent, 60 or more but less than 70 percent, 70 or more but less than 80 percent, 80 or more but less than 90 percent, 90 or more but less than 100 percent, 100 or more but less than 110 percent, 110 or more but less than 120 percent, and 120 percent or more;

(iii)   A list showing each geography in which the bank reported a small business or small farm loan; and

(iv)   The number and amount of small business and small farm loans to businesses and farms with gross annual revenues of $1 million or less;

(3) The number and amount of small business and small farm loans located inside each assessment area reported by the bank and the number and amount of small business and small farm loans located outside the assessment area(s) reported by the bank; and

(4) The number and amount of community development loans reported as originated or purchased.

(i) Aggregate disclosure statements. The OCC, in conjunction with the Board of Governors of the Federal Reserve System, the Federal Deposit Insurance Corporation, and the Office of Thrift Supervision, prepares annually, for each MSA (including an MSA that crosses a state boundary) and the non-MSA portion of each state, an aggregate disclosure statement of small business and small farm lending by all institutions subject to reporting under this part or parts 228, 345, or 563e of this title. These disclosure statements indicate, for each geography, the number and amount of all small business and small farm loans originated or purchased by reporting institutions, except that the OCC may adjust the form of the disclosure if necessary, because of special circumstances, to protect the privacy of a borrower or the competitive position of an institution.

* * *

§ 25.43. Content and availability of public file.

(a) Information available to the public. A bank shall maintain a public file that includes the following information:

(1) All written comments received from the public for the current year and each of the prior two calendar years that specifically relate to the bank's performance in helping to meet community credit needs, and any response to the comments by the bank, if neither the comments nor the responses contain statements that reflect adversely on the good name or reputation of any persons other than the bank or publication of which would violate specific provisions of law;

(2) A copy of the public section of the bank's most recent CRA Performance Evaluation prepared by the OCC. The bank shall place this copy in the public file within 30 business days after its receipt from the OCC;

(3) A list of the bank's branches, their street addresses, and geographies;

(4)   A list of branches opened or closed by the bank during the current year and each of the prior two calendar years, their street addresses, and geographies;

(5)   A list of services (including hours of operation, available loan and deposit products, and transaction fees) generally offered at the bank's branches and descriptions of material differences in the availability or cost of services at particular branches, if any. At its option, a bank may include information regarding the availability of alternative systems for delivering retail banking services (e.g., ATMs, ATMs not owned or operated by or exclusively for the bank, banking by telephone or computer, loan production offices, and bank-at-work or bank-by-mail programs);

(6)   A map of each assessment area showing the boundaries of the area and identifying the geographies contained within the area, either on the map or in a separate list; and

(7)   Any other information the bank chooses.

(b)   Additional information available to the public.–

(1)   Banks other than small banks. A bank, except a small bank or a bank that was a small bank during the prior calendar year, shall include in its public file the following information pertaining to the bank and its affiliates, if applicable, for each of the prior two calendar years:

(i)   If the bank has elected to have one or more categories of its consumer loans considered under the lending test, for each of these categories, the number and amount of loans:

(A)   To low-, moderate-, middle-, and upper-income individuals;

(B)   Located in low-, moderate-, middle-, and upper-income census tracts; and

(C)   Located inside the bank's assessment area(s) and outside the bank's assessment area(s); and

(ii)   The bank's CRA Disclosure Statement. The bank shall place the statement in the public file within three business days of its receipt from the OCC.

(2)   Banks required to report Home Mortgage Disclosure Act (HMDA) data. A bank required to report home mortgage loan data pursuant part 203 of this title shall include in its public file a copy of the HMDA Disclosure Statement provided by the Federal Financial Institutions Examination Council pertaining to the bank for each of

the prior two calendar years. In addition, a bank that elected to have the OCC consider the mortgage lending of an affiliate for any of these years shall include in its public file the affiliate's HMDA Disclosure Statement for those years. The bank shall place the statement(s) in the public file within three business days after its receipt.

(3) Small banks. A small bank or a bank that was a small bank during the prior calendar year shall include in its public file:

    (i) The bank's loan-to-deposit ratio for each quarter of the prior calendar year and, at its option, additional data on its loan-to-deposit ratio; and

    (ii) The information required for other banks by paragraph (b)(1) of this section, if the bank has elected to be evaluated under the lending, investment, and service tests.

(4) Banks with strategic plans. A bank that has been approved to be assessed under a strategic plan shall include in its public file a copy of that plan. A bank need not include information submitted to the OCC on a confidential basis in conjunction with the plan.

(5) Banks with less than satisfactory ratings. A bank that received a less than satisfactory rating during its most recent examination shall include in its public file a description of its current efforts to improve its performance in helping to meet the credit needs of its entire community. The bank shall update the description quarterly.

* * *

PART 32–LENDING LIMITS

§ 32.1. Authority, purpose and scope.

* * *

(b) Purpose. The purpose of this part is to protect the safety and soundness of national banks by preventing excessive loans to one person, or to related persons that are financially dependent, and to promote diversification of loans and equitable access to banking services.

(c) Scope.

(1)   This part applies to all loans and extensions of credit made by national banks and their domestic operating subsidiaries. This part does not apply to loans made by a national bank and its domestic operating subsidiaries to the bank's "affiliates," as that term is defined in 12 U.S.C. 371c(b)(1), to the bank's operating subsidiaries, or to Edge Act or Agreement Corporation subsidiaries.

(2)   The lending limits in this part are separate and independent from the investment limits prescribed by 12 U.S.C. 24 (Seventh), and a national bank may make loans or extensions of credit to one borrower up to the full amount permitted by this part and also hold eligible securities of the same obligor up to the full amount permitted under 12 U.S.C. 24 (Seventh) and 12 CFR part 1.

(3)   Extensions of credit to executive officers, directors and principal shareholders of national banks, and their related interests are subject to limits prescribed by 12 U.S.C. 375a and 375b in addition to the lending limits established by 12 U.S.C. 84 and this part.

(4)   In addition to the foregoing, loans and extensions of credit made by national banks and their domestic operating subsidiaries must be consistent with safe and sound banking practices.

§ 32.2. Definitions.

* * *

(b)   Capital and surplus means–

(1)   A bank's Tier 1 and Tier 2 capital included in the bank's risk-based capital under the OCC's Minimum Capital Ratios in Appendix A of part 3 of this chapter; plus

(2)   The balance of a bank's allowance for loan and lease losses not included in the bank's Tier 2 capital, for purposes of the calculation of risk-based capital under part 3 of this chapter.

* * *

(f)   Contractual commitment to advance funds.

(1)   The term includes a bank's obligation to–

(i)   Make payment (directly or indirectly) to a third person contingent upon default by a customer of the bank in performing an obligation and to make such payment in keeping with the agreed upon terms of the customer's contract with the third person, or to make payments upon some other stated condition;

      (ii)   Guarantee or act as surety for the benefit of a person;

      (iii) Advance funds under a qualifying commitment to lend, as defined in paragraph (l) of this section; and

      (iv) Advance funds under a standby letter of credit as defined in paragraph (p) of this section, a put, or other similar arrangement.

  (2) The term does not include commercial letters of credit and similar instruments where the issuing bank expects the beneficiary to draw on the issuer, that do not guarantee payment, and that do not provide for payment in the event of a default by a third party.

(g) Control is presumed to exist when a person directly or indirectly, or acting through or together with one or more persons–

  (1) Owns, controls, or has the power to vote 25 percent or more of any class of voting securities of another person;

  (2) Controls, in any manner, the election of a majority of the directors, trustees, or other persons exercising similar functions of another person; or

  (3) Has the power to exercise a controlling influence over the management or policies of another person.

* * *

(i) Financial instrument means stocks, notes, bonds, and debentures traded on a national securities exchange, OTC margin stocks as defined in Regulation U, 12 CFR part 221, commercial paper, negotiable certificates of deposit, bankers' acceptances, and shares in money market and mutual funds of the type that issue shares in which banks may perfect a security interest. Financial instruments may be denominated in foreign currencies that are freely convertible to U.S. dollars. The term "financial instrument" does not include mortgages.

(j) Loans and extensions of credit means a bank's direct or indirect advance of funds to or on behalf of a borrower based on an obligation of the borrower to repay the funds or repayable from specific property pledged by or on behalf of the borrower.

  (1) Loans or extensions of credit for purposes of 12 U.S.C. 84 and this part include–

      (i) A contractual commitment to advance funds, as defined in paragraph (f) of this section;

      (ii) A maker or endorser's obligation arising from a bank's discount of commercial paper;

(iii) A bank's purchase of securities subject to an agreement that the seller will repurchase the securities at the end of a stated period, but not including a bank's purchase of Type I securities, as defined in part 1 of this chapter, subject to a repurchase agreement, where the purchasing bank has assured control over or has established its rights to the Type I securities as collateral;

(iv) A bank's purchase of third-party paper subject to an agreement that the seller will repurchase the paper upon default or at the end of a stated period. The amount of the bank's loan is the total unpaid balance of the paper owned by the bank less any applicable dealer reserves retained by the bank and held by the bank as collateral security. Where the seller's obligation to repurchase is limited, the bank's loan is measured by the total amount of the paper the seller may ultimately be obligated to repurchase. A bank's purchase of third party paper without direct or indirect recourse to the seller is not a loan or extension of credit to the seller;

(v) An overdraft, whether or not prearranged, but not an intra-day overdraft for which payment is received before the close of business of the bank that makes the funds available;

(vi) The sale of Federal funds with a maturity of more than one business day, but not Federal funds with a maturity of one day or less or Federal funds sold under a continuing contract; and

(vii) Loans or extensions of credit that have been charged off on the books of the bank in whole or in part, unless the loan or extension of credit–

(A) Is unenforceable by reason of discharge in bankruptcy;

(B) Is no longer legally enforceable because of expiration of the statute of limitations or a judicial decision; or

(C) Is no longer legally enforceable for other reasons, provided that the bank maintains sufficient records to demonstrate that the loan is unenforceable.

(2) The following items do not constitute loans or extensions of credit for purposes of 12 U.S.C. 84 and this part–

(i) Additional funds advanced for the benefit of a borrower by a bank for payment of taxes, insurance, utilities, security, and maintenance and operating expenses necessary to preserve the value of real property securing the loan, consistent with safe and

sound banking practices, but only if the advance is for the protection of the bank's interest in the collateral, and provided that such amounts must be treated as an extension of credit if a new loan or extension of credit is made to the borrower;

(ii) Accrued and discounted interest on an existing loan or extension of credit, including interest that has been capitalized from prior notes and interest that has been advanced under terms and conditions of a loan agreement;

(iii) Financed sales of a bank's own assets, including Other Real Estate Owned, if the financing does not put the bank in a worse position than when the bank held title to the assets;

(iv) A renewal or restructuring of a loan as a new "loan or extension of credit," following the exercise by a bank of reasonable efforts, consistent with safe and sound banking practices, to bring the loan into conformance with the lending limit, unless new funds are advanced by the bank to the borrower (except as permitted by § 32.3(b)(5)), or a new borrower replaces the original borrower, or unless the OCC determines that a renewal or restructuring was undertaken as a means to evade the bank's lending limit;

(v) Amounts paid against uncollected funds in the normal process of collection; and

(vi) (A) That portion of a loan or extension of credit sold as a participation by a bank on a nonrecourse basis, provided that the participation results in a pro rata sharing of credit risk proportionate to the respective interests of the originating and participating lenders. Where a participation agreement provides that repayment must be applied first to the portions sold, a pro rata sharing will be deemed to exist only if the agreement also provides that, in the event of a default or comparable event defined in the agreement, participants must share in all subsequent repayments and collections in proportion to their percentage participation at the time of the occurrence of the event.

* * *

(l) Qualifying commitment to lend means a legally binding written commitment to lend that, when combined with all other outstanding loans and qualifying commitments to a borrower, was within the bank's lending limit when entered into, and has not been disqualified.

* * *

(2)   If the bank subsequently chooses to make an additional loan and that subsequent loan, together with all outstanding loans and qualifying commitments to a borrower, exceeds the bank's applicable lending limit at that time, the bank's qualifying commitments to the borrower that exceed the bank's lending limit at that time are deemed to be permanently disqualified, beginning with the most recent qualifying commitment and proceeding in reverse chronological order. When a commitment is disqualified, the entire commitment is disqualified and the disqualified commitment is no longer considered a "loan or extension of credit." Advances of funds under a disqualifed or non-qualifying commitment may only be made to the extent that the advance, together with all other outstanding loans to the borrower, do not exceed the bank's lending limit at the time of the advance, calculated pursuant to § 32.4.

(m)   Readily marketable collateral means financial instruments and bullion that are salable under ordinary market conditions with reasonable promptness at a fair market value determined by quotations based upon actual transactions on an auction or similarly available daily bid and ask price market.

(n)   Readily marketable staple means an article of commerce, agriculture, or industry, such as wheat and other grains, cotton, wool, and basic metals such as tin, copper and lead, in the form of standardized interchangeable units, that is easy to sell in a market with sufficiently frequent price quotations.

(1)   An article comes within this definition if–

(i)   The exact price is easy to determine; and

(ii)   The staple itself is easy to sell at any time at a price that would not be considerably less than the amount at which it is valued as collateral.

(2)   Whether an article qualifies as a readily marketable staple is determined on the basis of the conditions existing at the time the loan or extension of credit that is secured by the staples is made.

(o)   Sale of Federal funds means any transaction between depository institutions involving the transfer of immediately available funds resulting from credits to deposit balances at Federal Reserve Banks, or from credits to new or existing deposit balances due from a correspondent depository institution.

(p)   Standby letter of credit means any letter of credit, or similar arrangement, that represents an obligation to the beneficiary on the part of the issuer:

   (1)   To repay money borrowed by or advanced to or for the account of the account party;

   (2)   To make payment on account of any indebtedness undertaken by the account party; or

   (3)   To make payment on account of any default by the account party in the performance of an obligation.

§ 32.3. Lending limits.

(a)   Combined general limit. A national bank's total outstanding loans and extensions of credit to one borrower may not exceed 15 percent of the bank's capital and surplus, plus an additional 10 percent of the bank's capital and surplus, if the amount that exceeds the bank's 15 percent general limit is fully secured by readily marketable collateral, as defined in § 32.2(m). To qualify for the additional 10 percent limit, the bank must perfect a security interest in the collateral under applicable law and the collateral must have a current market value at all times of at least 100 percent of the amount of the loan or extension of credit that exceeds the bank's 15 percent general limit.

(b)   Loans subject to special lending limits. The following loans or extensions of credit are subject to the lending limits set forth below. When loans and extensions of credit qualify for more than one special lending limit, the special limits are cumulative.

   (1)   Loans secured by bills of lading or warehouse receipts covering readily marketable staples.

      (i)   A national bank's loans or extensions of credit to one borrower secured by bills of lading, warehouse receipts, or similar documents transferring or securing title to readily marketable staples, as defined in § 32.2(n), may not exceed 35 percent of the bank's capital and surplus in addition to the amount allowed under the bank's combined general limit. The market value of the staples securing the loan must at all times equal at least 115 percent of the amount of the outstanding loan that exceeds the bank's combined general limit.

      (ii)   Staples that qualify for this special limit must be nonperishable, may be refrigerated or frozen, and must be fully covered by insurance if such insurance is customary. Whether a staple is

non-perishable must be determined on a case-by-case basis because of differences in handling and storing commodities.

(iii) This special limit applies to a loan or extension of credit arising from a single transaction or secured by the same staples, provided that the duration of the loan or extension of credit is:

    (A) Not more than ten months if secured by nonperishable staples; or

    (B) Not more than six months if secured by refrigerated or frozen staples.

* * *

(2) Discount of installment consumer paper.

(i) A national bank's loans and extensions of credit to one borrower that arise from the discount of negotiable or nonnegotiable installment consumer paper, as defined at § 32.2(e), that carries a full recourse endorsement or unconditional guarantee by the person selling the paper, may not exceed 10 percent of the bank's capital and surplus in addition to the amount allowed under the bank's combined general limit. An unconditional guarantee may be in the form of a repurchase agreement or separate guarantee agreement. A condition reasonably within the power of the bank to perform, such as the repossession of collateral, will not make conditional an otherwise unconditional guarantee.

(ii) Where the seller of the paper offers only partial recourse to the bank, the lending limits of this section apply to the obligation of the seller to the bank, which is measured by the total amount of paper the seller may be obligated to repurchase or has guaranteed.

(iii) Where the bank is relying primarily upon the maker of the paper for payment of the loans or extensions of credit and not upon any full or partial recourse endorsement or guarantee by the seller of the paper, the lending limits of this section apply only to the maker. The bank must substantiate its reliance on the maker with—

    (A) Records supporting the bank's independent credit analysis of the maker's ability to repay the loan or extension of credit, maintained by the bank or by a third party that is

contractually obligated to make those records available for examination purposes; and

(B) A written certification by an officer of the bank authorized by the bank's board of directors or any designee of that officer, that the bank is relying primarily upon the maker to repay the loan or extension of credit.

* * *

(c) Loans not subject to the lending limits. The following loans or extensions of credit are not subject to the lending limits of 12 U.S.C. 84 or this part.

(1) Loans arising from the discount of commercial or business paper.

(i) Loans or extensions of credit arising from the discount of negotiable commercial or business paper that evidences an obligation to the person negotiating the paper. The paper—

(A) Must be given in payment of the purchase price of commodities purchased for resale, fabrication of a product, or any other business purpose that may reasonably be expected to provide funds for payment of the paper; and

(B) Must bear the full recourse endorsement of the owner of the paper, except that paper discounted in connection with export transactions, that is transferred without recourse, or with limited recourse, must be supported by an assignment of appropriate insurance covering the political, credit, and transfer risks applicable to the paper, such as insurance provided by the Export-Import Bank.

(ii) A failure to pay principal or interest on commercial or business paper when due does not result in a loan or extension of credit to the maker or endorser of the paper; however, the amount of such paper thereafter must be counted in determining whether additional loans or extensions of credit to the same borrower may be made within the limits of 12 U.S.C. 84 and this part.

(2) Bankers' acceptances. A bank's acceptance of drafts eligible for rediscount under 12 U.S.C. 372 and 373, or a bank's purchase of acceptances created by other banks that are eligible for rediscount under those sections; but not including—

(i) A bank's acceptance of drafts ineligible for rediscount (which constitutes a loan by the bank to the customer for whom the acceptance was made, in the amount of the draft);

(ii)   A bank's purchase of ineligible acceptances created by other banks (which constitutes a loan from the purchasing bank to the accepting bank, in the amount of the purchase price); and

(iii)   A bank's purchase of its own acceptances (which constitutes a loan to the bank's customer for whom the acceptance was made, in the amount of the purchase price).

(3) (i)   Loans secured by U.S. obligations. Loans or extensions of credit, or portions thereof, to the extent fully secured by the current market value of:

(A)   Bonds, notes, certificates of indebtedness, or Treasury bills of the United States or by similar obligations fully guaranteed as to principal and interest by the United States;

(B)   Loans to the extent guaranteed as to repayment of principal by the full faith and credit of the U.S. government, as set forth in paragraph (c)(4)(ii) of this section.

(ii)   To qualify under this paragraph, the bank must perfect a security interest in the collateral under applicable law.

* * *

§ 32.4. Calculation of lending limits.

(a)   Calculation date. For purposes of determining compliance with 12 U.S.C. 84 and this part, a bank's lending limit shall be calculated as of the most recent of the following dates–

(1)   When the bank's Consolidated Report of Condition and Income is required to be filed; or

(2)   When there is a change in the bank's capital category for purposes of 12 U.S.C. 1831o and part 6 of this chapter.

(b)   Authority of OCC to require more frequent calculations. If the OCC determines for safety and soundness reasons that a bank should calculate its lending limit more frequently than required by paragraph (a) of this section, the OCC may provide written notice to the bank directing the bank to calculate its lending limit at a more frequent interval, and the bank shall thereafter calculate its lending limit at that interval until further notice.

§ 32.5. Combination rules.

(a) General rule. Loans or extensions of credit to one borrower will be attributed to another person and each person will be deemed a borrower–

    (1) When proceeds of a loan or extension of credit are to be used for the direct benefit of the other person, to the extent of the proceeds so used; or

    (2) When a common enterprise is deemed to exist between the persons.

(b) Direct benefit. The proceeds of a loan or extension of credit to a borrower will be deemed to be used for the direct benefit of another person and will be attributed to the other person when the proceeds, or assets purchased with the proceeds, are transferred to another person, other than in a bona fide arm's length transaction where the proceeds are used to acquire property, goods, or services.

(c) Common enterprise. A common enterprise will be deemed to exist and loans to separate borrowers will be aggregated:

    (1) When the expected source of repayment for each loan or extension of credit is the same for each borrower and neither borrower has another source of income from which the loan (together with the borrower's other obligations) may be fully repaid. An employer will not be treated as a source of repayment under this paragraph because of wages and salaries paid to an employee, unless the standards of paragraph (c)(2) of this section are met;

    (2) When loans or extensions of credit are made–

        (i) To borrowers who are related directly or indirectly through common control, including where one borrower is directly or indirectly controlled by another borrower; and

        (ii) Substantial financial interdependence exists between or among the borrowers. Substantial financial interdependence is deemed to exist when 50 percent or more of one borrower's gross receipts or gross expenditures (on an annual basis) are derived from transactions with the other borrower. Gross receipts and expenditures include gross revenues/expenses, intercompany loans, dividends, capital contributions, and similar receipts or payments;

    (3) When separate persons borrow from a bank to acquire a business enterprise of which those borrowers will own more than 50 percent of the voting securities or voting interests, in which case a common

enterprise is deemed to exist between the borrowers for purposes of combining the acquisition loans; or

(4)   When the OCC determines, based upon an evaluation of the facts and circumstances of particular transactions, that a common enterprise exists.

(d)   Special rule for loans to a corporate group.

(1)   Loans or extensions of credit by a bank to a corporate group may not exceed 50 percent of the bank's capital and surplus. This limitation applies only to loans subject to the combined general limit. A corporate group includes a person and all of its subsidiaries. For purposes of this paragraph, a corporation or a limited liability company is a subsidiary of a person if the person owns or beneficially owns directly or indirectly more than 50 percent of the voting securities or voting interests of the corporation or company.

(2)   Except as provided in paragraph (d)(1) of this section, loans or extensions of credit to a person and its subsidiary, or to different subsidiaries of a person, are not combined unless either the direct benefit or the common enterprise test is met.

(e)   Special rules for loans to partnerships, joint ventures, and associations.–

(1)   Partnership loans. Loans or extensions of credit to a partnership, joint venture, or association are deemed to be loans or extensions of credit to each member of the partnership, joint venture, or association. This rule does not apply to limited partners in limited partnerships or to members of joint ventures or associations if the partners or members, by the terms of the partnership or membership agreement, are not held generally liable for the debts or actions of the partnership, joint venture, or association, and those provisions are valid under applicable law.

(2)   Loans to partners.

(i)   Loans or extensions of credit to members of a partnership, joint venture, or association are not attributed to the partnership, joint venture, or association unless either the direct benefit or the common enterprise tests are met. Both the direct benefit and common enterprise tests are met between a member of a partnership, joint venture or association and such partnership, joint venture or association, when loans or extensions of credit are made to the member to purchase an interest in the partnership, joint venture or association.

(ii) Loans or extensions of credit to members of a partnership, joint venture, or association are not attributed to other members of the partnership, joint venture, or association unless either the direct benefit or common enterprise test is met.

* * *

§ 32.6. Nonconforming loans.

(a) A loan, within a bank's legal lending limit when made, will not be deemed a violation but will be treated as nonconforming if the loan is no longer in conformity with the bank's lending limit because–

(1) The bank's capital has declined, borrowers have subsequently merged or formed a common enterprise, lenders have merged, the lending limit or capital rules have changed; or

(2) Collateral securing the loan to satisfy the requirements of a lending limit exception has declined in value.

(b) A bank must use reasonable efforts to bring a loan that is nonconforming as a result of paragraph (a)(1) of this section into conformity with the bank's lending limit unless to do so would be inconsistent with safe and sound banking practices.

(c) A bank must bring a loan that is nonconforming as a result of circumstances described in paragraph (a)(2) of this section into conformity with the bank's lending limit within 30 calendar days, except when judicial proceedings, regulatory actions or other extraordinary circumstances beyond the bank's control prevent the bank from taking action.

CHAPTER II–FEDERAL RESERVE SYSTEM
SUBCHAPTER A–BOARD OF GOVERNORS OF THE FEDERAL RESERVE SYSTEM

PART 215–LOANS TO EXECUTIVE OFFICERS, DIRECTORS, AND PRINCIPAL SHAREHOLDERS OF MEMBER BANKS (REGULATION O)

SUBPART A–LOANS BY MEMBER BANKS TO THEIR EXECUTIVE OFFICERS, DIRECTORS, AND PRINCIPAL SHAREHOLDERS

§ 215.1. Authority, purpose, and scope.

* * *

(b)   Purpose and scope. This subpart A governs any extension of credit by a member bank to an executive officer, director, or principal shareholder of: The member bank; a bank holding company of which the member bank is a subsidiary; and any other subsidiary of that bank holding company. It also applies to any extension of credit by a member bank to: A company controlled by such a person; and a political or campaign committee that benefits or is controlled by such a person. This subpart A also implements the reporting requirements of 12 U.S.C. 375a concerning extensions of credit by a member bank to its executive officers and of 12 U.S.C. 1817(k) concerning extensions of credit by a member bank to its executive officers or principal shareholders, or the related interests of such persons.

§ 215.2. Definitions.

For the purposes of this subpart A, the following definitions apply unless otherwise specified:

* * *

(c)   (1)   Control of a company or bank means that a person directly or indirectly, or acting through or in concert with one or more persons:

(i)   Owns, controls, or has the power to vote 25 percent or more of any class of voting securities of the company or bank;

        (ii)   Controls in any manner the election of a majority of the directors of the company or bank; or

        (iii) Has the power to exercise a controlling influence over the management or policies of the company or bank.

  (2) A person is presumed to have control, including the power to exercise a controlling influence over the management or policies, of a company or bank if:

        (i)   The person is:

              (A) An executive officer or director of the company or bank; and

              (B) Directly or indirectly owns, controls, or has the power to vote more than 10 percent of any class of voting securities of the company or bank; or

        (ii)   (A) The person directly or indirectly owns, controls, or has the power to vote more than 10 percent of any class of voting securities of the company or bank; and

              (B) No other person owns, controls, or has the power to vote a greater percentage of that class of voting securities.

  (3) An individual is not considered to have control, including the power to exercise a controlling influence over the management or policies, of a company or bank solely by virtue of the individual's position as an officer or director of the company or bank.

  (4) A person may rebut a presumption established by paragraph (c)(2) of this section by submitting to the appropriate Federal banking agency (as defined in 12 U.S.C. 1813(q)) written materials that, in the agency's judgment, demonstrate an absence of control.

(d) Director of a company or bank means any director of the company or bank, whether or not receiving compensation. An advisory director is not considered a director if the advisory director:

  (1) Is not elected by the shareholders of the company or bank;

  (2) Is not authorized to vote on matters before the board of directors; and

  (3) Provides solely general policy advice to the board of directors.

(e) (1) Executive officer of a company or bank means a person who participates or has authority to participate (other than in the capacity of a director) in major policymaking functions of the company or bank, whether or not: the officer has an official title; the title designates the officer an assistant; or the officer is serving without

salary or other compensation.[1] The chairman of the board, the president, every vice president, the cashier, the secretary, and the treasurer of a company or bank are considered executive officers, unless the officer is excluded, by resolution of the board of directors or by the bylaws of the bank or company, from participation (other than in the capacity of a director) in major policymaking functions of the bank or company, and the officer does not actually participate therein.

(2)   Extensions of credit to an executive officer of an affiliate of a member bank (other than a company that controls the bank) shall not be subject to §§ 215.4, 215.6 and 215.8 of this part, provided that:

(i)   The executive officer of the affiliate is excluded (by name or by title) from participation in major policymaking functions of the member bank by resolutions of the boards of directors of both the affiliate and the member bank, and does not actually participate in such major policymaking functions; and

(ii)   The executive officer is not otherwise subject to such requirements as a director or principal shareholder.

(f)   Foreign bank has the meaning given in 12 U.S.C. 3101(7).

(g)   Immediate family means the spouse of an individual, the individual's minor children, and any of the individual's children (including adults) residing in the individual's home.

(h)   Insider means an executive officer, director, or principal shareholder, and includes any related interest of such a person.

(i)   Lending limit. The lending limit for a member bank is an amount equal to the limit of loans to a single borrower established by section 5200 of the Revised Statutes, 12 U.S.C. 84. This amount is 15 percent of the bank's unimpaired capital and unimpaired surplus in the case of loans that are not fully secured, and an additional 10 percent of the bank's unimpaired capital and unimpaired surplus in the case of loans that are fully secured by readily marketable collateral having a market value, as determined by reliable and

---

[3]   The term is not intended to include persons who may have official titles and may exercise a certain measure of discretion in the performance of their duties, including discretion in the making of loans, but who do not participate in the determination of major policies of the bank or company and whose decisions are limited by policy standards fixed by the senior management of the bank or company. For example, the term does not include a manager or assistant manager of a branch of a bank unless that individual participates, or is authorized to participate, in major policymaking functions of the bank or company.

continuously available price quotations, at least equal to the amount of the loan. The lending limit also includes any higher amounts that are permitted by section 5200 of the Revised Statutes for the types of obligations listed therein as exceptions to the limit. A member bank's unimpaired capital and unimpaired surplus equals:

(1) The bank's Tier 1 and Tier 2 capital included in the bank's risk-based capital under the capital guidelines of the appropriate Federal banking agency, based on the bank's most recent consolidated report of condition filed under 12 USC 1817(a)(3); and

(2) The balance of the bank's allowance for loan and lease losses not included in the bank's Tier 2 capital for purposes of the calculation of risk-based capital by the appropriate Federal banking agency, based on the bank's most recent consolidated report of condition filed under 12 U.S.C. 1817(a)(3).

* * *

(m) (1) Principal shareholder means a person (other than an insured bank) that directly or indirectly, or acting through or in concert with one or more persons, owns, controls, or has the power to vote more than 10 percent of any class of voting securities of a member bank or company. Shares owned or controlled by a member of an individual's immediate family are considered to be held by the individual.

(2) A principal shareholder of a member bank does not include a company of which a member bank is a subsidiary.

(n) Related interest of a person means:

(1) A company that is controlled by that person; or

(2) A political or campaign committee that is controlled by that person or the funds or services of which will benefit that person.

(o) Subsidiary has the meaning given in 12 U.S.C. 1841(d), but does not include a subsidiary of a member bank.

§ 215.3. Extension of credit.

(a) An extension of credit is a making or renewal of any loan, a granting of a line of credit, or an extending of credit in any manner whatsoever, and includes:

(1) A purchase under repurchase agreement of securities, other assets, or obligations;

(2) An advance by means of an overdraft, cash item, or otherwise;

(3) Issuance of a standby letter of credit (or other similar arrangement regardless of name or description) or an ineligible acceptance, as those terms are defined in § 208.8(d) of this chapter;

(4) An acquisition by discount, purchase, exchange, or otherwise of any note, draft, bill of exchange, or other evidence of indebtedness upon which an insider may be liable as maker, drawer, endorser, guarantor, or surety;

(5) An increase of an existing indebtedness, but not if the additional funds are advanced by the bank for its own protection for:

(i) Accrued interest; or

(ii) Taxes, insurance, or other expenses incidental to the existing indebtedness;

(6) An advance of unearned salary or other unearned compensation for a period in excess of 30 days; and

(7) Any other similar transaction as a result of which a person becomes obligated to pay money (or its equivalent) to a bank, whether the obligation arises directly or indirectly, or because of an endorsement on an obligation or otherwise, or by any means whatsoever.

(b) An extension of credit does not include:

(1) An advance against accrued salary or other accrued compensation, or an advance for the payment of authorized travel or other expenses incurred or to be incurred on behalf of the bank;

(2) A receipt by a bank of a check deposited in or delivered to the bank in the usual course of business unless it results in the carrying of a cash item for or the granting of an overdraft (other than an inadvertent overdraft in a limited amount that is promptly repaid, as described in § 215.4(e) of this part);

(3) An acquisition of a note, draft, bill of exchange, or other evidence of indebtedness through:

(i) A merger or consolidation of banks or a similar transaction by which a bank acquires assets and assumes liabilities of another bank or similar organization; or

(ii) Foreclosure on collateral or similar proceeding for the protection of the bank, provided that such indebtedness is not held for a period of more than three years from the date of the acquisition, subject to extension by the appropriate Federal banking agency for good cause;

(4) (i) An endorsement or guarantee for the protection of a bank of any loan or other asset previously acquired by the bank in good faith; or

(ii) Any indebtedness to a bank for the purpose of protecting the bank against loss or of giving financial assistance to it;

(5) Indebtedness of $15,000 or less arising by reason of any general arrangement by which a bank:

(i) Acquires charge or time credit accounts; or

(ii) Makes payments to or on behalf of participants in a bank credit card plan, check credit plan, or similar open-end credit plan, provided:

(A) The indebtedness does not involve prior individual clearance or approval by the bank other than for the purposes of determining authority to participate in the arrangement and compliance with any dollar limit under the arrangement; and

(B) The indebtedness is incurred under terms that are not more favorable than those offered to the general public;

(6) Indebtedness of $5,000 or less arising by reason of an interest-bearing overdraft credit plan of the type specified in § 215.4(e) of this part; or

(7) A discount of promissory notes, bills of exchange, conditional sales contracts, or similar paper, without recourse.

* * *

§ 215.4. General prohibitions.

(a) Terms and creditworthiness. No member bank may extend credit to any insider of the bank or insider of its affiliates unless the extension of credit:

(1) Is made on substantially the same terms (including interest rates and collateral) as, and following credit underwriting procedures that are not less stringent than, those prevailing at the time for comparable transactions by the bank with other persons that are not covered by this part and who are not employed by the bank; and

(2) Does not involve more than the normal risk of repayment or present other unfavorable features.

(b) Prior approval.

    (1) No member bank may extend credit (which term includes granting a line of credit) to any insider of the bank or insider of its affiliates in an amount that, when aggregated with the amount of all other extensions of credit to that person and to all related interests of that person, exceeds the higher of $25,000 or 5 percent of the member bank's unimpaired capital and unimpaired surplus, unless:

        (i) The extension of credit has been approved in advance by a majority of the entire board of directors of that bank; and

        (ii) The interested party has abstained from participating directly or indirectly in the voting.

    (2) In no event may a member bank extend credit to any insider of the bank or insider of its affiliates in an amount that, when aggregated with all other extensions of credit to that person, and all related interests of that person, exceeds $500,000, except by complying with the requirements of this paragraph (b).

    (3) Approval by the board of directors under paragraphs (b)(1) and (b)(2) of this section is not required for an extension of credit that is made pursuant to a line of credit that was approved under paragraph (b)(1) of this section within 14 months of the date of the extension of credit. The extension of credit must also be in compliance with the requirements of § 215.4(a) of this part.

    (4) Participation in the discussion, or any attempt to influence the voting, by the board of directors regarding an extension of credit constitutes indirect participation in the voting by the board of directors on an extension of credit.

(c) Individual lending limit–No member bank may extend credit to any insider of the bank or insider of its affiliates in an amount that, when aggregated with the amount of all other extensions of credit by the member bank to that person and to all related interests of that person, exceeds the lending limit of the member bank specified in § 215.2(i) of this part. This prohibition does not apply to an extension of credit by a member bank to a company of which the member bank is a subsidiary or to any other subsidiary of that company.

(d) Aggregate lending limit–

    (1) General limit. A member bank may not extend credit to any insider of the bank or insider of its affiliates unless the extension of credit is in an amount that, when aggregated with the amount of all outstanding extensions of credit by that bank to all such insiders, does not exceed

the bank's unimpaired capital and unimpaired surplus (as defined in § 215.2(i) of this part).

(2) Member banks with deposits of less than $100,000,000.

(i) A member bank with deposits of less than $100,000,000 may by an annual resolution of its board of directors increase the general limit specified in paragraph (d)(1) of this section to a level not to exceed two times the bank's unimpaired capital and unimpaired surplus, if:

(A) The board of directors determines that such higher limit is consistent with prudent, safe, and sound banking practices in light of the bank's experience in lending to its insiders and is necessary to attract or retain directors or to prevent restricting the availability of credit in small communities;

(B) The resolution sets forth the facts and reasoning on which the board of directors bases the finding, including the amount of the bank's lending to its insiders as a percentage of the bank's unimpaired capital and unimpaired surplus as of the date of the resolution;

(C) The bank meets or exceeds, on a fully-phased in basis, all applicable capital requirements established by the appropriate Federal banking agency; and

(D) The bank received a satisfactory composite rating in its most recent report of examination.

(ii) If a member bank has adopted a resolution authorizing a higher limit pursuant to paragraph (d)(2)(i) of this section and subsequently fails to meet the requirements of paragraph (d)(2)(i)(C) or (d)(2)(i)(D) of this section, the member bank shall not extend any additional credit (including a renewal of any existing extension of credit) to any insider of the bank or its affiliates unless such extension or renewal is consistent with the general limit in paragraph (d)(1) of this section.

* * *

§ 215.5. Additional restrictions on loans to executive officers of member banks.

The following restrictions on extensions of credit by a member bank to any of its executive officers apply in addition to any restrictions on extensions of credit by a member bank to insiders of itself or its affiliates set forth elsewhere in this part. The restrictions of this section apply only to executive officers of the member bank and not to executive officers of its affiliates.

(a) No member bank may extend credit to any of its executive officers, and no executive officer of a member bank shall borrow from or otherwise become indebted to the bank, except in the amounts, for the purposes, and upon the conditions specified in paragraphs (c) and (d) of this section.

(b) No member bank may extend credit in an aggregate amount greater than the amount permitted in paragraph (c)(4) of this section to a partnership in which one or more of the bank's executive officers are partners and, either individually or together, hold a majority interest. For the purposes of paragraph (c)(4) of this section, the total amount of credit extended by a member bank to such partnership is considered to be extended to each executive officer of the member bank who is a member of the partnership.

(c) A member bank is authorized to extend credit to any executive officer of the bank:

    (1) In any amount to finance the education of the executive officer's children;

    (2) In any amount to finance or refinance the purchase, construction, maintenance, or improvement of a residence of the executive officer, provided:

        (i) The extension of credit is secured by a first lien on the residence and the residence is owned (or expected to be owned after the extension of credit) by the executive officer; and

        (ii) In the case of a refinancing, that only the amount thereof used to repay the original extension of credit, together with the closing costs of the refinancing, and any additional amount thereof used for any of the purposes enumerated in this paragraph (c)(2), are included within this category of credit;

    (3) In any amount, if the extension of credit is secured in a manner described in § 215.4(d)(3)(i)(A) through (d)(3)(i)(C) of this part; and

    (4) For any other purpose not specified in paragraphs (c)(1) through (c)(3) of this section, if the aggregate amount of extensions of credit to that executive officer under this paragraph does not exceed at any

one time the higher of 2.5 per cent of the bank's unimpaired capital and unimpaired surplus or $25,000, but in no event more than $100,000.

* * *

PART 225–BANK HOLDING COMPANIES AND CHANGE IN BANK CONTROL (REGULATION Y)

---

§ 225.2 Definitions.

Except as modified in this regulation or unless the context otherwise requires, the terms used in this regulation have the same meaning as set forth in the relevant statutes.

  (e) (1) "Control" of a bank or other company means (except for the purposes of Subpart E of this part):

     (i) Ownership, control, or power to vote 25 percent or more of the outstanding shares of any class of voting securities of the bank or other company, directly or indirectly or acting through one or more other persons;

     (ii) Control in any manner over the election of a majority of the directors, trustees, or general partners (or individuals exercising similar functions) of the bank or other company;

     (iii) The power to exercise, directly or indirectly, a controlling influence over the management or policies of the bank or other company, as determined by the Board after notice and opportunity for hearing in accordance with § 225.31 of Subpart D of this regulation; or

     (iv) Conditioning in any manner the transfer of 25 percent or more of the outstanding shares of any class of voting securities of a bank or other company upon the transfer of 25 percent or more of the outstanding shares of any class of voting securities of another bank or other company.

    (2) A bank or other company is deemed to control voting securities or assets owned, controlled, or held, directly or indirectly:

     (i) By any subsidiary of the bank or other company;

(ii)   In a fiduciary capacity (including by pension and profit-sharing trusts) for the benefit of the shareholders, members, or employees (or individuals serving in similar capacities) of the bank or other company or of any of its subsidiaries; or

(iii) In a fiduciary capacity for the benefit of the bank or other company or any of its subsidiaries.

§ 225.28 List of permissible nonbanking activities.

(a)   Closely related nonbanking activities. The activities listed in paragraph (b) of this section are so closely related to banking or managing or controlling banks as to be a proper incident thereto, and may be engaged in by a bank holding company or its subsidiary in accordance with the requirements of this regulation.

(b)   Activities determined by regulation to be permissible—

(1)   Extending credit and servicing loans. Making, acquiring, brokering, or servicing loans or other extensions of credit (including factoring, issuing letters of credit and accepting drafts) for the company's account or for the account of others.

(2)   Activities related to extending credit. Any activity usual in connection with making, acquiring, brokering or servicing loans or other extensions of credit, as determined by the Board. The Board has determined that the following activities are usual in connection with making, acquiring, brokering or servicing loans or other extensions of credit:

(i)   Real estate and personal property appraising. Performing appraisals of real estate and tangible and intangible personal property, including securities.

(ii)   Arranging commercial real estate equity financing. Acting as intermediary for the financing of commercial or industrial income-producing real estate by arranging for the transfer of the title, control, and risk of such a real estate project to one or more investors, if the bank holding company and its affiliates do not have an interest in or participate in managing or developing, a real estate project for which it arranges equity financing, and do not promote or sponsor the development of the property.

(iii) Check-guaranty services. Authorizing a subscribing merchant to accept personal checks tendered by the merchant's customers in payment for goods and services, and purchasing from the

merchant validly authorized checks that are subsequently dishonored.

(iv) Collection agency services. Collecting overdue accounts receivable, either retail or commercial.

(v) Credit bureau services. Maintaining information related to the credit history of consumers and providing the information to a credit grantor who is considering a borrower's application for credit or who has extended credit to the borrower.

(vi) Asset management, servicing, and collection activities. Engaging under contract with a third party in asset management, servicing, and collection 2 of assets of a type that an insured depository institution may originate and own, if the company does not engage in real property management or real estate brokerage services as part of these services.

(vii) Acquiring debt in default. Acquiring debt that is in default at the time of acquisition, if the company:

(A) Divests shares or assets securing debt in default that are not permissible, investments for bank holding companies, within the time period required for divestiture of property acquired in satisfaction of a debt previously contracted under § 225.12(b);

(B) Stands only in the position of a creditor and does not purchase equity of obligers of debt in default (other than equity that may be collateral for such debt); and

(C) Does not acquire debt in default secured by shares of a bank or bank holding company.

(viii) Real estate settlement servicing. Providing real estate settlement services.

(3) Leasing personal or real property. Leasing personal or real property or acting as agent, broker, or adviser in leasing such property if:

(i) The lease is on a nonoperating basis,[5]

---

[5] The requirement that the lease be on a nonoperating basis means that the bank holding company may not, directly or indirectly, engage in operating, servicing, maintaining, or repairing leased property during the lease term. For purposes of the leasing of automobiles, the requirement that the lease be on a nonoperating basis means that the bank holding company may not, directly or indirectly: (1) Provide servicing, repair, or maintenance of the leased vehicle during the lease term; (2) purchase parts and accessories in bulk or for an

    (ii)   The initial term of the lease is at least go days;

    (iii)   In the case of leases involving real property:

        (A)   At the inception of the initial lease, the effect of the transaction will yield a return that will compensate the lessor for not less than the lessor's full investment in the property plus the estimated total cost of financing the property over the term of the lease from rental payments, estimated tax benefits, and the estimated residual value of the property at the expiration of the initial lease; and

        (B)   The estimated residual value of property for purposed of paragraph (b)(3)(iii)(A) of this section shall not exceed 25 percent of the acquisition cost of the property to the lessor.

* * *

    (6)   Financial and investment advisory activities. Acting as investment or financial advisor to any person, including (without, in any way, limiting the foregoing):

        (i)   Serving as investment advisor (as defined in section 2(a)(20) of the Investment Company Act of 1940, 15 U.S.C. 80a-2(a)(20)), to an investment company registered under the act, including sponsoring, organizing, and managing a closed-end investment company;

        (ii)   Furnishing general economic information and advice, general economic statistical forecasting services, and industry studies;

        (iii)   Providing advice in connection with mergers, acquisitions, divestitures, investments, joint ventures, leveraged buyouts, recapitalizations, capital structurings, financing transactions and similar transactions, and conduction financial feasibility studies;[6]

        (iv)   Providing information, statistical forecasting, and advice with respect to any transaction in foreign exchange, swaps, and

---

individual vehicle after the lessee has taken delivery of the vehicle; (3) provide the loan of an automobile during servicing of the leased vehicle; (4) purchase insurance for the lessee; or (5) provide for the renewal of the vehicle's licensed merely as a service to the lessee where the lessee could renew the license without authorization from the lessor. The bank holding company may arrange for a third party to provide these services or products.

    [6]   Feasibility studies do not include assisting management with the planning or marketing for a given project or providing general operational or management advice.

similar transactions, commodities, and any forward contract, option, future, option on a future, and similar instruments;

(v) Providing educational courses, and instructional materials to consumers on individual financial management matters; and

(vi) Providing tax-planning and tax-preparation services to any person.

(7) Agency transactional services for customer investments—

(i) Securities brokerage. Providing securities brokerage services (including securities clearing and/or securities execution services on an exchange), whether alone or in combination with investment advisory services, and incidental activities (including related securities credit activities and custodial services), if the securities brokerage services are restricted to buying and selling securities solely as agent for the account of customers and do not include securities underwriting or dealing.

(ii) Riskless principal transactions. Buying and selling in the secondary market all types of securities on the order of customers as a "riskless principal" to the extent of engaging in a transaction in which the company, after receiving an order to buy (or sell) a security from a customer, purchases (or sells) the security for its own account to offset a contemporaneous sale to (or purchase from) the customer. This does not include:

(A) Selling bank-ineligible securities[7] at the order of a customer that is the issuer of the securities, or selling bank-ineligible securities in any transaction where the company has a contractual agreement to place the securities as agent of the issuer; or

(B) Acting as a riskless principal in any transaction involving a bank-ineligible security for which the company or any of its affiliates acts as underwriter (during the period of the underwriting or for 30 days thereafter) or dealer.[8]

---

[7] A bank-ineligible security is any security that a State member bank is not permitted to underwrite or deal in under 12 U.S.C. 24 and 335.

[8] A company or its affiliates may not enter quotes for specific bank-ineligible securities in any dealer quotation system in connection with the company's riskless principal transactions; except that the company or its affiliates may enter "bid" or "ask" quotations, or publish "offering wanted" or "bid wanted" notices on trading systems other than NASDAQ or an exchange, if the company or its affiliate does not enter price quotations on different sides of

(iii)   Private placement services. Acting as agent for the private placement of securities in accordance with the requirements of the Securities Act of 1933 (1933 Act) and the rules of the Securities and Exchange Commission, if the company engaged in the activity does not purchase or repurchase for its own account the securities being placed, or hold in inventory unsold portions of issues of these securities.

(iv)   Futures commission merchant. Acting as a futures commission merchant (FCM) for unaffiliated persons in the execution, clearance, or execution and clearance of any futures contract and option on a futures contract traded on an exchange in the United States or abroad if:

(A)   The activity is conducted through a separately incorporated subsidiary of the bank holding company, which may engage in activities other than FCM activities (including, but not limited to, permissible advisory and trading activities); and

(B)   The parent bank holding company does not provide a guarantee or otherwise become liable to the exchange or clearing association other than for those trades conducted by the subsidiary for its own account or for the account of any affiliate.

(v)   Other transactional services. Providing to customers as agent transactional services with respect to swaps and similar transactions, any transaction described in paragraph (b)(8) of this section, any transaction that is permissible for a state member bank, and any other transaction involving a forward contract, option, futures, option on a futures or similar contract (whether traded on an exchange or not) relating to a commodity that is traded on an exchange.

(8)   Investment transactions as principal—

(i)   Underwriting and dealing in government obligations and money market instruments. Underwriting and dealing in obligations of the United States, general obligations of states and their political subdivisions, and other obligations that state member banks of the Federal Reserve System may be authorized to underwrite and deal in under 12 U.S.C. 24 and 335, including banker's acceptances and certificates of deposit, under the same

---

the market for a particular security during any two-day period.

limitations as would be applicable if the activity were performed by the bank holding company's subsidiary member banks or its subsidiary nonmember banks as if they were member banks.

(ii) Investing and trading activities. Engaging as principal in:

(A) Foreign exchange;

(B) Forward contracts, options, futures, options on futures, swaps, and similar contracts, whether traded on exchanges or not, based on any rate, price, financial asset (including gold, silver, platinum, palladium, copper, or any other metal approved by the Board), nonfinancial asset, or group of assets, other than a bank-ineligible security,[9] if:

(1) A state member bank is authorized to invest in the asset underlying the contract;

(2) The contract requires cash settlement; or

(3) The contract allows for assignment, termination, or offset prior to delivery or expiration, and the company makes every reasonable effort to avoid taking or making delivery; and

(C) Forward contracts, options,[10] futures, options on futures, swaps, and similar contracts, whether traded on exchanges or not, based. on an index of a rate, a price, or the value of any financial asset, nonfinancial asset, or group of assets, if the contract requires cash settlement.

(iii) Buying and selling bullion, and related activities. Buying, selling and storing bars, rounds, bullion, and coins of gold, silver, platinum, palladium, copper, and any other metal approved by the Board, for the company's own account and the account of others, and providing incidental services such as arranging for storage, safe custody, assaying, and shipment.

---

[9] A bank-ineligible security is any security that a state member bank is not permitted to underwrite or deal in under 12 U.S.C. 24 and 33s.

[10] This reference does not include acting as a dealer in options based on indices of bank-ineligible securities when the options are traded on securities exchanges. These options are securities for purposes of the federal securities laws and bank-ineligible securities for purposes of section 20 of the Glass-Steagall Act. 12 U.S.C. 337. Similarly, this reference does not include acting as a dealer in any other instrument that is a bank-ineligible security for purposes of section 20. A bank holding company may deal in these instruments in accordance with the Boards orders on dealing in bank-ineligible securities.

    (9)   Management consulting and counseling activities—

        (i)   Management consulting.

            (A)   Providing management consulting advice:[11]

                (1)   On any matter to unaffiliated depository institutions, including commercial banks, savings and loan associations, savings banks, credit unions, industrial banks, Morris Plan banks, cooperative banks, industrial loan companies, trust companies, and branches or agencies of foreign banks;

                (2)   On any financial, economic, accounting, or audit matter to any other company.

            (B)   A company conducting management consulting activities under this subparagraph and any affiliate of such company may not:

                (1)   Own or control, directly or indirectly, more than 5 percent of the voting securities of the client institution, and

                (2)   Allow a management official, as defined in 12 CFR 212.2(h), of the company or any of its affiliates to serve as a management official of the client institution, except where such interlocking relationship is permitted pursuant to an exemption granted under 12 CFR 212.4(b) or otherwise permitted by the Board.

            (C)   A company conducting management consulting activities may provide management consulting services to customers not described in paragraph (b)(9)(i)(A)(1) of this section or regarding matters not described in paragraph (b)(9)(i)(A)(2) of this section, if the total annual revenue derived from those management consulting services does not exceed 30 percent of the company's total annual revenue derived from management consulting activities.

        (ii)   Employee benefits consulting services. Providing consulting services to employee benefit, compensation and insurance plans,

---

[11]   In performing this activity, bank holding companies are not authorized to perform tasks or operations or provide services to client institutions either on a daily or continuing basis, except as necessary to instruct the client institution on how to perform such services for itself. See also the Board's interpretation of bank management consulting advice (12 CFR 225.131).

including designing plans, assisting in the implementation of plans, providing administrative services to plans, and developing employee communication programs for plans.

(iii) Career counseling services. Providing career counseling services to:

    (A) A financial organization[12] and individuals currently employed by, or recently displaced from a financed organization;

    (B) Individuals who are seeking employment at a financial organization; and

    (C) Individuals who are currently employed in or who seek positions in the finance, accounting, and audit departments of any company.

(10) Support services—

    (i) Courier services. Providing courier services for:

        (A) Checks, commercial papers, documents, and written instruments (excluding currency or bearer-type negotiable instruments) that are exchanged among banks and financial institutions; and

        (B) Audit and accounting media of a banking or financial nature and other business records and documents used in processing such media.[13]

    (ii) Printing and selling MICR-encoded items. Printing and selling checks and related documents, including corporate image checks, cash tickets, voucher checks, deposit slips, savings withdrawal packages, and other forms that require Magnetic Ink Character Recognition (MICR) encoding.

* * *

(14) Data processing.

---

[12] *Financial organization* refers to insured depository institution holding companies and their subsidiaries, other than nonbanking affiliates of diversified savings and loan holding companies that engage in activities not permissible under section 4(c)(8) of the Bank Holding Company Act (12 U.S.C. 1842(C)(8)).

[13] See also the Board's interpretation on courier activities (12 CFR 225.129), which sets forth conditions for bank holding company entry into the activity.

(i)   Providing data processing and data transmission services, facilities (including data processing and data transmission hardware, software, documentation, or operating personnel), data bases, advice, and access to such services, facilities, or data bases by any technological means, if:

(A)   The data to be processed or furnished are financial, banking, or economic; and

(B)   The hardware provided in connection therewith is offered only in conjunction with software designed and marketed for the processing and transmission of financial, banking, or economic data, and where the general purpose hardware does not constitute more than 30 percent of the cost of any packaged offering.

(ii)   A company conducting data processing and data transmission activities may conduct data processing and data transmission activities not described in paragraph (b)(14)(i) of this section if the total annual revenue derived from those activities does not exceed 30 percent of the company's total annual revenues derived from data processing and data transmission activities.

§ 225.31.   Control proceedings.

(a)   Preliminary determination of control.

(1)   The Board may issue a preliminary determination of control under the procedures set forth in this section in any case in which:

(i)   Any of the presumptions of control set forth in paragraph (d) of this section is present; or

(ii)   It otherwise appears that a company has the power to exercise a controlling influence over the management or policies of a bank or other company.

(2)   If the Board makes a preliminary determination of control under this section, the Board shall send notice to the controlling company containing a statement of the facts upon which the preliminary determination is based.

* * *

(d)   Rebuttable presumptions of control. The following rebuttable presumptions shall be used in any proceeding under this section:

(1) Control of voting securities–

    (i) Securities convertible into voting securities. A company that owns, controls, or holds securities that are immediately convertible, at the option of the holder or owner, into voting securities of a bank or other company, controls the voting securities.

    (ii) Option or restriction on voting securities. A company that enters into an agreement or understanding under which the rights of a holder of voting securities of a bank or other company are restricted in any manner controls the securities. This presumption does not apply where the agreement or understanding:

        (A) Is a mutual agreement among shareholders granting to each other a right of first refusal with respect to their shares;

        (B) Is incident to a bona fide loan transaction; or

        (C) Relates to restrictions on transferability and continues only for the time necessary to obtain approval from the appropriate federal supervisory authority with respect to acquisition by the company of the securities.

(2) Control over company–

    (i) Management agreement. A company that enters into any agreement or understanding with a bank or other company (other than an investment advisory agreement), such as a management contract, under which the first company or any of its subsidiaries directs or exercises significant influence over the general management or overall operations of the bank or other company controls the bank or other company.

    (ii) Shares controlled by company and associated individuals. A company that, together with its management officials or controlling shareholders (including members of the immediate families of either), owns, controls, or holds with power to vote 25 percent or more of the outstanding shares of any class of voting securities of a bank or other company controls the bank or other company, if the first company owns, controls, or holds with power to vote more than 5 percent of the outstanding shares of any class of voting securities of the bank or other company.

    (iii) Common management officials. A company that has one or more management officials in common with a bank or other

company controls the bank or other company, if the first company owns, controls or holds with power to vote more than 5 percent of the outstanding shares of any class of voting securities of the bank or other company, and no other person controls as much as 5 percent of the outstanding shares of any class of voting securities of the bank or other company.

(iv)   Shares held as fiduciary. The presumptions in paragraphs (d)(2) (ii) and (iii) of this section do not apply if the securities are held by the company in a fiduciary capacity without sole discretionary authority to exercise the voting rights.

(e) Presumption of non-control–

(1)   In any proceeding under this section, there is a presumption that any company that directly or indirectly owns, controls, or has power to vote less than 5 percent of the outstanding shares of any class of voting securities of a bank or other company does not have control over that bank or other company.

(2)   In any proceeding under this section, or judicial proceeding under the BHC Act, other than a proceeding in which the Board has made a preliminary determination that a company has the power to exercise a controlling influence over the management or policies of the bank or other company, a company may not be held to have had control over the bank or other company at any given time, unless that company, at the time in question, directly or indirectly owned, controlled, or had power to vote 5 percent or more of the outstanding shares of any class of voting securities of the bank or other company, or had already been found to have control on the basis of the existence of a controlling influence relationship.

* * *

CHAPTER TEN

McCARRAN-FERGUSON ACT

(codified at 15 U.S.C. § 1021 *et seq.*)

§ 1. Declaration of policy

Congress hereby declares that the continued regulation and taxation by the several States of the business of insurance is in the public interest, and that silence on the part of the Congress shall not be construed to impose any barrier to the regulation or taxation of such business by the several States.

§ 2. Regulation by State law; Federal law relating specifically to insurance; applicability of certain Federal laws after June 30, 1948

(a) State regulation

The business of insurance, and every person engaged therein, shall be subject to the laws of the several States which relate to the regulation or taxation of such business.

(b) Federal regulation

No Act of Congress shall be construed to invalidate, impair, or supersede any law enacted by any State for the purpose of regulating the business of insurance, or which imposes a fee or tax upon such business, unless such Act specifically relates to the business of insurance: Provided, That after June 30, 1948, the Act of July 2, 1890, as amended, known as the Sherman Act, and the Act of October 15, 1914, as amended, known as the Clayton Act, and the Act of September 26, 1914, known as the Federal Trade Commission Act, as amended, shall be applicable to the business of insurance to the extent that such business is not regulated by State law.

§ 3. Suspension until June 30, 1948, of application of certain Federal laws; Sherman Act applicable to agreements to, or acts of, boycott, coercion, or intimidation

(a)   Until June 30, 1948, the Act of July 2, 1890, as amended, known as the Sherman Act, and the Act of October 15, 1914, as amended, known as the Clayton Act, and the Act of September 26, 1914, known as the Federal Trade Commission Act, and the Act of June 19, 1936, known as the Robinson-Patman Anti-Discrimination Act, shall not apply to the business of insurance or to acts in the conduct thereof.

(b)   Nothing contained in this chapter shall render the said Sherman Act inapplicable to any agreement to boycott, coerce, or intimidate, or act of boycott, coercion, or intimidation.

§ 4. Effect on other laws

Nothing contained in this chapter shall be construed to affect in any manner the application to the business of insurance of the Act of July 5, 1935, as amended, known as the National Labor Relations Act, or the Act of June 25, 1938, as amended, known as the Fair Labor Standards Act of 1938, or the Act of June 5, 1920, known as the Merchant Marine Act, 1920.

§ 5. "State" defined

As used in this chapter, the term "State" includes the several States, Alaska, Hawaii, Puerto Rico, Guam, and the District of Columbia.

EMPLOYEE RETIREMENT INCOME SECURITY ACT OF 1974

(codified at 29 U.S.C. § 1001 *et seq.*)

§ 2. Congressional findings and declaration of policy

(a) Benefit plans as affecting interstate commerce and the Federal taxing power[1]

The Congress finds that the growth in size, scope, and numbers of employee benefit plans in recent years has been rapid and substantial; that the operational scope and economic impact of such plans is increasingly interstate; that the continued well-being and security of millions of employees and their dependents are directly affected by these plans; that they are affected with a national public interest; that they have become an important factor affecting the stability of employment and the successful development of industrial relations; that they have become an important factor in commerce because of the interstate character of their activities, and of the activities of their participants, and the employers, employee organizations, and other entities by which they are established or maintained; that a large volume of the activities of such plans are carried on by means of the mails and instrumentalities of interstate commerce; that owing to the lack of employee information and adequate safeguards concerning their operation, it is desirable in the interests of employees and their beneficiaries, and to provide for the general welfare and the free flow of commerce, that disclosure be made and safeguards be provided with respect to the establishment, operation, and administration of such plans; that they substantially affect the revenues of the United States because they are afforded preferential Federal tax treatment; that despite the enormous growth in such plans many employees with long years of employment are losing anticipated retirement benefits owing to the lack of vesting provisions in such plans; that owing to the inadequacy of current minimum standards, the soundness and stability of plans with respect to adequate funds to pay promised benefits may be endangered; that owing to the termination of plans before requisite funds have been accumulated, employees and their beneficiaries have been deprived of anticipated benefits; and that it is therefore desirable in the interests of employees and

their beneficiaries, for the protection of the revenue of the United States, and to provide for the free flow of commerce, that minimum standards be provided assuring the equitable character of such plans and their financial soundness.

(b)   Protection of interstate commerce and beneficiaries by requiring disclosure and reporting, setting standards of conduct, etc., for fiduciaries

It is hereby declared to be the policy of this chapter to protect interstate commerce and the interests of participants in employee benefit plans and their beneficiaries, by requiring the disclosure and reporting to participants and beneficiaries of financial and other information with respect thereto, by establishing standards of conduct, responsibility, and obligation for fiduciaries of employee benefit plans, and by providing for appropriate remedies, sanctions, and ready access to the Federal courts.

(c)   Protection of interstate commerce, the Federal taxing power, and beneficiaries by vesting of accrued benefits, setting minimum standards of funding, requiring termination insurance

It is hereby further declared to be the policy of this chapter to protect interstate commerce, the Federal taxing power, and the interests of participants in private pension plans and their beneficiaries by improving the equitable character and the soundness of such plans by requiring them to vest the accrued benefits of employees with significant periods of service, to meet minimum standards of funding, and by requiring plan termination insurance.

§ 3. Definitions

For purposes of this subchapter:

(1)   The terms "employee welfare benefit plan" and "welfare plan" mean any plan, fund, or program which was heretofore or is hereafter established or maintained by an employer or by an employee organization, or by both, to the extent that such plan, fund, or program was established or is maintained for the purpose of providing for its participants or their beneficiaries, through the purchase of insurance or otherwise, (A) medical, surgical, or hospital care or benefits, or benefits in the event of sickness, accident, disability, death or unemployment, or vacation benefits, apprenticeship or other training programs, or day care centers, scholarship funds, or prepaid legal services, or (B) any benefit described in section 186(c) of this title (other than pensions on retirement or death, and insurance to provide such pensions).

(2) (A) Except as provided in subparagraph (B), the terms "employee pension benefit plan" and "pension plan" mean any plan, fund, or program which was heretofore or is hereafter established or maintained by an employer or by an employee organization, or by both, to the extent that by its express terms or as a result of surrounding circumstances such plan, fund, or program—

    (i) provides retirement income to employees, or

    (ii) results in a deferral of income by employees for periods extending to the termination of covered employment or beyond, regardless of the method of calculating the contributions made to the plan, the method of calculating the benefits under the plan or the method of distributing benefits from the plan.

(B) The Secretary may by regulation prescribe rules consistent with the standards and purposes of this chapter providing one or more exempt categories under which—

    (i) severance pay arrangements, and

    (ii) supplemental retirement income payments, under which the pension benefits of retirees or their beneficiaries are supplemented to take into account some portion or all of the increases in the cost of living (as determined by the Secretary of Labor) since retirement, shall, for purposes of this subchapter, be treated as welfare plans rather than pension plans. In the case of any arrangement or payment a principal effect of which is the evasion of the standards or purposes of this chapter applicable to pension plans, such arrangement or payment shall be treated as a pension plan.

(3) The term "employee benefit plan" or "plan" means an employee welfare benefit plan or an employee pension benefit plan or a plan which is both an employee welfare benefit plan and an employee pension benefit plan.

* * *

(34) The term "individual account plan" or "defined contribution plan" means a pension plan which provides for an individual account for each participant and for benefits based solely upon the amount contributed to the participant's account, and any income, expenses, gains and losses, and any forfeitures of accounts of other participants which may be allocated to such participant's account.

(35) The term "defined benefit plan" means a pension plan other than an individual account plan; except that a pension plan which is not an individual account plan and which provides a benefit derived from

employer contributions which is based partly on the balance of the separate account of a participant—

(A) for the purposes of section 1052 of this title, shall be treated as an individual account plan, and

(B) for the purposes of paragraph (23) of this section and section 1054 of this title, shall be treated as an individual account plan to the extent benefits are based upon the separate account of a participant and as a defined benefit plan with respect to the remaining portion of benefits under the plan.

* * *

§ 4. Coverage

(a) Except as provided in subsection (b) of this section and in sections 201, 301, and 401 of this title, this subchapter shall apply to any employee benefit plan if it is established or maintained—

(1) by any employer engaged in commerce or in any industry or activity affecting commerce; or

(2) by any employee organization or organizations representing employees engaged in commerce or in any industry or activity affecting commerce; or

(3) by both.

(b) The provisions of this subchapter shall not apply to any employee benefit plan if—

(1) such plan is a governmental plan (as defined in section 3(32) of this title);

(2) such plan is a church plan (as defined in section 3(33) of this title) with respect to which no election has been made under section 410(d) of the Internal Revenue Code of 1986;

(3) such plan is maintained solely for the purpose of complying with applicable workmen's compensation laws or unemployment compensation or disability insurance laws;

(4) such plan is maintained outside of the United States primarily for the benefit of persons substantially all of whom are nonresident aliens; or

(5) such plan is an excess benefit plan (as defined in section 3(36) of this title) and is unfunded.

The provisions of part 7 of subtitle B shall not apply to a health insurance issuer (as defined in section 706(b)(2) of this title) solely by reason of health insurance coverage (as defined in section 703(b)(1) of this title) provided by such issuer in connection with a group health plan (as defined in section 706(a)(1) of this title) if the provisions of this subchapter do not apply to such group health plan.

* * *

§ 203. Minimum vesting standards

(a) Nonforfeitability requirements

Each pension plan shall provide that an employee's right to his normal retirement benefit is nonforfeitable upon the attainment of normal retirement age and in addition shall satisfy the requirements of paragraphs (1) and (2) of this subsection.

(1) A plan satisfies the requirements of this paragraph if an employee's rights in his accrued benefit derived from his own contributions are nonforfeitable.

(2) A plan satisfies the requirements of this paragraph if it satisfies the requirements of subparagraph (A) or (B).

(A) A plan satisfies the requirements of this subparagraph if an employee who has completed at least 5 years of service has a nonforfeitable right to 100 percent of the employee's accrued benefit derived from employer contributions.

(B) A plan satisfies the requirements of this subparagraph if an employee has a nonforfeitable right to a percentage of the employee's accrued benefit derived from employer contributions determined under the following table:

Years of service:	The nonforfeitable percentage is:
3	20
4	40
5	60
6	80
7 or more	100.

* * *

§ 401. Coverage

(a)   Scope of coverage

This part shall apply to any employee benefit plan described in section 1003(a) of this title (and not exempted under section 1003(b) of this title), other than—

(1)   a plan which is unfunded and is maintained by an employer primarily for the purpose of providing deferred compensation for a select group of management or highly compensated employees; or

(2)   any agreement described in section 736 of Title 26, which provides payments to a retired partner or deceased partner or a deceased partner's successor in interest.

(b)   Securities or policies deemed to be included in plan assets

For purposes of this part:

(1)   In the case of a plan which invests in any security issued by an investment company registered under the Investment Company Act of 1940, the assets of such plan shall be deemed to include such security but shall not, solely by reason of such investment, be deemed to include any assets of such investment company.

(2)   In the case of a plan to which a guaranteed benefit policy is issued by an insurer, the assets of such plan shall be deemed to include such policy, but shall not, solely by reason of the issuance of such policy, be deemed to include any assets of such insurer. For purposes of this paragraph:

(A)   The term "insurer" means an insurance company, insurance service, or insurance organization, qualified to do business in a State.

(B)   The term "guaranteed benefit policy" means an insurance policy or contract to the extent that such policy or contract provides for benefits the amount of which is guaranteed by the insurer. Such term includes any surplus in a separate account, but excludes any other portion of a separate account.

(c)   Clarification of application of ERISA to insurance company general accounts

(1)   (A)   Not later than June 30, 1997, the Secretary shall issue proposed regulations to provide guidance for the purpose of determining, in cases where an insurer issues 1 or more policies to or for the benefit of an employee benefit plan (and such policies are

supported by assets of such insurer's general account), which assets held by the insurer (other than plan assets held in its separate accounts) constitute assets of the plan for purposes of this part and section 4975 of Title 26 and to provide guidance with respect to the application of this subchapter to the general account assets of insurers.

(B) The proposed regulations under subparagraph (A) shall be subject to public notice and comment until September 30, 1997.

(C) The Secretary shall issue final regulations providing the guidance described in subparagraph (A) not later than December 31, 1997.

(D) Such regulations shall only apply with respect to policies which are issued by an insurer on or before December 31, 1998, to or for the benefit of an employee benefit plan which is supported by assets of such insurer's general account. With respect to policies issued on or before December 31, 1998, such regulations shall take effect at the end of the 18-month period following the date on which such regulations become final.

(2) The Secretary shall ensure that the regulations issued under paragraph(1)—

(A) are administratively feasible, and

(B) protect the interests and rights of the plan and of its participants and beneficiaries (including meeting the requirements of paragraph (3)).

(3) The regulations prescribed by the Secretary pursuant to paragraph (1) shall require, in connection with any policy issued by an insurer to or for the benefit of an employee benefit plan to the extent that the policy is not a guaranteed benefit policy (as defined in subsection (b)(2)(B) of this section)—

(A) that a plan fiduciary totally independent of the insurer authorize the purchase of such policy (unless such purchase is a transaction exempt under section 408(b)(5) of this title),

(B) that the insurer describe (in such form and manner as shall be prescribed in such regulations), in annual reports and in policies issued to the policyholder after the date on which such regulations are issued in final form pursuant to paragraph (1)(C)—

(i)   a description of the method by which any income and expenses of the insurer's general account are allocated to the policy during the term of the policy and upon the termination of the policy, and

(ii)   for each report, the actual return to the plan under the policy and such other financial information as the Secretary may deem appropriate for the period covered by each such annual report,

(C)   that the insurer disclose to the plan fiduciary the extent to which alternative arrangements supported by assets of separate accounts of the insurer (which generally hold plan assets) are available, whether there is a right under the policy to transfer funds to a separate account and the terms governing any such right, and the extent to which support by assets of the insurer's general account and support by assets of separate accounts of the insurer might pose differing risks to the plan, and

(D)   that the insurer manage those assets of the insurer which are assets of such insurer's general account (irrespective of whether any such assets are plan assets) with the care, skill, prudence, and diligence under the circumstances then prevailing that a prudent man acting in a like capacity and familiar with such matters would use in the conduct of an enterprise of a like character and with like aims, taking into account all obligations supported by such enterprise.

(4)   Compliance by the insurer with all requirements of the regulations issued by the Secretary pursuant to paragraph (1) shall be deemed compliance by such insurer with sections 1104, 1106, and 1107 of this title with respect to those assets of the insurer's general account which support a policy described in paragraph (3).

(5)   (A)   Subject to subparagraph (B), any regulations issued under paragraph (1) shall not take effect before the date on which such regulations become final.

(B)   No person shall be subject to liability under this part or section 4975 of Title 26 for conduct which occurred before the date which is 18 months following the date described in subparagraph (A) on the basis of a claim that the assets of an insurer (other than plan assets held in a separate account) constitute assets of the plan, except—

(i) as otherwise provided by the Secretary in regulations intended to prevent avoidance of the regulations issued under paragraph (1), or

(ii) as provided in an action brought by the Secretary pursuant to paragraph (2) or (5) of section 1132(a) of this title for a breach of fiduciary responsibilities which would also constitute a violation of Federal or State criminal law.

The Secretary shall bring a cause of action described in clause (ii) if a participant, beneficiary, or fiduciary demonstrates to the satisfaction of the Secretary that a breach described in clause (ii) has occurred.

(6) Nothing in this subsection shall preclude the application of any Federal criminal law.

(7) For purposes of this subsection, the term "policy" includes a contract.

§ 402. Establishment of plan

(a) Named fiduciaries

(1) Every employee benefit plan shall be established and maintained pursuant to a written instrument. Such instrument shall provide for one or more named fiduciaries who jointly or severally shall have authority to control and manage the operation and administration of the plan.

(2) For purposes of this subchapter, the term "named fiduciary" means a fiduciary who is named in the plan instrument, or who, pursuant to a procedure specified in the plan, is identified as a fiduciary (A) by a person who is an employer or employee organization with respect to the plan or (B) by such an employer and such an employee organization acting jointly.

(b) Requisite features of plan

Every employee benefit plan shall—

(1) provide a procedure for establishing and carrying out a funding policy and method consistent with the objectives of the plan and the requirements of this subchapter,

(2) describe any procedure under the plan for the allocation of responsibilities for the operation and administration of the plan (including any procedure described in section 1105(c)(1) of this title),

(3) provide a procedure for amending such plan, and for identifying the persons who have authority to amend the plan, and

(4) specify the basis on which payments are made to and from the plan.

(c) Optional features of plan

Any employee benefit plan may provide—

(1) that any person or group of persons may serve in more than one fiduciary capacity with respect to the plan (including service both as trustee and administrator);

(2) that a named fiduciary, or a fiduciary designated by a named fiduciary pursuant to a plan procedure described in section 1105(c)(1) of this title, may employ one or more persons to render advice with regard to any responsibility such fiduciary has under the plan; or

(3) that a person who is a named fiduciary with respect to control or management of the assets of the plan may appoint an investment manager or managers to manage (including the power to acquire and dispose of) any assets of a plan.

§ 403. Establishment of trust

(a) Benefit plan assets to be held in trust; authority of trustees

Except as provided in subsection (b) of this section, all assets of an employee benefit plan shall be held in trust by one or more trustees. Such trustee or trustees shall be either named in the trust instrument or in the plan instrument described in section 1102(a) of this title or appointed by a person who is a named fiduciary, and upon acceptance of being named or appointed, the trustee or trustees shall have exclusive authority and discretion to manage and control the assets of the plan, except to the extent that—

(1) the plan expressly provides that the trustee or trustees are subject to the direction of a named fiduciary who is not a trustee, in which case the trustees shall be subject to proper directions of such fiduciary which are made in accordance with the terms of the plan and which are not contrary to this chapter, or

(2) authority to manage, acquire, or dispose of assets of the plan is delegated to one or more investment managers pursuant to section 1102(c)(3) of this title.

(b) Exceptions

The requirements of subsection (a) of this section shall not apply—

(1) to any assets of a plan which consist of insurance contracts or policies issued by an insurance company qualified to do business in a State;

(2) to any assets of such an insurance company or any assets of a plan which are held by such an insurance company;

(3) to a plan—

(A) some or all of the participants of which are employees described in section 401(c)(1) of Title 26; or

(B) which consists of one or more individual retirement accounts described in section 408 of Title 26; to the extent that such plan's assets are held in one or more custodial accounts which qualify under section 401(f) or 408(h) of Title 26, whichever is applicable.

(4) to a plan which the Secretary exempts from the requirement of subsection (a) of this section and which is not subject to any of the following provisions of this chapter—

(A) part 2 of this subtitle,

(B) part 3 of this subtitle, or

(C) subchapter III of this chapter; or

(5) to a contract established and maintained under section 403(b) of Title 26 to the extent that the assets of the contract are held in one or more custodial accounts pursuant to section 403(b)(7) of Title 26.

(6) Any plan, fund or program under which an employer, all of whose stock is directly or indirectly owned by employees, former employees or their beneficiaries, proposes through an unfunded arrangement to compensate retired employees for benefits which were forfeited by such employees under a pension plan maintained by a former employer prior to the date such pension plan became subject to this chapter.

* * *

§ 404. Fiduciary duties

(a) Prudent man standard of care

(1) Subject to sections 1103(c) and (d), 1342, and 1344 of this title, a fiduciary shall discharge his duties with respect to a plan solely in the interest of the participants and beneficiaries and—

(A) for the exclusive purpose of:

(i) providing benefits to participants and their beneficiaries; and

(ii) defraying reasonable expenses of administering the plan;

(B) with the care, skill, prudence, and diligence under the circumstances then prevailing that a prudent man acting in a like capacity and familiar with such matters would use in the conduct of an enterprise of a like character and with like aims;

(C) by diversifying the investments of the plan so as to minimize the risk of large losses, unless under the circumstances it is clearly prudent not to do so; and

(D) in accordance with the documents and instruments governing the plan insofar as such documents and instruments are consistent with the provisions of this subchapter and subchapter III of this chapter.

(2) In the case of an eligible individual account plan (as defined in section 407(d)(3) of this title), the diversification requirement of paragraph (1)(C) and the prudence requirement (only to the extent that it requires diversification) of paragraph (1)(B) is not violated by acquisition or holding of qualifying employer real property or qualifying employer securities (as defined in section 407(d)(4) and (5) of this title).

* * *

(c) Control over assets by participant or beneficiary

(1) In the case of a pension plan which provides for individual accounts and permits a participant or beneficiary to exercise control over the assets in his account, if a participant or beneficiary exercises control over the assets in his account (as determined under regulations of the Secretary)—

(A) such participant or beneficiary shall not be deemed to be a fiduciary by reason of such exercise, and

(B) no person who is otherwise a fiduciary shall be liable under this part for any loss, or by reason of any breach, which results from such participant's or beneficiary's exercise of control.

* * *

§ 406. Prohibited transactions

(a) Transactions between plan and party in interest

Except as provided in section 408 of this title:

(1) A fiduciary with respect to a plan shall not cause the plan to engage in a transaction, if he knows or should know that such transaction constitutes a direct or indirect—

    (A) sale or exchange, or leasing, of any property between the plan and a party in interest;

    (B) lending of money or other extension of credit between the plan and a party in interest;

    (C) furnishing of goods, services, or facilities between the plan and a party in interest;

    (D) transfer to, or use by or for the benefit of, a party in interest, of any assets of the plan; or

    (E) acquisition, on behalf of the plan, of any employer security or employer real property in violation of section 407(a) of this title.

(2) No fiduciary who has authority or discretion to control or manage the assets of a plan shall permit the plan to hold any employer security or employer real property if he knows or should know that holding such security or real property violates section 407(a) of this title.

* * *

§ 407. Limitation with respect to acquisition and holding of employer securities and employer real property by certain plans

(a) Percentage limitation

Except as otherwise provided in this section and section 1114 of this title:

(1) A plan may not acquire or hold—

    (A) any employer security which is not a qualifying employer security, or

    (B) any employer real property which is not qualifying employer real property.

(2) A plan may not acquire any qualifying employer security or qualifying employer real property, if immediately after such acquisition the aggregate fair market value of employer securities and employer real property held by the plan exceeds 10 percent of the fair market value of the assets of the plan.

(3) (A) After December 31, 1984, a plan may not hold any qualifying employer securities or qualifying employer real property (or both) to the extent that the aggregate fair market value of such

securities and property determined on December 31, 1984, exceeds 10 percent of the greater of—

    (i)   the fair market value of the assets of the plan, determined on December 31, 1984, or

    (ii)   the fair market value of the assets of the plan determined on January 1, 1975.

(B)   Subparagraph (A) of this paragraph shall not apply to any plan which on any date after December 31, 1974; and before January 1, 1985, did not hold employer securities or employer real property (or both) the aggregate fair market value of which determined on such date exceeded 10 percent of the greater of

    (i)   the fair market value of the assets of the plan, determined on such date, or

    (ii)   the fair market value of the assets of the plan determined on January 1, 1975.

(4) (A)   After December 31, 1979, a plan may not hold any employer securities or employer real property in excess of the amount specified in regulations under subparagraph (B). This subparagraph shall not apply to a plan after the earliest date after December 31, 1974, on which it complies with such regulations.

    (B)   Not later than December 31, 1976, the Secretary shall prescribe regulations which shall have the effect of requiring that a plan divest itself of 50 percent of the holdings of employer securities and employer real property which the plan would be required to divest before January 1, 1985, under paragraph (2) or subsection (c) of this section (whichever is applicable).

* * *

§ 408. Exemptions from prohibited transactions

(a)   Grant of exemptions

The Secretary shall establish an exemption procedure for purposes of this subsection. Pursuant to such procedure, he may grant a conditional or unconditional exemption of any fiduciary or transaction, or class of fiduciaries or transactions, from all or part of the restrictions imposed by sections 406 and 407(a) of this title. Action under this subsection may be taken only after consultation and coordination with the Secretary of the Treasury. An exemption granted under this section shall not relieve a

fiduciary from any other applicable provision of this chapter. The Secretary may not grant an exemption under this subsection unless he finds that such exemption is—

(1) administratively feasible,

(2) in the interests of the plan and of its participants and beneficiaries, and

(3) protective of the rights of participants and beneficiaries of such plan.

Before granting an exemption under this subsection from section 406(a) or 407(a) of this title, the Secretary shall publish notice in the Federal Register of the pendency of the exemption, shall require that adequate notice be given to interested persons, and shall afford interested persons opportunity to present views. The Secretary may not grant an exemption under this subsection from section 406(b) of this title unless he affords an opportunity for a hearing and makes a determination on the record with respect to the findings required by paragraphs (1), (2), and (3) of this subsection.

* * *

§ 409. Liability for breach of fiduciary duty

(a) Any person who is a fiduciary with respect to a plan who breaches any of the responsibilities, obligations, or duties imposed upon fiduciaries by this subchapter shall be personally liable to make good to such plan any losses to the plan resulting from each such breach, and to restore to such plan any profits of such fiduciary which have been made through use of assets of the plan by the fiduciary, and shall be subject to such other equitable or remedial relief as the court may deem appropriate, including removal of such fiduciary. A fiduciary may also be removed for a violation of section 1111 of this title.

(b) No fiduciary shall be liable with respect to a breach of fiduciary duty under this subchapter if such breach was committed before he became a fiduciary or after he ceased to be a fiduciary.

* * *

§ 501. Criminal penalties

Any person who willfully violates any provision of part 1 of this subtitle, or any regulation or order issued under any such provision, shall upon conviction be fined not more than $5,000 or imprisoned not more than one year, or both; except that in the case of such violation by a person not an individual, the fine imposed upon such person shall be a fine not exceeding $100,000.

§ 502. Civil enforcement

(a)　Persons empowered to bring a civil action

A civil action may be brought—

(1)　by a participant or beneficiary—

(A)　for the relief provided for in subsection (c) of this section, or

(B)　to recover benefits due to him under the terms of his plan, to enforce his rights under the terms of the plan, or to clarify his rights to future benefits under the terms of the plan;

(2)　by the Secretary, or by a participant, beneficiary or fiduciary for appropriate relief under section 1109 of this title;

(3)　by a participant, beneficiary, or fiduciary (A) to enjoin any act or practice which violates any provision of this subchapter or the terms of the plan, or (B) to obtain other appropriate equitable relief (i) to redress such violations or (ii) to enforce any provisions of this subchapter or the terms of the plan;

(4)　by the Secretary, or by a participant, or beneficiary for appropriate relief in the case of a violation of 105(c) of this title;

(5)　except as otherwise provided in subsection (b) of this section, by the Secretary (A) to enjoin any act or practice which violates any provision of this subchapter, or (B) to obtain other appropriate equitable relief (i) to redress such violation or (ii) to enforce any provision of this subchapter;

(6)　by the Secretary to collect any civil penalty under paragraph (2), (4), (5), or (6) of subsection (c) of this section or under subsection (i) or (l) of this section;

(7)　by a State to enforce compliance with a qualified medical child support order (as defined in section 609(a)(2)(A) of this title);

(8)　by the Secretary, or by an employer or other person referred to in section 101(f)(1) of this title, (A) to enjoin any act or practice which violates subsection (f) of section 101 of this title, or (B) to obtain appropriate equitable relief (i) to redress such violation or (ii) to enforce such subsection; or

(9)　in the event that the purchase of an insurance contract or insurance annuity in connection with termination of an individual's status as a participant covered under a pension plan with respect to all or any portion of the participant's pension benefit under such plan constitutes a violation of part 4 of this subtitle or the terms of the plan, by the

Secretary, by any individual who was a participant or beneficiary at the time of the alleged violation, or by a fiduciary, to obtain appropriate relief, including the posting of security if necessary, to assure receipt by the participant or beneficiary of the amounts provided or to be provided by such insurance contract or annuity, plus reasonable prejudgment interest on such amounts.

* * *

§ 503. Claims procedure

In accordance with regulations of the Secretary, every employee benefit plan shall—

(1)   provide adequate notice in writing to any participant or beneficiary whose claim for benefits under the plan has been denied, setting forth the specific reasons for such denial, written in a manner calculated to be understood by the participant, and

(2)   afford a reasonable opportunity to any participant whose claim for benefits has been denied for a full and fair review by the appropriate named fiduciary of the decision denying the claim.

§ 504. Investigative authority

(a)   Investigation and submission of reports, books, etc.

The Secretary shall have the power, in order to determine whether any person has violated or is about to violate any provision of this subchapter or any regulation or order thereunder—

(1)   to make an investigation, and in connection therewith to require the submission of reports, books, and records, and the filing of data in support of any information required to be filed with the Secretary under this subchapter, and

(2)   to enter such places, inspect such books and records and question such persons as he may deem necessary to enable him to determine the facts relative to such investigation, if he has reasonable cause to believe there may exist a violation of this subchapter or any rule or regulation issued thereunder or if the entry is pursuant to an agreement with the plan.

The Secretary may make available to any person actually affected by any matter which is the subject of an investigation under this section, and to any department or agency of the United States, information concerning any

matter which may be the subject of such investigation; except that any information obtained by the Secretary pursuant to section 6103(g) of Title 26 shall be made available only in accordance with regulations prescribed by the Secretary of the Treasury.

* * *

§ 514. Other laws

(a) Supersedure; effective date

Except as provided in subsection (b) of this section, the provisions of this subchapter and subchapter III of this chapter shall supersede any and all State laws insofar as they may now or hereafter relate to any employee benefit plan described in section 1003(a) of this title and not exempt under section 1003(b) of this title. This section shall take effect on January 1, 1975.

(b) Construction and application

(1) This section shall not apply with respect to any cause of action which arose, or any act or omission which occurred, before January 1, 1975.

(2) (A) Except as provided in subparagraph (B), nothing in this subchapter shall be construed to exempt or relieve any person from any law of any State which regulates insurance, banking, or securities.

(B) Neither an employee benefit plan described in section 1003(a) of this title, which is not exempt under section 1003(b) of this title (other than a plan established primarily for the purpose of providing death benefits), nor any trust established under such a plan, shall be deemed to be an insurance company or other insurer, bank, trust company, or investment company or to be engaged in the business of insurance or banking for purposes of any law of any State purporting to regulate insurance companies, insurance contracts, banks, trust companies, or investment companies.

(3) Nothing in this section shall be construed to prohibit use by the Secretary of services or facilities of a State agency as permitted under section 506 of this title.

(4) Subsection (a) of this section shall not apply to any generally applicable criminal law of a State.

(5) (A) Except as provided in subparagraph (B), subsection (a) of this section shall not apply to the Hawaii Prepaid Health Care Act.

(B) Nothing in subparagraph (A) shall be construed to exempt from subsection (a) of this section—

    (i) any State tax law relating to employee benefit plans, or

    (ii) any amendment of the Hawaii Prepaid Health Care Act enacted after September 2, 1974, to the extent it provides for more than the effective administration of such Act as in effect on such date.

(C) Notwithstanding subparagraph (A), parts 1 and 4 of this subtitle, and the preceding sections of this part to the extent they govern matters which are governed by the provisions of such parts 1 and 4, shall supersede the Hawaii Prepaid Health Care Act (as in effect on or after January 14, 1983), but the Secretary may enter into cooperative arrangements under this paragraph and section 506 of this title with officials of the State of Hawaii to assist them in effectuating the policies of provisions of such Act which are superseded by such parts 1 and 4 and the preceding sections of this part.

(6) (A) Notwithstanding any other provision of this section—

    (i) in the case of an employee welfare benefit plan which is a multiple employer welfare arrangement and is fully insured (or which is a multiple employer welfare arrangement subject to an exemption under subparagraph (B)), any law of any State which regulates insurance may apply to such arrangement to the extent that such law provides—

        (I) standards, requiring the maintenance of specified levels of reserves and specified levels of contributions, which any such plan, or any trust established under such a plan, must meet in order to be considered under such law able to pay benefits in full when due, and

        (II) provisions to enforce such standards, and

    (ii) in the case of any other employee welfare benefit plan which is a multiple employer welfare arrangement, in addition to this subchapter, any law of any State which regulates insurance may apply to the extent not inconsistent with the preceding sections of this subchapter.

(B) The Secretary may, under regulations which may be prescribed by the Secretary, exempt from subparagraph (A)(ii), individually or by class, multiple employer welfare arrangements which are

not fully insured. Any such exemption may be granted with respect to any arrangement or class of arrangements only if such arrangement or each arrangement which is a member of such class meets the requirements of section 3(1) and section 4 of this title necessary to be considered an employee welfare benefit plan to which this subchapter applies.

(C) Nothing in subparagraph (A) shall affect the manner or extent to which the provisions of this subchapter apply to an employee welfare benefit plan which is not a multiple employer welfare arrangement and which is a plan, fund, or program participating in, subscribing to, or otherwise using a multiple employer welfare arrangement to fund or administer benefits to such plan's participants and beneficiaries.

(D) For purposes of this paragraph, a multiple employer welfare arrangement shall be considered fully insured only if the terms of the arrangement provide for benefits the amount of all of which the Secretary determines are guaranteed under a contract, or policy of insurance, issued by an insurance company, insurance service, or insurance organization, qualified to conduct business in a State.

(7) Subsection (a) of this section shall not apply to qualified domestic relations orders (within the meaning of section 206(d)(3)(B)(i) of this title), qualified medical child support orders (within the meaning of section 609(a)(2)(A) of this title), and the provisions of law referred to in section 609(a)(2)(B)(ii) of this title to the extent enforced by qualified medical child support orders.

* * *

CHAPTER TWELVE

SECURITIES ACT OF 1933

(codified at 15 U.S.C. § 77a *et seq.*)

§ 1. Short title

This chapter may be cited as the "Securities Act of 1933."

§ 2(a). Definitions

When used in this subchapter, unless the context otherwise requires—

(1)   The term "security" means any note, stock, treasury stock, bond, debenture, evidence of indebtedness, certificate of interest or participation in any profit-sharing agreement, collateral-trust certificate, preorganization certificate or subscription, transferable share, investment contract, voting-trust certificate, certificate of deposit for a security, fractional undivided interest in oil, gas, or other mineral rights, any put, call, straddle, option, or privilege on any security, certificate of deposit, or group or index of securities (including any interest therein or based on the value thereof), or any put, call, straddle, option, or privilege entered into on a national securities exchange relating to foreign currency, or, in general, any interest or instrument commonly known as a "security", or any certificate of interest or participation in, temporary or interim certificate for, receipt for, guarantee of, or warrant or right to subscribe to or purchase, any of the foregoing.

* * *

(4)   The term "issuer" means every person who issues or proposes to issue any security; except that with respect to certificates of deposit, voting-trust certificates, or collateral-trust certificates, or with respect to certificates of interest or shares in an unincorporated investment trust not having a board of directors (or persons performing similar functions) or of the fixed, restricted management, or unit type, the term "issuer" means the person or persons performing the acts and assuming the duties of depositor or manager pursuant to the provisions of the trust or other agreement or instrument under which such securities are issued; except that in the case of an unincorporated association which provides by its articles for limited liability of any or all of its members, or in the case of a trust, committee, or other legal entity, the trustees or members thereof shall not be individually

liable as issuers of any security issued by the association, trust, committee, or other legal entity; except that with respect to equipment-trust certificates or like securities, the term "issuer" means the person by whom the equipment or property is or is to be used; and except that with respect to fractional undivided interests in oil, gas, or other mineral rights, the term "issuer" means the owner of any such right or of any interest in such right (whether whole or fractional) who creates fractional interests therein for the purpose of public offering.

* * *

(11) The term "underwriter" means any person who has purchased from an issuer with a view to, or offers or sells for an issuer in connection with, the distribution of any security, or participates or has a direct or indirect participation in any such undertaking, or participates or has a participation in the direct or indirect underwriting of any such undertaking; but such term shall not include a person whose interest is limited to a commission from an underwriter or dealer not in excess of the usual and customary distributors' or sellers' commission. As used in this paragraph the term "issuer" shall include, in addition to an issuer, any person directly or indirectly controlling or controlled by the issuer, or any person under direct or indirect common control with the issuer.

* * *

§ 3. Exempted securities

(a) Except as hereinafter expressly provided, the provisions of this subchapter shall not apply to any of the following classes of securities:

(1) Reserved.

(2) Any security issued or guaranteed by the United States or any territory thereof, or by the District of Columbia, or by any State of the United States, or by any political subdivision of a State or territory, or by any public instrumentality of one or more States or territories, or by any person controlled or supervised by and acting as an instrumentality of the Government of the United States pursuant to authority granted by the Congress of the United States; or any certificate of deposit for any of the foregoing; or any security issued or guaranteed by any bank . . . .

(3) Any note, draft, bill of exchange, or banker's acceptance which arises out of a current transaction or the proceeds of which have been or are to be used for current transactions, and which has a maturity at the time of issuance of not exceeding nine months, exclusive of days of

grace, or any renewal thereof the maturity of which is likewise limited;

(4) Any security issued by a person organized and operated exclusively for religious, educational, benevolent, fraternal, charitable, or reformatory purposes and not for pecuniary profit, and no part of the net earnings of which inures to the benefit of any person, private stockholder, or individual; or any security of a fund that is excluded from the definition of an investment company under section 3(c)(10)(B) of the Investment Company Act of 1940;

* * *

(8) Any insurance or endowment policy or annuity contract or optional annuity contract, issued by a corporation subject to the supervision of the insurance commissioner, bank commissioner, or any agency or officer performing like functions, of any State or Territory of the United States or the District of Columbia;

* * *

§ 4. Exempted Transactions

The provisions of section 5 shall not apply to—

(1) transactions by any person other than an issuer, underwriter, or dealer.

(2) transactions by an issuer not involving any public offering.

* * *

§ 5. Prohibitions relating to interstate commerce and the mails

(a) Sale or delivery after sale of unregistered securities

Unless a registration statement is in effect as to a security, it shall be unlawful for any person, directly or indirectly—

(1) to make use of any means or instruments of transportation or communication in interstate commerce or of the mails to sell such security through the use or medium of any prospectus or otherwise; or

(2) to carry or cause to be carried through the mails or in interstate commerce, by any means or instruments of transportation, any such security for the purpose of sale or for delivery after sale.

(b) Necessity of prospectus meeting requirements of section 10 of this title

It shall be unlawful for any person, directly or indirectly—

(1)   to make use of any means or instruments of transportation or communication in interstate commerce or of the mails to carry or transmit any prospectus relating to any security with respect to which a registration statement has been filed under this subchapter, unless such prospectus meets the requirements of section 10 of this title; or

(2)   to carry or cause to be carried through the mails or in interstate commerce any such security for the purpose of sale or for delivery after sale, unless accompanied or preceded by a prospectus that meets the requirements of subsection (a) of section 10 of this title.

(c)   Necessity of filing registration statement

It shall be unlawful for any person, directly or indirectly, to make use of any means or instruments of transportation or communication in interstate commerce or of the mails to offer to sell or offer to buy through the use or medium of any prospectus or otherwise any security, unless a registration statement has been filed as to such security, or while the registration statement is the subject of a refusal order or stop order or (prior to the effective date of the registration statement) any public proceeding or examination under section 8 of this title.

* * *

§ 8. Taking effect of registration statements and amendments thereto

(a)   Effective date of registration statement

Except as hereinafter provided, the effective date of a registration statement shall be the twentieth day after the filing thereof or such earlier date as the Commission may determine, having due regard to the adequacy of the information respecting the issuer theretofore available to the public, to the facility with which the nature of the securities to be registered, their relationship to the capital structure of the issuer and the rights of holders thereof can be understood, and to the public interest and the protection of investors.

* * *

§ 11. Civil liabilities on account of false registration statement

(a) Persons possessing cause of action; persons liable

In case any part of the registration statement, when such part became effective, contained an untrue statement of a material fact or omitted to state a material fact required to be stated therein or necessary to make the statements therein not misleading, any person acquiring such security (unless it is proved that at the time of such acquisition he knew of such untruth or omission) may, either at law or in equity, in any court of competent jurisdiction, sue—

(1) every person who signed the registration statement;

(2) every person who was a director of (or person performing similar functions) or partner in the issuer at the time of the filing of the part of the registration statement with respect to which his liability is asserted;

(3) every person who, with his consent, is named in the registration statement as being or about to become a director, person performing similar functions, or partner;

(4) every accountant, engineer, or appraiser, or any person whose profession gives authority to a statement made by him, who has with his consent been named as having prepared or certified any part of the registration statement, or as having prepared or certified any report or valuation which is used in connection with the registration statement, with respect to the statement in such registration statement, report, or valuation, which purports to have been prepared or certified by him;

(5) every underwriter with respect to such security.

If such person acquired the security after the issuer has made generally available to its security holders an earning statement covering a period of at least twelve months beginning after the effective date of the registration statement, then the right of recovery under this subsection shall be conditioned on proof that such person acquired the security relying upon such untrue statement in the registration statement or relying upon the registration statement and not knowing of such omission, but such reliance may be established without proof of the reading of the registration statement by such person.

(b)   Persons exempt from liability upon proof of issues

Notwithstanding the provisions of subsection (a) of this section no person, other than the issuer, shall be liable as provided therein who shall sustain the burden of proof—

(1)   that before the effective date of the part of the registration statement with respect to which his liability is asserted (A) he had resigned from or had taken such steps as are permitted by law to resign from, or ceased or refused to act in, every office, capacity, or relationship in which he was described in the registration statement as acting or agreeing to act, and (B) he had advised the Commission and the issuer in writing that he had taken such action and that he would not be responsible for such part of the registration statement; or

(2)   that if such part of the registration statement became effective without his knowledge, upon becoming aware of such fact he forthwith acted and advised the Commission, in accordance with paragraph (1) of this subsection, and, in addition, gave reasonable public notice that such part of the registration statement had become effective without his knowledge; or

* * *

§ 14. Contrary stipulations void

Any condition, stipulation, or provision binding any person acquiring any security to waive compliance with any provision of this subchapter or of the rules and regulations of the Commission shall be void.

§ 15. Liability of controlling persons

Every person who, by or through stock ownership, agency, or otherwise, or who, pursuant to or in connection with an agreement or understanding with one or more other persons by or through stock ownership, agency, or otherwise, controls any person liable under sections 11 or 12 of this title, shall also be liable jointly and severally with and to the same extent as such controlled person to any person to whom such controlled person is liable, unless the controlling person had no knowledge of or reasonable ground to believe in the existence of the facts by reason of which the liability of the controlled person is alleged to exist.

§ 17. Fraudulent interstate transactions

(a) Use of interstate commerce for purpose of fraud or deceit

It shall be unlawful for any person in the offer or sale of any securities by the use of any means or instruments of transportation or communication in interstate commerce or by the use of the mails, directly or indirectly--

(1) to employ any device, scheme, or artifice to defraud, or

(2) to obtain money or property by means of any untrue statement of a material fact or any omission to state a material fact necessary in order to make the statements made, in the light of the circumstances under which they were made, not misleading, or

(3) to engage in any transaction, practice, or course of business which operates or would operate as a fraud or deceit upon the purchaser.

(b) Use of interstate commerce for purpose of offering for sale

It shall be unlawful for any person, by the use of any means or instruments of transportation or communication in interstate commerce or by the use of the mails, to publish, give publicity to, or circulate any notice, circular, advertisement, newspaper, article, letter, investment service, or communication which, though not purporting to offer a security for sale, describes such security for a consideration received or to be received, directly or indirectly, from an issuer, underwriter, or dealer, without fully disclosing the receipt, whether past or prospective, of such consideration and the amount thereof.

(c) Exemptions, of section 3 not applicable to this section

The exemptions provided in section 3 of this title shall not apply to the provisions of this section.

Rule 151. Safe harbor definition of certain "annuity contracts or optional annuity contracts" within the meaning of Section 3(a)(8) (codified at 17 C.F.R. § 230.151).

(a) Any annuity contract or optional annuity contract (a "contract") shall be deemed to be within the provisions of section 3(a)(8) of the Securities Act of 1933, Provided, That

(1) The annuity or optional annuity contract is issued by a corporation (the "insurer") subject to the supervision of the insurance commissioner, bank commissioner, or any agency or officer

performing like functions, of any State or Territory of the United States or the District of Columbia;

(2)   The insurer assumes the investment risk under the contract as prescribed in paragraph (b) of this section; and

(3)   The contract is not marketed primarily as an investment.

(b)   The insurer shall be deemed to assume the investment risk under the contract if:

(1)   The value of the contract does not vary according to the investment experience of a separate account;

(2)   The insurer for the life of the contract

(i)   Guarantees the principal amount of purchase payments and interest credited thereto, less any deduction (without regard to its timing) for sales, administrative or other expenses or charges; and

(ii)   Credits a specified rate of interest (as defined in paragraph (c) of this section to net purchase payments and interest credited thereto; and

(3)   The insurer guarantees that the rate of any interest to be credited in excess of that described in paragraph (b)(2)(ii) of this section will not be modified more frequently than once per year.

(c)   The term "specified rate of interest," as used in paragraph (b)(2)(ii) of this section, means a rate of interest under the contract that is at least equal to the minimum rate required to be credited by the relevant nonforfeiture law in the jurisdiction in which the contract is issued. If that jurisdiction does not have any applicable nonforfeiture law at the time the contract is issued (or if the minimum rate applicable to an existing contract is no longer mandated in that jurisdiction), the specified rate under the contract must at least be equal to the minimum rate then required for individual annuity contracts by the NAIC Standard Nonforfeiture Law.

* * *

CHAPTER THIRTEEN

SECURITIES EXCHANGE ACT OF 1934

(codified at 15 U.S.C. § 78a *et seq.*)

§ 1. Short title

This chapter may be cited as the "Securities Exchange Act of 1934."

§ 2. Necessity for regulation

For the reasons hereinafter enumerated, transactions in securities as commonly conducted upon securities exchanges and over-the-counter markets are affected with a national public interest which makes it necessary to provide for regulation and control of such transactions and of practices and matters related thereto, including transactions by officers, directors, and principal security holders, to require appropriate reports, to remove impediments to and perfect the mechanisms of a national market system for securities and a national system for the clearance and settlement of securities transactions and the safeguarding of securities and funds related thereto, and to impose requirements necessary to make such regulation and control reasonably complete and effective, in order to protect interstate commerce, the national credit, the Federal taxing power, to protect and make more effective the national banking system and Federal Reserve System, and to insure the maintenance of fair and honest markets in such transactions:

(1) Such transactions (a) are carried on in large volume by the public generally and in large part originate outside the States in which the exchanges and over-the-counter markets are located and/or are effected by means of the mails and instrumentalities of interstate commerce; (b) constitute an important part of the current of interstate commerce; (c) involve in large part the securities of issuers engaged in interstate commerce; (d) involve the use of credit, directly affect the financing of trade, industry, and transportation in interstate commerce, and directly affect and influence the volume of interstate commerce; and affect the national credit.

(2) The prices established and offered in such transactions are generally disseminated and quoted throughout the United States and foreign countries and constitute a basis for determining and establishing the prices at which securities are bought and sold, the amount of certain taxes owing

to the United States and to the several States by owners, buyers, and sellers of securities, and the value of collateral for bank loans.

(3) Frequently the prices of securities on such exchanges and markets are susceptible to manipulation and control, and the dissemination of such prices gives rise to excessive speculation, resulting in sudden and unreasonable fluctuations in the prices of securities which (a) cause alternately unreasonable expansion and unreasonable contraction of the volume of credit available for trade, transportation, and industry in interstate commerce, (b) hinder the proper appraisal of the value of securities and thus prevent a fair calculation of taxes owing to the United States and to the several States by owners, buyers, and sellers of securities, and (c) prevent the fair valuation of collateral for bank loans and/or obstruct the effective operation of the national banking system and Federal Reserve System.

(4) National emergencies, which produce widespread unemployment and the dislocation of trade, transportation, and industry, and which burden interstate commerce and adversely affect the general welfare, are precipitated, intensified, and prolonged by manipulation and sudden and unreasonable fluctuations of security prices and by excessive speculation on such exchanges and markets, and to meet such emergencies the Federal Government is put to such great expense as to burden the national credit.

§ 3. Definitions and application

(a) Definitions

When used in this chapter, unless the context otherwise requires—

(1) The term "exchange" means any organization, association, or group of persons, whether incorporated or unincorporated, which constitutes, maintains, or provides a market place or facilities for bringing together purchasers and sellers of securities or for otherwise performing with respect to securities the functions commonly performed by a stock exchange as that term is generally understood, and includes the market place and the market facilities maintained by such exchange.

* * *

(4) The term "broker" means any person engaged in the business of effecting transactions in securities for the account of others, but does not include a bank.

(5) The term "dealer" means any person engaged in the business of buying and selling securities for his own account, through a broker or otherwise, but does not include a bank, or any person insofar as he buys or sells securities for his own account, either individually or in some fiduciary capacity, but not as a part of a regular business.

(6) The term "bank" means (A) a banking institution organized under the laws of the United States, (B) a member bank of the Federal Reserve System, (C) any other banking institution, whether incorporated or not, doing business under the laws of any State or of the United States, a substantial portion of the business of which consists of receiving deposits or exercising fiduciary powers similar to those permitted to national banks under the authority of the Comptroller of the currency pursuant to section 92a of Title 12, and which is supervised and examined by State or Federal authority having supervision over banks, and which is not operated for the purpose of evading the provisions of this chapter, and (D) a receiver, conservator, or other liquidating agent of any institution or firm included in clauses (A), (B), or (C) of this paragraph.

* * *

(10) The term "security" means any note, stock, treasury stock, bond, debenture, certificate of interest or participation in any profit-sharing agreement or in any oil, gas, or other mineral royalty or lease, any collateral-trust certificate, preorganization certificate or subscription, transferable share, investment contract, voting-trust certificate, certificate of deposit, for a security, any put, call, straddle, option, or privilege on any security, certificate of deposit, or group or index of securities (including any interest therein or based on the value thereof), or any put, call, straddle, option, or privilege entered into on a national securities exchange relating to foreign currency, or in general, any instrument commonly known as a "security"; or any certificate of interest or participation in, temporary or interim certificate for, receipt for, or warrant or right to subscribe to or purchase, any of the foregoing; but shall not include currency or any note, draft, bill of exchange, or banker's acceptance which has a maturity at the time of issuance of not exceeding nine months, exclusive of days of grace, or any renewal thereof the maturity of which is likewise limited.

§ 4. Securities and Exchange Commission

(a)   Establishment; composition; limitations on commissioners; terms of office

There is hereby established a Securities and Exchange Commission (hereinafter referred to as the "Commission") to be composed of five commissioners to be appointed by the President by and with the advice and consent of the Senate. Not more than three of such commissioners shall be members of the same political party, and in making appointments members of different political parties shall be appointed alternately as nearly as may be practicable. No commissioner shall engage in any other business, vocation, or employment than that of serving as commissioner, nor shall any commissioner participate, directly or indirectly, in any stock-market operations or transactions of a character subject to regulation by the Commission pursuant to this chapter. Each commissioner shall hold office for a term of five years and until his successor is appointed and has qualified, except that he shall not so continue to serve beyond the expiration of the next session of Congress subsequent to the expiration of said fixed term of office, and except (1) any commissioner appointed to fill a vacancy occurring prior to the expiration of the term for which his predecessor was appointed shall be appointed for the remainder of such term, and (2) the terms of office of the commissioners first taking office after June 6, 1934, shall expire as designated by the President at the time of nomination, one at the end of one year, one at the end of two years, one at the end of three years, one at the end of four years, and one at the end of five years, after June 6, 1934.

(b)   Appointment and compensation of staff and leasing authority

(1)   Appointment and compensation

The Commission is authorized to appoint and fix the compensation of such officers, attorneys, examiners, and other experts as may be necessary for carrying out its functions under this chapter, and the Commission may, subject to the civil-service laws, appoint such other officers and employees as are necessary in the execution of its functions and fix their salaries in accordance with chapter 51 and subchapter III of chapter 53 of Title 5.

(2)   Leasing authority

Notwithstanding any other provision of law, the Commission is authorized to enter directly into leases for real property for office, meeting, storage, and such other space as is necessary to carry out its functions, and shall be exempt from any General Services Administration space management regulations or directives.

(c) Acceptance of travel support for Commission activities from non-Federal sources; regulations

Notwithstanding any other provision of law, in accordance with regulations which the Commission shall prescribe to prevent conflicts of interest, the Commission may accept payment and reimbursement, in cash or in kind, from non- Federal agencies, organizations, and individuals for travel, subsistence, and other necessary expenses incurred by Commission members and employees in attending meetings and conferences concerning the functions or activities of the Commission. Any payment or reimbursement accepted shall be credited to the appropriated funds of the Commission. The amount of travel, subsistence, and other necessary expenses for members and employees paid or reimbursed under this subsection may exceed per diem amounts established in official travel regulations, but the Commission may include in its regulations under this subsection a limitation on such amounts.

(d) Acceptance of relocation expenses from former employers by professional fellows program participants

Notwithstanding any other provision of law, former employers of participants in the Commission's professional fellows programs may pay such participants their actual expenses for relocation to Washington, District of Columbia, to facilitate their participation in such programs, and program participants may accept such payments.

(e) Fee payments

Notwithstanding any other provision of law, whenever any fee is required to be paid to the Commission pursuant to any provision of the securities laws or any other law, the Commission may provide by rule that such fee shall be paid in a manner other than in cash and the Commission may also specify the time that such fee shall be determined and paid relative to the filing of any statement or document with the Commission.

(f) Reimbursement of expenses for assisting foreign securities authorities

Notwithstanding any other provision of law, the Commission may accept payment and reimbursement, in cash or in kind, from a foreign securities authority, or made on behalf of such authority, for necessary expenses incurred by the Commission, its members, and employees in carrying out any investigation pursuant to section 78u(a)(2) of this title or in providing any other assistance to a foreign securities authority. Any payment or reimbursement accepted shall be considered a reimbursement to the appropriated funds of the Commission.

§ 5. Transactions on unregistered exchanges

It shall be unlawful for any broker, dealer, or exchange, directly or indirectly, to make use of the mails or any means or instrumentality of interstate commerce for the purpose of using any facility of an exchange within or subject to the jurisdiction of the United States to effect any transaction in a security, or to report any such transaction, unless such exchange (1) is registered as a national securities exchange under section 78f of this title, or (2) is exempted from such registration upon application by the exchange because, in the opinion of the Commission, by reason of the limited volume of transactions effected on such exchange, it is not practicable and not necessary or appropriate in the public interest or for the protection of investors to require such registration.

§ 6. National securities exchanges

(a)   Registration; application

An exchange may be registered as a national securities exchange under the terms and conditions hereinafter provided in this section and in accordance with the provisions of section 78s(a) of this title, by filing with the Commission an application for registration in such form as the Commission, by rule, may prescribe containing the rules of the exchange and such other information and documents as the Commission, by rule, may prescribe as necessary or appropriate in the public interest or for the protection of investors.

(b)   Determination by Commission requisite to registration of applicant as a national securities exchange

An exchange shall not be registered as a national securities exchange unless the Commission determines that--

(1)   Such exchange is so organized and has the capacity to be able to carry out the purposes of this chapter and to comply, and (subject to any rule or order of the Commission pursuant to section 78q(d) or 78s(g)(2) of this title) to enforce compliance by its members and persons associated with its members, with the provisions of this chapter, the rules and regulations thereunder, and the rules of the exchange.

(2)   Subject to the provisions of subsection (c) of this section, the rules of the exchange provide that any registered broker or dealer or natural person associated with a registered broker or dealer may become a member of such exchange and any person may become associated with a member thereof.

(3) The rules of the exchange assure a fair representation of its members in the selection of its directors and administration of its affairs and provide that one or more directors shall be representative of issuers and investors and not be associated with a member of the exchange, broker, or dealer.

(4) The rules of the exchange provide for the equitable allocation of reasonable dues, fees, and other charges among its members and issuers and other persons using its facilities.

(5) The rules of the exchange are designed to prevent fraudulent and manipulative acts and practices, to promote just and equitable principles of trade, to foster cooperation and coordination with persons engaged in regulating, clearing, settling, processing information with respect to, and facilitating transactions in securities, to remove impediments to and perfect the mechanism of a free and open market and a national market system, and, in general, to protect investors and the public interest; and are not designed to permit unfair discrimination between customers, issuers, brokers, or dealers, or to regulate by virtue of any authority conferred by this chapter matters not related to the purposes of this chapter or the administration of the exchange.

(6) The rules of the exchange provide that (subject to any rule or order of the Commission pursuant to section 78q(d) or 78s(g)(2) of this title) its members and persons associated with its members shall be appropriately disciplined for violation of the provisions of this chapter, the rules or regulations thereunder, or the rules of the exchange, by expulsion, suspension, limitation of activities, functions, and operations, fine, censure, being suspended or barred from being associated with a member, or any other fitting sanction.

(7) The rules of the exchange are in accordance with the provisions of subsection (d) of this section, and in general, provide a fair procedure for the disciplining of members and persons associated with members, the denial of membership to any person seeking membership therein, the barring of any person from becoming associated with a member thereof, and the prohibition or limitation by the exchange of any person with respect to access to services offered by the exchange or a member thereof.

(8) The rules of the exchange do not impose any burden on competition not necessary or appropriate in furtherance of the purposes of this chapter.

(9)   The rules of the exchange prohibit the listing of any security issued in a limited partnership rollup transaction (as such term is defined in paragraphs (4) and (5) of section 78n(h) of this title), unless such transaction was conducted in accordance with procedures designed to protect the rights of limited partners, including—

(A)   the right of dissenting limited partners to one of the following:

(i)   an appraisal and compensation;

(ii)   retention of a security under substantially the same terms and conditions as the original issue;

(iii)   approval of the limited partnership rollup transaction by not less than 75 percent of the outstanding securities of each of the participating limited partnerships;

(iv)   the use of a committee of limited partners that is independent, as determined in accordance with rules prescribed by the exchange, of the general partner or sponsor, that has been approved by a majority of the outstanding units of each of the participating limited partnerships, and that has such authority as is necessary to protect the interest of limited partners, including the authority to hire independent advisors, to negotiate with the general partner or sponsor on behalf of the limited partners, and to make a recommendation to the limited partners with respect to the proposed transaction; or

(v)   other comparable rights that are prescribed by rule by the exchange and that are designed to protect dissenting limited partners;

(B)   the right not to have their voting power unfairly reduced or abridged;

(C)   the right not to bear an unfair portion of the costs of a proposed limited partnership rollup transaction that is rejected; and

(D)   restrictions on the conversion of contingent interests or fees into non- contingent interests or fees and restrictions on the receipt of a non- contingent equity interest in exchange for fees for services which have not yet been provided.

As used in this paragraph, the term "dissenting limited partner" means a person who, on the date on which soliciting material is mailed to investors, is a holder of a beneficial interest in a limited partnership that is the subject of a limited partnership rollup

transaction, and who casts a vote against the transaction and complies with procedures established by the exchange, except that for purposes of an exchange or tender offer, such person shall file an objection in writing under the rules of the exchange during the period during which the offer is outstanding.

* * *

(e) Commissions, allowances, discounts, and other fees

    (1) On and after June 4, 1975, no national securities exchange may impose any schedule or fix rates of commissions, allowances, discounts, or other fees to be charged by its members: Provided, however, That until May 1, 1976, the preceding provisions of this paragraph shall not prohibit any such exchange from imposing or fixing any schedule of commissions, allowances, discounts, or other fees to be charged by its members for acting as broker on the floor of the exchange or as odd-lot dealer: And provided further, That the Commission, in accordance with the provisions of section 78s(b) of this title as modified by the provisions of paragraph (3) of this subsection, may—

        (A) permit a national securities exchange, by rule, to impose a reasonable schedule or fix reasonable rates of commissions, allowances, discounts, or other fees to be charged by its members for effecting transactions on such exchange prior to November 1, 1976, if the Commission finds that such schedule or fixed rates of commissions, allowances, discounts, or other fees are in the public interest; and

        (B) permit a national securities exchange, by rule, to impose a schedule or fix rates of commissions, allowances, discounts, or other fees to be charged by its members for effecting transactions on such exchange after November 1, 1976, if the Commission finds that such schedule or fixed rates of commissions, allowances, discounts, or other fees (i) are reasonable in relation to the costs of providing the service for which such fees are charged (and the Commission publishes the standards employed in adjudging reasonableness) and (ii) do not impose any burden on competition not necessary or appropriate in furtherance of the purposes of this chapter, taking into consideration the competitive effects of permitting such schedule or fixed rates weighed against the competitive effects of other lawful actions which the Commission is authorized to take under this chapter.

(2)   Notwithstanding the provisions of section 78s(c) of this title, the Commission, by rule, may abrogate any exchange rule which imposes a schedule or fixes rates of commissions, allowances, discounts, or other fees, if the Commission determines that such schedule or fixed rates are no longer reasonable, in the public interest, or necessary to accomplish the purposes of this chapter.

(3)   (A)   Before approving or disapproving any proposed rule change submitted by a national securities exchange which would impose a schedule or fix rates of commissions, allowances, discounts, or other fees to be charged by its members for effecting transactions on such exchange, the Commission shall afford interested persons (i) an opportunity for oral presentation of data, views, and arguments and (ii) with respect to any such rule concerning transactions effected after November 1, 1976, if the Commission determines there are disputed issues of material fact, to present such rebuttal submissions and to conduct (or have conducted under subparagraph (B) of this paragraph) such cross-examination as the Commission determines to be appropriate and required for full disclosure and proper resolution of such disputed issues of material fact.

(B)   The Commission shall prescribe rules and make rulings concerning any proceeding in accordance with subparagraph (A) of this paragraph designed to avoid unnecessary costs or delay. Such rules or rulings may (i) impose reasonable time limits on each interested person's oral presentations, and (ii) require any cross-examination to which a person may be entitled under subparagraph (A) of this paragraph to be conducted by the Commission on behalf of that person in such manner as the Commission determines to be appropriate and required for full disclosure and proper resolution of disputed issues of material fact.

(C)   (i)   If any class of persons, the members of which are entitled to conduct (or have conducted) cross-examination under subparagraphs (A) and (B) of this paragraph and which have, in the view of the Commission, the same or similar interests in the proceeding, cannot agree upon a single representative of such interests for purposes of cross-examination, the Commission may make rules and

rulings specifying the manner in which such interests shall be represented and such cross-examination conducted.

(ii) No member of any class of persons with respect to which the Commission has specified the manner in which its interests shall be represented pursuant to clause (i) of this subparagraph shall be denied, pursuant to such clause (i), the opportunity to conduct (or have conducted) cross-examination as to issues affecting his particular interests if he satisfies the Commission that he has made a reasonable and good faith effort to reach agreement upon group representation and there are substantial and relevant issues which would not be presented adequately by group representation.

(D) A transcript shall be kept of any oral presentation and cross-examination.

(E) In addition to the bases specified in section 78y(a) of this title, a reviewing Court may set aside an order of the Commission under section 78s(b) of this title approving an exchange rule imposing a schedule or fixing rates of commissions, allowances, discounts, or other fees, if the Court finds—

(1) a Commission determination under subparagraph (A) of this paragraph that an interested person is not entitled to conduct cross-examination or make rebuttal submissions, or

(2) a Commission rule or ruling under subparagraph (B) of this paragraph limiting the petitioner's cross-examination or rebuttal submissions,

has precluded full disclosure and proper resolution of disputed issues of material fact which were necessary for fair determination by the Commission.

* * *

§ 9. Manipulation of security prices

(a) Transactions relating to purchase or sale of security

It shall be unlawful for any person, directly or indirectly, by the use of the mails or any means or instrumentality of interstate commerce, or of any facility of any national securities exchange, or for any member of a national securities exchange—

(1)   For the purpose of creating a false or misleading appearance of active trading in any security registered on a national securities exchange, or a false or misleading appearance with respect to the market for any such security,

   (A)   to effect any transaction in such security which involves no change in the beneficial ownership thereof, or

   (B)   to enter an order or orders for the purchase of such security with the knowledge that an order or orders of substantially the same size, at substantially the same time, and at substantially the same price, for the sale of any such security, has been or will be entered by or for the same or different parties, or

   (C)   to enter any order or orders for the sale of any such security with the knowledge that an order or orders of substantially the same size, at substantially the same time, and at substantially the same price, for the purchase of such security, has been or will be entered by or for the same or different parties.

(2)   To effect, alone or with one or more other persons, a series of transactions in any security registered on a national securities exchange creating actual or apparent active trading in such security or raising or depressing the price of such security, for the purpose of inducing the purchase or sale of such security by others.

(3)   If a dealer or broker, or other person selling or offering for sale or purchasing or offering to purchase the security, to induce the purchase or sale of any security registered on a national securities exchange by the circulation or dissemination in the ordinary course of business of information to the effect that the price of any such security will or is likely to rise or fall because of market operations of any one or more persons conducted for the purpose of raising or depressing the prices of such security.

(4)   If a dealer or broker, or other person selling or offering for sale or purchasing or offering to purchase the security, to make, regarding any security registered on a national securities exchange, for the purpose of inducing the purchase or sale of such security, any statement which was at the time and in the light of the circumstances under which it was made, false or misleading with respect to any material fact, and which he knew or had reasonable ground to believe was so false or misleading.

(5)   For a consideration, received directly or indirectly from a dealer or broker, or other person selling or offering for sale or purchasing or

offering to purchase the security, to induce the purchase or sale of any security registered on a national securities exchange by the circulation or dissemination of information to the effect that the price of any such security will or is likely to rise or fall because of the market operations of any one or more persons conducted for the purpose of raising or depressing the price of such security.

(6) To effect either alone or with one or more other persons any series of transactions for the purchase and/or sale of any security registered on a national securities exchange for the purpose of pegging, fixing, or stabilizing the price of such security in contravention of such rules and regulations as the Commission may prescribe as necessary or appropriate in the public interest or for the protection of investors.

* * *

§ 10. Manipulative and deceptive devices

It shall be unlawful for any person, directly or indirectly, by the use of any means or instrumentality of interstate commerce or of the mails, or of any facility of any national securities exchange—

(a) To effect a short sale, or to use or employ any stop-loss order in connection with the purchase or sale, of any security registered on a national securities exchange, in contravention of such rules and regulations as the Commission may prescribe as necessary or appropriate in the public interest or for the protection of investors.

(b) To use or employ, in connection with the purchase or sale of any security registered on a national securities exchange or any security not so registered, any manipulative or deceptive device or contrivance in contravention of such rules and regulations as the Commission may prescribe as necessary or appropriate in the public interest or for the protection of investors.

* * *

§ 11A. National market system for securities; securities information processors

(a) Congressional findings; facilitating establishment of national market system for securities; designation of qualified securities

(1) The Congress finds that—

(A) The securities markets are an important national asset which must be preserved and strengthened.

(B) New data processing and communications techniques create the opportunity for more efficient and effective market operations.

(C) It is in the public interest and appropriate for the protection of investors and the maintenance of fair and orderly markets to assure—

   (i) economically efficient execution of securities transactions;

   (ii) fair competition among brokers and dealers, among exchange markets, and between exchange markets and markets other than exchange markets;

   (iii) the availability to brokers, dealers, and investors of information with respect to quotations for and transactions in securities;

   (iv) the practicability of brokers executing investors' orders in the best market; and

   (v) an opportunity, consistent with the provisions of clauses (i) and (iv) of this subparagraph, for investors' orders to be executed without the participation of a dealer.

(D) The linking of all markets for qualified securities through communication and data processing facilities will foster efficiency, enhance competition, increase the information available to brokers, dealers, and investors, facilitate the offsetting of investors' orders, and contribute to best execution of such orders.

(2) The Commission is directed, therefore, having due regard for the public interest, the protection of investors, and the maintenance of fair and orderly markets, to use its authority under this chapter to facilitate the establishment of a national market system for securities (which may include subsystems for particular types of securities with unique trading characteristics) in accordance with the findings and to carry out the objectives set forth in paragraph (1) of this subsection. The Commission, by rule, shall designate the securities or classes of securities qualified for trading in the national market system from among securities other than exempted securities. (Securities or classes of securities so designated hereinafter in this section referred to as "qualified securities".)

(3)   The Commission is authorized in furtherance of the directive in paragraph (2) of this subsection—

   (A)   to create one or more advisory committees pursuant to the Federal Advisory Committee Act (which shall be in addition to the National Market Advisory Board established pursuant to subsection (d) of this section) and to employ one or more outside experts;

   (B)   by rule or order, to authorize or require self-regulatory organizations to act jointly with respect to matters as to which they share authority under this chapter in planning, developing, operating, or regulating a national market system (or a subsystem thereof) or one or more facilities thereof; and

   (C)   to conduct studies and make recommendations to the Congress from time to time as to the possible need for modifications of the scheme of self- regulation provided for in this chapter so as to adapt it to a national market system.

* * *

§ 12. Registration requirements for securities

(a)   General requirement of registration

It shall be unlawful for any member, broker, or dealer to effect any transaction in any security (other than an exempted security) on a national securities exchange unless a registration is effective as to such security for such exchange in accordance with the provisions of this chapter and the rules and regulations thereunder.

* * *

(g)   Registration of securities by issuer; exemptions

   (1)   Every issuer which is engaged in interstate commerce, or in a business affecting interstate commerce, or whose securities are traded by use of the mails or any means or instrumentality of interstate commerce shall—

      (A)   within one hundred and twenty days after the last day of its first fiscal year ended after July 1, 1964, on which the issuer has total assets exceeding $1,000,000 and a class of equity security (other than an exempted security) held of record by seven hundred and fifty or more persons; and

(B) within one hundred and twenty days after the last day of its first fiscal year ended after two years from July 1, 1964, on which the issuer has total assets exceeding $1,000,000 and a class of equity security (other than an exempted security) held of record by five hundred or more but less than seven hundred and fifty persons,

register such security by filing with the Commission a registration statement (and such copies thereof as the Commission may require) with respect to such security containing such information and documents as the Commission may specify comparable to that which is required in an application to register a security pursuant to subsection (b) of this section. Each such registration statement shall become effective sixty days after filing with the Commission or within such shorter period as the Commission may direct. Until such registration statement becomes effective it shall not be deemed filed for the purposes of section 78r of this title. Any issuer may register any class of equity security not required to be registered by filing a registration statement pursuant to the provisions of this paragraph. The Commission is authorized to extend the date upon which any issuer or class of issuers is required to register a security pursuant to the provisions of this paragraph.

(2) The provisions of this subsection shall not apply in respect of—

(A) any security listed and registered on a national securities exchange.

(B) any security issued by an investment company registered pursuant to section 80a-8 of this title.

(C) any security, other than permanent stock, guaranty stock, permanent reserve stock, or any similar certificate evidencing nonwithdrawable capital, issued by a savings and loan association, building and loan association, cooperative bank, homestead association, or similar institution, which is supervised and examined by State or Federal authority having supervision over any such institution.

(D) any security of an issuer organized and operated exclusively for religious, educational, benevolent, fraternal, charitable, or reformatory purposes and not for pecuniary profit, and no part of the net earnings of which inures to the benefit of any private shareholder or individual; or any security of a fund that is excluded from the definition of an investment company under section 80a-3(c)(10)(B) of this title.

(E)   any security of an issuer which is a "cooperative association" as defined in the Agricultural Marketing Act, approved June 15, 1929, as amended, or a federation of such cooperative associations, if such federation possesses no greater powers or purposes than cooperative associations so defined.

(F)   any security issued by a mutual or cooperative organization which supplies a commodity or service primarily for the benefit of its members and operates not for pecuniary profit, but only if the security is part of a class issuable only to persons who purchase commodities or services from the issuer, the security is transferable only to a successor in interest or occupancy of premises serviced or to be served by the issuer, and no dividends are payable to the holder of the security.

(G)   any security issued by an insurance company if all of the following conditions are met:

    (i)   Such insurance company is required to and does file an annual statement with the Commissioner of Insurance (or other officer or agency performing a similar function) of its domiciliary State, and such annual statement conforms to that prescribed by the National Association of Insurance Commissioners or in the determination of such State commissioner, officer or agency substantially conforms to that so prescribed.

    (ii)   Such insurance company is subject to regulation by its domiciliary State of proxies, consents, or authorizations in respect of securities issued by such company and such regulation conforms to that prescribed by the National Association of Insurance Commissioners.

    (iii)   After July 1, 1966, the purchase and sales of securities issued by such insurance company by beneficial owners, directors, or officers of such company are subject to regulation (including reporting) by its domiciliary State substantially in the manner provided in section 78p of this title.

(H)   any interest or participation in any collective trust funds maintained by a bank or in a separate account maintained by an insurance company which interest or participation is issued in connection with (i) a stock-bonus, pension, or profit-sharing plan which meets the requirements for qualification under section 401 of Title 26, or (ii) an annuity plan which meets the

requirements for deduction of the employer's contribution under section 404(a)(2) of Title 26.

(3)   The Commission may by rules or regulations or, on its own motion, after notice and opportunity for hearing, by order, exempt from this subsection any security of a foreign issuer, including any certificate of deposit for such a security, if the Commission finds that such exemption is in the public interest and is consistent with the protection of investors.

(4)   Registration of any class of security pursuant to this subsection shall be terminated ninety days, or such shorter period as the Commission may determine, after the issuer files a certification with the Commission that the number of holders of record of such class of security is reduced to less than three hundred persons. The Commission shall after notice and opportunity for hearing deny termination of registration if it finds that the certification is untrue. Termination of registration shall be deferred pending final determination on the question of denial.

(5)   For the purposes of this subsection the term "class" shall include all securities of an issuer which are of substantially similar character and the holders of which enjoy substantially similar rights and privileges. The Commission may for the purpose of this subsection define by rules and regulations the terms "total assets" and "held of record" as it deems necessary or appropriate in the public interest or for the protection of investors in order to prevent circumvention of the provisions of this subsection.

* * *

§ 13. Periodical and other reports

(a)   Reports by issuer of security; contents

Every issuer of a security registered pursuant to section 78l of this title shall file with the Commission, in accordance with such rules and regulations as the Commission may prescribe as necessary or appropriate for the proper protection of investors and to insure fair dealing in the security--

(1)   such information and documents (and such copies thereof) as the Commission shall require to keep reasonably current the information and documents required to be included in or filed with an application or registration statement filed pursuant to section 78l of this title,

except that the Commission may not require the filing of any material contract wholly executed before July 1, 1962.

(2) such annual reports (and such copies thereof), certified if required by the rules and regulations of the Commission by independent public accountants, and such quarterly reports (and such copies thereof), as the Commission may prescribe.

Every issuer of a security registered on a national securities exchange shall also file a duplicate original of such information, documents, and reports with the exchange.

* * *

(d) Reports by persons acquiring more than five per centum of certain classes of securities

(1) Any person who, after acquiring directly or indirectly the beneficial ownership of any equity security of a class which is registered pursuant to section 78l of this title, or any equity security of an insurance company which would have been required to be so registered except for the exemption contained in section 78l(g)(2)(G) of this title, or any equity security issued by a closed-end investment company registered under the Investment Company Act of 1940 or any equity security issued by a Native Corporation pursuant to section 1629c(d)(6) of Title 43, is directly or indirectly the beneficial owner of more than 5 per centum of such class shall, within ten days after such acquisition, send to the issuer of the security at its principal executive office, by registered or certified mail, send to each exchange where the security is traded, and filed with the Commission, a statement containing such of the following information, and such additional information, as the Commission may by rules and regulations, prescribe as necessary or appropriate in the public interest or for the protection of investors—

(A) the background, and identity, residence, and citizenship of, and the nature of such beneficial ownership by, such person and all other persons by whom or on whose behalf the purchases have been or are to be effected;

(B) the source and amount of the funds or other consideration used or to be used in making the purchases, and if any part of the purchase price is represented or is to be represented by funds or other consideration borrowed or otherwise obtained for the purpose of acquiring, holding, or trading such security, a description of the transaction and the names of the parties

thereto, except that where a source of funds is a loan made in the ordinary course of business by a bank, as defined in section 78c(a)(6) of this title, if the person filing such statement so requests, the name of the bank shall not be made available to the public;

(C)   if the purpose of the purchases or prospective purchases is to acquire control of the business of the issuer of the securities, any plans or proposals which such persons may have to liquidate such issuer, to sell its assets to or merge it with any other persons, or to make any other major change in its business or corporate structure;

(D)   the number of shares of such security which are beneficially owned, and the number of shares concerning which there is a right to acquire, directly or indirectly, by (i) such person, and (ii) by each associate of such person, giving the background, identity, residence, and citizenship of each such associate; and

(E)   information as to any contracts, arrangements, or understandings with any person with respect to any securities of the issuer, including but not limited to transfer of any of the securities, joint ventures, loan or option arrangements, puts or calls, guaranties of loans, guaranties against loss or guaranties of profits, division of losses or profits, or the giving or withholding of proxies, naming the persons with whom such contracts, arrangements, or understandings have been entered into, and giving the details thereof.

(2)   If any material change occurs in the facts set forth in the statements to the issuer and the exchange, and in the statement filed with the Commission, an amendment shall be transmitted to the issuer and the exchange and shall be filed with the Commission, in accordance with such rules and regulations as the Commission may prescribe as necessary or appropriate in the public interest or for the protection of investors.

(3)   When two or more persons act as a partnership, limited partnership, syndicate, or other group for the purpose of acquiring, holding, or disposing of securities of an issuer, such syndicate or group shall be deemed a "person" for the purposes of this subsection.

(4)   In determining, for purposes of this subsection, any percentage of a class of any security, such class shall be deemed to consist of the amount of the outstanding securities of such class, exclusive of any

securities of such class held by or for the account of the issuer or a subsidiary of the issuer.

(5) The Commission, by rule or regulation or by order, may permit any person to file in lieu of the statement required by paragraph (1) of this subsection or the rules and regulations thereunder, a notice stating the name of such person, the number of shares of any equity securities subject to paragraph (1) which are owned by him, the date of their acquisition and such other information as the Commission may specify, if it appears to the Commission that such securities were acquired by such person in the ordinary course of his business and were not acquired for the purpose of and do not have the effect of changing or influencing the control of the issuer nor in connection with or as a participant in any transaction having such purpose or effect.

(6) The provisions of this subsection shall not apply to—

(A) any acquisition or offer to acquire securities made or proposed to be made by means of a registration statement under the Securities Act of 1933;

(B) any acquisition of the beneficial ownership of a security which, together with all other acquisitions by the same person of securities of the same class during the preceding twelve months, does not exceed 2 per centum of that class;

(C) any acquisition of an equity security by the issuer of such security;

(D) any acquisition or proposed acquisition of a security which the Commission, by rules or regulations or by order, shall exempt from the provisions of this subsection as not entered into for the purpose of, and not having the effect of, changing or influencing the control of the issuer or otherwise as not comprehended within the purposes of this subsection.

* * *

§ 14. Proxies

(a) Solicitation of proxies in violation of rules and regulations

It shall be unlawful for any person, by the use of the mails or by any means or instrumentality of interstate commerce or of any facility of a national securities exchange or otherwise, in contravention of such rules and regulations as the Commission may prescribe as necessary or

appropriate in the public interest or for the protection of investors, to solicit or to permit the use of his name to solicit any proxy or consent or authorization in respect of any security (other than an exempted security) registered pursuant to section 78l of this title.

* * *

§ 15. Registration and regulation of brokers and dealers

(a)   Registration of all persons utilizing exchange facilities to effect transactions; exemptions

(1)   It shall be unlawful for any broker or dealer which is either a person other than a natural person or a natural person not associated with a broker or dealer which is a person other than a natural person (other than such a broker or dealer whose business is exclusively intrastate and who does not make use of any facility of a national securities exchange) to make use of the mails or any means or instrumentality of interstate commerce to effect any transactions in, or to induce or attempt to induce the purchase or sale of, any security (other than an exempted security or commercial paper, bankers' acceptances, or commercial bills) unless such broker or dealer is registered in accordance with subsection (b) of this section.

(2)   The Commission, by rule or order, as it deems consistent with the public interest and the protection of investors, may conditionally or unconditionally exempt from paragraph (1) of this subsection any broker or dealer or class of brokers or dealers specified in such rule or order.

(b)   Manner of registration of brokers and dealers

(1)   A broker or dealer may be registered by filing with the Commission an application for registration in such form and containing such information and documents concerning such broker or dealer and any persons associated with such broker or dealer as the Commission, by rule, may prescribe as necessary or appropriate in the public interest or for the protection of investors. Within forty-five days of the date of the filing of such application (or within such longer period as to which the applicant consents), the Commission shall—

(A)   by order grant registration, or

(B)   institute proceedings to determine whether registration should be denied. Such proceedings shall include notice of the grounds for denial under consideration and opportunity for hearing and shall

be concluded within one hundred twenty days of the date of the filing of the application for registration. At the conclusion of such proceedings, the Commission, by order, shall grant or deny such registration. The order granting registration shall not be effective until such broker or dealer has become a member of a registered securities association, or until such broker or dealer has become a member of a national securities exchange if such broker or dealer effects transactions solely on that exchange, unless the Commission has exempted such broker or dealer, by rule or order, from such membership. The Commission may extend the time for conclusion of such proceedings for up to ninety days if it finds good cause for such extension and publishes its reasons for so finding or for such longer period as to which the applicant consents.

The Commission shall grant such registration if the Commission finds that the requirements of this section are satisfied. The Commission shall deny such registration if it does not make such a finding or if it finds that if the applicant were so registered, its registration would be subject to suspension or revocation under paragraph (4) of this subsection.

(2) (A) An application for registration of a broker or dealer to be formed or organized may be made by a broker or dealer to which the broker or dealer to be formed or organized is to be the successor. Such application, in such form as the Commission, by rule, may prescribe, shall contain such information and documents concerning the applicant, the successor, and any persons associated with the applicant or the successor, as the Commission, by rule, may prescribe as necessary or appropriate in the public interest or for the protection of investors. The grant or denial of registration to such an applicant shall be in accordance with the procedures set forth in paragraph (1) of this subsection. If the Commission grants such registration, the registration shall terminate on the forty-fifth day after the effective date thereof, unless prior thereto the successor shall, in accordance with such rules and regulations as the Commission may prescribe, adopt the application for registration as its own.

(B) Any person who is a broker or dealer solely by reason of acting as a municipal securities dealer or municipal securities broker, who so acts through a separately identifiable department or division, and who so acted in such a manner on June 4, 1975, may, in accordance with such terms and conditions as the

Commission, by rule, prescribes as necessary and appropriate in the public interest and for the protection of investors, register such separately identifiable department or division in accordance with this subsection. If any such department or division is so registered, the department or division and not such person himself shall be the broker or dealer for purposes of this chapter.

(C) Within six months of the date of the granting of registration to a broker or dealer, the Commission, or upon the authorization and direction of the Commission, a registered securities association or national securities exchange of which such broker or dealer is a member, shall conduct an inspection of the broker or dealer to determine whether it is operating in conformity with the provisions of this chapter and the rules and regulations thereunder: Provided, however, That the Commission may delay such inspection of any class of brokers or dealers for a period not to exceed six months.

(3) Any provision of this chapter (other than section 78e of this title and subsection (a) of this section) which prohibits any act, practice, or course of business if the mails or any means or instrumentality of interstate commerce is used in connection therewith shall also prohibit any such act, practice, or course of business by any registered broker or dealer or any person acting on behalf of such a broker or dealer, irrespective of any use of the mails or any means or instrumentality of interstate commerce in connection therewith.

(4) The Commission, by order, shall censure, place limitations on the activities, functions, or operations of, suspend for a period not exceeding twelve months, or revoke the registration of any broker or dealer if it finds, on the record after notice and opportunity for hearing, that such censure, placing of limitations, suspension, or revocation is in the public interest and that such broker or dealer, whether prior or subsequent to becoming such, or any person associated with such broker or dealer, whether prior or subsequent to becoming so associated—

(A) has willfully made or caused to be made in any application for registration or report required to be filed with the Commission or with any other appropriate regulatory agency under this chapter, or in any proceeding before the Commission with respect to registration, any statement which was at the time and in the light of the circumstances under which it was made false or misleading with respect to any material fact, or has omitted to

state in any such application or report any material fact which is required to be stated therein.

(B) has been convicted within ten years preceding the filing of any application for registration or at any time thereafter of any felony or misdemeanor or of a substantially equivalent crime by a foreign court of competent jurisdiction which the Commission finds—

    (i) involves the purchase or sale of any security, the taking of a false oath, the making of a false report, bribery, perjury, burglary, any substantially equivalent activity however denominated by the laws of the relevant foreign government, or conspiracy to commit any such offense;

    (ii) arises out of the conduct of the business of a broker, dealer, municipal securities dealer, government securities broker, government securities dealer, investment adviser, bank, insurance company, fiduciary, transfer agent, foreign person performing a function substantially equivalent to any of the above, or entity or person required to be registered under the Commodity Exchange Act or any substantially equivalent foreign statute or regulation;

    (iii) involves the larceny, theft, robbery, extortion, forgery, counterfeiting, fraudulent concealment, embezzlement, fraudulent conversion, or misappropriation of funds, or securities, or substantially equivalent activity however denominated by the laws of the relevant foreign government; or

    (iv) involves the violation of section 152, 1341, 1342, or 1343 or chapter 25 or 47 of Title 18, or a violation of a substantially equivalent foreign statute.

(C) is permanently or temporarily enjoined by order, judgment, or decree of any court of competent jurisdiction from acting as an investment adviser, underwriter, broker, dealer, municipal securities dealer, government securities broker, government securities dealer, transfer agent, foreign person performing a function substantially equivalent to any of the above, or entity or person required to be registered under the Commodity Exchange Act or any substantially equivalent foreign statute or regulation, or as an affiliated person or employee of any investment company, bank, insurance company, foreign entity substantially equivalent to any of the above, or entity or person required to be

registered under the Commodity Exchange Act or any substantially equivalent foreign statute or regulation or from engaging in or continuing any conduct or practice in connection with any such activity, or in connection with the purchase or sale of any security.

(D) has willfully violated any provision of the Securities Act of 1933, the Investment Advisers Act of 1940, the Investment Company Act of 1940, the Commodity Exchange Act, this chapter, the rules or regulations under any of such statutes, or the rules of the Municipal Securities Rulemaking Board, or is unable to comply with any such provision.

(E) has willfully aided, abetted, counseled, commanded, induced, or procured the violation by any other person of any provision of the Securities Act of 1933, the Investment Advisers Act of 1940, the Investment Company Act of 1940, the Commodity Exchange Act, this chapter, the rules or regulations under any of such statutes, or the rules of the Municipal Securities Rulemaking Board, or has failed reasonably to supervise, with a view to preventing violations of the provisions of such statutes, rules, and regulations, another person who commits such a violation, if such other person is subject to his supervision. For the purposes of this subparagraph (E) no person shall be deemed to have failed reasonably to supervise any other person, if—

   (i) there have been established procedures, and a system for applying such procedures, which would reasonably be expected to prevent and detect, insofar as practicable, any such violation by such other person, and

   (ii) such person has reasonably discharged the duties and obligations incumbent upon him by reason of such procedures and system without reasonable cause to believe that such procedures and system were not being complied with.

(F) is subject to an order of the Commission entered pursuant to paragraph (6) of this subsection (b) barring or suspending the right of such person to be associated with a broker or dealer.

(G) has been found by a foreign financial regulatory authority to have—

   (i) made or caused to be made in any application for registration or report required to be filed with a foreign

financial regulatory authority, or in any proceeding before a foreign financial regulatory authority with respect to registration, any statement that was at the time and in the light of the circumstances under which it was made false or misleading with respect to any material fact, or has omitted to state in any application or report to the foreign financial regulatory authority any material fact that is required to be stated therein;

(ii) violated any foreign statute or regulation regarding transactions in securities, or contracts of sale of a commodity for future delivery, traded on or subject to the rules of a contract market or any board of trade;

(iii) aided, abetted, counseled, commanded, induced, or procured the violation by any person of any provision of any statutory provisions enacted by a foreign government, or rules or regulations thereunder, empowering a foreign financial regulatory authority regarding transactions in securities, or contracts of sale of a commodity for future delivery, traded on or subject to the rules of a contract market or any board of trade, or has been found, by a foreign financial regulatory authority, to have failed reasonably to supervise, with a view to preventing violations of such statutory provisions, rules, and regulations, another person who commits such a violation, if such other person is subject to his supervision.

(5) Pending final determination whether any registration under this subsection shall be revoked, the Commission, by order, may suspend such registration, if such suspension appears to the Commission, after notice and opportunity for hearing, to be necessary or appropriate in the public interest or for the protection of investors. Any registered broker or dealer may, upon such terms and conditions as the Commission deems necessary or appropriate in the public interest or for the protection of investors, withdraw from registration by filing a written notice of withdrawal with the Commission. If the Commission finds that any registered broker or dealer is no longer in existence or has ceased to do business as a broker or dealer, the Commission, by order, shall cancel the registration of such broker or dealer.

(6) (A) With respect to any person who is associated, who is seeking to become associated, or, at the time of the alleged misconduct,

who was associated or was seeking to become associated with a broker or dealer, or any person participating, or, at the time of the alleged misconduct, who was participating, in an offering of any penny stock, the Commission, by order, shall censure, place limitations on the activities or functions of such person, or suspend for a period not exceeding 12 months, or bar such person from being associated with a broker or dealer, or from participating in an offering of penny stock, if the Commission finds, on the record after notice and opportunity for a hearing, that such censure, placing of limitations, suspension, or bar is in the public interest and that such person—

(i) has committed or omitted any act or omission enumerated in subparagraph (A), (D), or (E) of paragraph (4) of this subsection;

(ii) has been convicted of any offense specified in subparagraph (B) of such paragraph (4) within 10 years of the commencement of the proceedings under this paragraph; or

(iii) is enjoined from any action, conduct, or practice specified in subparagraph (C) of such paragraph (4).

(B) It shall be unlawful—

(i) for any person as to whom an order under subparagraph (A) is in effect, without the consent of the Commission, willfully to become, or to be, associated with a broker or dealer in contravention of such order, or to participate in an offering of penny stock in contravention of such order;

(ii) for any broker or dealer to permit such a person, without the consent of the Commission, to become or remain, a person associated with the broker or dealer in contravention of such order, if such broker or dealer knew, or in the exercise of reasonable care should have known, of such order; or

(iii) for any broker or dealer to permit such a person, without the consent of the Commission, to participate in an offering of penny stock in contravention of such order, if such broker or dealer knew, or in the exercise of reasonable care should have known, of such order and of such participation.

(C) For purposes of this paragraph, the term "person participating in an offering of penny stock" includes any person acting as any promoter, finder, consultant, agent, or other person who engages in activities with a broker, dealer, or issuer for purposes of the issuance or trading in any penny stock, or inducing or attempting to induce the purchase or sale of any penny stock. The Commission may, by rule or regulation, define such term to include other activities, and may, by rule, regulation, or order, exempt any person or class of persons, in whole or in part, conditionally or unconditionally, from such term.

(7) No registered broker or dealer or government securities broker or government securities dealer registered (or required to register) under section 78o-5(a)(1)(A) of this title shall effect any transaction in, or induce the purchase or sale of, any security unless such broker or dealer meets such standards of operational capability and such broker or dealer and all natural persons associated with such broker or dealer meet such standards of training, experience, competence, and such other qualifications as the Commission finds necessary or appropriate in the public interest or for the protection of investors. The Commission shall establish such standards by rules and regulations, which may—

(A) specify that all or any portion of such standards shall be applicable to any class of brokers and dealers and persons associated with brokers and dealers;

(B) require persons in any such class to pass tests prescribed in accordance with such rules and regulations, which tests shall, with respect to any class of partners, officers, or supervisory employees (which latter term may be defined by the Commission's rules and regulations and as so defined shall include branch managers of brokers or dealers) engaged in the management of the broker or dealer, include questions relating to bookkeeping, accounting, internal control over cash and securities, supervision of employees, maintenance of records, and other appropriate matters; and

(C) provide that persons in any such class other than brokers and dealers and partners, officers, and supervisory employees of brokers or dealers, may be qualified solely on the basis of compliance with such standards of training and

such other qualifications as the Commission finds appropriate.

The Commission, by rule, may prescribe reasonable fees and charges to defray its costs in carrying out this paragraph, including, but not limited to, fees for any test administered by it or under its direction. The Commission may cooperate with registered securities associations and national securities exchanges in devising and administering tests and may require registered brokers and dealers and persons associated with such brokers and dealers to pass tests administered by or on behalf of any such association or exchange and to pay such association or exchange reasonable fees or charges to defray the costs incurred by such association or exchange in administering such tests.

(8)   It shall be unlawful for any registered broker or dealer to effect any transaction in, or induce or attempt to induce the purchase or sale of, any security (other than or commercial paper, bankers' acceptances, or commercial bills), unless such broker or dealer is a member of a securities association registered pursuant to section 78o-3 of this title or effects transactions in securities solely on a national securities exchange of which it is a member.

(9)   The Commission by rule or order, as it deems consistent with the public interest and the protection of investors, may conditionally or unconditionally exempt from paragraph (8) of this subsection any broker or dealer or class of brokers or dealers specified in such rule or order.

(10) For the purposes of determining whether a person is subject to a statutory disqualification under section 78f(c)(2), 78o-3(g)(2), or 78q- 1(b)(4)(A) of this title, the term "Commission" in paragraph (4)(B) of this subsection shall mean "exchange", "association", or "clearing agency", respectively.

(c)   Use of manipulative or deceptive devices; contravention of rules and regulations

(1)   (A)   No broker or dealer shall make use of the mails or any means or instrumentality of interstate commerce to effect any transaction in, or to induce or attempt to induce the purchase or sale of, any security (other than commercial paper, bankers' acceptances, or commercial bills) otherwise than on a national securities exchange of which it is a member by means of any manipulative, deceptive, or other fraudulent device or contrivance.

(B) No municipal securities dealer shall make use of the mails or any means or instrumentality of interstate commerce to effect any transaction in, or to induce or attempt to induce the purchase or sale of, any municipal security by means of any manipulative, deceptive, or other fraudulent device or contrivance.

(C) No government securities broker or government securities dealer shall make use of the mails or any means or instrumentality of interstate commerce to effect any transaction in, or to induce or attempt to induce the purchase or sale of, any government security by means of any manipulative, deceptive, or other fraudulent device or contrivance.

(D) The Commission shall, for the purposes of this paragraph, by rules and regulations define such devices or contrivances as are manipulative, deceptive, or otherwise fraudulent.

(E) The Commission shall, prior to adopting any rule or regulation under subparagraph (C), consult with and consider the views of the Secretary of the Treasury and each appropriate regulatory agency. If the Secretary of the Treasury or any appropriate regulatory agency comments in writing on a proposed rule or regulation of the Commission under such subparagraph (C) that has been published for comment, the Commission shall respond in writing to such written comment before adopting the proposed rule. If the Secretary of the Treasury determines, and notifies the Commission, that such rule or regulation, if implemented, would, or as applied does (i) adversely affect the liquidity or efficiency of the market for government securities; or (ii) impose any burden on competition not necessary or appropriate in furtherance of the purposes of this section, the Commission shall, prior to adopting the proposed rule or regulation, find that such rule or regulation is necessary and appropriate in furtherance of the purposes of this section notwithstanding the Secretary's determination.

(2) (A) No broker or dealer shall make use of the mails or any means or instrumentality of interstate commerce to effect any transaction in, or to induce or attempt to induce the purchase or sale of, any security (other than an exempted security or commercial paper, bankers' acceptances, or commercial bills) otherwise than on a national securities exchange of which it is a member, in connection with which such broker or dealer engages in any

fraudulent, deceptive, or manipulative act or practice, or makes any fictitious quotation.

(B)   No municipal securities dealer shall make use of the mails or any means or instrumentality of interstate commerce to effect any transaction in, or to induce or attempt to induce the purchase or sale of, any municipal security in connection with which such municipal securities dealer engages in any fraudulent, deceptive, or manipulative act or practice, or makes any fictitious quotation.

(C)   No government securities broker or government securities dealer shall make use of the mails or any means or instrumentality of interstate commerce to effect any transaction in, or induce or attempt to induce the purchase or sale of, any government security in connection with which such government securities broker or government securities dealer engages in any fraudulent, deceptive, or manipulative act or practice, or makes any fictitious quotation.

(D)   The Commission shall, for the purposes of this paragraph, by rules and regulations define, and prescribe means reasonably designed to prevent, such acts and practices as are fraudulent, deceptive, or manipulative and such quotations as are fictitious.

(E)   The Commission shall, prior to adopting any rule or regulation under subparagraph (C), consult with and consider the views of the Secretary of the Treasury and each appropriate regulatory agency. If the Secretary of the Treasury or any appropriate regulatory agency comments in writing on a proposed rule or regulation of the Commission under such subparagraph (C) that has been published for comment, the Commission shall respond in writing to such written comment before adopting the proposed rule. If the Secretary of the Treasury determines, and notifies the Commission, that such rule or regulation, if implemented, would, or as applied does (i) adversely affect the liquidity or efficiency of the market for government securities; or (ii) impose any burden on competition not necessary or appropriate in furtherance of the purposes of this section, the Commission shall, prior to adopting the proposed rule or regulation, find that such rule or regulation is necessary and appropriate in furtherance of the purposes of this section notwithstanding the Secretary's determination.

(3)   No broker or dealer (other than a government securities broker or government securities dealer, except a registered broker or dealer) shall make use of the mails or any means or instrumentality of interstate commerce to effect any transaction in, or to induce or attempt to induce the purchase or sale of, any security (other than an exempted security (except a government security) or commercial paper, bankers' acceptances, or commercial bills) in contravention of such rules and regulations as the Commission shall prescribe as necessary or appropriate in the public interest or for the protection of investors to provide safeguards with respect to the financial responsibility and related practices of brokers and dealers including, but not limited to, the acceptance of custody and use of customers' securities and the carrying and use of customers' deposits or credit balances. Such rules and regulations shall (A) require the maintenance of reserves with respect to customers' deposits or credit balances, and (B) no later than September 1, 1975, establish minimum financial responsibility requirements for all brokers and dealers.

(4)   If the Commission finds, after notice and opportunity for a hearing, that any person subject to the provisions of section 78l, 78m, 78n of this tile, or subsection (d) of this section or any rule or regulation thereunder has failed to comply with any such provision, rule, or regulation in any material respect, the Commission may publish its findings and issue an order requiring such person, and any person who was a cause of the failure to comply due to an act or omission the person knew or should have known would contribute to the failure to comply, to comply, or to take steps to effect compliance, with such provision or such rule or regulation thereunder upon such terms and conditions and within such time as the Commission may specify in such order.

(5)   No dealer (other than a specialist registered on a national securities exchange) acting in the capacity of market maker or otherwise shall make use of the mails or any means or instrumentality of interstate commerce to effect any transaction in, or to induce or attempt to induce the purchase or sale of, any security (other than an exempted security or a municipal security) in contravention of such specified and appropriate standards with respect to dealing as the Commission, by rule, shall prescribe as necessary or appropriate in the public interest and for the protection of investors, to maintain fair and orderly markets, or to remove impediments to and perfect the mechanism of a national market system. Under the rules of the

Commission a dealer in a security may be prohibited from acting as a broker in that security.

(6)   No broker or dealer shall make use of the mails or any means or instrumentality of interstate commerce to effect any transaction in, or to induce or attempt to induce the purchase or sale of, any security (other than an exempted security, municipal security, commercial paper, bankers' acceptances, or commercial bills) in contravention of such rules and regulations as the Commission shall prescribe as necessary or appropriate in the public interest and for the protection of investors or to perfect or remove impediments to a national system for the prompt and accurate clearance and settlement of securities transactions, with respect to the time and method of, and the form and format of documents used in connection with, making settlements of and payments for transactions in securities, making transfers and deliveries of securities, and closing accounts. Nothing in this paragraph shall be construed (A) to affect the authority of the Board of Governors of the Federal Reserve System, pursuant to section 78g of this title, to prescribe rules and regulations for the purpose of preventing the excessive use of credit for the purchase or carrying of securities, or (B) to authorize the Commission to prescribe rules or regulations for such purpose.

(7)   In connection with any bid for or purchase of a government security related to an offering of government securities by or on behalf of an issuer, no government securities broker, government securities dealer, or bidder for or purchaser of securities in such offering shall knowingly or willfully make any false or misleading written statement or omit any fact necessary to make any written statement made not misleading.

(8)   Prohibition of referral fees

No broker or dealer, or person associated with a broker or dealer, may solicit or accept, directly or indirectly, remuneration for assisting an attorney in obtaining the representation of any person in any private action arising under this chapter or under the Securities Act of 1933

* * *

(g)   Requirements for transactions in penny stocks

(1)   In general

No broker or dealer shall make use of the mails or any means or instrumentality of interstate commerce to effect any transaction in, or

to induce or attempt to induce the purchase or sale of, any penny stock by any customer except in accordance with the requirements of this subsection and the rules and regulations prescribed under this subsection.

(2) Risk disclosure with respect to penny stocks

Prior to effecting any transaction in any penny stock, a broker or dealer shall give the customer a risk disclosure document that—

(A) contains a description of the nature and level of risk in the market for penny stocks in both public offerings and secondary trading;

(B) contains a description of the broker's or dealer's duties to the customer and of the rights and remedies available to the customer with respect to violations of such duties or other requirements of Federal securities laws;

(C) contains a brief, clear, narrative description of a dealer market, including "bid" and "ask" prices for penny stocks and the significance of the spread between the bid and ask prices;

(D) contains the toll free telephone number for inquiries on disciplinary   actions established pursuant to section 78o-3(i) of this title;

(E) defines significant terms used in the disclosure document or in the conduct of trading in penny stocks; and

(F) contains such other information, and is in such form (including language, type size, and format), as the Commission shall require by rule or regulation.

(3) Commission rules relating to disclosure

The Commission shall adopt rules setting forth additional standards for the disclosure by brokers and dealers to customers of information concerning transactions in penny stocks. Such rules—

(A) shall require brokers and dealers to disclose to each customer, prior to effecting any transaction in, and at the time of confirming any transaction with respect to any penny stock, in accordance with such procedures and methods as the Commission may require consistent with the public interest and the protection of investors—

(i) the bid and ask prices for penny stock, or such other information as the Commission may, by rule, require to

provide customers with more useful and reliable
information relating to the price of such stock;

(ii)   the number of shares to which such bid and ask prices
apply, or other comparable information relating to the
depth and liquidity of the market for such stock; and

(iii)   the amount and a description of any compensation that the
broker or dealer and the associated person thereof will
receive or has received in connection with such transaction;

(B)   shall require brokers and dealers to provide, to each customer
whose account with the broker or dealer contains penny stocks,
a monthly statement indicating the market value of the penny
stocks in that account or indicating that the market value of such
stock cannot be determined because of the unavailability of firm
quotes; and

(C)   may, as the Commission finds necessary or appropriate in the
public interest or for the protection of investors, require brokers
and dealers to disclose to customers additional information
concerning transactions in penny stocks.

(4)   Exemptions

The Commission, as it determines consistent with the public
interest and the protection of investors, may by rule, regulation, or
order exempt in whole or in part, conditionally or unconditionally,
any person or class of persons, or any transaction or class of
transactions, from the requirements of this subsection. Such
exemptions shall include an exemption for brokers and dealers based
on the minimal percentage of the broker's or dealer's commissions,
commission-equivalents, and markups received from transactions in
penny stocks.

(5)   Regulations

It shall be unlawful for any person to violate such rules and
regulations as the Commission shall prescribe in the public interest or
for the protection of investors or to maintain fair and orderly
markets—

(A)   as necessary or appropriate to carry out this subsection; or

(B)   as reasonably designed to prevent fraudulent, deceptive, or
manipulative acts and practices with respect to penny stocks.

(h) Limitations on State law

    (1) Capital, margin, books and records, bonding, and reports

        No law, rule, regulation, or order, or other administrative action of any State or political subdivision thereof shall establish capital, custody, margin, financial responsibility, making and keeping records, bonding, or financial or operational reporting requirements for brokers, dealers, municipal securities dealers, government securities brokers, or government securities dealers that differ from, or are in addition to, the requirements in those areas established under this chapter. The Commission shall consult periodically the securities commissions (or any agency or office performing like functions) of the States concerning the adequacy of such requirements as established under this chapter.

    (2) De minimis transactions by associated persons

        No law, rule, regulation, or order, or other administrative action of any State or political subdivision thereof may prohibit an associated person of a broker or dealer from affecting a transaction described in paragraph (3) for a customer in such State if—

        (A) such associated person is not ineligible to register with such State for any reason other than such a transaction;

        (B) such associated person is registered with a registered securities association and at least one State; and

        (C) the broker or dealer with which such person is associated is registered with such State.

    (3) Described transactions

        (A) In general

        A transaction is described in this paragraph if—

        (i) such transaction is effected—

        (I) on behalf of a customer that, for 30 days prior to the day of the transaction, maintained an account with the broker or dealer; and

        (II) by an associated person of the broker or dealer—

        (aa) to which the customer was assigned for 14 days prior to the day of the transaction; and

        (bb) who is registered with a State in which the customer was a resident or was present for at

least 30 consecutive days during the 1-year period prior to the day of the transaction;

(ii)   the transaction is effected—

(I)   on behalf of a customer that, for 30 days prior to the day of the transaction, maintains an account with the broker or dealer; and

(II)   during the period beginning on the date on which such associated person files an application for registration with the State in which the transaction is effected and ending on the earlier of—

(aa)   60 days after the date on which the application is filed; or

(bb)   the date on which such State notifies the associated person that it has denied the application for registration or has stayed the pendency of the application for cause.

(B)   Rules of construction

For purposes of subparagraph (A)(i)(II)—

(i)   each of up to 3 associated persons of a broker or dealer who are designated to effect transactions during the absence or unavailability of the principal associated person for a customer may be treated as an associated person to which such customer is assigned; and

(ii)   if the customer is present in another State for 30 or more consecutive days or has permanently changed his or her residence to another State, a transaction is not described in this paragraph, unless the association person of the broker or dealer files an application for registration with such State not later than 10 business days after the later of the date of the transaction, or the date of the discovery of the presence of the customer in the other State for 30 or more consecutive days or the change in the customer's residence.

§ 15A. Registered securities associations

(a)   Registration; application

An association of brokers and dealers may be registered as a national securities association pursuant to subsection (b) of this section, or as an

affiliated securities association pursuant to subsection (d) of this section, under the terms and conditions hereinafter provided in this section and in accordance with the provisions of section 78s(a) of this title, by filing with the Commission an application for registration in such form as the Commission, by rule, may prescribe containing the rules of the association and such other information and documents as the Commission, by rule, may prescribe as necessary or appropriate in the public interest or for the protection of investors.

(b) Determinations by Commission requisite to registration of applicant as national securities association

An association of brokers and dealers shall not be registered as a national securities association unless the Commission determines that—

(1) By reason of the number and geographical distribution of its members and the scope of their transactions, such association will be able to carry out the purposes of this section.

(2) Such association is so organized and has the capacity to be able to carry out the purposes of this chapter and to comply, and (subject to any rule or order of the Commission pursuant to section 78q(d) or 78s(g)(2) of this title) to enforce compliance by its members and persons associated with its members, with the provisions of this chapter, the rules and regulations thereunder, the rules of the Municipal Securities Rulemaking Board, and the rules of the association.

(3) Subject to the provisions of subsection (g) of this section, the rules of the association provide that any registered broker or dealer may become a member of such association and any person may become associated with a member thereof.

(4) The rules of the association assure a fair representation of its members in the selection of its directors and administration of its affairs and provide that one or more directors shall be representative of issuers and investors and not be associated with a member of the association, broker, or dealer.

(5) The rules of the association provide for the equitable allocation of reasonable dues, fees, and other charges among members and issuers and other persons using any facility or system which the association operates or controls.

(6) The rules of the association are designed to prevent fraudulent and manipulative acts and practices, to promote just and equitable principles of trade, to foster cooperation and coordination with

persons engaged in regulating, clearing, settling, processing information with respect to, and facilitating transactions in securities, to remove impediments to and perfect the mechanism of a free and open market and a national market system, and, in general, to protect investors and the public interest; and are not designed to permit unfair discrimination between customers, issuers, brokers, or dealers, to fix minimum profits, to impose any schedule or fix rates of commissions, allowances, discounts, or other fees to be charged by its members, or to regulate by virtue of any authority conferred by this chapter matters not related to the purposes of this chapter or the administration of the association.

(7)   The rules of the association provide that (subject to any rule or order of the Commission pursuant to section 78q(d) or 78s(g)(2) of this title) its members and persons associated with its members shall be appropriately disciplined for violation of any provision of this chapter, the rules or regulations thereunder, the rules of the Municipal Securities Rulemaking Board, or the rules of the association, by expulsion, suspension, limitation of activities, functions, and operations, fine, censure, being suspended or barred from being associated with a member, or any other fitting sanction.

(8)   The rules of the association are in accordance with the provisions of subsection (h) of this section, and, in general, provide a fair procedure for the disciplining of members and persons associated with members, the denial of membership to any person seeking membership therein, the barring of any person from becoming associated with a member thereof, and the prohibition or limitation by the association of any person with respect to access to services offered by the association or a member thereof.

(9)   The rules of the association do not impose any burden on competition not necessary or appropriate in furtherance of the purposes of this chapter.

(10) The requirements of subsection (c) of this section, insofar as these may be applicable, are satisfied.

(11) The rules of the association include provisions governing the form and content of quotations relating to securities sold otherwise than on a national securities exchange which may be distributed or published by any member or person associated with a member, and the persons to whom such quotations may be supplied. Such rules relating to quotations shall be designed to produce fair and informative quotations, to prevent fictitious or misleading quotations, and to

promote orderly procedures for collecting, distributing, and publishing quotations.

(12) The rules of the association to promote just and equitable principles of trade, as required by paragraph (6), include rules to prevent members of the association from participating in any limited partnership rollup transaction (as such term is defined in paragraphs (4) and (5) of section 78n(h) of this title) unless such transaction was conducted in accordance with procedures designed to protect the rights of limited partners, including—

(A) the right of dissenting limited partners to one of the following:

(i) an appraisal and compensation;

(ii) retention of a security under substantially the same terms and conditions as the original issue;

(iii) approval of the limited partnership rollup transaction by not less than 75 percent of the outstanding securities of each of the participating limited partnerships;

(iv) the use of a committee that is independent, as determined in accordance with rules prescribed by the association, of the general partner or sponsor, that has been approved by a majority of the outstanding securities of each of the participating partnerships, and that has such authority as is necessary to protect the interest of limited partners, including the authority to hire independent advisors, to negotiate with the general partner or sponsor on behalf of the limited partners, and to make a recommendation to the limited partners with respect to the proposed transaction; or

(v) other comparable rights that are prescribed by rule by the association and that are designed to protect dissenting limited partners;

(B) the right not to have their voting power unfairly reduced or abridged;

(C) the right not to bear an unfair portion of the costs of a proposed limited partnership rollup transaction that is rejected; and

(D) restrictions on the conversion of contingent interests or fees into non-contingent interests or fees and restrictions on the receipt of a non-contingent equity interest in exchange for fees for services which have not yet been provided.

As used in this paragraph, the term "dissenting limited partner" means a person who, on the date on which soliciting material is mailed to investors, is a holder of a beneficial interest in a limited partnership that is the subject of a limited partnership rollup transaction, and who casts a vote against the transaction and complies with procedures established by the association, except that for purposes of an exchange or tender offer, such person shall file an objection in writing under the rules of the association during the period in which the offer is outstanding.

(13) The rules of the association prohibit the authorization for quotation on an automated interdealer quotation system sponsored by the association of any security designated by the Commission as a national market system security resulting from a limited partnership rollup transaction (as such term is defined in paragraphs (4) and (5) of section 78n(h) of this title), unless such transaction was conducted in accordance with procedures designed to protect the rights of limited partners, including--

(A) the right of dissenting limited partners to one of the following:

(i) an appraisal and compensation;

(ii) retention of a security under substantially the same terms and conditions as the original issue;

(iii) approval of the limited partnership rollup transaction by not less than 75 percent of the outstanding securities of each of the participating limited partnerships;

(iv) the use of a committee that is independent, as determined in accordance with rules prescribed by the association, of the general partner or sponsor, that has been approved by a majority of the outstanding securities of each of the participating partnerships, and that has such authority as is necessary to protect the interest of limited partners, including the authority to hire independent advisors, to negotiate with the general partner or sponsor on behalf of the limited partners, and to make a recommendation to the limited partners with respect to the proposed transaction; or

(v) other comparable rights that are prescribed by rule by the association and that are designed to protect dissenting limited partners;

(B) the right not to have their voting power unfairly reduced or abridged;

(C) the right not to bear an unfair portion of the costs of a proposed limited partnership rollup transaction that is rejected; and

(D) restrictions on the conversion of contingent interests or fees into non-contingent interests or fees and restrictions on the receipt of a non-contingent equity interest in exchange for fees for services which have not yet been provided.

As used in this paragraph, the term "dissenting limited partner" means a person who, on the date on which soliciting material is mailed to investors, is a holder of a beneficial interest in a limited partnership that is the subject of a limited partnership rollup transaction, and who casts a vote against the transaction and complies with procedures established by the association, except that for purposes of an exchange or tender offer, such person shall file an objection in writing under the rules of the association during the period during which the offer is outstanding.

* * *

§ 17. Records and reports

(a) Rules and regulations

(1) Every national securities exchange, member thereof, broker or dealer who transacts a business in securities through the medium of any such member, registered securities association, registered broker or dealer, registered municipal securities dealer, registered securities information processor, registered transfer agent, and registered clearing agency and the Municipal Securities Rulemaking Board shall make and keep for prescribed periods such records, furnish such copies thereof, and make and disseminate such reports as the Commission, by rule, prescribes as necessary or appropriate in the public interest, for the protection of investors, or otherwise in furtherance of the purposes of this chapter.

(2) Every registered clearing agency shall also make and keep for prescribed periods such records, furnish such copies thereof, and make and disseminate such reports, as the appropriate regulatory agency for such clearing agency, by rule, prescribes as necessary or appropriate for the safeguarding of securities and funds in the custody or control of such clearing agency or for which it is responsible.

(3)   Every registered transfer agent shall also make and keep for prescribed periods such records, furnish such copies thereof, and make such reports as the appropriate regulatory agency for such transfer agent, by rule, prescribes as necessary or appropriate in furtherance of the purposes of section 78q-1 of this title.

(b)   Examination of records; notice; avoidance of duplication and undue regulatory burden

All records of persons described in subsection (a) of this section are subject at any time, or from time to time, to such reasonable periodic, special, or other examinations by representatives of the Commission and the appropriate regulatory agency for such persons as the Commission or the appropriate regulatory agency for such persons deems necessary or appropriate in the public interest, for the protection of investors, or otherwise in furtherance of the purposes of this chapter: Provided, however, That the Commission shall, prior to conducting any such examination of a registered clearing agency, registered transfer agent, or registered municipal securities dealer for which it is not the appropriate regulatory agency, give notice to the appropriate regulatory agency for such clearing agency, transfer agent, or municipal securities dealer of such proposed examination and consult with such appropriate regulatory agency concerning the feasibility and desirability of coordinating such examination with examinations conducted by such appropriate regulatory agency with a view to avoiding unnecessary regulatory duplication or undue regulatory burdens for such clearing agency, transfer agent, or municipal securities dealer. Nothing in the proviso to the preceding sentence shall be construed to impair or limit (other than by the requirement of prior consultation) the power of the Commission under this subsection to examine any clearing agency, transfer agent, or municipal securities dealer or to affect in any way the power of the Commission under any other provision of this chapter or otherwise to inspect, examine, or investigate any such clearing agency, transfer agent, or municipal securities dealer.

(c)   Copies of reports filed with other regulatory agencies

(1)   Every clearing agency, transfer agent, and municipal securities dealer for which the Commission is not the appropriate regulatory agency shall (A) file with the appropriate regulatory agency for such clearing agency, transfer agent, or municipal securities dealer a copy of any application, notice, proposal, report, or document filed with the Commission by reason of its being a clearing agency, transfer agent, or municipal securities dealer and (B) file with the Commission a copy of any application, notice, proposal, report, or document filed with

such appropriate regulatory agency by reason of its being a clearing agency, transfer agent, or municipal securities dealer. The Municipal Securities Rulemaking Board shall file with each agency enumerated in section 78c(a)(34)(A) of this title copies of every proposed rule change filed with the Commission pursuant to section 78s(b) of this title.

(2) The appropriate regulatory agency for a clearing agency, transfer agent, or municipal securities dealer for which the Commission is not the appropriate regulatory agency shall file with the Commission notice of the commencement of any proceeding and a copy of any order entered by such appropriate regulatory agency against any clearing agency, transfer agent, municipal securities dealer, or person associated with a transfer agent or municipal securities dealer, and the Commission shall file with such appropriate regulatory agency, if any, notice of the commencement of any proceeding and a copy of any order entered by the Commission against the clearing agency, transfer agent, or municipal securities dealer, or against any person associated with a transfer agent or municipal securities dealer for which the agency is the appropriate regulatory agency.

(3) The Commission and the appropriate regulatory agency for a clearing agency, transfer agent, or municipal securities dealer for which the Commission is not the appropriate regulatory agency shall each notify the other and make a report of any examination conducted by it of such clearing agency, transfer agent, or municipal securities dealer, and, upon request, furnish to the other a copy of such report and any data supplied to it in connection with such examination.

(4) The Commission or the appropriate regulatory agency may specify that documents required to be filed pursuant to this subsection with the Commission or such agency, respectively, may be retained by the originating clearing agency, transfer agent, or municipal securities dealer, or filed with another appropriate regulatory agency. The Commission or the appropriate regulatory agency (as the case may be) making such a specification shall continue to have access to the document on request.

(d) Self-regulatory organizations

(1) The Commission, by rule or order, as it deems necessary or appropriate in the public interest and for the protection of investors, to foster cooperation and coordination among self-regulatory organizations, or to remove impediments to and foster the

development of a national market system and national system for the clearance and settlement of securities transactions, may—

(A)   with respect to any person who is a member of or participant in more than one self-regulatory organization, relieve any such self-regulatory organization of any responsibility under this chapter (i) to receive regulatory reports from such person, (ii) to examine such person for compliance, or to enforce compliance by such person, with specified provisions of this chapter, the rules and regulations thereunder, and its own rules, or (iii) to carry out other specified regulatory functions with respect to such person, and

(B)   allocate among self-regulatory organizations the authority to adopt rules with respect to matters as to which, in the absence of such allocation, such self-regulatory organizations share authority under this chapter.

In making any such rule or entering any such order, the Commission shall take into consideration the regulatory capabilities and procedures of the self- regulatory organizations, availability of staff, convenience of location, unnecessary regulatory duplication, and such other factors as the Commission may consider germane to the protection of investors, cooperation and coordination among self-regulatory organizations, and the development of a national market system and a national system for the clearance and settlement of securities transactions. The Commission, by rule or order, as it deems necessary or appropriate in the public interest and for the protection of investors, may require any self-regulatory organization relieved of any responsibility pursuant to this paragraph, and any person with respect to whom such responsibility relates, to take such steps as are specified in any such rule or order to notify customers of, and persons doing business with, such person of the limited nature of such self-regulatory organization's responsibility for such person's acts, practices, and course of business.

(2)   A self-regulatory organization shall furnish copies of any report of examination of any person who is a member of or a participant in such self- regulatory organization to any other self-regulatory organization of which such person is a member or in which such person is a participant upon the request of such person, such other self-regulatory organization, or the Commission.

(e) Balance sheet and income statement; other financial statements and information

   (1) (A) Every registered broker or dealer shall annually file with the Commission a balance sheet and income statement certified by an independent public accountant, prepared on a calendar or fiscal year basis, and such other financial statements (which shall, as the Commission specifies, be certified) and information concerning its financial condition as the Commission, by rule may prescribe as necessary or appropriate in the public interest or for the protection of investors.

        (B) Every registered broker and dealer shall annually send to its customers its certified balance sheet and such other financial statements and information concerning its financial condition as the Commission, by rule, may prescribe pursuant to subsection (a) of this section.

        (C) The Commission, by rule or order, may conditionally or unconditionally exempt any registered broker or dealer, or class of such brokers or dealers, from any provision of this paragraph if the Commission determines that such exemption is consistent with the public interest and the protection of investors.

   (2) The Commission, by rule, as it deems necessary or appropriate in the public interest or for the protection of investors, may prescribe the form and content of financial statements filed pursuant to this chapter and the accounting principles and accounting standards used in their preparation.

* * *

(h) Risk assessment for holding company systems

   (1) Obligations to obtain, maintain, and report information

        Every person who is (A) a registered broker or dealer, or (B) a registered municipal securities dealer for which the Commission is the appropriate regulatory agency, shall obtain such information and make and keep such records as the Commission by rule prescribes concerning the registered person's policies, procedures, or systems for monitoring and controlling financial and operational risks to it resulting from the activities of any of its associated persons, other than a natural person. Such records shall describe, in the aggregate, each of the financial and securities activities conducted by, and the customary sources of capital and funding of, those of its associated persons whose business activities are reasonably likely to have a

material impact on the financial or operational condition of such registered person, including its net capital, its liquidity, or its ability to conduct or finance its operations. The Commission, by rule, may require summary reports of such information to be filed with the Commission no more frequently than quarterly.

(2)   Authority to require additional information

If, as a result of adverse market conditions or based on reports provided to the Commission pursuant to paragraph (1) of this subsection or other available information, the Commission reasonably concludes that it has concerns regarding the financial or operational condition of (A) any registered broker or dealer, or (B) any registered municipal securities dealer, government securities broker, or government securities dealer for which the Commission is the appropriate regulatory agency, the Commission may require the registered person to make reports concerning the financial and securities activities of any of such person's associated persons, other than a natural person, whose business activities are reasonably likely to have a material impact on the financial or operational condition of such registered person. The Commission, in requiring reports pursuant to this paragraph, shall specify the information required, the period for which it is required, the time and date on which the information must be furnished, and whether the information is to be furnished directly to the Commission or to a self-regulatory organization with primary responsibility for examining the registered person's financial and operational condition.

(3)   Special provisions with respect to associated persons subject to Federal banking agency regulation

(A)   Cooperation in implementation

In developing and implementing reporting requirements pursuant to paragraph (1) of this subsection with respect to associated persons subject to examination by or reporting requirements of a Federal banking agency, the Commission shall consult with and consider the views of each such Federal banking agency. If a Federal banking agency comments in writing on a proposed rule of the Commission under this subsection that has been published for comment, the Commission shall respond in writing to such written comment before adopting the proposed rule. The Commission shall, at the request of the Federal banking agency, publish such comment

and response in the Federal Register at the time of publishing the adopted rule.

(B) Use of banking agency reports

A registered broker, dealer, or municipal securities dealer shall be in compliance with any recordkeeping or reporting requirement adopted pursuant to paragraph (1) of this subsection concerning an associated person that is subject to examination by or reporting requirements of a Federal banking agency if such broker, dealer, or municipal securities dealer utilizes for such recordkeeping or reporting requirement copies of reports filed by the associated person with the Federal banking agency pursuant to section 161 of Title 12, subchapter VIII of chapter 3 of Title 12, section 1817(a) of Title 12, section 1467a(b) of Title 12, or section 1847 of Title 12. The Commission may, however, by rule adopted pursuant to paragraph (1), require any broker, dealer, or municipal securities dealer filing such reports with the Commission to obtain, maintain, or report supplemental information if the Commission makes an explicit finding that such supplemental information is necessary to inform the Commission regarding potential risks to such broker, dealer, or municipal securities dealer. Prior to requiring any such supplemental information, the Commission shall first request the Federal banking agency to expand its reporting requirements to include such information.

(C) Procedure for requiring additional information

Prior to making a request pursuant to paragraph (2) of this subsection for information with respect to an associated person that is subject to examination by or reporting requirements of a Federal banking agency, the Commission shall--

(i) notify such agency of the information required with respect to such associated person; and

(ii) consult with such agency to determine whether the information required is available from such agency and for other purposes, unless the Commission determines that any delay resulting from such consultation would be inconsistent with ensuring the financial and operational condition of the broker, dealer, municipal securities dealer, government securities broker, or government securities dealer or the stability or integrity of the securities markets.

(D) Exclusion for examination reports

Nothing in this subsection shall be construed to permit the Commission to require any registered broker or dealer, or any registered municipal securities dealer, government securities broker, or government securities dealer for which the Commission is the appropriate regulatory agency, to obtain, maintain, or furnish any examination report of any Federal banking agency or any supervisory recommendations or analysis contained therein.

(E) Confidentiality of information provided

No information provided to or obtained by the Commission from any Federal banking agency pursuant to a request by the Commission under subparagraph (C) of this paragraph regarding any associated person which is subject to examination by or reporting requirements of a Federal banking agency may be disclosed to any other person (other than a self-regulatory organization), without the prior written approval of the Federal banking agency. Nothing in this subsection shall authorize the Commission to withhold information from Congress, or prevent the Commission from complying with a request for information from any other Federal department or agency requesting the information for purposes within the scope of its jurisdiction, or complying with an order of a court of the United States in an action brought by the United States or the Commission.

(F) Notice to banking agencies concerning financial and operational condition concerns

The Commission shall notify the Federal banking agency of any concerns of the Commission regarding significant financial or operational risks resulting from the activities of any registered broker or dealer, or any registered municipal securities dealer, government securities broker, or government securities dealer for which the Commission is the appropriate regulatory agency, to any associated person thereof which is subject to examination by or reporting requirements of the Federal banking agency.

(G) "Federal banking agency" defined

For purposes of this paragraph, the term "Federal banking agency" shall have the same meaning as the term "appropriate Federal bank agency" in section 1813(q) of Title 12.

(4) Exemptions

The Commission by rule or order may exempt any person or class of persons, under such terms and conditions and for such periods as the Commission shall provide in such rule or order, from the provisions of this subsection, and the rules thereunder. In granting such exemptions, the Commission shall consider, among other factors—

(A) whether information of the type required under this subsection is available from a supervisory agency (as defined in section 3401(6) of Title 12), a State insurance commission or similar State agency, the Commodity Futures Trading Commission, or a similar foreign regulator;

(B) the primary business of any associated person;

(C) the nature and extent of domestic or foreign regulation of the associated person's activities;

(D) the nature and extent of the registered person's securities activities; and

(E) with respect to the registered person and its associated persons, on a consolidated basis, the amount and proportion of assets devoted to, and revenues derived from, activities in the United States securities markets.

(5) Authority to limit disclosure of information

Notwithstanding any other provision of law, the Commission shall not be compelled to disclose any information required to be reported under this subsection, or any information supplied to the Commission by any domestic or foreign regulatory agency that relates to the financial or operational condition of any associated person of a registered broker, dealer, government securities broker, government securities dealer, or municipal securities dealer. Nothing in this subsection shall authorize the Commission to withhold information from Congress, or prevent the Commission from complying with a request for information from any other Federal department or agency requesting the information for purposes within the scope of its jurisdiction, or complying with an order of a court of the United States in an action brought by the United States or

the Commission. For purposes of section 552 of Title 5, this subsection shall be considered a statute described in subsection (b)(3)(B) of such section 552. In prescribing regulations to carry out the requirements of this subsection, the Commission shall designate information described in or obtained pursuant to subparagraph (B) or (C) of paragraph (3) of this subsection as confidential information for purposes of section 78x(b)(2) of this title.

* * *

§ 19. Registration, responsibilities, and oversight of self-regulatory organizations

(a)   Registration procedures; notice of filing; other regulatory agencies

(1)   The Commission shall, upon the filing of an application for registration as a national securities exchange, registered securities association, or registered clearing agency, pursuant to section 78f, 78o-3, or 78q-1 of this title, respectively, publish notice of such filing and afford interested persons an opportunity to submit written data, views, and arguments concerning such application. Within ninety days of the date of publication of such notice (or within such longer period as to which the applicant consents), the Commission shall—

(A) by order grant such registration, or

(B) institute proceedings to determine whether registration should be denied. Such proceedings shall include notice of the grounds for denial under consideration and opportunity for hearing and shall be concluded within one hundred eighty days of the date of a publication of notice of the filing of the application for registration. At the conclusion of such proceedings the Commission, by order, shall grant or deny such registration. The Commission may extend the time for conclusion of such proceedings for up to ninety days if it finds good cause for such extension and publishes its reasons for so finding or for such longer period as to which the applicant consents.

The Commission shall grant such registration if it finds that the requirements of this chapter and the rules and regulations thereunder with respect to the applicant are satisfied. The Commission shall deny such registration if it does not make such finding.

(2) With respect to an application for registration filed by a clearing agency for which the Commission is not the appropriate regulatory agency—

(A) The Commission shall not grant registration prior to the sixtieth day after the date of publication of notice of the filing of such application unless the appropriate regulatory agency for such clearing agency has notified the Commission of such appropriate regulatory agency's determination that such clearing agency is so organized and has the capacity to be able to safeguard securities and funds in its custody or control or for which it is responsible and that the rules of such clearing agency are designed to assure the safeguarding of such securities and funds.

(B) The Commission shall institute proceedings in accordance with paragraph (1)(B) of this subsection to determine whether registration should be denied if the appropriate regulatory agency for such clearing agency notifies the Commission within sixty days of the date of publication of notice of the filing of such application of such appropriate regulatory agency's (i) determination that such clearing agency may not be so organized or have the capacity to be able to safeguard securities or funds in its custody or control or for which it is responsible or that the rules of such clearing agency may not be designed to assure the safeguarding of such securities and funds and (ii) reasons for such determination.

(C) The Commission shall deny registration if the appropriate regulatory agency for such clearing agency notifies the Commission prior to the conclusion of proceedings instituted in accordance with paragraph (1)(B) of this subsection of such appropriate regulatory agency's (i) determination that such clearing agency is not so organized or does not have the capacity to be able to safeguard securities or funds in its custody or control or for which it is responsible or that the rules of such clearing agency are not designed to assure the safeguarding of such securities or funds and (ii) reasons for such determination.

(3) A self-regulatory organization may, upon such terms and conditions as the Commission, by rule, deems necessary or appropriate in the public interest or for the protection of investors, withdraw from registration by filing a written notice of withdrawal with the Commission. If the Commission finds that any self-regulatory organization is no longer in existence or has ceased to do business in

the capacity specified in its application for registration, the Commission, by order, shall cancel its registration. Upon the withdrawal of a national securities association from registration or the cancellation, suspension, or revocation of the registration of a national securities association, the registration of any association affiliated therewith shall automatically terminate.

(b)   Proposed rule changes; notice; proceedings

(1)   Each self-regulatory organization shall file with the Commission, in accordance with such rules as the Commission may prescribe, copies of any proposed rule or any proposed change in, addition to, or deletion from the rules of such self-regulatory organization (hereinafter in this subsection collectively referred to as a "proposed rule change") accompanied by a concise general statement of the basis and purpose of such proposed rule change. The Commission shall, upon the filing of any proposed rule change, publish notice thereof together with the terms of substance of the proposed rule change or a description of the subjects and issues involved. The Commission shall give interested persons an opportunity to submit written data, views, and arguments concerning such proposed rule change. No proposed rule change shall take effect unless approved by the Commission or otherwise permitted in accordance with the provisions of this subsection.

* * *

(c)   Amendment by Commission of rules of self-regulatory organizations

The Commission, by rule, may abrogate, add to, and delete from (hereinafter in this subsection collectively referred to as "amend") the rules of a self- regulatory organization (other than a registered clearing agency) as the Commission deems necessary or appropriate to insure the fair administration of the self-regulatory organization, to conform its rules to requirements of this chapter and the rules and regulations thereunder applicable to such organization, or otherwise in furtherance of the purposes of this chapter, in the following manner:

(1)   The Commission shall notify the self-regulatory organization and publish notice of the proposed rulemaking in the Federal Register. The notice shall include the text of the proposed amendment to the rules of the self-regulatory organization and a statement of the Commission's reasons, including any pertinent facts, for commencing such proposed rulemaking.

(2) The Commission shall give interested persons an opportunity for the oral presentation of data, views, and arguments, in addition to an opportunity to make written submissions. A transcript shall be kept of any oral presentation.

(3) A rule adopted pursuant to this subsection shall incorporate the text of the amendment to the rules of the self-regulatory organization and a statement of the Commission's basis for and purpose in so amending such rules. This statement shall include an identification of any facts on which the Commission considers its determination so to amend the rules of the self-regulatory agency to be based, including the reasons for the Commission's conclusions as to any of such facts which were disputed in the rulemaking.

(4) (A) Except as provided in paragraphs (1) through (3) of this subsection, rulemaking under this subsection shall be in accordance with the procedures specified in section 553 of Title 5 for rulemaking not on the record.

(B) Nothing in this subsection shall be construed to impair or limit the Commission's power to make, or to modify or alter the procedures the Commission may follow in making, rules and regulations pursuant to any other authority under this chapter.

(C) Any amendment to the rules of a self-regulatory organization made by the Commission pursuant to this subsection shall be considered for all purposes of this chapter to be part of the rules of such self-regulatory organization and shall not be considered to be a rule of the Commission.

(5) With respect to rules described in subsection (b)(5) of this section, the Commission shall consult with and consider the views of the Secretary of the Treasury before abrogating, adding to, and deleting from such rules, except where the Commission determines that an emergency exists requiring expeditious or summary action and publishes its reasons therefor.

* * *

(g) Compliance with rules and regulations

(1) Every self-regulatory organization shall comply with the provisions of this chapter, the rules and regulations thereunder, and its own rules, and (subject to the provisions of section 78q(d) of this title, paragraph (2) of this subsection, and the rules thereunder) absent reasonable justification or excuse enforce compliance--

(A)   in the case of a national securities exchange, with such provisions by its members and persons associated with its members;

(B)   in the case of a registered securities association, with such provisions and the provisions of the rules of the Municipal Securities Rulemaking Board by its members and persons associated with its members; and

(C)   in the case of a registered clearing agency, with its own rules by its participants.

(2)   The Commission, by rule, consistent with the public interest, the protection of investors, and the other purposes of this chapter, may relieve any self-regulatory organization of any responsibility under this chapter to enforce compliance with any specified provision of this chapter or the rules or regulations thereunder by any member of such organization or person associated with such a member, or any class of such members or persons associated with a member.

(h)   Suspension or revocation of self-regulatory organization's registration; censure; other sanctions

(1)   The appropriate regulatory agency for a self-regulatory organization is authorized, by order, if in its opinion such action is necessary or appropriate in the public interest, for the protection of investors, or otherwise in furtherance of the purposes of this chapter, to suspend for a period not exceeding twelve months or revoke the registration of such self-regulatory organization, or to censure or impose limitations upon the activities, functions, and operations of such self-regulatory organization, if such appropriate regulatory agency finds, on the record after notice and opportunity for hearing, that such self-regulatory organization has violated or is unable to comply with any provision of this chapter, the rules or regulations thereunder, or its own rules or without reasonable justification or excuse has failed to enforce compliance—

(A)   in the case of a national securities exchange, with any such provision by a member thereof or a person associated with a member thereof;

(B)   in the case of a registered securities association, with any such provision or any provision of the rules of the Municipal Securities Rulemaking Board by a member thereof or a person associated with a member thereof; or

(C) in the case of a registered clearing agency, with any provision of its own rules by a participant therein.

(2) The appropriate regulatory agency for a self-regulatory organization is authorized, by order, if in its opinion such action is necessary or appropriate in the public interest, for the protection of investors, or otherwise in furtherance of the purposes of this chapter, to suspend for a period not exceeding twelve months or expel from such self-regulatory organization any member thereof or participant therein, if such member or participant is subject to an order of the Commission pursuant to section 78o(b)(4) of this title or if such appropriate regulatory agency finds, on the record after notice and opportunity for hearing, that such member or participant has willfully violated or has effected any transaction for any other person who, such member or participant had reason to believe, was violating with respect to such transaction—

(A) in the case of a national securities exchange, any provision of the Securities Act of 1933, the Investment Advisers Act of 1940, the Investment Company Act of 1940, this chapter, or the rules or regulations under any of such statutes;

(B) in the case of a registered securities association, any provision of the Securities Act of 1933, the Investment Advisers Act of 1940, the Investment Company Act of 1940, this chapter, the rules or regulations under any of such statutes, or the rules of the Municipal Securities Rulemaking Board; or

(C) in the case of a registered clearing agency, any provision of the rules of the clearing agency.

(3) The appropriate regulatory agency for a national securities exchange or registered securities association is authorized, by order, if in its opinion such action is necessary or appropriate in the public interest, for the protection of investors, or otherwise in furtherance of the purposes of this chapter, to suspend for a period not exceeding twelve months or to bar any person from being associated with a member of such national securities exchange or registered securities association, if such person is subject to an order of the Commission pursuant to section 78o(b)(6) of this title or if such appropriate regulatory agency finds, on the record after notice and opportunity for hearing, that such person has willfully violated or has effected any transaction for any other person who, such person associated with a member had reason to believe, was violating with respect to such transaction—

(A)　in the case of a national securities exchange, any provision of the Securities Act of 1933, the Investment Advisers Act of 1940, the Investment Company Act of 1940, this chapter, or the rules or regulations under any of such statutes; or

(B)　in the case of a registered securities association, any provision of the Securities Act of 1933, the Investment Advisers Act of 1940, the Investment Company Act of 1940, this chapter, the rules or regulations under any of the statutes, or the rules of the Municipal Securities Rulemaking Board.

(4)　The appropriate regulatory agency for a self-regulatory organization is authorized, by order, if in its opinion such action is necessary or appropriate in the public interest, for the protection of investors, or otherwise in furtherance of the purposes of this chapter, to remove from office or censure any officer or director of such self-regulatory organization, if such appropriate regulatory agency finds, on the record after notice and opportunity for hearing, that such officer or director has willfully violated any provision of this chapter, the rules or regulations thereunder, or the rules of such self-regulatory organization, willfully abused his authority, or without reasonable justification or excuse has failed to enforce compliance--

(A)　in the case of a national securities exchange, with any such provision by any member or person associated with a member;

(B)　in the case of a registered securities association, with any such provision or any provision of the rules of the Municipal Securities Rulemaking Board by any member or person associated with a member; or

(C)　in the case of a registered clearing agency, with any provision of the rules of the clearing agency by any participant.

§ 20. Liability of controlling persons and persons who aid and abet violations

(a)　Joint and several liability; good faith defense

Every person who, directly or indirectly, controls any person liable under any provision of this chapter or of any rule or regulation thereunder shall also be liable jointly and severally with and to the same extent as such controlled person to any person to whom such controlled person is liable, unless the controlling person acted in good faith and did not directly or

indirectly induce the act or acts constituting the violation or cause of action.

* * *

§ 21. Investigations and actions

(a) Authority and discretion of Commission to investigate violations

    (1) The Commission may, in its discretion, make such investigations as it deems necessary to determine whether any person has violated, is violating, or is about to violate any provision of this chapter, the rules or regulations thereunder, the rules of a national securities exchange or registered securities association of which such person is a member or a person associated with a member, the rules of a registered clearing agency in which such person is a participant, or the rules of the Municipal Securities Rulemaking Board, and may require or permit any person to file with it a statement in writing, under oath or otherwise as the Commission shall determine, as to all the facts and circumstances concerning the matter to be investigated. The Commission is authorized in its discretion, to publish information concerning any such violations, and to investigate any facts, conditions, practices, or matters which it may deem necessary or proper to aid in the enforcement of such provisions, in the prescribing of rules and regulations under this chapter, or in securing information to serve as a basis for recommending further legislation concerning the matters to which this chapter relates.

    (2) On request from a foreign securities authority, the Commission may provide assistance in accordance with this paragraph if the requesting authority states that the requesting authority is conducting an investigation which it deems necessary to determine whether any person has violated, is violating, or is about to violate any laws or rules relating to securities matters that the requesting authority administers or enforces. The Commission may, in its discretion, conduct such investigation as the Commission deems necessary to collect information and evidence pertinent to the request for assistance. Such assistance may be provided without regard to whether the facts stated in the request would also constitute a violation of the laws of the United States. In deciding whether to provide such assistance, the Commission shall consider whether (A) the requesting authority has agreed to provide reciprocal assistance in

securities matters to the Commission; and (B) compliance with the request would prejudice the public interest of the United States.

* * *

(d)   Injunction proceedings; authority of court to prohibit persons from serving as officers and directors; money penalties in civil actions

(1)   Whenever it shall appear to the Commission that any person is engaged or is about to engage in acts or practices constituting a violation of any provision of this chapter, the rules or regulations thereunder, the rules of a national securities exchange or registered securities association of which such person is a member or a person associated with a member, the rules of a registered clearing agency in which such person is a participant, or the rules of the Municipal Securities Rulemaking Board, it may in its discretion bring an action in the proper district court of the United States, the United States District Court for the District of Columbia, or the United States courts of any territory or other place subject to the jurisdiction of the United States, to enjoin such acts or practices, and upon a proper showing a permanent or temporary injunction or restraining order shall be granted without bond. The Commission may transmit such evidence as may be available concerning such acts or practices as may constitute a violation of any provision of this chapter or the rules or regulations thereunder to the Attorney General, who may, in his discretion, institute the necessary criminal proceedings under this chapter.

(2)   Authority of court to prohibit persons from serving as officers and directors

In any proceeding under paragraph (1) of this subsection, the court may prohibit, conditionally or unconditionally, and permanently or for such period of time as it shall determine, any person who violated section 78j(b) of this title or the rules or regulations thereunder from acting as an officer or director of any issuer that has a class of securities registered pursuant to section 78l of this title or that is required to file reports pursuant to section 78o(d) of this title if the person's conduct demonstrates substantial unfitness to serve as an officer or director of any such issuer.

(3)   Money penalties in civil actions

(A)   Authority of Commission

Whenever it shall appear to the Commission that any person has violated any provision of this chapter, the rules or

regulations thereunder, or a cease- and-desist order entered by the Commission pursuant to section 78u-3 of this title, other than by committing a violation subject to a penalty pursuant to section 78u-1 of this title, the Commission may bring an action in a United States district court to seek, and the court shall have jurisdiction to impose, upon a proper showing, a civil penalty to be paid by the person who committed such violation.

(B) Amount of penalty

(i) First tier

The amount of the penalty shall be determined by the court in light of the facts and circumstances. For each violation, the amount of the penalty shall not exceed the greater of (I) $5,000 for a natural person or $50,000 for any other person, or (II) the gross amount of pecuniary gain to such defendant as a result of the violation.

(ii) Second tier

Notwithstanding clause (i), the amount of penalty for each such violation shall not exceed the greater of (I) $50,000 for a natural person or $250,000 for any other person, or (II) the gross amount of pecuniary gain to such defendant as a result of the violation, if the violation described in subparagraph (A) involved fraud, deceit, manipulation, or deliberate or reckless disregard of a regulatory requirement.

(iii) Third tier

Notwithstanding clauses (i) and (ii), the amount of penalty for each such violation shall not exceed the greater of (I) $100,000 for a natural person or $500,000 for any other person, or (II) the gross amount of pecuniary gain to such defendant as a result of the violation, if—

(aa) the violation described in subparagraph (A) involved fraud, deceit, manipulation, or deliberate or reckless disregard of a regulatory requirement; and

(bb) such violation directly or indirectly resulted in substantial losses or created a significant risk of substantial losses to other persons.

(C) Procedures for collection

(i) Payment of penalty to treasury

A penalty imposed under this section shall be payable into the Treasury of the United States.

(ii)   Collection of penalties

If a person upon whom such a penalty is imposed shall fail to pay such penalty within the time prescribed in the court's order, the Commission may refer the matter to the Attorney General who shall recover such penalty by action in the appropriate United States district court.

(iii)   Remedy not exclusive

The actions authorized by this paragraph may be brought in addition to any other action that the Commission or the Attorney General is entitled to bring.

(iv)   Jurisdiction and venue

For purposes of section 78aa of this title, actions under this paragraph shall be actions to enforce a liability or a duty created by this chapter.

(D)   Special provisions relating to a violation of a cease-and-desist order

In an action to enforce a cease-and-desist order entered by the Commission pursuant to section 78u-3 of this title, each separate violation of such order shall be a separate offense, except that in the case of a violation through a continuing failure to comply with the order, each day of the failure to comply shall be deemed a separate offense.

(4)   Prohibition of attorneys' fees paid from Commission disgorgement funds

Except as otherwise ordered by the court upon motion by the Commission, or, in the case of an administrative action, as otherwise ordered by the Commission, funds disgorged as the result of an action brought by the Commission in Federal court, or as a result of any Commission administrative action, shall not be distributed as payment for attorneys' fees or expenses incurred by private parties seeking distribution of the disgorged funds.

* * *

§ 21A. Civil penalties for insider trading

(a)   Authority to impose civil penalties

    (1)   Judicial actions by Commission authorized

          Whenever it shall appear to the Commission that any person has violated any provision of this chapter or the rules or regulations thereunder by purchasing or selling a security while in possession of material, nonpublic information in, or has violated any such provision by communicating such information in connection with, a transaction on or through the facilities of a national securities exchange or from or through a broker or dealer, and which is not part of a public offering by an issuer of securities other than standardized options, the Commission—

        (A)   may bring an action in a United States district court to seek, and the court shall have jurisdiction to impose, a civil penalty to be paid by the person who committed such violation; and

        (B)   may, subject to subsection (b)(1) of this section, bring an action in a United States district court to seek, and the court shall have jurisdiction to impose, a civil penalty to be paid by a person who, at the time of the violation, directly or indirectly controlled the person who committed such violation.

    (2)   Amount of penalty for person who committed violation

          The amount of the penalty which may be imposed on the person who committed such violation shall be determined by the court in light of the facts and circumstances, but shall not exceed three times the profit gained or loss avoided as a result of such unlawful purchase, sale, or communication.

    (3)   Amount of penalty for controlling person

          The amount of the penalty which may be imposed on any person who, at the time of the violation, directly or indirectly controlled the person who committed such violation, shall be determined by the court in light of the facts and circumstances, but shall not exceed the greater of $1,000,000, or three times the amount of the profit gained or loss avoided as a result of such controlled person's violation. If such controlled person's violation was a violation by communication, the profit gained or loss avoided as a result of the violation shall, for purposes of this paragraph only, be deemed to be limited to the profit gained or loss avoided by the person or persons to whom the controlled person directed such communication.

(b)   Limitations on liability

(1)   Liability of controlling persons

No controlling person shall be subject to a penalty under subsection (a)(1)(B) of this section unless the Commission establishes that—

(A)   such controlling person knew or recklessly disregarded the fact that such controlled person was likely to engage in the act or acts constituting the violation and failed to take appropriate steps to prevent such act or acts before they occurred; or

(B)   such controlling person knowingly or recklessly failed to establish, maintain, or enforce any policy or procedure required under section 78o(f) of this title or section 80b-4a of this title and such failure substantially contributed to or permitted the occurrence of the act or acts constituting the violation.

(2)   Additional restrictions on liability

No person shall be subject to a penalty under subsection (a) of this section solely by reason of employing another person who is subject to a penalty under such subsection, unless such employing person is liable as a controlling person under paragraph (1) of this subsection. Section 78t(a) of this title shall not apply to actions under subsection (a) of this section.

* * *

§ 28. Effect on existing law

(a)   Addition of rights and remedies; recovery of actual damages; State securities commissions

The rights and remedies provided by this chapter shall be in addition to any and all other rights and remedies that may exist at law or in equity; but no person permitted to maintain a suit for damages under the provisions of this chapter shall recover, through satisfaction of judgment in one or more actions, a total amount in excess of his actual damages on account of the act complained of. Except as otherwise specifically provided in this chapter, nothing in this chapter shall affect the jurisdiction of the securities commission (or any agency or officer performing like functions) of any State over any security or any person insofar as it does not conflict with the provisions of this chapter or the rules and regulations thereunder. No State law which prohibits or regulates the making or promoting of wagering or gaming contracts, or the operation of "bucket shops" or other similar or related activities, shall invalidate any put, call,

straddle, option, privilege, or other security, or apply to any activity which is incidental or related to the offer, purchase, sale, exercise, settlement, or closeout of any such instrument, if such instrument is traded pursuant to rules and regulations of a self-regulatory organization that are filed with the Commission pursuant to section 19(b) of this Act.

(b) Modification of disciplinary procedures

Nothing in this chapter shall be construed to modify existing law with regard to the binding effect (1) on any member of or participant in any self-regulatory organization of any action taken by the authorities of such organization to settle disputes between its members or participants, (2) on any municipal securities dealer or municipal securities broker of any action taken pursuant to a procedure established by the Municipal Securities Rulemaking Board to settle disputes between municipal securities dealers and municipal securities brokers, or (3) of any action described in paragraph (1) or (2) on any person who has agreed to be bound thereby.

(c) Continuing validity of disciplinary sanctions

The stay, setting aside, or modification pursuant to section 78s(e) of this title of any disciplinary sanction imposed by a self-regulatory organization on a member thereof, person associated with a member, or participant therein, shall not affect the validity or force of any action taken as a result of such sanction by the self-regulatory organization prior to such stay, setting aside, or modification: Provided, That such action is not inconsistent with the provisions of this chapter or the rules or regulations thereunder. The rights of any person acting in good faith which arise out of any such action shall not be affected in any way by such stay, setting aside, or modification.

(d) Physical location of facilities of registered clearing agencies or registered transfer agents not to subject changes in beneficial or record ownership of securities to State or local taxes

No State or political subdivision thereof shall impose any tax on any change in beneficial or record ownership of securities effected through the facilities of a registered clearing agency or registered transfer agent or any nominee thereof or custodian therefor or upon the delivery or transfer of securities to or through or receipt from such agency or agent or any nominee thereof or custodian therefor, unless such change is in beneficial or record ownership or such transfer or delivery or receipt would otherwise be taxable by such State or political subdivision if the facilities of such registered clearing agency, registered transfer agent, or any nominee thereof or custodian therefor were not physically located in the taxing State or political subdivision. No State or political subdivision thereof shall

impose any tax on securities which are deposited in or retained by a registered clearing agency, registered transfer agent, or any nominee thereof or custodian therefor, unless such securities would otherwise be taxable by such State or political subdivision if the facilities of such registered clearing agency, registered transfer agent, or any nominee thereof or custodian therefor were not physically located in the taxing State or political subdivision.

(e)   Exchange, broker, and dealer commissions; brokerage and research services

(1)   No person using the mails, or any means or instrumentality of interstate commerce, in the exercise of investment discretion with respect to an account shall be deemed to have acted unlawfully or to have breached a fiduciary duty under State or Federal law unless expressly provided to the contrary by a law enacted by the Congress or any State subsequent to June 4, 1975, solely by reason of his having caused the account to pay a member of an exchange, broker, or dealer an amount of commission for effecting a securities transaction in excess of the amount of commission another member of an exchange, broker, or dealer would have charged for effecting that transaction, if such person determined in good faith that such amount of commission was reasonable in relation to the value of the brokerage and research services provided by such member, broker, or dealer, viewed in terms of either that particular transaction or his overall responsibilities with respect to the accounts as to which he exercises investment discretion. This subsection is exclusive and plenary insofar as conduct is covered by the foregoing, unless otherwise expressly provided by contract: Provided, however, That nothing in this subsection shall be construed to impair or limit the power of the Commission under any other provision of this chapter or otherwise.

(2)   A person exercising investment discretion with respect to an account shall make such disclosure of his policies and practices with respect to commissions that will be paid for effecting securities transactions, at such times and in such manner, as the appropriate regulatory agency, by rule, may prescribe as necessary or appropriate in the public interest or for the protection of investors.

(3)   For purposes of this subsection a person provides brokerage and research services insofar as he--

(A)   furnishes advice, either directly or through publications or writings, as to the value of securities, the advisability of

investing in, purchasing, or selling securities, and the availability of securities or purchasers or sellers of securities;

(B) furnishes analyses and reports concerning issuers, industries, securities, economic factors and trends, portfolio strategy, and the performance of accounts; or

(C) effects securities transactions and performs functions incidental thereto (such as clearance, settlement, and custody) or required in connection therewith by rules of the Commission or a self-regulatory organization of which such person is a member or person associated with a member or in which such person is a participant.

§ 29. Validity of contracts

(a) Waiver provisions

Any condition, stipulation, or provision binding any person to waive compliance with any provision of this chapter or of any rule or regulation thereunder, or of any rule of an exchange required thereby shall be void.

* * *

§ 32. Penalties

(a) Willful violations; false and misleading statements

Any person who willfully violates any provision of this chapter (other than section 78dd-1 of this title), or any rule or regulation thereunder the violation of which is made unlawful or the observance of which is required under the terms of this chapter, or any person who willfully and knowingly makes, or causes to be made, any statement in any application, report, or document required to be filed under this chapter or any rule or regulation thereunder or any undertaking contained in a registration statement as provided in subsection (d) of section 78o of this title, or by any self-regulatory organization in connection with an application for membership or participation therein or to become associated with a member thereof, which statement was false or misleading with respect to any material fact, shall upon conviction be fined not more than $1,000,000, or imprisoned not more than 10 years, or both, except that when such person is a person other than a natural person, a fine not exceeding $2,500,000 may be imposed; but no person shall be subject to

imprisonment under this section for the violation of any rule or regulation if he proves that he had no knowledge of such rule or regulation.

(b)   Failure to file information, documents, or reports

Any issuer which fails to file information, documents, or reports required to be filed under subsection (d) of section 78o of this title or any rule or regulation thereunder shall forfeit to the United States the sum of $100 for each and every day such failure to file shall continue. Such forfeiture, which shall be in lieu of any criminal penalty for such failure to file which might be deemed to arise under subsection (a) of this section, shall be payable into the Treasury of the United States and shall be recoverable in a civil suit in the name of the United States.

(c)   Violations by issuers, officers, directors, stockholders, employees, or agents of issuers

(1)   (A)   Any issuer that violates section 78dd-1(a) of this title shall be fined not more than $2,000,000.

(B)   Any issuer that violates section 78dd-1(a) of this title shall be subject to a civil penalty of not more than $10,000 imposed in an action brought by the Commission.

(2)   (A)   Any officer or director of an issuer, or stockholder acting on behalf of such issuer, who willfully violates section 78dd-1(a) of this title shall be fined not more than $100,000, or imprisoned not more than 5 years, or both.

(B)   Any employee or agent of an issuer who is a United States citizen, national, or resident or is otherwise subject to the jurisdiction of the United States (other than an officer, director, or stockholder acting on behalf of such issuer), and who willfully violates section 78dd-1(a) of this title, shall be fined not more than $100,000, or imprisoned not more than 5 years, or both.

(C)   Any officer, director, employee, or agent of an issuer, or stockholder acting on behalf of such issuer, who violates section 78dd-1(a) of this title shall be subject to a civil penalty of not more than $10,000 imposed in an action brought by the Commission.

(3)   Whenever a fine is imposed under paragraph (2) upon any officer, director, employee, agent, or stockholder of an issuer, such fine may not be paid, directly or indirectly, by such issuer.

* * *

SELECTED RULES AND REGULATIONS UNDER THE SECURITIES EXCHANGE ACT OF 1934

_____

(codified at 17 C.F.R. § 240.___)

* * *

3a4-1. Associated persons of an issuer deemed not to be brokers.

(a) An associated person of an issuer of securities shall not be deemed to be a broker solely by reason of his participation in the sale of the securities of such issuer if the associated person:

    (1) Is not subject to a statutory disqualification, as that term is defined in section 3(a)(39) of the Act, at the time of his participation; and

    (2) Is not compensated in connection with his participation by the payment of commissions or other remuneration based either directly or indirectly on transactions in securities; and

    (3) Is not at the time of his participation an associated person of a broker or dealer; and

    (4) Meets the conditions of any one of paragraphs (a)(4) (i), (ii), or (iii) of this section.

        (i) The associated person restricts his participation to transactions involving offers and sales of securities:

            (A) To a registered broker or dealer; a registered investment company (or registered separate account); an insurance company; a bank; a savings and loan association; a trust company or similar institution supervised by a state or federal banking authority; or a trust for which a bank, a savings and loan association, a trust company, or a registered investment adviser either is the trustee or is authorized in writing to make investment decisions; or

            (B) That are exempted by reason of sections 3(a)(7), 3(a)(9) or 3(a)(10) of the Securities Act of 1933 from the registration provisions of that Act; or

            (C) That are made pursuant to a plan or agreement submitted for the vote or consent of the security holders who will receive securities of the issuer in connection with a reclassification of securities of the issuer, a merger or consolidation or a similar plan of acquisition involving an

exchange of securities, or a transfer of assets of any other person to the issuer in exchange for securities of the issuer; or

(D) That are made pursuant to a bonus, profit-sharing, pension, retirement, thrift, savings, incentive, stock purchase, stock ownership, stock appreciation, stock option, dividend reinvestment or similar plan for employees of an issuer or a subsidiary of the issuer;

(ii) The associated person meets all of the following conditions:

(A) The associated person primarily performs, or is intended primarily to perform at the end of the offering, substantial duties for or on behalf of the issuer otherwise than in connection with transactions in securities; and

(B) The associated person was not a broker or dealer, or an associated person of a broker or dealer, within the preceding 12 months; and

(C) The associated person does not participate in selling an offering of securities for any issuer more than once every 12 months other than in reliance on paragraphs (a)(4)(i) or (a)(4)(iii) of this section, except that for securities issued pursuant to Rule 415 under the Securities Act of 1933, the 12 months shall begin with the last sale of any security included within one Rule 415 registration.

(iii) The associated person restricts his participation to any one or more of the following activities:

(A) Preparing any written communication or delivering such communication through the mails or other means that does not involve oral solicitation by the associated person of a potential purchaser; provided, however, that the content of such communication is approved by a partner, officer or director of the issuer;

(B) Responding to inquiries of a potential purchaser in a communication initiated by the potential purchaser; provided, however, that the content of such responses are limited to information contained in a registration statement filed under the Securities Act of 1933 or other offering document; or

(C) Performing ministerial and clerical work involved in effecting any transaction.

(b)   No presumption shall arise that an associated person of an issuer has violated section 15(a) of the Act solely by reason of his participation in the sale of securities of the issuer if he does not meet the conditions specified in paragraph (a) of this section.

(c)   Definitions. When used in this section:

   (1)   The term "associated person of an issuer" means any natural person who is a partner, officer, director, or employee of:

      (i)   The issuer;

      (ii)   A corporate general partner of a limited partnership that is the issuer;

      (iii)   A company or partnership that controls, is controlled by, or is under common control with, the issuer; or

      (iv)   An investment adviser registered under the Investment Advisers Act of 1940 to an investment company registered under the Investment Company Act of 1940 which is the issuer.

   (2)   The term "associated person of a broker or dealer" means any partner, officer, director, or branch manager of such broker or dealer (or any person occupying a similar status or performing similar functions), any person directly or indirectly controlling, controlled by, or under common control with such broker or dealer, or any employee of such broker or dealer, except that any person associated with a broker or dealer whose functions are solely clerical or ministerial and any person who is required under the laws of any state to register as a broker or dealer in that state solely because such person is an issuer of securities or associated person of an issuer of securities shall not be included in the meaning of such term for purposes of this section.

* * *

10b-5. Employment of manipulative and deceptive devices.

   It shall be unlawful for any person, directly or indirectly, by the use of any means or instrumentality of interstate commerce, or of the mails or of any facility of any national securities exchange,

(a)   To employ any device, scheme, or artifice to defraud,

(b)   To make any untrue statement of a material fact or to omit to state a material fact necessary in order to make the statements made, in the light of the circumstances under which they were made, not misleading, or

(c)   To engage in any act, practice, or course of business which operates or would operate as a fraud or deceit upon any person, in connection with the purchase or sale of any security.

* * *

10b-10. Confirmation of transactions.

Preliminary Note. This section requires broker-dealers to disclose specified information in writing to customers at or before completion of a transaction. The requirements under this section that particular information be disclosed is not determinative of a broker-dealer's obligation under the general antifraud provisions of the federal securities laws to disclose additional information to a customer at the time of the customer's investment decision.

(a)   Disclosure Requirement. It shall be unlawful for any broker or dealer to effect for or with an account of a customer any transaction in, or to induce the purchase or sale by such customer of, any security (other than U.S. Savings Bonds or municipal securities) unless such broker or dealer, at or before completion of such transaction, gives or sends to such customer written notification disclosing:

(1)   The date and time of the transaction (or the fact that the time of the transaction will be furnished upon written request to such customer) and the identity, price, and number of shares or units (or principal amount) of such security purchased or sold by such customer; and

(2)   Whether the broker or dealer is acting as agent for such customer, as agent for some other person, as agent for both such customer and some other person, or as principal for its own account; and if the broker or dealer is acting as principal, whether it is a market maker in the security (other than by reason of acting as a block positioner); and

(i)   If the broker or dealer is acting as agent for such customer, for some other person, or for both such customer and some other person:

(A)   The name of the person from whom the security was purchased, or to whom it was sold, for such customer or the fact that the information will be furnished upon written request of such customer; and

(B)   The amount of any remuneration received or to be received by the broker from such customer in connection with the transaction unless remuneration paid by such customer is determined pursuant to written agreement with such customer, otherwise than on a transaction basis; and

(C)   For a transaction in any subject security as defined in Rule 11Ac1-2 or a security authorized for quotation on an automated interdealer quotation system that has the characteristics set forth in Section 17B of this Act, a

statement whether payment for order flow is received by the broker or dealer for transactions in such securities and the fact that the source and nature of the compensation received in connection with the particular transaction will be furnished upon written request of the customer; and

(D) The source and amount of any other remuneration received or to be received by the broker in connection with the transaction: Provided, however, that if, in the case of a purchase, the broker was not participating in a distribution, or in the case of a sale, was not participating in a tender offer, the written notification may state whether any other remuneration has been or will be received and the fact that the source and amount of such other remuneration will be furnished upon written request of such customer; or

(ii) If the broker or dealer is acting as principal for its own account:

(A) In the case where such broker or dealer is not a market maker in an equity security and, if, after having received an order to buy from a customer, the broker or dealer purchased the equity security from another person to offset a contemporaneous sale to such customer or, after having received an order to sell from a customer, the broker or dealer sold the security to another person to offset a contemporaneous purchase from such customer, the difference between the price to the customer and the dealer's contemporaneous purchase (for customer purchases) or sale price (for customer sales); or

(B) In the case of any other transaction in a reported security, or an equity security that is quoted on NASDAQ or traded on a national securities exchange and that is subject to last sale reporting, the reported trade price, the price to the customer in the transaction, and the difference, if any, between the reported trade price and the price to the customer.

(3) Whether any odd-lot differential or equivalent fee has been paid by such customer in connection with the execution of an order for an odd-lot number of shares or units (or principal amount) of a security and the fact that the amount of any such differential or fee will be furnished upon oral or written request: Provided, however, that such disclosure need not be made if the differential or fee is included in the remuneration disclosure, or exempted from disclosure, pursuant to paragraph (a)(2)(i)(B) of this section; and

(4)   In the case of any transaction in a debt security subject to redemption before maturity, a statement to the effect that such debt security may be redeemed in whole or in part before maturity, that such a redemption could affect the yield represented and the fact that additional information is available upon request; and

(5)   In the case of a transaction in a debt security effected exclusively on the basis of a dollar price:

(i)   The dollar price at which the transaction was effected, and

(ii)   The yield to maturity calculated from the dollar price: Provided, however, that this paragraph (a)(5)(ii) shall not apply to a transaction in a debt security that either:

(A)   Has a maturity date that may be extended by the issuer thereof, with a variable interest payable thereon; or

(B)   Is an asset-backed security, that represents an interest in or is secured by a pool of receivables or other financial assets that are subject continuously to prepayment; and

(6)   In the case of a transaction in a debt security effected on the basis of yield:

(i)   The yield at which the transaction was effected, including the percentage amount and its characterization (e.g., current yield, yield to maturity, or yield to call) and if effected at yield to call, the type of call, the call date and call price; and

(ii)   The dollar price calculated from the yield at which the transaction was effected; and

(iii)   If effected on a basis other than yield to maturity and the yield to maturity is lower than the represented yield, the yield to maturity as well as the represented yield; Provided, however, that this paragraph (a)(6)(iii) shall not apply to a transaction in a debt security that either:

(A)   Has a maturity date that may be extended by the issuer thereof, with a variable interest rate payable thereon; or

(B)   Is an asset-backed security, that represents an interest in or is secured by a pool of receivables or other financial assets that are subject continuously to prepayment; and

(7)   In the case of a transaction in a debt security that is an asset-backed security, which represents an interest in or is secured by a pool of receivables or other financial assets that are subject continuously to prepayment, a statement indicating that the actual yield of such asset-backed security may vary according to the rate at which the underlying receivables or other financial assets are prepaid and a

statement of the fact that information concerning the factors that affect yield (including at a minimum estimated yield, weighted average life, and the prepayment assumptions underlying yield) will be furnished upon written request of such customer; and

(i), (ii) [Reserved]

(iii) For a transaction in any subject security as defined in Rule 11Ac1-2 or a security authorized for quotation on an automated interdealer quotation system that has the characteristics set forth in Section 17B of the Act (> 15 U.S.C. 78q-2), a statement whether payment for order flow is received by the broker or dealer for transactions in such securities and that the source and nature of the compensation received in connection with the particular transaction will be furnished upon written request of the customer; and

(iv) The source and amount of any other remuneration received or to be received by him in connection with the transaction: Provided, however, That if, in the case of a purchase, the broker was not participating in a distribution, or in the case of a sale, was not participating in a tender offer, the written notification may state whether any other remuneration has been or will be received and that the source and amount of such other remuneration will be furnished upon written request of such customer; and

(8) If he is acting as principal for his own account.

(i) (A) If he is not a market maker in that security and, if, after having received an order to buy from such customer, he purchased the security from another person to offset a contemporaneous sale to such customer or, after having received an order to sell from such customer, he sold the security to another person to offset a contemporaneous purchase from such a customer, the amount of any mark-up, mark-down, or similar remuneration received in an equity security; or

(B) In any other case of a transaction in a reported security, the trade price reported in accordance with an effective transaction reporting plan, the price to the customer in the transaction, and the difference, if any, between the reported trade price and the price to the customer.

(ii) In the case of transaction in an equity security, whether he is a market maker in that security (otherwise than by reason of his action as a block positioner in that security).

(9)   That the broker or dealer is not a member of the Securities Investor Protection Corporation (SIPC), or that the broker or dealer clearing or carrying the customer account is not a member of SIPC, if such is the case: Provided, however, That this paragraph (a)(9) shall not apply in the case of a transaction in shares of a registered open-end investment company or unit investment trust if:

(i)   The customer sends funds or securities directly to, or receives funds or securities directly from, the registered open-end investment company or unit investment trust, its transfer agent, its custodian, or other designated agent, and such person is not an associated person of the broker or dealer required by paragraph (a) of this section to send written notification to the customer; and

(ii)   The written notification required by paragraph (a) of this section is sent on behalf of the broker or dealer to the customer by a person described in paragraph (a)(9)(i) of this section.

(b)   Alternative Periodic Reporting. A broker or dealer may effect transactions for or with the account of a customer without giving or sending to such customer the written notification described in paragraph (a) of this section if:

(1)   Such transactions are effected pursuant to a periodic plan or an investment company plan, or effected in shares of any open-end management investment company registered under the Investment Company Act of 1940 that holds itself out as a money market fund and attempts to maintain a stable net asset value per share: Provided, however, that no sales load is deducted upon the purchase or redemption of shares in the money market fund; and

(2)   Such broker or dealer gives or sends to such customer within five business days after the end of each quarterly period, for transactions involving investment company and periodic plans, and after the end of each monthly period, for other transactions described in paragraph (c)(1) of this section, a written statement disclosing each purchase or redemption, effected for or with, and each dividend or distribution credited to or reinvested for, the account of such customer during the month; the date of such transaction; the identity, number, and price of any securities purchased or redeemed by such customer in each such transaction; the total number of shares of such securities in such customer's account; any remuneration received or to be received by the broker or dealer in connection therewith; and that any other information required by paragraph (a) of this section will be furnished upon written request: Provided, however, that the written statement

may be delivered to some other person designated by the customer for distribution to the customer; and

(3) Such customer is provided with prior notification in writing disclosing the intention to send the written information referred to in paragraph (c)(1) of this section in lieu of an immediate confirmation.

(c) A broker or dealer shall give or send to a customer information requested pursuant to this rule within 5 business days of receipt of the request; Provided, however, That in the case of information pertaining to a transaction effected more than 30 days prior to receipt of the request, the information shall be given or sent to the customer within 15 business days.

(d) Definitions. For the purposes of this section:

(1) Customer shall not include a broker or dealer;

(2) Completion of the transaction shall have the meaning provided in rule 15c1-1 under the Act;

(3) Time of the transaction means the time of execution, to the extent feasible, of the customer's order;

(4) Debt security as used in paragraphs (a)(3), (a)(4), and (a)(5) only, means any security, such as a bond, debenture, note, or any other similar instrument which evidences a liability of the issuer (including any such security that is convertible into stock or a similar security) and fractional or participation interests in one or more of any of the foregoing: Provided, however, that securities issued by an investment company registered under the Investment Company Act of 1940 shall not be included in this definition:

(5) Periodic plan means any written authorization for a broker acting as agent to purchase or sell for a customer a specific security or securities (other than securities issued by an open end investment company or unit investment trust registered under the Investment Company Act of 1940), in specific amounts (calculated in security units or dollars), at specific time intervals and setting forth the commissions or charges to be paid by the customer in connection therewith (or the manner of calculating them); and

(6) Investment company plan means any plan under which securities issued by an open-end investment company or unit investment trust registered under the Investment Company Act of 1940 are purchased by a customer (the

payments being made directly to, or made payable to, the registered investment company, or the principal underwriter, custodian, trustee, or other designated agent of the registered investment company), or sold by a customer pursuant to:

(i)   An individual retirement or individual pension plan qualified under the Internal Revenue Code;

(ii) A contractual or systematic agreement under which the customer purchases at the applicable public offering price, or redeems at the applicable redemption price, such securities in specified amounts (calculated in security units or dollars) at specified time intervals and setting forth the commissions or charges to be paid by such customer in connection therewith (or the manner of calculating them; or

(iii) Any other arrangement involving a group of two or more customers and contemplating periodic purchases of such securities by each customer through a person designated by the group; Provided, That such arrangement requires the registered investment company or its agent—

(A) To give or send to the designated person, at or before the completion of the transaction for the purchase of such securities, a written notification of the receipt of the total amount paid by the group;

(B) To send to anyone in the group who was a customer in the prior quarter and on whose behalf payment has not been received in the current quarter a quarterly written statement reflecting that a payment was not received on his behalf; and

(C) To advise each customer in the group if a payment is not received from the designated person on behalf of the group within 10 days of a date certain specified in the arrangement for delivery of that payment by the designated person and thereafter to send to each such customer the written notification described in paragraph (a) of this section for the next three succeeding payments.

(7) Reported security shall have the meaning provided in Rule 11Aa3-1 under the Act.

(8) Effective transaction reporting plan shall have the meaning provided in Rule 11Aa3-1 under the Act.

(9) Payment for order flow shall mean any monetary payment, service, property, or other benefit that results in remuneration, compensation, or consideration to a broker or dealer from any broker or dealer, national securities exchange, registered securities association, or exchange member in return for the routing of customer orders by such broker or dealer to any broker or dealer, national securities exchange, registered securities association, or exchange member for execution, including but not limited to: research, clearance, custody, products or services; reciprocal agreements for the provision of order flow; adjustment of a broker or dealer's unfavorable trading errors; offers to participate as underwriter in public offerings; stock loans or shared interest accrued thereon; discounts, rebates, or any other reductions of or credits against any fee to, or expense or other financial obligation of, the broker or dealer routing a customer order that exceeds that fee, expense or financial obligation.

(10) Asset-backed security means a security that is primarily serviced by the cashflows of a discrete pool of receivables or other financial assets, either fixed or revolving, that by their terms convert into cash within a finite time period plus any rights or other assets designed to assure the servicing or timely distribution of proceeds to the security holders.

(e) The Commission may exempt any broker or dealer from the requirements of paragraphs (a) and (b) of this section with regard to specific transactions of specific classes of transactions for which the broker or dealer will provide alternative procedures to effect the purposes of this section; any such exemption may be granted subject to compliance with such alternative procedures and upon such other stated terms and conditions as the Commission may impose.

* * *

11Ac1-3. Customer account statements.

(a) No broker or dealer acting as agent for a customer may effect any transaction in, induce or attempt to induce the purchase or sale of, or direct orders for purchase or sale of, any subject security as defined in Rule 11Ac1-2 or a security authorized for quotation on an automated

inter-dealer quotation system that has the characteristics set forth in section 17B of the Act (15 U.S.C. § 78q-2), unless such broker or dealer informs such customer, in writing, upon opening a new account and on an annual basis thereafter, of the following:

(1)   The broker's or dealer's policies regarding receipt of payment for order flow as defined in Rule 10b-10(e)(9), from any broker or dealer, national securities exchange, registered securities association, or exchange member to which it routes customers' orders for execution, including a statement as to whether any payment for order flow is received for routing customer orders and a detailed description of the nature of the compensation received; and

(2)   The broker's or dealer's policies for determining where to route customer orders that are the subject of payment for order flow as defined in Rule 10b-10(e)(9) absent specific instructions from customers, including a description of the extent to which orders can be executed prices superior to the best bid or best offer as defined in Rule 11Ac1-2.

(b)   Exemptions. The Commission, upon request or upon its own motion, may exempt by rule or by order, any broker or dealer or any class of brokers or dealers, security or class of securities from the requirements of paragraph (a) of this section with respect to any transaction or class of transactions, either unconditionally or on specified terms and conditions, if the Commission determines that such exemption is consistent with the pubic interest and the protection of investors.

* * *

11Ac1-4. Display of customer limit orders.

(a)   Definitions. For purposes of this section:

(1)   The term association shall mean any association of brokers and dealers registered pursuant to Section 15A of the Act (15 U.S.C. § 78o-3).

(2)   The terms best bid and best offer shall have the meaning provided in Rule 11Ac1-1(a)(3).

(3)   The terms bid and offer shall have the meaning provided in Rule 11Ac1- 1(a)(4).

(4)   The term block size shall mean any order:

(i)   Of at least 10,000 shares; or

(ii)   For a quantity of stock having a market value of at least $200,000.

(5)   The term covered security shall mean any "reported security" and any other security for which a transaction report, last sale data or quotation information is disseminated through an automated quotation system as described in section 3(a)(51)(A)(ii) of the Act (15 U.S.C. § 78c(a)(51)(A)(ii)).

(6)   The term customer limit order shall mean an order to buy or sell a covered security at a specified price that is not for the account of either a broker or dealer; provided, however, That the term customer limit order shall include an order transmitted by a broker or dealer on behalf of a customer.

(7)   The term electronic communications network shall have the meaning provided in Rule 11Ac1-1(a)(8).

(8)   The term exchange-traded security shall have the meaning provided in Rule 11Ac1-1(a)(10).

(9)   The term OTC market maker shall mean any dealer who holds itself out as being willing to buy from and sell to its customers, or otherwise, a covered security for its own account on a regular or continuous basis otherwise than on a national securities exchange in amounts of less than block size.

(10) The term reported security shall have the meaning provided in Rule 11Ac1-1(a)(20).

(b)   Specialists and OTC market makers. For all covered securities:

(1)   Each member of an exchange that is registered by that exchange as a specialist, or is authorized by that exchange to perform functions substantially similar to that of a specialist, shall publish immediately a bid or offer that reflects:

(i)   The price and the full size of each customer limit order held by the specialist that is at a price that would improve the bid or offer of such specialist in such security; and

(ii)   The full size of each customer limit order held by the specialist that:

(A) Is priced equal to the bid or offer of such specialist for such security;

(B) Is priced equal to the national best bid or offer; and

(C) Represents more than a de minimis change in relation to the size associated with the specialist's bid or offer.

(2)   Each registered broker or dealer that acts as an OTC market maker shall publish immediately a bid or offer that reflects:

       (i)   The price and the full size of each customer limit order held by the OTC market maker that is at a price that would improve the bid or offer of such OTC market maker in such security; and

      (ii)   The full size of each customer limit order held by the OTC market maker that:

          (A) Is priced equal to the bid or offer of such OTC market maker for such security;

          (B) Is priced equal to the national best bid or offer; and

          (C) Represents more than a de minimis change in relation to the size associated with the OTC market maker's bid or offer.

(c)   Exceptions. The requirements in paragraph (b) of this section shall not apply to any customer limit order:

      (1)   That is executed upon receipt of the order.

      (2)   That is placed by a customer who expressly requests, either at the time that the order is placed or prior thereto pursuant to an individually negotiated agreement with respect to such customer's orders, that the order not be displayed.

      (3)   That is an odd-lot order.

      (4)   That is a block size order, unless a customer placing such order requests that the order be displayed.

      (5)   That is delivered immediately upon receipt to an exchange or association-sponsored system, or an electronic communications network that complies with the requirements of Rule 11Ac1-1(c)(5)(ii) with respect to that order.

      (6)   That is delivered immediately upon receipt to another exchange member or OTC market maker that complies with the requirements of this section with respect to that order.

      (7)   That is an "all or none" order.

(d)   Exemptions. The Commission may exempt from the provisions of this section, either unconditionally or on specified terms and conditions, any responsible broker or dealer, electronic communications network, exchange, or association if the Commission determines that such exemption is consistent with the public interest, the protection of investors and the removal of impediments to and perfection of the mechanism of a national market system.

* * *

15c1-2. Fraud and misrepresentation.

(a) The term "manipulative, deceptive, or other fraudulent device or contrivance", as used in section 15(c)(1) of the act is hereby defined to include any act, practice, or course of business which operates or would operate as a fraud or deceit upon any person.

(b) The term "manipulative, deceptive, or other fraudulent device or contrivance", as used in section 15(c)(1) of the act, is hereby defined to include any untrue statement of a material fact and any omission to state a material fact necessary in order to make the statements made, in the light of the circumstances under which they are made, not misleading, which statement or omission is made with knowledge or reasonable grounds to believe that it is untrue or misleading.

(c) The scope of this section shall not be limited by any specific definitions of the term "manipulative, deceptive, or other fraudulent device or contrivance" contained in other rules adopted pursuant to section 15(c)(1) of the act.

* * *

15c2-11. Initiation or resumption of quotations without specific information.

Preliminary Note: Brokers and dealers may wish to refer to Securities Exchange Act Release No. 29094 (April 17, 1991), for a discussion of procedures for gathering and reviewing the information required by this rule and the requirement that a broker or dealer have a reasonable basis for believing that the information is accurate and obtained from reliable sources.

(a) As a means reasonably designed to prevent fraudulent, deceptive, or manipulative acts or practices, it shall be unlawful for a broker or dealer to publish any quotation for a security or, directly or indirectly, to submit any such quotation for publication, in any quotation medium (as defined in this section) unless such broker or dealer has in its records the documents and information required by this paragraph (for purposes of this section, "paragraph (a) information"), and, based upon a review of the paragraph (a) information together with any other documents and information required by paragraph (b) of this section, has a reasonable basis under the circumstances for believing that the paragraph (a) information is accurate in all material respects, and that the sources of the paragraph (a) information are reliable. The information required pursuant to this paragraph is:

    (1) A copy of the prospectus specified by section 10(a) of the Securities Act of 1933 for an issuer that has filed a registration statement under the Securities Act of 1933, other than a registration statement on Form F-6, which became effective less than 90 calendar days prior to

the day on which such broker or dealer publishes or submits the quotation to the quotation medium, Provided That such registration statement has not thereafter been the subject of a stop order which is still in effect when the quotation is published or submitted; or

(2)   A copy of the offering circular provided for under Regulation A under the Securities Act of 1933 for an issuer that has filed a notification under Regulation A and was authorized to commence the offering less than 40 calendar days prior to the day on which such broker or dealer publishes or submits the quotation to the quotation medium, Provided That the offering circular provided for under Regulation A has not thereafter become the subject of a suspension order which is still in effect when the quotation is published or submitted; or

(3)   A copy of the issuer's most recent annual report filed pursuant to section 13 or 15(d) of the Act or a copy of the annual statement referred to in section 12(g)(2)(G)(i) of the Act, in the case of an issuer required to file reports pursuant to section 13 or 15(d) of the Act or an issuer of a security covered by section 12(g)(2)(B) or (G) of the Act, together with any quarterly and current reports that have been filed under the provisions of the Act by the issuer after such annual report or annual statement; Provided, however, That until such issuer has filed its first annual report pursuant to section 13 or 15(d) of the Act or annual statement referred to in section 12(g)(2)(G)(i) of the Act, the broker or dealer has in its records a copy of the prospectus specified by section 10(a) of the Securities Act of 1933 included in a registration statement filed by the issuer under the Securities Act of 1933, other than a registration statement on Form F-6, that became effective within the prior 16 months, or a copy of any registration statement filed by the issuer under section 12 of the Act that became effective within the prior 16 months, together with any quarterly and current reports filed thereafter under section 13 or 15(d) of the Act; and Provided further, That the broker or dealer has a reasonable basis under the circumstances for believing that the issuer is current in filing annual, quarterly, and current reports filed pursuant to section 13 or 15(d) of the Act, or, in the case of an insurance company exempted from section 12(g) of the Act by reason of section 12(g)(2)(G) thereof, the annual statement referred to in section 12(g)(2)(G)(i) of the Act; or

(4)   The information furnished to the Commission pursuant to Rule 12g3-2(b) since the beginning of the issuer's last fiscal year, in the case of an issuer exempt from section 12(g) of the Act by reason of compliance with the provisions of Rule 12g3-2(b), which information the broker or dealer shall make reasonably available upon request to

any person expressing an interest in a proposed transaction in the security with such broker or dealer; or

(5) The following information, which shall be reasonably current in relation to the day the quotation is submitted and which the broker or dealer shall make reasonably available upon request to any person expressing an interest in a proposed transaction in the security with such broker or dealer:

(i)   The exact name of the issuer and its predecessor (if any);

(ii)   the address of its principal executive offices;

(iii) the state of incorporation, if it is a corporation;

(iv)   the exact title and class of the security;

(v)   the par or stated value of the security;

(vi)   the number of shares or total amount of the securities outstanding as of the end of the issuer's most recent fiscal year;

(vii) the name and address of the transfer agent;

(viii) the nature of the issuer's business;

(ix)   the nature of products or services offered;

(x)   the nature and extent of the issuer's facilities;

(xi)   the name of the chief executive officer and members of the board of directors;

(xii) the issuer's most recent balance sheet and profit and loss and retained earnings statements;

(xiii) similar financial information for such part of the 2 preceding fiscal   years as the issuer or its predecessor has been in existence;

(xiv) whether the broker or dealer or any associated person is affiliated,   directly or indirectly with the issuer;

(xv)   whether the quotation is being published or submitted on behalf of any other broker or dealer, and, if so, the name of such broker or dealer; and

(xvi)   whether the quotation is being submitted or published directly or   indirectly on behalf of the issuer, or any director, officer or any person, directly or indirectly the beneficial owner of more than 10 percent of the outstanding units or shares of any equity security of the issuer, and, if so, the name of such person, and the basis for any exemption under the federal securities laws for any sales of such securities on behalf of such person.

If such information is made available to others upon request pursuant to this paragraph, such delivery, unless otherwise

represented, shall not constitute a representation by such broker or dealer that such information is accurate, but shall constitute a representation by such broker or dealer that the information is reasonably current in relation to the day the quotation is submitted, that the broker or dealer has a reasonable basis under the circumstances for believing the information is accurate in all material respects, and that the information was obtained from sources which the broker or dealer has a reasonable basis for believing are reliable. This paragraph (a)(5) shall not apply to any security of an issuer included in paragraph (a)(3) of this section unless a report or statement of such issuer described in paragraph (a)(3) of this section is not reasonably available to the broker or dealer. A report or statement of an issuer described in paragraph (a)(3) of this section shall be "reasonably available" when such report or statement is filed with the Commission.

(b) With respect to any security the quotation of which is within the provisions of this section, the broker or dealer submitting or publishing such quotation shall have in its records the following documents and information:

(1) A record of the circumstances involved in the submission of publication of such quotation, including the identity of the person or persons for whom the quotation is being submitted or published and any information regarding the transactions provided to the broker or dealer by such person or persons;

(2) A copy of any trading suspension order issued by the Commission pursuant to section 12(k) of the Act respecting any securities of the issuer or its predecessor (if any) during the 12 months preceding the date of the publication or submission of the quotation, or a copy of the public release issued by the Commission announcing such trading suspension order; and

(3) A copy or a written record of any other material information (including adverse information) regarding the issuer which comes to the broker's or dealer's knowledge or possession before the publication or submission of the quotation.

(c) The broker or dealer shall preserve the documents and information required under paragraphs (a) and (b) of this section for a period of not less than three years, the first two years in an easily accessible place.

* * *

15c3-1. Net capital requirements for brokers or dealers.

(a) Every broker or dealer shall at all times have and maintain net capital no less than the greater of the highest minimum requirement applicable to its

ratio requirement under paragraph (a)(1) of this section, or to any of its activities under paragraph (a)(2) of this section. Each broker or dealer also shall comply with the supplemental requirements of paragraphs (a)(4) and (a)(9) of this section, to the extent either paragraph is applicable to its activities. In addition, a broker or dealer shall maintain net capital of not less than its own net capital requirement plus the sum of each broker's or dealer's subsidiary or affiliate minimum net capital requirements, which is consolidated pursuant to Appendix C, Rule 15c3-1c.

* * *

15g-1. Exemptions for certain transactions.

The following transactions shall be exempt from 15g-2, 15g-3, 15g-4, 15g-5, and 15g-6:

(a) Transactions by a broker or dealer:

    (1) Whose commissions, commission equivalents, mark-ups, and mark-downs from transactions in penny stocks during each of the immediately preceding three months and during eleven or more of the preceding twelve months, or during the immediately preceding six months, did not exceed five percent of its total commissions, commission equivalents, mark-ups, and mark-downs from transactions in securities during those months; and

    (2) Who has not been a market maker in the penny stock that is the subject of the transaction in the immediately preceding twelve months.

        Note: Prior to April 28, 1993, commissions, commission equivalents, mark-ups, and mark-downs from transactions in designated securities, as defined in 15c2-6(d)(2) as of April 15, 1992, may be considered to be commissions, commission equivalents, mark-ups, and mark-downs from transactions in penny stocks for purposes of paragraph (a)(1) of this section.

(b) Transactions in which the customer is an institutional accredited investor, as defined in 17 CFR 230.501(a) (1), (2), (3), (7), or (8).

(c) Transactions that meet the requirements of Regulation D (17 CFR 230.501- 230.508), or transactions with an issuer not involving any public offering pursuant to section 4(2) of the Securities Act of 1933.

(d) Transactions in which the customer is the issuer, or a director, officer, general partner, or direct or indirect beneficial owner of more than five percent of any class of equity security of the issuer, of the penny stock that is the subject of the transaction.

(e) Transactions that are not recommended by the broker or dealer.

(f)   Any other transaction or class of transactions or persons or class of persons that, upon prior written request or upon its own motion, the Commission conditionally or unconditionally exempts by order as consistent with the public interest and the protection of investors.

* * *

15g-2. Risk disclosure document relating to the penny stock market.

(a)   It shall be unlawful for a broker or dealer to effect a transaction in any penny stock for or with the account of a customer unless, prior to effecting such transaction, the broker or dealer has furnished to the customer a document containing the information set forth in Schedule 15G, 15g-100, and has obtained from the customer a manually signed and dated written acknowledgement of receipt of the document.

(b)   The broker or dealer shall preserve, as part of its records, a copy of the written acknowledgment required by paragraph (a) of this section for the period specified in 17a-4(b) of this chapter.

* * *

15g-3. Broker or dealer disclosure of quotations and other information relating to the penny stock market.

(a)   Requirement. It shall be unlawful for a broker or dealer to effect a transaction in any penny stock with or for the account of a customer unless such broker or dealer discloses to such customer, within the time periods and in the manner required by paragraph (b) of this section, the following information:

(1)   The inside bid quotation and the inside offer quotation for the penny stock.

(2)   If paragraph (a)(1) of this section does not apply because of the absence of an inside bid quotation and an inside offer quotation:

(i)   With respect to a transaction effected with or for a customer on a principal basis (other than as provided in paragraph (a)(2)(ii) of this section):

(A)   The dealer shall disclose its offer price for the security:

(1)   If during the previous five days the dealer has effected no fewer than three bona fide sales to other dealers consistently at its offer price for the security current at the time of those sales, and

(2)   If the dealer reasonably believes in good faith at the time of the transaction with the customer that its offer

price accurately reflects the price at which it is willing to sell one or more round lots to another dealer. For purposes of paragraph (a)(2)(i)(A) of this section, "consistently" shall constitute, at a minimum, seventy-five percent of the dealer's bona fide interdealer sales during the previous five-day period, and, if the dealer has effected only three bona fide inter-dealer sales during such period, all three of such sales.

(B)   The dealer shall disclose its bid price for the security:

    (1)   If during the previous five days the dealer has effected no fewer than three bona fide purchases from other dealers consistently at its bid price for the security current at the time of those purchases, and

    (2)   If the dealer reasonably believes in good faith at the time of the transaction with the customer that its bid price accurately reflects the price at which it is willing to buy one or more round lots from another dealer. For purposes of paragraph (a)(2)(i)(B) of this section, "consistently" shall constitute, at a minimum, seventy-five percent of the dealer's bona fide interdealer purchases during the previous five-day period, and, if the dealer has effected only three bona fide inter-dealer purchases during such period, all three of such purchases.

(C)   If the dealer's bid or offer prices to the customer do not satisfy the criteria of paragraphs (a)(2)(i)(A) or (a)(2)(i)(B) of this section, the dealer shall disclose to the customer:

    (1)   That it has not effected inter-dealer purchases or sales of the penny stock consistently at its bid or offer price, and

    (2)   The price at which it last purchased the penny stock from, or sold the penny stock to, respectively, another dealer in a bona fide transaction.

(ii)   With respect to transactions effected by a broker or dealer with or for the account of the customer:

(A)   On an agency basis or

(B)   On a basis other than as a market maker in the security, where, after having received an order from the customer to purchase a penny stock, the dealer effects the purchase

from another person to offset a contemporaneous sale of the penny stock to such customer, or, after having received an order from the customer to sell the penny stock, the dealer effects the sale to another person to offset a contemporaneous purchase from such customer, the broker or dealer shall disclose the best independent interdealer bid and offer prices for the penny stock that the broker or dealer obtains through reasonable diligence. A broker-dealer shall be deemed to have exercised reasonable diligence if it obtains quotations from three market makers in the security (or all known market makers if there are fewer than three).

(3)   With respect to bid or offer prices and transaction prices disclosed pursuant to paragraph (a) of this section, the broker or dealer shall disclose the number of shares to which the bid and offer prices apply.

(b)   Timing.

(1)   The information described in paragraph (a) of this section:

(i)   Shall be provided to the customer orally or in writing prior to effecting any transaction with or for the customer for the purchase or sale of such penny stock; and

(ii)   Shall be given or sent to the customer in writing, at or prior to the time that any written confirmation of the transaction is given or sent to the customer pursuant to 10b-10 of this chapter.

(2)   A broker or dealer, at the time of making the disclosure pursuant to paragraph (b)(1)(i) of this section, shall make and preserve as part of its records, a record of such disclosure for the period specified in 17a-4(b).

(c)   Definitions. For purposes of this section:

(1)   The term bid price shall mean the price most recently communicated by the dealer to another broker or dealer at which the dealer is willing to purchase one or more round lots of the penny stock, and shall not include indications of interest.

(2)   The term offer price shall mean the price most recently communicated by the dealer to another broker or dealer at which the dealer is willing to sell one or more round lots of the penny stock, and shall not include indications of interest.

(3)   The term inside bid quotation for a security shall mean the highest bid quotation for the security displayed by a market maker in the security on a Qualifying Electronic Quotation System, at any time in which at

least two market makers are contemporaneously displaying on such system bid and offer quotations for the security at specified prices.

(4) The term inside offer quotation for a security shall mean the lowest offer quotation for the security displayed by a market maker in the security on a Qualifying Electronic Quotation System, at any time in which at least two market makers are contemporaneously displaying on such system bid and offer quotations for the security at specified prices.

(5) The term Qualifying Electronic Quotation System shall mean an automated interdealer quotation system that has the characteristics set forth in section 17B(b)(2) of the Act, or such other automated interdealer quotation system designated by the Commission for purposes of this section.

* * *

15g-4. Disclosure of compensation to brokers or dealers.

Preliminary NOTE: Brokers and dealers may wish to refer to Securities Exchange Act Release No. 30608 (April 20, 1992) for a discussion of the procedures for computing compensation in active and competitive markets, inactive and competitive markets, and dominated and controlled markets.

(a) Disclosure requirement. It shall be unlawful for any broker or dealer to effect a transaction in any penny stock for or with the account of a customer unless such broker or dealer discloses to such customer, within the time periods and in the manner required by paragraph (b) of this section, the aggregate amount of any compensation received by such broker or dealer in connection with such transaction.

(b) Timing.

(1) The information described in paragraph (a) of this section:

(i) Shall be provided to the customer orally or in writing prior to effecting any transaction with or for the customer for the purchase or sale of such penny stock; and

(ii) Shall be given or sent to the customer in writing, at or prior to the time that any written confirmation of the transaction is given or sent to the customer pursuant to > 17 CFR 240.10b-10.

(2) A broker or dealer, at the time of making the disclosure pursuant to paragraph (b)(1)(i) of this section, shall make and preserve as part of its records, a record of such disclosure for the period specified in > 17 CFR 240.17a-4(b).

(c) Definition of Compensation. For purposes of this section, compensation means, with respect to a transaction in a penny stock:

(1) If a broker is acting as agent for a customer, the amount of any remuneration received or to be received by it from such customer in connection with such transaction;

(2) If, after having received a buy order from a customer, a dealer other than a market maker purchased the penny stock as principal from another person to offset a contemporaneous sale to such customer or, after having received a sell order from a customer, sold the penny stock as principal to another person to offset a contemporaneous purchase from such customer, the difference between the price to the customer and such contemporaneous purchase or sale price; or

(3) If the dealer otherwise is acting as principal for its own account, the difference between the price to the customer and the prevailing market price.

(d) "Active and competitive" market. For purposes of this section only, a market may be deemed to be "active and competitive" in determining the prevailing market price with respect to a transaction by a market maker in a penny stock if the aggregate number of transactions effected by such market maker in the penny stock in the five business days preceding such transaction is less than twenty percent of the aggregate number of all transactions in the penny stock reported on a Qualifying Electronic Quotation System (as defined in 15g-3(c)(5)) during such five-day period. No presumption shall arise that a market is not "active and competitive" solely by reason of a market maker not meeting the conditions specified in this paragraph.

* * *

15g-5. Disclosure of compensation of associated persons in connection with penny stock transactions.

(a) General. It shall be unlawful for a broker or dealer to effect a transaction in any penny stock for or with the account of a customer unless the broker or dealer discloses to such customer, within the time periods and in the manner required by paragraph (b) of this section, the aggregate amount of cash compensation that any associated person of the broker or dealer who is a natural person and has communicated with the customer concerning the transaction at or prior to receipt of the customer's transaction order, other than any person whose function is solely clerical or ministerial, has received or will receive from any source in connection with the transaction and that is determined at or prior to the time of the transaction, including

separate disclosure, if applicable, of the source and amount of such compensation that is not paid by the broker or dealer.

(b) Timing.

    (1) The information described in paragraph (a) of this section:

        (i) Shall be provided to the customer orally or in writing prior to effecting any transaction with or for the customer for the purchase or sale of such penny stock; and

        (ii) Shall be given or sent to the customer in writing, at or prior to the time that any written confirmation of the transaction is given or sent to the customer pursuant to 10b-10.

    (2) A broker or dealer, at the time of making the disclosure pursuant to paragraph (b)(1)(i) of this section, shall make and preserve as part of its records, a record of such disclosure for the period specified in 17a-4(b).

(c) Contingent compensation arrangements. Where a portion or all of the cash or other compensation that the associated person may receive in connection with the transaction may be determined and paid following the transaction based on aggregate sales volume levels or other contingencies, the written disclosure required by paragraph (b)(1)(ii) of this section shall state that fact and describe the basis upon which such compensation is determined.

* * *

15g-6. Account statements for penny stock customers.

(a) Requirement. It shall be unlawful for any broker or dealer that has effected the sale to any customer, other than in a transaction that is exempt pursuant to 15g-1, of any security that is a penny stock on the last trading day of any calendar month, or any successor of such broker or dealer, to fail to give or send to such customer a written statement containing the information described in paragraphs (c) and (d) of this section with respect to each such month in which such security is held for the customer's account with the broker or dealer, within ten days following the end of such month.

(b) Exemptions. A broker or dealer shall be exempted from the requirement of paragraph (a) of this section under either of the following circumstances:

    (1) If the broker or dealer does not effect any transactions in penny stocks for or with the account of the customer during a period of six consecutive calendar months, then the broker or dealer shall not be required to provide monthly statements for each quarterly period that is immediately subsequent to such six-month period and in which the broker or dealer does not effect any transaction in penny stocks for or

with the account of the customer, provided that the broker or dealer gives or sends to the customer written statements containing the information described in paragraphs (d) and (e) of this section on a quarterly basis, within ten days following the end of each such quarterly period.

(2) If, on all but five or fewer trading days of any quarterly period, a security has a price of five dollars or more, the broker or dealer shall not be required to provide a monthly statement covering the security for subsequent quarterly periods, until the end of any such subsequent quarterly period on the last trading day of which the price of the security is less than five dollars.

(c) Price Determinations. For purposes of paragraphs (a) and (b) of this section, the price of a security on any trading day shall be determined at the close of business in accordance with the provisions of 3a51- 1(d)(1).

(d) Market and price information. The statement required by paragraph (a) of this section shall contain at least the following information with respect to each penny stock covered by paragraph (a) of this section, as of the last trading day of the period to which the statement relates:

(1) The identity and number of shares or units of each such security held for the customer's account; and

(2) The estimated market value of the security, to the extent that such estimated market value can be determined in accordance with the following provisions:

(i) The highest inside bid quotation for the security on the last trading day of the period to which the statement relates, multiplied by the number of shares or units of the security held for the customer's account; or

(ii) If paragraph (d)(2)(i) of this section is not applicable because of the absence of an inside bid quotation, and if the broker or dealer furnishing the statement has effected at least ten separate Qualifying Purchases in the security during the last five trading days of the period to which the statement relates, the weighted average price per share paid by the broker or dealer in all Qualifying Purchases effected during such five-day period, multiplied by the number of shares or units of the security held for the customer's account; or

(iii) If neither of paragraphs (d)(2)(i) nor (d)(2)(ii) of this section is applicable, a statement that there is "no estimated market value" with respect to the security.

(e) Legend. In addition to the information required by paragraph (d) of this section, the written statement required by paragraph (a) of this section shall include a conspicuous legend that is identified with the penny stocks described in the statement and that contains the following language:

If this statement contains an estimated value, you should be aware that this value may be based on a limited number of trades or quotes. Therefore, you may not be able to sell these securities at a price equal or near to the value shown. However, the broker-dealer furnishing this statement may not refuse to accept your order to sell these securities. Also, the amount you receive from a sale generally will be reduced by the amount of any commissions or similar charges. If an estimated value is not shown for a security, a value could not be determined because of a lack of information.

(f) Preservation of records. Any broker or dealer subject to this section shall preserve, as part of its records, copies of the written statements required by paragraph (a) of this section and keep such records for the periods specified in 17a-4(b).

(g) Definitions. For purposes of this section:

 (1) The term Quarterly period shall mean any period of three consecutive full calendar months.

 (2) The inside bid quotation for a security shall mean the highest bid quotation for the security displayed by a market maker in the security on a Qualifying Electronic Quotation System, at any time in which at least two market makers are contemporaneously displaying on such system bid and offer quotations for the security at specified prices.

 (3) The term Qualifying Electronic Quotation System shall mean an automated interdealer quotation system that has the characteristics set forth in section 17B(b)(2) of the Act, or such other automated interdealer quotation system designated by the Commission for purposes of this section.

 (4) The term Qualifying Purchases shall mean bona fide purchases by a broker or dealer of a penny stock for its own account, each of which involves at least 100 shares, but excluding any block purchase involving more than one percent of the outstanding shares or units of the security.

* * *

15g-8. Sales of escrowed securities of blank check companies.

As a means reasonably designed to prevent fraudulent, deceptive, or manipulative acts or practices, it shall be unlawful for any person to sell or offer to

sell any security that is deposited and held in an escrow or trust account pursuant to Rule 419 under the Securities Act of 1933, or any interest in or related to such security, other than pursuant to a qualified domestic relations order as defined by the Internal Revenue Code of 1986, as amended, or Title I of the Employee Retirement Income Security Act, or the rules thereunder.

15g-9. Sales practice requirements for certain low-priced securities.

(a)   As a means reasonably designed to prevent fraudulent, deceptive, or manipulative acts or practices, it shall be unlawful for a broker or dealer to sell a penny stock to, or to effect the purchase of a penny stock by, any person unless:

    (1)   The transaction is exempt under paragraph (c) of this section; or

    (2)   Prior to the transaction:

        (i)   The broker or dealer has approved the person's account for transactions in penny stocks in accordance with the procedures set forth in paragraph (b) of this section; and

        (ii)   The broker or dealer has received from the person a written agreement to the transaction setting forth the identity and quantity of the penny stock to be purchased.

(b)   In order to approve a person's account for transactions in penny stock, the broker or dealer must:

    (1)   Obtain from the person information concerning the person's financial situation, investment experience, and investment objectives;

    (2)   Reasonably determine, based on the information required by paragraph (b)(1) of this section and any other information known by the broker-dealer, that transactions in penny stocks are suitable for the person, and that the person (or the person's independent adviser in these transactions) has sufficient knowledge and experience in financial matters that the person (or the person's independent adviser in these transactions) reasonably may be expected to be capable of evaluating the risks of transactions in penny stocks;

    (3)   Deliver to the person a written statement:

        (i)   Setting forth the basis on which the broker or dealer made the determination required by paragraph (b)(2) of this section;

        (ii)   Stating in a highlighted format that it is unlawful for the broker or dealer to effect a transaction in a penny stock subject to the provisions of paragraph (a)(2) of this section unless the broker or dealer has received, prior to the transaction, a written agreement to the transaction from the person; and

(iii) Stating in a highlighted format immediately preceding the customer signature line that:

   (A) The broker or dealer is required by this section to provide the person with the written statement; and

   (B) The person should not sign and return the written statement to the broker or dealer if it does not accurately reflect the person's financial situation, investment experience, and investment objectives; and

(4) Obtain from the person a manually signed and dated copy of the written statement required by paragraph (b)(3) of this section.

(c) For purposes of this section, the following transactions shall be exempt:

(1) Transactions that are exempt under 15g-1 (a), (b), (d), (e), and (f).

(2) Transactions that meet the requirements of 17 CFR 230.505 or 230.506 (including, where applicable, the requirements of 17 CFR 230.501 through 230.503, and 17 CFR 230.507 through 230.508), or transactions with an issuer not involving any public offering pursuant to section 4(2) of the Securities Act of 1933.

(3) Transactions in which the purchaser is an established customer of the broker or dealer.

(d) For purposes of this section:

(1) The term penny stock shall have the same meaning as in 3a51- 1.

(2) The term established customer shall mean any person for whom the broker or dealer, or a clearing broker on behalf of such broker or dealer, carries an account, and who in such account:

   (i) Has effected a securities transaction, or made a deposit of funds or securities, more than one year previously; or

   (ii) Has made three purchases of penny stocks that occurred on separate days and involved different issuers.

* * *

19c-4. Governing certain listing or authorization determinations by national securities exchanges and associations.

(a) The rules of each exchange shall provide as follows: No rule, stated policy, practice, or interpretation of this exchange shall permit the listing, or the continuance of the listing, of any common stock or other equity security of a domestic issuer, if the issuer of such security issues any class of security, or takes other corporate action, with the effect of nullifying, restricting or disparately reducing the per share voting rights of holders of an

outstanding class or classes of common stock of such issuer registered pursuant to section 12 of the Act.

(b)   The rules of each association shall provide as follows: No rule, stated policy, practice, or interpretation of this association shall permit the authorization for quotation and/or transaction reporting through an automated inter-dealer quotation system ("authorization"), or the continuance of authorization, of any common stock or other equity security of a domestic issuer, if the issuer of such security issues any class of security, or takes other corporate action, with the effect of nullifying, restricting, or disparately reducing the per share voting rights of holders of an outstanding class or classes of common stock of such issuer registered pursuant to section 12 of the Act.

(c)   For the purposes of paragraphs (a) and (b) of this section, the following shall be presumed to have the effect of nullifying, restricting, or disparately reducing the per share voting rights of an outstanding class or classes of common stock:

(1)   Corporate action to impose any restriction on the voting power of shares of the common stock of the issuer held by a beneficial or record holder based on the number of shares held by such beneficial or record holder;

(2)   Corporate action to impose any restriction on the voting power of shares of the common stock of the issuer held by a beneficial or record holder based on the length of time such shares have been held by such beneficial or record holder;

(3)   Any issuance of securities through an exchange offer by the issuer for shares of an outstanding class of the common stock of the issuer, in which the securities issued have voting rights greater than or less than the per share voting rights of any outstanding class of the common stock of the issuer.

(4)   Any issuance of securities pursuant to a stock dividend, or any other type of distribution of stock, in which the securities issued have voting rights greater than the per share voting rights of any outstanding class of the common stock of the issuer.

(d)   For the purpose of paragraphs (a) and (b) of this section, the following, standing alone, shall be presumed not to have the effect of nullifying, restricting, or disparately reducing the per share voting rights of holders of an outstanding class or classes of common stock:

(1)   The issuance of securities pursuant to an initial registered public offering;

(2) The issuance of any class of securities, through a registered public offering, with voting rights not greater than the per share voting rights of any outstanding class of the common stock of the issuer;

(3) The issuance of any class of securities to effect a bona fide merger or acquisition, with voting rights not greater than the per share voting rights of any outstanding class of the common stock of the issuer.

(4) Corporate action taken pursuant to state law requiring a state's domestic corporation to condition the voting rights of a beneficial or record holder of a specified threshold percentage of the corporation's voting stock on the approval of the corporation's independent shareholders.

(e) Definitions. The following terms shall have the following meanings for purposes of this section, and the rules of each exchange and association shall include such definitions for the purposes of the prohibition in paragraphs (a) and (b), respectively, of this section:

(1) The term "Act" shall mean the Securities Exchange Act of 1934, as amended.

(2) The term "common stock" shall include any security of an issuer designated as common stock and any security of an issuer, however designated, which, by statute or by its terms, is a common stock (e.g., a security which entitles the holders thereof to vote generally on matters submitted to the issuer's security holders for a vote).

(3) The term "equity security" shall include any equity security defined as such pursuant to Rule 3a11-1 under the Act.

(4) The term "domestic issuer" shall mean an issuer that is not a "foreign private issuer" as defined in Rule 3b-4 under the Act.

(5) The term "security" shall include any security defined as such pursuant to section 3(a)(10) of the Act, but shall exclude any class of security having a preference or priority over the issuer's common stock as to dividends, interest payments, redemption or payments in liquidation, if the voting rights of such securities only become effective as a result of specified events, not relating to an acquisition of the common stock of the issuer, which reasonably can be expected to jeopardize the issuer's financial ability to meet its payment obligations to the holders of that class of securities.

(6) The term "exchange" shall mean a national securities exchange, registered as such with the Securities and Exchange Commission pursuant to section 6 of the Act, which makes transaction reports available pursuant to Rule 11Aa3-1 under the Act; and

(7)   The term "association" shall mean a national securities association registered as such with the Securities and Exchange Commission pursuant to section 15A of the Act.

(f)   An exchange or association may adopt a rule, stated policy, practice, or interpretation, subject to the procedures specified by section 19(b) of the Act, specifying what types of securities issuances and other corporate actions are covered by, or excluded from, the prohibition in paragraphs (a) and (b) of this section, respectively, if such rule, stated policy, practice, or interpretation is consistent with the protection of investors and the public interest, and otherwise in furtherance of the purposes of the Act and this section.

* * *

CHAPTER FIFTEEN

INVESTMENT ADVISERS ACT OF 1940

(codified at 15 U.S.C. § 81b-1 *et seq.*)

§ 201. Findings

Upon the basis of facts disclosed by the record and report of the Securities and Exchange Commission made pursuant to section 30 of the Public Utility Holding Company Act of 1935, and facts otherwise disclosed and ascertained, it is found that investment advisers are of national concern, in that, among other things—

(1) their advice, counsel, publications, writings, analyses, and reports are furnished and distributed, and their contracts, subscription agreements, and other arrangements with clients are negotiated and performed, by the use of the mails and means and instrumentalities of interstate commerce;

(2) their advice, counsel, publications, writings, analyses, and reports customarily relate to the purchase and sale of securities traded on national securities exchanges and in interstate over-the-counter markets, securities issued by companies engaged in business in interstate commerce, and securities issued by national banks and member banks of the Federal Reserve System; and

(3) the foregoing transactions occur in such volume as substantially to affect interstate commerce, national securities exchanges, and other securities markets, the national banking system and the national economy.

§ 202. Definitions

(a) When used in this Act, unless the context otherwise requires, the following definitions shall apply:

* * *

(11) "Investment adviser" means any person who, for compensation, engages in the business of advising others, either directly or through publications or writings, as to the value of securities or as to the advisability of investing in, purchasing, or selling securities, or who, for compensation and as part of a regular

business, issues or promulgates analyses or reports concerning securities; but does not include

(A)   a bank, or any bank holding company as defined in the Bank Holding Company Act of 1956 which is not an investment company;

(B)   any lawyer, accountant, engineer, or teacher whose performance of such services is solely incidental to the practice of his profession;

(C)   any broker or dealer whose performance of such services is solely incidental to the conduct of his business as a broker or dealer and who receives no special compensation therefor;

(D)   the publisher of any bona fide newspaper, news magazine or business or financial publication of general and regular circulation;

(E)   any person whose advice, analyses, or reports relate to no securities other than securities which are direct obligations of or obligations guaranteed as to principal or interest by the United States, or securities issued or guaranteed by corporations in which the United States has a direct or indirect interest which shall have been designated by the Secretary of the Treasury, pursuant to section 3(a)(12) of the Securities Exchange Act of 1934, as exempted securities for the purposes of that Act; or

(F)   such other persons not within the intent of this paragraph, as the Commission may designate by rules and regulations or order.

* * *

§ 203. Registration of investment advisers

(a)   Necessity of registration. Except as provided in subsection (b) and section 203A, it shall be unlawful for any investment adviser, unless registered under this section, to make use of the mails or any means or instrumentality of interstate commerce in connection with his or its business as an investment adviser.

(b)   Investment advisers who need not be registered. The provisions of subsection (a) of this section shall not apply to —

(1) any investment adviser all of whose clients are residents of the State within which such investment adviser maintains his or its principal office and place of business, and who does not furnish advice or issue analyses or reports with respect to securities listed or admitted to unlisted trading privileges on any national securities exchange;

(2) any investment adviser whose only clients are insurance companies;

(3) any investment adviser who during the course of the preceding twelve months has had fewer than fifteen clients and who neither holds himself out generally to the public as an investment adviser nor acts as an investment adviser to any investment company registered under the Investment Company Act of 1940. . . .

(c) Procedure for registration.

    (1) An investment adviser, or any person who presently contemplates becoming an investment adviser, may be registered by filing with the Commission an application for registration in such form and containing such of the following information and documents as the Commission, by rule, may prescribe as necessary or appropriate in the public interest or for the protection of investors:

    (A) the name and form of organization under which the investment adviser engages or intends to engage in business; the name of the State or other sovereign power under which such investment adviser is organized; the location of his or its principal business office and branch offices, if any; the names and addresses of his or its partners, officers, directors, and persons performing similar functions or, if such an investment adviser be an individual, of such individual; and the number of his or its employees;

    (B) the education, the business affiliations for the past ten years, and the present business affiliations of such investment adviser and of his or its partners, officers, directors, and persons performing similar functions and of any controlling person thereof;

    (C) the nature of the business of such investment adviser, including the manner of giving advice and rendering analyses or reports;

    (D) a balance sheet certified by an independent public accountant and other financial statements (which shall, as the Commission specifies, be certified);

    (E) the nature and scope of the authority of such investment adviser with respect to clients' funds and accounts;

(F)   the basis or bases upon which such investment adviser is compensated;

(G)   whether such investment adviser, or any person associated with such investment adviser, is subject to any disqualification which would be a basis for denial, suspension, or revocation of registration of such investment adviser under the provisions of subsection (e) of this section; and

(H)   a statement as to whether the principal business of such investment adviser consists or is to consist of acting as investment adviser and a statement as to whether a substantial part of the business of such investment adviser, consists or is to consist of rendering investment supervisory services.

(2)   Within forty-five days of the date of the filing of such application (or within such longer period as to which the applicant consents) the Commission shall—

(A)   by order grant such registration; or

(B)   institute proceedings to determine whether registration should be denied. Such proceedings shall include notice of the grounds for denial under consideration and opportunity for hearing and shall be concluded within one hundred twenty days of the date of the filing of the application for registration. At the conclusion of such proceedings the Commission, by order, shall grant or deny such registration. The Commission may extend the time for conclusion of such proceedings for up to ninety days if it finds good cause for such extension and publishes its reasons for so finding or for such longer period as to which the applicant consents.

The Commission shall grant such registration if the Commission finds that the requirements of this section are satisfied and that the applicant is not prohibited from registering as an investment adviser under section 203A. The Commission shall deny such registration if it does not make such a finding or if it finds that if the applicant were so registered, its registration would be subject to suspension or revocation under subsection (e) of this section [establishing grounds for discipline of investment advisers] .

* * *

§ 203A. State and Federal responsibilities

(a) Advisers subject to State authorities

    (1) In general. No investment adviser that is regulated or required to be regulated as an investment adviser in the State in which it maintains its principal office and place of business shall register under section 203, unless the investment adviser—

        (A) has assets under management of not less than $25,000,000, or such higher amount as the Commission may, by rule, deem appropriate in accordance with the purposes of this Act; or

        (B) is an adviser to an investment company registered under the Investment Company Act of 1940.

    (2) Definition. For purposes of this subsection, the term "assets under management" means the securities portfolios with respect to which an investment adviser provides continuous and regular supervisory or management services.

(b) Advisers subject to Commission authority

    (1) In general. No law of any State or political subdivision thereof requiring the registration, licensing, or qualification as an investment adviser or supervised person of an investment adviser shall apply to any person—

        (A) that is registered under section 203 as an investment adviser, or that is a supervised person of such person, except that a State may license, register, or otherwise qualify any investment adviser representative who has a place of business located within that State; or

        (B) that is not registered under section 293 because that person is excepted from the definition of an investment adviser under section 202(a)(11) of this title.

    (2) Limitation. Nothing in this subsection shall prohibit the securities commission (or any agency or office performing like functions) of any State from investigating and bringing enforcement actions with respect to fraud or deceit against an investment adviser or person associated with an investment adviser.

(c) Exemptions. Notwithstanding subsection (a) of this section, the Commission, by rule or regulation upon its own motion, or by order upon application, may permit the registration with the Commission of any person or class of persons to which the application of subsection (a) of this section

would be unfair, a burden on interstate commerce, or otherwise inconsistent with the purposes of this section.

(d) Filing depositories. The Commission may, by rule, require an investment adviser—

    (1) to file with the Commission any fee, application, report, or notice required by this subchapter or by the rules issued under this subchapter through any entity designated by the Commission for that purpose; and

    (2) to pay the reasonable costs associated with such filing.

(e) State assistance. Upon request of the securities commissioner (or any agency or officer performing like functions) of any State, the Commission may provide such training, technical assistance, or other reasonable assistance in connection with the regulation of investment advisers by the State.

§ 205. Investment advisory contracts

(a) Compensation, assignment, and partnership-membership provisions. No investment adviser, unless exempt from registration pursuant to section 203A, shall make use of the mails or any means or instrumentality of interstate commerce, directly or indirectly, to enter into, extend, or renew any investment advisory contract, or in any way to perform any investment advisory contract entered into, extended, or renewed on or after November 1, 1940, if such contract--

    (1) provides for compensation to the investment adviser on the basis of a share of capital gains upon or capital appreciation of the funds or any portion of the funds of the client;

    (2) fails to provide, in substance, that no assignment of such contract shall be made by the investment adviser without the consent of the other party to the contract; or

    (3) fails to provide, in substance, that the investment adviser, if a partnership, will notify the other party to the contract of any change in the membership of such partnership within a reasonable time after such change.

(b) Compensation prohibition inapplicable to certain compensation computations. Paragraph (1) of subsection (a) of this section shall not —

    (1) be construed to prohibit an investment advisory contract which provides for compensation based upon the total value of a fund

averaged over a definite period, or as of definite dates, or taken as of a definite date; [or]

(2) apply to an investment advisory contract with—

    (A) an investment company registered under the Investment Company Act of 1940, or

    (B) any other person (except a trust, governmental plan, collective trust fund, or separate account referred to in section 203(c)(11) of this title), provided that the contract relates to the investment of assets in excess of $1 million, if the contract provides for compensation based on the asset value of the company or fund under management averaged over a specified period and increasing and decreasing proportionately with the investment performance of the company or fund over a specified period in relation to the investment record of an appropriate index of securities prices or such other measure of investment performance as the Commission by rule, regulation, or order may specify . . . .

(4) apply to an investment advisory contract with a company excepted from the definition of an investment company under section 80a-3(c)(7) of this title; or

(5) apply to an investment advisory contract with a person who is not a resident of the United States.

(c) Measurement of changes in compensation. For purposes of paragraph (2) of subsection (b) of this section, the point from which increases and decreases in compensation are measured shall be the fee which is paid or earned when the investment performance of such company or fund is equivalent to that of the index or other measure of performance, and an index of securities prices shall be deemed appropriate unless the Commission by order shall determine otherwise.

(d) "Investment advisory contract" defined. As used in paragraphs (2) and (3) of subsection (a) of this section, "investment advisory contract" means any contract or agreement whereby a person agrees to act as investment adviser to or to manage any investment or trading account of another person other than an investment company registered under the Investment Company Act of 1940.

(e) Exempt persons and transactions. The Commission, by rule or regulation, upon its own motion, or by order upon application, may conditionally or unconditionally exempt any person or transaction, or any class or classes of persons or transactions, from subsection (a)(1) of this section, if and to the

extent that the exemption relates to an investment advisory contract with any person that the Commission determines does not need the protections of subsection (a)(1) of this section, on the basis of such factors as financial sophistication, net worth, knowledge of and experience in financial matters, amount of assets under management, relationship with a registered investment adviser, and such other factors as the Commission determines are consistent with this section.

§ 206. Prohibited transactions by investment advisers

It shall be unlawful for any investment adviser, by use of the mails or any means or instrumentality of interstate commerce, directly or indirectly--

(1) to employ any device, scheme, or artifice to defraud any client or prospective client;

(2) to engage in any transaction, practice, or course of business which operates as a fraud or deceit upon any client or prospective client;

(3) acting as principal for his own account, knowingly to sell any security to or purchase any security from a client, or acting as broker for a person other than such client, knowingly to effect any sale or purchase of any security for the account of such client, without disclosing to such client in writing before the completion of such transaction the capacity in which he is acting and obtaining the consent of the client to such transaction. The prohibitions of this paragraph shall not apply to any transaction with a customer of a broker or dealer if such broker or dealer is not acting as an investment adviser in relation to such transaction;

(4) to engage in any act, practice, or course of business which is fraudulent, deceptive, or manipulative. The Commission shall, for the purposes of this paragraph (4) by rules and regulations define, and prescribe means reasonably designed to prevent, such acts, practices, and courses of business as are fraudulent, deceptive, or manipulative.

CHAPTER SIXTEEN

SELECTED RULES AND REGULATIONS UNDER THE INVESTMENT ADVISERS ACT OF 1940

(Codified at 17 C.F.R. § 275.___)

* * *

203-1. Application for registration of investment adviser.

(a) An application for registration of an investment adviser filed pursuant to section 203(c) of the Act shall be filed on Form ADV in accordance with the instructions contained therein.

(b) A Form ADV filed by an investment-adviser partnership which is not registered when such form is filed and which succeeds to and continues the business of a predecessor partnership registered as an investment adviser shall be deemed to be an application for registration even though designated as an amendment if it is filed to reflect the changes in the partnership and to furnish required information concerning any new partners.

(c) A Form ADV filed by an investment adviser corporation, which is not registered when such form is filed and which succeeds to and continues the business of a predecessor corporation registered as an investment adviser shall be deemed to be an application for registration even though designated as an amendment if the succession is based solely on a change in the predecessor's state of incorporation and the amendment is filed to reflect that change.

(d) A Form ADV filed by an investment adviser corporation, partnership, sole proprietorship or other entity which is not registered when such form is filed and which succeeds to and continues the business of a predecessor corporation, partnership, sole proprietorship or other entity registered as an investment adviser shall be deemed to be an application for registration even though designated as an amendment if the succession is based solely on a change in the predecessor's form of organization and the amendment is filed to reflect that change.

203-2. Withdrawal from registration.

(a)   Notice of withdrawal from registration as an investment adviser pursuant to section 203(h) shall be filed on Form ADV-W in accordance with the instructions contained therein.

(b)   Except as hereinafter provided, a notice to withdraw from registration filed by an investment adviser pursuant to section 203(h) shall become effective on the 60th day after the filing thereof with the Commission or within such shorter period of time as the Commission may determine. If, prior to the effective date of a notice of withdrawal from registration, the Commission has instituted a proceeding pursuant to section 203(e) to suspend or revoke registration, or a proceeding pursuant to section 203(h) to impose terms or conditions upon withdrawal, the notice of withdrawal shall not become effective except at such time and upon such terms and conditions as the Commission deems necessary or appropriate in the public interest or for the protection of investors.

(c)   Every notice of withdrawal filed pursuant to this rule shall constitute a "report" within the meaning of sections 204 and 207 and other applicable provisions of the Act.

* * *

Rule 203(b)(3)-1. Definition of "client" of an investment adviser.

Preliminary Note to Rule 203(b)(3)-1: This rule is a safe harbor and is not intended to specify the exclusive method for determining who may be deemed a single client for purposes of section 203(b)(3) of the Act.

(a) General.

For purposes of section 203(b)(3) of the Act [15 U.S.C. § 80b-3(b)(3)], the following are deemed a single client:

(1)   A natural person, and:

   (i)   Any minor child of the natural person;

   (ii)   Any relative, spouse, or relative of the spouse of the natural person who has the same principal residence;

   (iii)   All accounts of which the natural person and/or the persons referred to in this paragraph (a)(1) are the only primary beneficiaries; and

    (iv)   All trusts of which the natural person and/or the persons referred to in this paragraph (a)(1) are the only primary beneficiaries;

(2)

    (i)   A corporation, general partnership, limited partnership, limited liability company, trust (other than a trust referred to in paragraph (a)(1)(iv) of this section), or other legal organization (any of which are referred to hereinafter as a "legal organization") that receives investment advice based on its investment objectives rather than the individual investment objectives of its shareholders, partners, limited partners, members, or beneficiaries (any of which are referred to hereinafter as an "owner"); and

    (ii)   Two or more legal organizations referred to in paragraph (a)(2)(i) of this section that have identical owners.

(b) Special Rules.

For purposes of this section:

(1)   An owner must be counted as a client if the investment adviser provides investment advisory services to the owner separate and apart from the investment advisory services provided to the legal organization, Provided, however, that the determination that an owner is a client will not affect the applicability of this section with regard to any other owner;

(2)   An owner need not be counted as a client of an investment adviser solely because the investment adviser, on behalf of the legal organization, offers, promotes, or sells interests in the legal organization to the owner, or reports periodically to the owners as a group solely with respect to the performance of or plans for the legal organization's assets or similar matters;

(3)   A limited partnership is a client of any general partner or other person acting as investment adviser to the partnership;

(4)   Any person for whom an investment adviser provides investment advisory services without compensation need not be counted as a client; and

(5)   An investment adviser that has its principal office and place of business outside of the United States must count only clients that are United States residents; an investment adviser that has its

principal office and place of business in the United States must count all clients.

(c) Holding Out.

Any investment adviser relying on this section shall not be deemed to be holding itself out generally to the public as an investment adviser, within the meaning of section 203(b)(3) of the Act [15 U.S.C. § 80b-3(b)(3)], solely because such investment adviser participates in a non-public offering of interests in a limited partnership under the Securities Act of 1933.

* * *

203A-1. Eligibility for commission registration.

(a) Threshold Increased to $30 Million of Assets Under Management.

No investment adviser that is registered or required to be registered as an investment adviser in the State in which it maintains its principal office and place of business shall register with the Commission under section 203 of the Act [15 U.S.C. § 80b-3], unless the investment adviser:

(1)   Has assets under management of not less than $30,000,000, as reported on the Form ADV of the investment adviser; or

(2)   Is an investment adviser to an investment company registered under the Investment Company Act of 1940 [15 U.S.C. § 80a-1 et seq.].

(b) Exemption for Investment Advisers Having Between $25 and $30 Million of Assets Under Management.

Notwithstanding paragraph (a) of this section, an investment adviser that is registered or required to be registered as an investment adviser in the State in which it maintains its principal office and place of business may register with the Commission if the investment adviser has assets under management of not less than $25,000,000 but not more than $30,000,000, as reported on the Form ADV of the investment adviser. This paragraph (b) shall not apply to an investment adviser:

(1)   To an investment company registered under the Investment Company Act of 1940 [15 U.S.C. § 80a-1 et seq.]; or

(2)   That is exempted by Rule 203A-2 from the prohibition in section 203A(a) of the Act [15 U.S.C. § 80b-3a(a)] on registering with the Commission.

Note to paragraphs (a) and (b): Paragraphs (a) and (b) together make registration with the Commission optional for certain investment advisers that have between $25 and $30 million of assets under management.

(c) Grace Period for Transition From Commission to State Registration.

An investment adviser registered with the Commission, upon filing an amendment to Form ADV that indicates that it would be prohibited by section 203A(a) of the Act [15 U.S.C. § 80b-3a(a)] from registering with the Commission, shall be subject to having its registration cancelled pursuant to section 203(h) of the Act [15 U.S.C. § 80b-3(h)], Provided, That the Commission shall not commence any cancellation proceeding on the basis of the amendment until the expiration of a period of not less than 90 days from the date the investment adviser was required by Rule 204-1(a) to file the amendment.

(d) Transition From State to Commission Registration.

An investment adviser that is registered with a securities commissioner (or any agency or officer performing like functions) of any State that requires such investment adviser annually to report to it the amount of assets under management pursuant to a form or rule substantially similar to Schedule I to Form ADV must register with the Commission within 90 days after the date on which the investment adviser is required to report assets under management of $30,000,000 or more to the state securities commissioner, unless, at the time of registration with the Commission, the investment adviser is prohibited by section 203A(a) of the Act [15 U.S.C. § 80b-3a(a)] from registering with the Commission.

Notes to paragraph (d):

1.   An investment adviser may be prohibited by section 203A(a) from registering with the Commission if its assets under management have decreased to an amount less than $25,000,000 during the 90-day period.

2.   An investment adviser not eligible to rely on paragraph (d) must register with the Commission promptly when no

longer prohibited by section 203A(a) from registering with the Commission.

203A-2. Exemptions from prohibition on commission registration.

The prohibition of section 203A(a) of the Act [15 U.S.C. § 80b-3a(a)] shall not apply to:

(a) Nationally Recognized Statistical Rating Organizations.

An investment adviser that is a nationally recognized statistical rating organization, as that term is used in paragraphs (c)(2)(vi)(E), (F), and (H) of Rule 15c3-1 of this chapter.

(b) Pension Consultants.

(1)   An investment adviser that is a "pension consultant," as defined in this section, with respect to assets of plans having an aggregate value of at least $50,000,000.

(2)   An investment adviser is a pension consultant, for purposes of paragraph (b) of this section, if the investment adviser provides investment advice to:

(i)   Any employee benefit plan described in section 3(3) of the Employee Retirement Income Security Act of 1974 ("ERISA") [29 U.S.C. § 1002(3)];

(ii)   Any governmental plan described in section 3(32) of ERISA [29 U.S.C. § 1002(32)]; or

(iii)   Any church plan described in section 3(33) of ERISA [29 U.S.C. § 1002(33)].

(3)   In determining the aggregate value of assets of plans, include only that portion of a plan's assets for which the investment adviser provided investment advice (including any advice with respect to the selection of an investment adviser to manage such assets). Determine the aggregate value of assets by cumulating the value of assets of plans with respect to which the investment adviser was last employed or retained by contract to provide investment advice during a 12-month period ended within 90 days of filing Schedule I to Form ADV.

(c) Investment Advisers Controlling, Controlled By, or Under Common Control with an Investment Adviser Registered with the Commission.

An investment adviser that controls, is controlled by, or is under common control with, an investment adviser eligible to register, and registered with, the Commission ("registered adviser"), provided that the principal office and place of business of the investment adviser is the same as that of the registered adviser. For purposes of this paragraph, control means the power to direct or cause the direction of the management or policies of an investment adviser, whether through ownership of securities, by contract, or otherwise. Any person that directly or indirectly has the right to vote 25 percent or more of the voting securities, or is entitled to 25 percent or more of the profits, of an investment adviser is presumed to control that investment adviser.

(d) Investment Advisers Expecting to Be Eligible for Commission Registration Within 120 Days.

An investment adviser that:

(1)   Immediately before it registers with the Commission, is not registered or required to be registered with the Commission or a securities commissioner (or any agency or officer performing like functions) of any State and has a reasonable expectation that it would be eligible to register with the Commission within 120 days after the date the investment adviser's registration with the Commission becomes effective;

(2)   Includes on Schedule E to its Form ADV an undertaking to withdraw from registration with the Commission if, on the 120th day after the date the investment adviser's registration with the Commission becomes effective, the investment adviser would be prohibited by section 203A(a) of the Act [15 U.S.C. § 80b-3a(a)] from registering with the Commission; and

(3)   Within 120 days after the date the investment adviser's registration with the Commission becomes effective, files an amendment to Form ADV revising Schedule I thereto and, if the amendment indicates that the investment adviser would be prohibited by section 203A(a) of the Act [15 U.S.C. § 80b-3a(a)] from registering with the Commission, the amendment is accompanied by a completed Form ADV-W whereby it withdraws from registration with the Commission.

(e)   Multi-State Investment Advisers.

An investment adviser that:

(1)   Upon submission of its application for registration with the Commission, is required by the laws of 30 or more States to

register as an investment adviser with the securities commissioners (or any agencies or officers performing like functions) in the respective States, and thereafter would, but for this section, be required by the laws of at least 25 States to register as an investment adviser with the securities commissioners (or any agencies or officers performing like functions) in the respective States;

(2)   Attaches a representation to Schedule I to Form ADV that the investment adviser has reviewed the applicable State and federal laws and has concluded that, in the case of an application for registration with the Commission, it is required by the laws of 30 or more States to register as an investment adviser with the securities commissioners (or any agencies or officers performing like functions) in the respective States or, in the case of an amendment to Form ADV revising Schedule I to Form ADV, it would be required by the laws of at least 25 States to register as an investment adviser with the securities commissioners (or any agencies or officers performing like functions) in the respective States, within 90 days prior to the date of filing Schedule I;

(3)   Includes on Schedule E to Form ADV an undertaking to withdraw from registration with the Commission if an amendment to Form ADV revising Schedule I to Form ADV indicates that the investment adviser would be required by the laws of fewer than 25 States to register as an investment adviser with the securities commissioners (or any agencies or officers performing like functions) in the respective States, and, if an amendment to Form ADV revising Schedule I indicates that the investment adviser would be prohibited by section 203A(a) of the Act [15 U.S.C. § 80b-3a(a)] from registering with the Commission, files a completed Form ADV-W within 90 days from the date the investment adviser was required by Rule 204-1(a) to file the amendment to Form ADV revising Schedule I, whereby the investment adviser withdraws from registration with the Commission; and

(4)   Maintains in an easily accessible place a record of the States in which the investment adviser has determined it would, but for the exemption, be required to register for a period of not less than five years from the filing of a Schedule I to Form ADV that includes a representation that is based on such record.

* * *

204-1. Amendments to application for registration.

(a) Every investment adviser whose registration with the Commission is effective on the last day of its fiscal year shall, within 90 days of the end of its fiscal year, unless its registration has been withdrawn, cancelled, or revoked prior to that day, file:

(1) Schedule I to Form ADV;

(2) A balance sheet if the balance sheet is required by Item 14 of Part II of Form ADV; and

(3) An executed page one of Part I of Form ADV.

(b)

(1) If the information contained in the response to Items 1, 2, 3, 4, 5, 8, 11, 13A, 13B, 14A and 14B of Part I of any application for registration as an investment adviser, or in any amendment thereto, becomes inaccurate for any reason, or if the information contained in response to any question in Items 9 and 10 of Part I, all of Part II (except Item 14), and all of Schedule H of any application for registration as an investment adviser, or in any amendment thereto, becomes inaccurate in a material manner, the investment adviser shall promptly file an amendment on Form ADV correcting the information.

(2) For all other changes not designated in paragraph (b)(1) of this section, the investment adviser shall file an amendment on Form ADV updating the information together with the amendments required by paragraph (a) of this section.

204-2. Books and records to be maintained by investment advisers.

(a) Every investment adviser registered or required to be registered under section 203 of the Act [15 U.S.C. § 80b-3] shall make and keep true, accurate and current the following books and records relating to its investment advisory business:

(1) A journal or journals, including cash receipts and disbursements records, and any other records of original entry forming the basis of entries in any ledger.

(2) General and auxiliary ledgers (or other comparable records) reflecting asset, liability, reserve, capital, income and expense accounts.

(3)   A memorandum of each order given by the investment adviser
for the purchase or sale of any security, of any instruction
received by the investment adviser from the client concerning the
purchase, sale, receipt or delivery of a particular security, and of
any modification or cancellation of any such order or instruction.
Such memoranda shall show the terms and conditions of the
order, instruction, modification or cancellation; shall identify the
person connected with the investment adviser who
recommended the transaction to the client and the person who
placed such order; and shall show the account for which entered,
the date of entry, and the bank, broker or dealer by or through
whom executed where appropriate. Orders entered pursuant to
the exercise of discretionary power shall be so designated.

(4)   All check books, bank statements, cancelled checks and cash
reconciliations of the investment adviser.

(5)   All bills or statements (or copies thereof), paid or unpaid,
relating to the business of the investment adviser as such.

(6)   All trial balances, financial statements, and internal audit
working papers relating to the business of such investment
adviser.

(7)   Originals of all written communications received and copies of
all written communications sent by such investment adviser
relating to (A) any recommendation made or proposed to be
made and any advice given or proposed to be given, (B) any
receipt, disbursement or delivery of funds or securities, or (C)
the placing or execution of any order to purchase or sell any
security: Provided, however, (i) that the investment adviser shall
not be required to keep any unsolicited market letters and other
similar communications of general public distribution not
prepared by or for the investment adviser, and (ii) that if the
investment adviser sends any notice, circular or other
advertisement offering any report, analysis, publication or other
investment advisory service to more than 10 persons, the
investment adviser shall not be required to keep a record of the
names and addresses of the persons to whom it was sent; except
that if such notice, circular or advertisement is distributed to
persons named on any list, the investment adviser shall retain
with the copy of such notice, circular or advertisement a
memorandum describing the list and the source thereof.

(8) A list or other record of all accounts in which the investment adviser is vested with any discretionary power with respect to the funds, securities or transactions of any client.

(9) All powers of attorney and other evidences of the granting of any discretionary authority by any client to the investment adviser, or copies thereof.

(10) All written agreements (or copies thereof) entered into by the investment adviser with any client or otherwise relating to the business of such investment adviser as such.

(11) A copy of each notice, circular, advertisement, newspaper article, investment letter, bulletin or other communication that the investment adviser circulates or distributes, directly or indirectly, to 10 or more persons (other than persons connected with such investment adviser), and if such notice, circular, advertisement, newspaper article, investment letter, bulletin or other communication recommends the purchase or sale of a specific security and does not state the reasons for such recommendation, a memorandum of the investment adviser indicating the reasons therefor.

(12) A record of every transaction in a security in which the investment adviser or any advisory representative (as hereinafter defined) of such investment adviser has, or by reason of such transaction acquires, any direct or indirect beneficial ownership, except (i) transactions effected in any account over which neither the investment adviser nor any advisory representative of the investment adviser has any direct or indirect influence or control; and (ii) transactions in securities which are direct obligations of the United States. Such record shall state the title and amount of the security involved; the date and nature of the transaction (i.e., purchase, sale or other acquisition or disposition); the price at which it was effected; and the name of the broker, dealer or bank with or through whom the transaction was effected. Such record may also contain a statement declaring that the reporting or recording of any such transaction shall not be construed as an admission that the investment adviser or advisory representative has any direct or indirect beneficial ownership in the security. A transaction shall be recorded not later than 10 days after the end of the calendar quarter in which the transaction was effected.

For purposes of this paragraph–

(A)   The term "advisory representative" shall mean any partner, officer or director of the investment adviser; any employee who makes any recommendation, who participates in the determination of which recommendation shall be made, or whose functions or duties relate to the determination of which recommendation shall be made; any employee who, in connection with his duties, obtains any information concerning which securities are being recommended prior to the effective dissemination of such recommendations or of the information concerning such recommendations; and any of the following persons who obtain information concerning securities recommendations being made by such investment adviser prior to the effective dissemination of such recommendations or of the information concerning such recommendations:

   (i)   any person in a control relationship to the investment adviser,

   (ii)   any affiliated person of such controlling person and

   (iii)   any affiliated person of such affiliated person.

(B)   "Control" shall have the same meaning as that set forth in section 2(a)(9) of the Investment Company Act of 1940, as amended.

An investment adviser shall not be deemed to have violated the provisions of subparagraph (12) because of his failure to record securities transactions of any advisory representative if he establishes that he instituted adequate procedures and used reasonable diligence to obtain promptly reports of all transactions required to be recorded.

(13) Notwithstanding the provisions of subparagraph (12) above, where the investment adviser is primarily engaged in a business or businesses other than advising registered investment companies or other advisory clients, a record must be maintained of every transaction in a security in which the investment adviser or any advisory representative (as hereinafter defined) of such investment adviser has, or by reason of such transaction acquires, any direct or indirect beneficial ownership, except

(i)   transactions effected in any account over which neither the investment adviser nor any advisory representative of the investment adviser has any direct or indirect influence or control; and

(ii) transactions in securities which are direct obligations of the United States. Such record shall state the title and amount of the security involved; the date and nature of the transaction (i.e., purchase, sale or other acquisition or disposition); the price at which it was effected; and the name of the broker, dealer or bank with or through whom the transaction was effected. Such record may also contain a statement declaring that the reporting or recording of any such transaction shall not be construed as an admission that the investment adviser or advisory representative has any direct or indirect beneficial ownership in the security. A transaction shall be recorded not later than 10 days after the end of the calendar quarter in which the transaction was effected.

For purposes of this paragraph–

(A) The term "advisory representative," when used in connection with a company primarily engaged in a business or businesses other than advising registered investment companies or other advisory clients, shall mean any partner, officer, director or employee of the investment adviser who makes any recommendation, who participates in the determination of which recommendation shall be made, or whose functions or duties relate to the determination of which recommendation shall be made, or who, in connection with his duties, obtains any information concerning which securities are being recommended prior to the effective dissemination of such recommendations or of the information concerning such recommendations; and any of the following persons who obtain information concerning securities recommendations being made by such investment adviser prior to the effective dissemination of such recommendations or of the information concerning such recommendations:

        (i)   any person in a control relationship to the investment adviser,

        (ii) any affiliated person of such controlling person and

        (iii) any affiliated person of such affiliated person.

(B)   "Control" shall have the same meaning as that set forth in section 2(a)(9) of the Investment Company Act of 1940, as amended.

(C)   An investment adviser is "primarily engaged in a business or businesses other than advising registered investment companies or other advisory clients" when, for each of its most recent three fiscal years or for the period of time since organization, whichever is lesser, the investment adviser derived, on an unconsolidated basis, more than 50% of (1) its total sales and revenues, and (2) its income (or loss) before income taxes and extraordinary items, from such other business or businesses.

An investment adviser shall not be deemed to have violated the provisions of this subparagraph (13) because of his failure to record securities transactions of any advisory representative if he establishes that he instituted adequate procedures and used reasonable diligence to obtain promptly reports of all transactions required to be recorded.

(14) A copy of each written statement and each amendment or revision thereof, given or sent to any client or prospective client of such investment adviser in accordance with the provisions of Rule 204-3 under the Act, and a record of the dates that each written statement, and each amendment or revision thereof, was given, or offered to be given, to any client or prospective client who subsequently becomes a client.

(15) All written acknowledgments of receipt obtained from clients pursuant to Rule 206(4)-3(a)(2)(iii)(B) of this chapter and copies of the disclosure documents delivered to clients by solicitors pursuant to Rule 206(4)-3 of this chapter.

(16) All accounts, books, internal working papers, and any other records or documents that are necessary to form the basis for or demonstrate the calculation of the performance or rate of return

of any or all managed accounts or securities recommendations in any notice, circular, advertisement, newspaper article, investment letter, bulletin or other communication that the investment adviser circulates or distributes, directly or indirectly, to 10 or more persons (other than persons connected with such investment adviser); provided, however, that, with respect to the performance of managed accounts, the retention of all account statements, if they reflect all debits, credits, and other transactions in a client's account for the period of the statement, and all worksheets necessary to demonstrate the calculation of the performance or rate of return of all managed accounts shall be deemed to satisfy the requirements of this paragraph.

(b)   If an investment adviser subject to paragraph (a) of this rule has custody or possession of securities or funds of any client, the records required to be made and kept under paragraph (a) above shall include:

(1)   A journal or other record showing all purchases, sales, receipts and deliveries of securities (including certificate numbers) for such accounts and all other debits and credits to such accounts.

(2)   A separate ledger account for each such client showing all purchases, sales, receipts and deliveries of securities, the date and price of each such purchase and sale, and all debits and credits.

(3)   Copies of confirmations of all transactions effected by or for the account of any such client.

(4)   A record for each security in which any such client has a position, which record shall show the name of each such client having any interest in each security, the amount or interest of each such client, and the location of each such security.

(c)   Every investment adviser subject to paragraph (a) of this rule who renders any investment supervisory or management service to any client shall, with respect to the portfolio being supervised or managed and to the extent that the information is reasonably available to or obtainable by the investment adviser, make and keep true, accurate and current:

(1)   Records showing separately for each such client the securities purchased and sold, and the date, amount and price of each such purchase and sale.

(2)   For each security in which any such client has a current position, information from which the investment adviser can promptly

furnish the name of each such client, and the current amount or interest of such client.

(d)   Any books or records required by this rule may be maintained by the investment adviser in such manner that the identity of any client to whom such investment adviser renders investment supervisory services is indicated by numerical or alphabetical code or some similar designation.

(e)

(1)   All books and records required to be made under the provisions of paragraph (a) to (c)(1), inclusive, of this rule (except for books and records required to be made under the provisions of paragraphs (a)(11) and (a)(16) of this rule), shall be maintained and preserved in an easily accessible place for a period of not less than five years from the end of the fiscal year during which the last entry was made on such record, the first two years in an appropriate office of the investment adviser.

(2)   Partnership articles and any amendments thereto, articles of incorporation, charters, minute books, and stock certificate books of the investment adviser and of any predecessor, shall be maintained in the principal office of the investment adviser and preserved until at least three years after termination of the enterprise.

(3)   Books and records required to be made under the provisions of paragraphs (a)(11) and (a)(16) of this rule shall be maintained and preserved in an easily accessible place for a period of not less than five years, the first two years in an appropriate office of the investment adviser, from the end of the fiscal year during which the investment adviser last published or otherwise disseminated, directly or indirectly, the notice, circular, advertisement, newspaper article, investment letter, bulletin or other communication.

(f)   An investment adviser subject to paragraph (a) of this rule, before ceasing to conduct or discontinuing business as an investment adviser shall arrange for and be responsible for the preservation of the books and records required to be maintained and preserved under this rule for the remainder of the period specified in this rule, and shall notify the Commission in writing, at its principal office, Washington, D.C. 20549, of the exact address where such books and records will be maintained during such period.

(g)

(1)   The records required to be maintained and preserved pursuant to this rule may be immediately produced or reproduced by photograph on film or, as provided in paragraph (g)(2) below, on magnetic disk, tape or other computer storage medium, and be maintained and preserved for the required time in that form. If records are produced or reproduced by photographic film or computer storage medium, the investment adviser shall:

(i)   arrange the records and index the films or computer storage medium so as to permit the immediate location of any particular record,

(ii)   be ready at all times to provide, and promptly provide, any facsimile enlargement of film or computer printout or copy of the computer storage medium which the Commission by its examiners or other representatives may request,

(iii)   store separately from the original one other copy of the film or computer storage medium for the time required,

(iv)   with respect to records stored on computer storage medium, maintain procedures for maintenance and preservation of, and access to, records so as to reasonably safeguard records from loss, alteration, or destruction, and

(v)   with respect to records stored on photographic film, at all times have available for Commission examination of its records pursuant to section 204 of the Investment Advisers Act of 1940, facilities for immediate, easily readable projection of the film and for producing easily readable facsimile enlargements.

(2)   Pursuant to paragraph (g)(1) an adviser may maintain and preserve on computer tape or disk or other computer storage medium records which, in the ordinary course of the adviser's business, are created by the adviser on electronic media or are received by the adviser solely on electronic media or by electronic data transmission.

(h)

(1)   Any book or other record made, kept, maintained and preserved in compliance with Rules 17a-3 and 17a-4 under the Securities Exchange Act of 1934, which is substantially the same as the book or other record required to be made, kept, maintained and

preserved under this rule, shall be deemed to be made, kept, maintained and preserved in compliance with this rule.

(2) A record made and kept pursuant to any provision of paragraph (a) of this rule, which contains all the information required under any other provision of paragraph (a), need not be maintained in duplicate in order to meet the requirements of the other provision of paragraph (a) of the rule.

(i) As used in this rule the term "discretionary power" shall not include discretion as to the price at which or the time when a transaction is or is to be effected, if, before the order is given by the investment adviser, the client has directed or approved the purchase or sale of a definite amount of the particular security.

(j)

(1) Except as provided in paragraph (j)(3) hereof, each non-resident investment adviser registered or applying for registration pursuant to section 203 of the Act shall keep, maintain and preserve, at a place within the United States designated in a notice from him as provided in paragraph (j)(2) hereof, true, correct, complete and current copies of books and records which he is required to make, keep current, maintain or preserve pursuant to any provision of any rule or regulation of the Commission adopted under the Act.

(2) Except as provided in paragraph (j)(3) hereof, each non-resident investment adviser subject to this paragraph (j) shall furnish to the Commission a written notice specifying the address of the place within the United States where the copies of the books and records required to be kept and preserved by him pursuant to paragraph (j)(1) hereof are located. Each non-resident investment adviser registered or applying for registration when this paragraph becomes effective shall file such notice within 30 days after such rule becomes effective. Each non-resident investment adviser who files an application for registration after this paragraph becomes effective shall file such notice with such application for registration.

(3) Notwithstanding the provisions of paragraphs (j)(1) and (j)(2) hereof, a non-resident investment adviser need not keep or preserve within the United States copies of the books and records referred to in said paragraphs (j)(1) and (j)(2), if:

(i)   Such non-resident investment adviser files with the Commission, at the time or within the period provided by paragraph (j)(2) hereof, a written undertaking, in form acceptable to the Commission and signed by a duly authorized person, to furnish to the Commission, upon demand, at its principal office in Washington, D.C., or at any Regional or District Office of the Commission designated in such demand, true, correct, complete and current copies of any or all of the books and records which he is required to make, keep current, maintain, or preserve pursuant to any provision of any rule or regulation of the Commission adopted under the Act, or any part of such books and records which may be specified in such demand. Such undertaking shall be in substantially the following form:

> The undersigned hereby undertakes to furnish at its own expense to the Securities and Exchange Commission at its principal office in Washington, D.C., or at any Regional or District Office of said Commission specified in a demand for copies of books and records made by or on behalf of said Commission, true, correct, complete, and current copies of any or all, or any part, of the books and records which the undersigned is required to make, keep current or preserve pursuant to any provision of any rule or regulation of the Securities and Exchange Commission under the Investment Advisers Act of 1940. This undertaking shall be suspended during any period when the undersigned is making, keeping current, and preserving copies of all of said books and records at a place within the United States in compliance with Rule 204-2(j) under the Investment Advisers Act of 1940. This undertaking shall be binding upon the undersigned and the heirs, successors and assigns of the undersigned, and the written irrevocable consents and powers of attorney of the undersigned, its general partners and managing agents filed with the Securities and Exchange Commission shall extend to and cover any action to enforce same.

and

(ii)   Such non-resident investment adviser furnishes to the Commission, at his own expense 14 days after written demand therefor forwarded to him by registered mail at his last address of record filed with the Commission and signed by the Secretary of the Commission or such other person as the Commission may authorize to act in its behalf, true, correct, complete and current copies of any or all books and records which such investment adviser is required to make, keep current or preserve pursuant to any provision of any rule or regulation of the Commission adopted under the Act, or any part of such books and records which may be specified in said written demand. Such copies shall be furnished to the Commission at its principal office in Washington, D.C., or at any Regional or District Office of the Commission which may be specified in said written demand.

(4)   For purposes of this rule the term "non-resident investment adviser" shall have the meaning set out in Rule 0-2(d)(3) under the Act.

(k)   Every investment adviser that registers under section 203 of the Act [15 U.S.C. § 80b-3] after July 8, 1997 shall be required to preserve in accordance with this section the books and records the investment adviser had been required to maintain by the State in which the investment adviser had its principal office and place of business prior to registering with the Commission.

204-3. Written disclosure statements.

(a) General Requirement.

Unless otherwise provided in this rule, an investment adviser, registered or required to be registered pursuant to section 203 of the Act shall, in accordance with the provisions of this section, furnish each advisory client and prospective advisory client with a written disclosure statement which may be either a copy of Part II of its Form ADV which complies with Rule 204-1(b) under the Act or a written document containing at least the information then so required by Part II of Form ADV.

(b) Delivery.

    (1)   An investment adviser, except as provided in paragraph (2), shall deliver the statement required by this section to an advisory client or prospective advisory client

        (i)   not less than 48 hours prior to entering into any written or oral investment advisory contract with such client or prospective client, or

        (ii)   at the time of entering into any such contract, if the advisory client has a right to terminate the contract without penalty within five business days after entering into the contract.

    (2)   Delivery of the statement required by paragraph (1) need not be made in connection with entering into (i) an investment company contract or (ii) a contract for impersonal advisory services.

(c) Offer to Deliver.

    (1)   An investment adviser, except as provided in paragraph (2), annually shall, without charge, deliver or offer in writing to deliver upon written request to each of its advisory clients the statement required by this section.

    (2)   The delivery or offer required by paragraph (1) need not be made to advisory clients receiving advisory services solely pursuant to

        (i)   an investment company contract or

        (ii)   a contract for impersonal advisory services requiring a payment of less than $200;

    (3)   With respect to an advisory client entering into a contract or receiving advisory services pursuant to a contract for impersonal advisory services which requires a payment of $200 or more, an offer of the type specified in paragraph (1) shall also be made at the time of entering into an advisory contract.

    (4)   Any statement requested in writing by an advisory client pursuant to an offer required by this paragraph must be mailed or delivered within seven days of the receipt of the request.

(d) Omission of Inapplicable Information.

If an investment adviser renders substantially different types of investment advisory services to different advisory clients, any information required by Part II of Form ADV may be omitted from

the statement furnished to an advisory client or prospective advisory client if such information is applicable only to a type of investment advisory service or fee which is not rendered or charged, or proposed to be rendered or charged, to that client or prospective client.

(e) Other disclosures.

Nothing in this rule shall relieve any investment advisor from any obligation pursuant to any provision of the Act or the rules and regulations thereunder or other federal or state law to disclose any information to its advisory clients or prospective advisory clients not specifically required by this rule.

(f) Sponsors of Wrap Fee Programs.

(1)   An investment adviser, registered or required to be registered pursuant to section 203 of the Act, that is compensated under a wrap fee program for sponsoring, organizing, or administering the program, or for selecting, or providing advice to clients regarding the selection of, other investment advisers in the program, shall, in lieu of the written disclosure statement required by paragraph (a) of this section and in accordance with the other provisions of this section, furnish each client and prospective client of the wrap fee program with a written disclosure statement containing at least the information required by Schedule H of Form ADV. Any additional information included in such disclosure statement should be limited to information concerning wrap fee programs sponsored by the investment adviser.

(2)   If an investment adviser is required under this paragraph (f) to furnish disclosure statements to clients or prospective clients of more than one wrap fee program, the investment adviser may omit from the disclosure statement furnished to clients and prospective clients of a wrap fee program or programs any information required by Schedule H that is not applicable to clients or prospective clients of that wrap fee program or programs.

(3)   An investment adviser need not furnish the written disclosure statement required by paragraph (f)(1) of this section to clients and prospective clients of a wrap fee program if another investment adviser is required to furnish and does furnish the written disclosure statement to all clients and prospective clients of the wrap fee program.

(4) An investment adviser that is required under this paragraph (f) to furnish a disclosure statement to clients of a wrap fee program shall furnish the disclosure statement to each client of the wrap fee program (including clients that have previously been furnished the brochure required under paragraph (a) of this section) no later than October 1, 1994.

(g) Definitions.

For the purpose of this rule:

(1) "contract for impersonal advisory services" means any contract relating solely to the provision of investment advisory services

(i) by means of written material or oral statements which do not purport to meet the objectives or needs of specific individuals or accounts;

(ii) through the issuance of statistical information containing no expression of opinion as to the investment merits of a particular security; or

(iii) any combination of the foregoing services.

(2) "entering into," in reference to an investment advisory contract, does not include an extension or renewal without material change of any such contract which is in effect immediately prior to such extension or renewal.

(3) "investment company contract" means a contract with an investment company registered under the Investment Company Act of 1940 which meets the requirements of section 15(c) of that Act.

(4) "wrap fee program" means a program under which any client is charged a specified fee or fees not based directly upon transactions in a client's account for investment advisory services (which may include portfolio management or advice concerning the selection of other investment advisers) and execution of client transactions.

205-1. Definition of "investment performance" of an investment company and "investment record" of an appropriate index of securities prices.

(a)   "Investment performance" of an investment company for any period shall mean the sum of:

(1)   the change in its net asset value per share during such period;

(2)   the value of its cash distributions per share accumulated to the end of such period; and

(3)   the value of capital gains taxes per share paid or payable on undistributed realized long-term capital gains accumulated to the end of such period; expressed as a percentage of its net asset value per share at the beginning of such period. For this purpose, the value of distributions per share of realized capital gains, of dividends per share paid from investment income and of capital gains taxes per share paid or payable on undistributed realized long-term capital gains shall be treated as reinvested in shares of the investment company at the net asset value per share in effect at the close of business on the record date for the payment of such distributions and dividends and the date on which provision is made for such taxes, after giving effect to such distributions, dividends and taxes.

(b)   "Investment record" of an appropriate index of securities prices for any period shall mean the sum of:

(1)   the change in the level of the index during such period; and

(2)   the value, computed consistently with the index, of cash distributions made by companies whose securities comprise the index accumulated to the end of such period; expressed as a percentage of the index level at the beginning of such period. For this purpose cash distributions on the securities which comprise the index shall be treated as reinvested in the index at least as frequently as the end of each calendar quarter following the payment of the dividend.

Rule 205-2. Definition of "specified period" over which the asset value of the company or fund under management is averaged.

(a) For purposes of this rule:

(1) "Fulcrum fee" shall mean the fee which is paid or earned when the investment company's performance is equivalent to that of the index or other measure of performance.

(2) "Rolling period" shall mean a period consisting of a specified number of subperiods of definite length in which the most recent subperiod is substituted for the earliest subperiod as time passes.

(b) The specified period over which the asset value of the company or fund under management is averaged shall mean the period over which the investment performance of the company or fund and the investment record of an appropriate index of securities prices or such other measure of investment performance are computed.

(c) Notwithstanding paragraph (b), the specified period over which the asset value of the company or fund is averaged for the purpose of computing the fulcrum fee may differ from the period over which the asset value is averaged for computing the performance related portion of the fee, only if

(1) The performance related portion of the fee is computed over a rolling period and the total fee is payable at the end of each subperiod of the rolling period; and

(2) The fulcrum fee is computed on the basis of the asset value averaged over the most recent subperiod or subperiods of the rolling period.

205-3. Exemption from the compensation prohibition of section 205(a)(1) for investment advisers.

(a) General.

The provisions of section 205(a)(1) of the Act [15 U.S.C. § 80b-5(a)(1)] will not be deemed to prohibit an investment adviser from entering into, performing, renewing or extending an investment advisory contract that provides for compensation to the investment adviser on the basis of a share of the capital gains upon, or the capital appreciation of, the funds, or any portion of the funds, of a client, Provided, That the client entering into the contract subject to this

section is a qualified client, as defined in paragraph (d)(1) of this section.

(b) Identification of the client.

In the case of a private investment company, as defined in paragraph (d)(3) of this section, an investment company registered under the Investment Company Act of 1940, or a business development company, as defined in section 202(a)(22) of the Act [15 U.S.C. § 80b-2(a)(22)], each equity owner of any such company (except for the investment adviser entering into the contract and any other equity owners not charged a fee on the basis of a share of capital gains or capital appreciation) will be considered a client for purposes of paragraph (a) of this section.

(c) Transition rule.

An investment adviser that entered into a contract before August 20, 1998, and satisfied the conditions of this section as in effect on the date that the contract was entered into will be considered to satisfy the conditions of this section;

> Provided, however, that this section will apply with respect to any natural person or company who is not a party to the contract prior to and becomes a party to the contract after August 20, 1998.

(d) Definitions.

For the purposes of this section:

(1)   The term "qualified client" means:

    (i)   A natural person who or a company that immediately after entering into the contract has at least $750,000 under the management of the investment adviser;

    (ii)   A natural person who or a company that the investment adviser entering into the contract (and any person acting on his behalf) reasonably believes, immediately prior to entering into the contract, either:

        (A)   Has a net worth (together, in the case of a natural person, with assets held jointly with a spouse) of more than $1,500,000 at the time the contract is entered into; or

        (B)   Is a qualified purchaser as defined in section 2(a)(51)(A) of the Investment Company Act of 1940

[15 U.S.C. § 80a-2(a)(51)(A)] at the time the contract is entered into; or

(iii) A natural person who immediately prior to entering into the contract is:

(A) An executive officer, director, trustee, general partner, or person serving in a similar capacity, of the investment adviser; or

(B) An employee of the investment adviser (other than an employee performing solely clerical, secretarial or administrative functions with regard to the investment adviser) who, in connection with his or her regular functions or duties, participates in the investment activities of such investment adviser, provided that such employee has been performing such functions and duties for or on behalf of the investment adviser, or substantially similar functions or duties for or on behalf of another company for at least 12 months.

(2) The term "company" has the same meaning as in section 202(a)(5) of the Act [15 U.S.C. 80b-2(a)(5)], but does not include a company that is required to be registered under the Investment Company Act of 1940 but is not registered.

(3) The term "private investment company" means a company that would be defined as an investment company under section 3(a) of the Investment Company Act of 1940 [15 U.S.C. § 80a-3(a)] but for the exception provided from that definition by section 3(c)(1) of such Act [15 U.S.C. § 80a-3(c)(1)].

(4) The term "executive officer" means the president, any vice president in charge of a principal business unit, division or function (such as sales, administration or finance), any other officer who performs a policy-making function, or any other person who performs similar policy-making functions, for the investment adviser.

206(3)-1. Exemption of investment advisers registered as broker-dealers in connection with the provision of certain investment advisory services.

(a)   An investment adviser which is a broker or dealer registered pursuant to section 15 of the Securities Exchange Act of 1934 shall be exempt from section 206(3) in connection with any transaction in relation to which such broker or dealer is acting as an investment adviser solely

    (1)   by means of publicly distributed written materials or publicly made oral statements;

    (2)   by means of written materials or oral statements which do not purport to meet the objectives or needs of specific individuals or accounts;

    (3)   through the issuance of statistical information containing no expressions of opinion as to the investment merits of a particular security; or

    (4)   any combination of the foregoing services:

        Provided, however, that such materials and oral statements include a statement that if the purchaser of the advisory communication uses the services of the adviser in connection with a sale or purchase of a security which is a subject of such communication, the adviser may act as principal for its own account or as agent for another person.

(b)   For the purpose of this rule, publicly distributed written materials are those which are distributed to 35 or more persons who pay for such materials, and publicly made oral statements are those made simultaneously to 35 or more persons who pay for access to such statements.

Note: The requirement that the investment adviser disclose that it may act as principal or agent for another person in the sale or purchase of a security that is the subject of investment advice does not relieve the investment adviser of any disclosure obligation which, depending upon the nature of the relationship between the investment adviser and the client, may be imposed by subparagraphs (1) or (2) of section 206 or the other provisions of the federal securities laws.

CHAPTER SEVENTEEN

INVESTMENT COMPANY ACT OF 1940

(codified at 15 U.S.C. § 80a-1 *et seq.*)

§ 1. Findings and Declaration of Policy

(a) Findings

Upon the basis of facts disclosed by the record and reports of the Securities and Exchange Commission made pursuant to the Public Utility Holding Company Act of 1935, and facts otherwise disclosed and ascertained, it is found that investment companies are affected with a national public interest in that, among other things—

(1) the securities issued by such companies, which constitute a substantial part of all securities publicly offered, are distributed, purchased, paid for, exchanged, transferred, redeemed, and repurchased by use of the mails and means and instrumentalities of interstate commerce, and in the case of the numerous companies which issue redeemable securities this process of distribution and redemption is continuous;

(2) the principal activities of such companies--investing, reinvesting, and trading in securities--are conducted by use of the mails and means and instrumentalities of interstate commerce, including the facilities of national securities exchanges, and constitute a substantial part of all transactions effected in the securities markets of the Nation;

(3) such companies customarily invest and trade in securities issued by, and may dominate and control or otherwise affect the policies and management of, companies engaged in business in interstate commerce;

(4) such companies are media for the investment in the national economy of a substantial part of the national savings and may have a vital effect upon the flow of such savings into the capital markets; and

(5) the activities of such companies, extending over many States, their use of the instrumentalities of interstate commerce and the wide geographic distribution of their security holders, make difficult, if not impossible, effective State regulation of such companies in the interest of investors.

(b) Policy

Upon the basis of facts disclosed by the record and reports of the Securities and Exchange Commission made pursuant to section 79z-4 of this title, and facts otherwise disclosed and ascertained, it is declared that the national public interest and the interest of investors are adversely affected—

(1) when investors purchase, pay for, exchange, receive dividends upon, vote, refrain from voting, sell, or surrender securities issued by investment companies without adequate, accurate, and explicit information, fairly presented, concerning the character of such securities and the circumstances, policies, and financial responsibility of such companies and their management;

(2) when investment companies are organized, operated, managed, or their portfolio securities are selected, in the interest of directors, officers, investment advisers, depositors, or other affiliated persons thereof, in the interest of underwriters, brokers, or dealers, in the interest of special classes of their security holders, or in the interest of other investment companies or persons engaged in other lines of business, rather than in the interest of all classes of such companies' security holders;

(3) when investment companies issue securities containing inequitable or discriminatory provisions, or fail to protect the preferences and privileges of the holders of their outstanding securities;

(4) when the control of investment companies is unduly concentrated through pyramiding or inequitable methods of control, or is inequitably distributed, or when investment companies are managed by irresponsible persons;

(5) when investment companies, in keeping their accounts, in maintaining reserves, and in computing their earnings and the asset value of their outstanding securities, employ unsound or misleading methods, or are not subjected to adequate independent scrutiny;

(6) when investment companies are reorganized, become inactive, or change the character of their business, or when the control or management thereof is transferred, without the consent of their security holders;

(7) when investment companies by excessive borrowing and the issuance of excessive amounts of senior securities increase unduly the speculative character of their junior securities; or

(8)   when investment companies operate without adequate assets or reserves.

It is declared that the policy and purposes of this Act, in accordance with which the provisions of this Act shall be interpreted, are to mitigate and, so far as is feasible, to eliminate the conditions enumerated in this section which adversely affect the national public interest and the interest of investors.

§ 2.   General Definitions

(a)   When used in this Act, unless the context otherwise requires—

* * *

(3)   "Affiliated person" of another person means (A) any person directly or indirectly owning, controlling, or holding with power to vote, 5 per centum or more of the outstanding voting securities of such other person; (B) any person 5 per centum or more of whose outstanding voting securities are directly or indirectly owned, controlled, or held with power to vote, by such other person; (C) any person directly or indirectly controlling, controlled by, or under common control with, such other person; (D) any officer, director, partner, copartner, or employee of such other person; (E) if such other person is an investment company, any investment adviser thereof or any member of an advisory board thereof; and (F) if such other person is an unincorporated investment company not having a board of directors, the depositor thereof.

(4)   "Assignment" includes any direct or indirect transfer or hypothecation of a contract or chose in action by the assignor, or of a controlling block of the assignor's outstanding voting securities by a security holder of the assignor; but does not include an assignment of partnership interests incidental to the death or withdrawal of a minority of the members of the partnership having only a minority interest in the partnership business or to the admission to the partnership of one or more members who, after such admission, shall be only a minority of the members and shall have only a minority interest in the business.

(5)   "Bank" means (A) a banking institution organized under the laws of the United States, (B) a member bank of the Federal Reserve System, (C) any other banking institution or trust company, whether incorporated or not, doing business under the laws of any State or of the United States, a substantial portion of the business of which

consists of receiving deposits or exercising fiduciary powers similar to those permitted to national banks under the authority of the Comptroller of the Currency, and which is supervised and examined by State or Federal authority having supervision over banks, and which is not operated for the purpose of evading the provisions of this Act, and (D) a receiver, conservator, or other liquidating agent of any institution or firm included in clauses (A), (B), or (C) of this paragraph.

* * *

(8) "Company" means a corporation, a partnership, an association, a joint- stock company, a trust, a fund, or any organized group of persons whether incorporated or not; or any receiver, trustee in a case under Title 11 or similar official or any liquidating agent for any of the foregoing, in his capacity as such.

* * *

(12) "Director" means any director of a corporation or any person performing similar functions with respect to any organization, whether incorporated or unincorporated, including any natural person who is a member of a board of trustees of a management company created as a common-law trust.

* * *

(17) "Insurance company" means a company which is organized as an insurance company, whose primary and predominant business activity is the writing of insurance or the reinsuring of risks underwritten by insurance companies, and which is subject to supervision by the insurance commissioner or a similar official or agency of a State; or any receiver or similar official or any liquidating agent for such a company, in his capacity as such.

* * *

(19) "Interested person" of another person means—

(A) when used with respect to an investment company—

(i)   any affiliated person of such company,

(ii) any member of the immediate family of any natural person who is an affiliated person of such company,

(iii) any interested person of any investment adviser of or principal underwriter for such company,

(iv)   any person or partner or employee of any person who at any time since the beginning of the last two completed fiscal years of such company has acted as legal counsel for such company,

(v)   any broker or dealer registered under the Securities Exchange Act of 1934 or any affiliated person of such a broker or dealer, and

(vi)   any natural person whom the Commission by order shall have determined to be an interested person by reason of having had, at any time since the beginning of the last two completed fiscal years of such company, a material business or professional relationship with such company or with the principal executive officer of such company or with any other investment company having the same investment adviser or principal underwriter or with the principal executive officer of such other investment company:

Provided, That no person shall be deemed to be an interested person of an investment company solely by reason of (aa) his being a member of its board of directors or advisory board or an owner of its securities, or (bb) his membership in the immediate family of any person specified in clause (aa) of this proviso; and

(B)   when used with respect to an investment adviser of or principal underwriter for any investment company—

(i)   any affiliated person of such investment adviser or principal underwriter,

(ii)   any member of the immediate family of any natural person who is an affiliated person of such investment adviser or principal underwriter,

(iii)   any person who knowingly has any direct or indirect beneficial interest in, or who is designated as trustee, executor, or guardian of any legal interest in, any security issued either by such investment adviser or principal underwriter or by a controlling person of such investment adviser or principal underwriter,

(iv)   any person or partner or employee of any person who at any time since the beginning of the last two completed fiscal years of such investment company has acted as legal counsel for such investment adviser or principal underwriter,

    (v)   any broker or dealer registered under the Securities Exchange Act of 1934 or any affiliated person of such a broker or dealer, and

    (vi)   any natural person whom the Commission by order shall have determined to be an interested person by reason of having had at any time since the beginning of the last two completed fiscal years of such investment company a material business or professional relationship with such investment adviser or principal underwriter or with the principal executive officer or any controlling person of such investment adviser or principal underwriter.

For the purposes of this paragraph (19), "member of the immediate family" means any parent, spouse of a parent, child, spouse of a child, spouse, brother, or sister, and includes step and adoptive relationships. The Commission may modify or revoke any order issued under clause (vi) of subparagraph (A) or (B) of this paragraph whenever it finds that such order is no longer consistent with the facts. No order issued pursuant to clause (vi) of subparagraph (A) or (B) of this paragraph shall become effective until at least sixty days after the entry thereof, and no such order shall affect the status of any person for the purposes of this subchapter or for any other purpose for any period prior to the effective date of such order.

(20)   "Investment adviser" of an investment company means (A) any person (other than a bona fide officer, director, trustee, member of an advisory board, or employee of such company, as such) who pursuant to contract with such company regularly furnishes advice to such company with respect to the desirability of investing in, purchasing or selling securities or other property, or is empowered to determine what securities or other property shall be purchased or sold by such company, and (B) any other person who pursuant to contract with a person described in clause (A) of this paragraph regularly performs substantially all of the duties undertaken by such person described in said clause (A); but does not include (i) a person whose advice is furnished solely through uniform publications distributed to subscribers thereto, (ii) a person who furnishes only statistical and other factual information, advice regarding economic factors and trends, or advice as to occasional transactions in specific securities, but without generally furnishing advice or making recommendations regarding the purchase or sale of securities, (iii) a company furnishing such services at cost to one or more investment companies, insurance companies, or other financial institutions, (iv) any person the

character and amount of whose compensation for such services must be approved by a court, or (v) such other persons as the Commission may by rules and regulations or order determine not to be within the intent of this definition.

* * *

(31) "Prospectus", as used in section 22 of this Act, means a written prospectus intended to meet the requirements of section 10(a) of the Securities Act of 1933 and currently in use. As used elsewhere, "prospectus" means a prospectus as defined in the Securities Act of 1933.

(32) "Redeemable security" means any security, other than short-term paper, under the terms of which the holder, upon its presentation to the issuer or to a person designated by the issuer, is entitled (whether absolutely or only out of surplus) to receive approximately his proportionate share of the issuer's current net assets, or the cash equivalent thereof.

* * *

(51) (A) "Qualified purchaser" means—

  (i)   any natural person (including any person who holds a joint, community property, or other similar shared ownership interest in an issuer that is excepted under section 80a-3(c)(7) of this title with that person's qualified purchaser spouse) who owns not less than $5,000,000 in investments, as defined by the Commission;

  (ii) any company that owns not less than $5,000,000 in investments and that is owned directly or indirectly by or for 2 or more natural persons who are related as siblings or spouse (including former spouses), or direct lineal descendants by birth or adoption, spouses of such persons, the estates of such persons, or foundations, charitable organizations, or trusts established by or for the benefit of such persons;

  (iii) any trust that is not covered by clause (ii) and that was not formed for the specific purpose of acquiring the securities offered, as to which the trustee or other person authorized to make decisions with respect to the trust, and each settlor or other person who has contributed assets to the trust, is a person described in clause (i), (ii), or (iv); or

(iv) any person, acting for its own account or the accounts of other qualified purchasers, who in the aggregate owns and invests on a discretionary basis, not less than $25,000,000 in investments.

(B) The Commission may adopt such rules and regulations applicable to the persons and trusts specified in clauses (i) through (iv) of subparagraph (A) as it determines are necessary or appropriate in the public interest or for the protection of investors.

* * *

§ 3. Definition of Investment Company

(a) Definitions

(1) When used in this Act, "investment company" means any issuer which—

(A) is or holds itself out as being engaged primarily, or proposes to engage primarily, in the business of investing, reinvesting, or trading in securities;

(B) is engaged or proposes to engage in the business of issuing face-amount certificates of the installment type, or has been engaged in such business and has any such certificate outstanding; or

(C) is engaged or proposes to engage in the business of investing, reinvesting, owning, holding, or trading in securities, and owns or proposes to acquire investment securities having a value exceeding 40 per centum of the value of such issuer's total assets (exclusive of Government securities and cash items) on an unconsolidated basis.

(2) As used in this section, "investment securities" includes all securities except (A) Government securities, (B) securities issued by employees' securities companies, and (C) securities issued by majority-owned subsidiaries of the owner which (i) are not investment companies, and (ii) are not relying on the exception from the definition of investment company in paragraph (1) or (7) of subsection (c) of this section.

(b) Exemption from Provisions

Notwithstanding paragraph (3) of subsection (a) of this section, none of the following persons is an investment company within the meaning of this Act:

(1) Any issuer primarily engaged, directly or through a wholly-owned subsidiary or subsidiaries, in a business or businesses other than that of investing, reinvesting, owning, holding, or trading in securities.

(2) Any issuer which the Commission, upon application by such issuer, finds and by order declares to be primarily engaged in a business or businesses other than that of investing, reinvesting, owning, holding, or trading in securities either directly or (A) through majority-owned subsidiaries or (B) through controlled companies conducting similar types of businesses. The filing of an application under this paragraph in good faith by an issuer other than a registered investment company shall exempt the applicant for a period of sixty days from all provisions of this Act applicable to investment companies as such. For cause shown, the Commission by order may extend such period of exemption for an additional period or periods. Whenever the Commission, upon its own motion or upon application, finds that the circumstances which gave rise to the issuance of an order granting an application under this paragraph no longer exist, the Commission shall by order revoke such order.

(3) Any issuer all the outstanding securities of which (other than short-term paper and directors' qualifying shares) are directly or indirectly owned by a company excepted from the definition of investment company by paragraph (1) or (2) of this subsection.

(c) Further Exemptions

Notwithstanding subsection (a) of this section, none of the following persons is an investment company within the meaning of this Act:

(1) Any issuer whose outstanding securities (other than short-term paper) are beneficially owned by not more than one hundred persons and which is not making and does not presently propose to make a public offering of its securities. Such issuer shall be deemed to be an investment company for purposes of the limitations set forth in subparagraphs (A)(i) and (B)(i) of section 12(d)(1) of this Act governing the purchase or other acquisition by such issuer of any security issued by any registered investment company and the sale of any security issued by any registered open-end investment company to any such issuer. For purposes of this paragraph:

(A) Beneficial ownership by a company shall be deemed to be beneficial ownership by one person, except that, if the company owns 10 per centum or more of the outstanding voting securities of the issuer. and is or, but for the exception provided for in this paragraph or paragraph (7), would be an investment company,

the beneficial ownership shall be deemed to be that of the holders of such company's outstanding securities (other than short-term paper).

(B)   Beneficial ownership by any person who acquires securities or interests in securities of an issuer described in the first sentence of this paragraph shall be deemed to be beneficial ownership by the person from whom such transfer was made, pursuant to such rules and regulations as the Commission shall prescribe as necessary or appropriate in the public interest and consistent with the protection of investors and the purposes fairly intended by the policy and provisions of this Act, where the transfer was caused by legal separation, divorce, death, or other involuntary event.

(2)   (A)   Any person primarily engaged in the business of underwriting and distributing securities issued by other persons, selling securities to customers, acting as broker, and acting as market intermediary, or any one or more of such activities, whose gross income normally is derived principally from such business and related activities.

* * *

(3)   Any bank or insurance company; any savings and loan association, building and loan association, cooperative bank, homestead association, or similar institution, or any receiver, conservator, liquidator, liquidating agent, or similar official or person thereof or therefor; or any common trust fund or similar fund maintained by a bank exclusively for the collective investment and reinvestment of moneys contributed thereto by the bank in its capacity as a trustee, executor, administrator, or guardian.

(4)   Any person substantially all of whose business is confined to making small loans, industrial banking, or similar businesses.

* * *

(7)   (A)   Any issuer, the outstanding securities of which are owned exclusively by persons who, at the time of acquisition of such securities, are qualified purchasers, and which is not making and does not at that time propose to make a public offering of such securities. Securities that are owned by persons who received the securities from a qualified purchaser as a gift or bequest, or in a case in which the transfer was caused by legal separation, divorce, death, or other involuntary event, shall be deemed to be owned by a qualified purchaser, subject to such rules,

regulations, and orders as the Commission may prescribe as necessary or appropriate in the public interest or for the protection of investors.

(B) Notwithstanding subparagraph (A), an issuer is within the exception provided by this paragraph if—

   (i) in addition to qualified purchasers, outstanding securities of that issuer are beneficially owned by not more than 100 persons who are not qualified purchasers, if--

      (I) such persons acquired any portion of the securities of such issuer on or before September 1, 1996; and

      (II) at the time at which such persons initially acquired the securities of such issuer, the issuer was excepted by paragraph (1); and

   (ii) prior to availing itself of the exception provided by this paragraph—

      (I) such issuer has disclosed to each beneficial owner, as determined under paragraph (1), that future investors will be limited to qualified purchasers, and that ownership in such issuer is no longer limited to not more than 100 persons; and

      (II) concurrently with or after such disclosure, such issuer has provided each beneficial owner, as determined under paragraph (1), with a reasonable opportunity to redeem any part or all of their interests in the issuer, notwithstanding any agreement to the contrary between the issuer and such persons, for that person's proportionate share of the issuer's net assets.

(C) Each person that elects to redeem under subparagraph (B)(ii)(II) shall receive an amount in cash equal to that person's proportionate share of the issuer's net assets, unless the issuer elects to provide such person with the option of receiving, and such person agrees to receive, all or a portion of such person's share in assets of the issuer. If the issuer elects to provide such persons with such an opportunity, disclosure concerning such opportunity shall be made in the disclosure required by subparagraph (B)(ii)(I).

(D) An issuer that is excepted under this paragraph shall nonetheless be deemed to be an investment company for purposes of the limitations set forth in subparagraphs (A)(i) and (B)(i) of section

80a-12(d)(1) of this title relating to the purchase or other acquisition by such issuer of any security issued by any registered investment company and the sale of any security issued by any registered open-end investment company to any such issuer.

(E)   For purposes of determining compliance with this paragraph and paragraph (1), an issuer that is otherwise excepted under this paragraph and an issuer that is otherwise excepted under paragraph (1) shall not be treated by the Commission as being a single issuer for purposes of determining whether the outstanding securities of the issuer excepted under paragraph (1) are beneficially owned by not more than 100 persons or whether the outstanding securities of the issuer excepted under this paragraph are owned by persons that are not qualified purchasers. Nothing in this subparagraph shall be construed to establish that a person is a bona fide qualified purchaser for purposes of this paragraph or a bona fide beneficial owner for purposes of paragraph (1).

* * *

§ 4. Classification of Investment Companies

For the purposes of this Act, investment companies are divided into three principal classes, defined as follows:

(1)   "Face-amount certificate company" means an investment company which is engaged or proposes to engage in the business of issuing face-amount certificates of the installment type, or which has been engaged in such business and has any such certificate outstanding.

(2)   "Unit investment trust" means an investment company which (A) is organized under a trust indenture, contract of custodianship or agency, or similar instrument, (B) does not have a board of directors, and (C) issues only redeemable securities, each of which represents an undivided interest in a unit of specified securities; but does not include a voting trust.

(3)   "Management company" means any investment company other than a face-amount certificate company or a unit investment trust.

§ 5. Subclassification of Management Companies

(a) Open-end and Closed-end Companies

For the purposes of this Act management companies are divided into open-end and closed-end companies, defined as follows:

(1) "Open-end company" means a management company which is offering for sale or has outstanding any redeemable security of which it is the issuer.

(2) "Closed-end company" means any management company other than an open-end company.

(b) Diversified and non-diversified companies

Management companies are further divided into diversified companies and non-diversified companies, defined as follows:

(1) "Diversified company" means a management company which meets the following requirements: At least 75 per centum of the value of its total assets is represented by cash and cash items (including receivables), Government securities, securities of other investment companies, and other securities for the purposes of this calculation limited in respect of any one issuer to an amount not greater in value than 5 per centum of the value of the total assets of such management company and to not more than 10 per centum of the outstanding voting securities of such issuer.

(2) "Non-diversified company" means any management company other than a diversified company.

(c) Loss of status as diversified company

A registered diversified company which at the time of its qualification as such meets the requirements of paragraph (1) of subsection (b) of this section shall not lose its status as a diversified company because of any subsequent discrepancy between the value of its various investments and the requirements of said paragraph, so long as any such discrepancy existing immediately after its acquisition of any security or other property is neither wholly nor partly the result of such acquisition.

* * *

§ 8. Registration of investment companies

(a) Notification of registration; effective date of registration

Any investment company organized or otherwise created under the laws of the United States or of a State may register for the purposes of this Act by

filing with the Commission a notification of registration, in such form as the Commission shall by rules and regulations prescribe as necessary or appropriate in the public interest or for the protection of investors. An investment company shall be deemed to be registered upon receipt by the Commission of such notification of registration.

(b) Registration statement; contents

Every registered investment company shall file with the Commission, within such reasonable time after registration as the Commission shall fix by rules and regulations, an original and such copies of a registration statement, in such form and containing such of the following information and documents as the Commission shall by rules and regulations prescribe as necessary or appropriate in the public interest or for the protection of investors:

(1)   a recital of the policy of the registrant in respect of each of the following types of activities, such recital consisting in each case of a statement whether the registrant reserves freedom of action to engage in activities of such type, and if such freedom of action is reserved, a statement briefly indicating, insofar as is practicable, the extent to which the registrant intends to engage therein: (A) the classification and subclassifications, as defined in sections 4 and 5 of this Act, within which the registrant proposes to operate; (B) borrowing money; (C) the issuance of senior securities; (D) engaging in the business of underwriting securities issued by other persons; (E) concentrating investments in a particular industry or group of industries; (F) the purchase and sale of real estate and commodities, or either of them; (G) making loans to other persons; and (H) portfolio turn-over (including a statement showing the aggregate dollar amount of purchases and sales of portfolio securities, other than Government securities, in each of the last three full fiscal years preceding the filing of such registration statement);

(2)   a recital of all investment policies of the registrant, not enumerated in paragraph (1), which are changeable only if authorized by shareholder vote;

(3)   a recital of all policies of the registrant, not enumerated in paragraphs (1) and (2), in respect of matters which the registrant deems matters of fundamental policy;

(4)   the name and address of each affiliated person of the registrant; the name and principal address of every company, other than the registrant, of which each such person is an officer, director, or partner; a brief statement of the business experience for the preceding five years of each officer and director of the registrant; and

(5) the information and documents which would be required to be filed in order to register under the Securities Act of 1933 and the Securities Exchange Act of 1934, all securities (other than short-term paper) which the registrant has outstanding or proposes to issue.

(c) Alternative information

The Commission shall make provision, by permissive rules and regulations or order, for the filing of the following, or so much of the following as the Commission may designate, in lieu of the information and documents required pursuant to subsection (b) of this section:

(1) copies of the most recent registration statement filed by the registrant under the Securities Act of 1933 and currently effective under such Act, or if the registrant has not filed such a statement, copies of a registration statement filed by the registrant under the Securities Exchange Act of 1934 and currently effective under such Act;

(2) copies of any reports filed by the registrant pursuant to section 13 or 15(d) of the Securities Exchange Act of 1934; and

(3) a report containing reasonably current information regarding the matters included in copies filed pursuant to paragraphs (1) and (2) of this subsection, and such further information regarding matters not included in such copies as the Commission is authorized to require under subsection (b) of this section.

(d) Registration of unit investment trusts

If the registrant is a unit investment trust substantially all of the assets of which are securities issued by another registered investment company, the Commission is authorized to prescribe for the registrant, by rules and regulations or order, a registration statement which eliminates inappropriate duplication of information contained in the registration statement filed under this section by such other investment company.

(e) Failure to file registration statement or omissions of material fact

If it appears to the Commission that a registered investment company has failed to file the registration statement required by this section or a report required pursuant to section 30(a) or (b) of this title, or has filed such a registration statement or report but omitted therefrom material facts required to be stated therein, or has filed such a registration statement or report in violation of section 80a-34(b) of this title, the Commission shall notify such company by registered mail or by certified mail of the failure to file such registration statement or report, or of the respects in which such registration statement or report appears to be materially incomplete or misleading, as the case may be, and shall fix a date (in no event earlier than thirty days after the

mailing of such notice) prior to which such company may file such registration statement or report or correct the same. If such registration statement or report is not filed or corrected within the time so fixed by the Commission or any extension thereof, the Commission, after appropriate notice and opportunity for hearing, and upon such conditions and with such exemptions as it deems appropriate for the protection of investors, may by order suspend the registration of such company until such statement or report is filed or corrected, or may by order revoke such registration, if the evidence establishes—

(1)   that such company has failed to file a registration statement required by this section or a report required pursuant to section 30(a) or (b) of this Act, or has filed such a registration statement or report but omitted therefrom material facts required to be stated therein, or has filed such a registration statement or report in violation of section 34(b) of this title; and

(2)   that such suspension or revocation is in the public interest.

(f)   Cessation of existence as investment company

Whenever the Commission, on its own motion or upon application, finds that a registered investment company has ceased to be an investment company, it shall so declare by order and upon the taking effect of such order the registration of such company shall cease to be in effect. If necessary for the protection of investors, an order under this subsection may be made upon appropriate conditions. The Commission's denial of any application under this subsection shall be by order.

* * *

§ 10. Affiliations or Interest of Directors, Officers, and Employees

(a)   Interested persons of company who may serve on board of directors

No registered investment company shall have a board of directors more than 60 per centum of the members of which are persons who are interested persons of such registered company.

(b)   Employment and use of directors, officers, etc., as regular broker, principal underwriter, or investment banker

No registered investment company shall—

(1)   employ as regular broker any director, officer, or employee of such registered company, or any person of which any such director, officer, or employee is an affiliated person, unless a majority of the board of

directors of such registered company shall be persons who are not such brokers or affiliated persons of any of such brokers;

(2) use as a principal underwriter of securities issued by it any director, officer, or employee of such registered company or any person of which any such director, officer, or employee is an interested person, unless a majority of the board of directors of such registered company shall be persons who are not such principal underwriters or interested persons of any of such principal underwriters; or

(3) have as director, officer, or employee any investment banker, or any affiliated person of an investment banker, unless a majority of the board of directors of such registered company shall be persons who are not investment bankers or affiliated persons of any investment banker. For the purposes of this paragraph, a person shall not be deemed an affiliated person of an investment banker solely by reason of the fact that he is an affiliated person of a company of the character described in section 12(d)(3)(A) and (B) of this Act.

(c) Officers, directors, or employees of one bank as majority of board of directors of company; exceptions

No registered investment company shall have a majority of its board of directors consisting of persons who are officers, directors, or employees of any one bank, except that, if on March 15, 1940, any registered investment company had a majority of its directors consisting of persons who are directors, officers, or employees of any one bank, such company may continue to have the same percentage of its board of directors consisting of persons who are directors, officers, or employees of such bank.

(d) Exception to limitation of number of interested persons who may serve on board of directors

Notwithstanding subsections (a) and (b)(2) of this section, a registered investment company may have a board of directors all the members of which, except one, are interested persons of the investment adviser of such company, or are officers or employees of such company, if—

(1) such investment company is an open-end company;

(2) such investment adviser is registered under the Investment Advisers Act of 1940 and is engaged principally in the business of rendering investment supervisory services as defined in that act;

(3) no sales load is charged on securities issued by such investment company;

(4)   any premium over net asset value charged by such company upon the issuance of any such security, plus any discount from net asset value charged on redemption thereof, shall not in the aggregate exceed 2 per centum;

(5)   no sales or promotion expenses are incurred by such registered company; but expenses incurred in complying with laws regulating the issue or sale of securities shall not be deemed sales or promotion expenses;

(6)   such investment adviser is the only investment adviser to such investment company, and such investment adviser does not receive a management fee exceeding 1 per centum per annum of the value of such company's net assets averaged over the year or taken as of a definite date or dates within the year;

(7)   all executive salaries and executive expenses and office rent of such investment company are paid by such investment adviser; and

(8)   such investment company has only one class of securities outstanding, each unit of which has equal voting rights with every other unit.

(e)   Death, disqualification, or resignation of directors as suspension of limitation provisions

If by reason of the death, disqualification, or bona fide resignation of any director or directors, the requirements of the foregoing provisions of this section or of section 15(f)(1) of this title in respect of directors shall not be met by a registered investment company, the operation of such provision shall be suspended as to such registered company--

(1)   for a period of thirty days if the vacancy or vacancies may be filled by action of the board of directors;

(2)   for a period of sixty days if a vote of stockholders is required to fill the vacancy or vacancies; or

(3)   for such longer period as the Commission may prescribe, by rules and regulations upon its own motion or by order upon application, as not inconsistent with the protection of investors.

(f)   Officer, director, etc., of company acting as principal underwriter of security acquired by company

No registered investment company shall knowingly purchase or otherwise acquire, during the existence of any underwriting or selling syndicate, any security (except a security of which such company is the issuer) a principal underwriter of which is an officer, director, member of an advisory board, investment adviser, or employee of such registered company, or is a

person (other than a company of the character described in section 12(d)(3)(A) and (B) of this Act) of which any such officer, director, member of an advisory board, investment adviser, or employee is an affiliated person, unless in acquiring such security such registered company is itself acting as a principal underwriter for the issuer.   The Commission, by rules and regulations upon its own motion or by order upon application, may conditionally or unconditionally exempt any transaction or classes of transactions from any of the provisions of this subsection, if and to the extent that such exemption is consistent with the protection of investors.

(g) Advisory boards; restrictions on membership

In the case of a registered investment company which has an advisory board, such board, as a distinct entity, shall be subject to the same restrictions as to its membership as are imposed upon a board of directors by this section.

(h) Application of section to unincorporated registered management companies

In the case of a registered management company which is an unincorporated company not having a board of directors, the provisions of this section shall apply as follows:

(1) the provisions of subsection (a) of this section, as modified by subsection (e) of this section, shall apply to the board of directors of the depositor of such company;

(2) the provisions of subsections (b) and (c) of this section, as modified by subsection (e) of this section, shall apply to the board of directors of the depositor and of every investment adviser of such company; and

(3) the provisions of subsection (f) of this section shall apply to purchases and other acquisitions for the account of such company of securities a principal underwriter of which is the depositor or an investment adviser of such company, or an affiliated person of such depositor or investment adviser.

§ 12. Functions and Activities of Investment Companies

(a) Purchase of securities on margin; joint trading accounts; short sales of securities; exceptions

It shall be unlawful for any registered investment company, in contravention of such rules and regulations or orders as the Commission may prescribe as necessary or appropriate in the public interest or for the protection of investors—

(1)   to purchase any security on margin, except such short-term credits as are necessary for the clearance of transactions;

(2)   to participate on a joint or a joint and several basis in any trading account in securities, except in connection with an underwriting in which such registered company is a participant; or

(3)   to effect a short sale of any security, except in connection with an underwriting in which such registered company is a participant.

(b)   Distribution by investment company of securities of which it is issuer

It shall be unlawful for any registered open-end company (other than a company complying with the provisions of section 10(d) of this Act) to act as a distributor of securities of which it is the issuer, except through an underwriter, in contravention of such rules and regulations as the Commission may prescribe as necessary or appropriate in the public interest or for the protection of investors.

(c)   Limitations on commitments as underwriter

It shall be unlawful for any registered diversified company to make any commitment as underwriter, if immediately thereafter the amount of its outstanding underwriting commitments, plus the value of its investments in securities of issuers (other than investment companies) of which it owns more than 10 per centum of the outstanding voting securities, exceeds 25 per centum of the value of its total assets.

(d)   Limitations on acquisition by investment companies of securities of other specific businesses

(1)   (A)   It shall be unlawful for any registered investment company (the "acquiring company") and any company or companies controlled by such acquiring company to purchase or otherwise acquire any security issued by any other investment company (the "acquired company"), and for any investment company (the "acquiring company") and any company or companies controlled by such acquiring company to purchase or otherwise acquire any security issued by any registered investment company (the "acquired company"), if the acquiring company and any company or companies controlled by it immediately after such purchase or acquisition own in the aggregate—

(i)   more than 3 per centum of the total outstanding voting stock of the acquired company;

(ii)   securities issued by the acquired company having an aggregate value in excess of 5 per centum of the value of the total assets of the acquiring company; or

   (iii) securities issued by the acquired company and all other investment companies (other than treasury stock of the acquiring company) having an aggregate value in excess of 10 per centum of the value of the total assets of the acquiring company.

 (B) It shall be unlawful for any registered open-end investment company (the "acquired company"), any principal underwriter therefor, or any broker or dealer registered under the Securities Exchange Act of 1934, knowingly to sell or otherwise dispose of any security issued by the acquired company to any other investment company (the "acquiring company") or any company or companies controlled by the acquiring company, if immediately after such sale or disposition--

   (i) more than 3 per centum of the total outstanding voting stock of the acquired company is owned by the acquiring company and any company or companies controlled by it; or

   (ii) more than 10 per centum of the total outstanding voting stock of the acquired company is owned by the acquiring company and other investment companies and companies controlled by them.

 (C) It shall be unlawful for any investment company (the "acquiring company") and any company or companies controlled by the acquiring company to purchase or otherwise acquire any security issued by a registered closed-end investment company, if immediately after such purchase or acquisition the acquiring company, other investment companies having the same investment adviser, and companies controlled by such investment companies, own more than 10 per centum of the total outstanding voting stock of such closed-end company.

 (D) The provisions of this paragraph shall not apply to a security received as a dividend or as a result of an offer of exchange approved pursuant to section 11 of this Act or of a plan of reorganization of any company (other than a plan devised for the purpose of evading the foregoing provisions).

 (E) The provisions of this paragraph shall not apply to a security (or securities) purchased or acquired by an investment company if--

   (i) the depositor of, or principal underwriter for, such investment company is a broker or dealer registered under the Securities Exchange Act of 1934, or a person controlled by such a broker or dealer;

    (ii)   such security is the only investment security held by such investment company (or such securities are the only investment securities held by such investment company, if such investment company is a registered unit investment trust that issues two or more classes or series of securities, each of which provides for the accumulation of shares of a different investment company); and

    (iii) the purchase or acquisition is made pursuant to an arrangement with the issuer of, or principal underwriter for the issuer of, the security whereby such investment company is obligated--

        (aa) either to seek instructions from its security holders with regard to the voting of all proxies with respect to such security and to vote such proxies only in accordance with such instructions, or to vote the shares held by it in the same proportion as the vote of all other holders of such security, and

        (bb) in the event that such investment company is not a registered investment company, to refrain from substituting such security unless the Commission shall have approved such substitution in the manner provided in section 26 of this Act.

(F)   The provisions of this paragraph shall not apply to securities purchased or otherwise acquired by a registered investment company if—

    (i)   immediately after such purchase or acquisition not more than 3 per centum of the total outstanding stock of such issuer is owned by such registered investment company and all affiliated persons of such registered investment company; and

    (ii)   such registered investment company has not offered or sold after January 1, 1971, and is not proposing to offer or sell any security issued by it through a principal underwriter or otherwise at a public offering price which includes a sales load of more than 1 1/2 per centum.

    No issuer of any security purchased or acquired by a registered investment company pursuant to this subparagraph shall be obligated to redeem such security in an amount exceeding 1 per centum of such issuer's total outstanding securities during any period of less than thirty days. Such investment company shall

exercise voting rights by proxy or otherwise with respect to any security purchased or acquired pursuant to this subparagraph in the manner prescribed by subparagraph (E) of this subsection.

(G) (i)   This paragraph does not apply to securities of a registered open-end investment company or a registered unit investment trust (hereafter in this subparagraph referred to as the "acquired company") purchased or otherwise acquired by a registered open-end investment company or a registered unit investment trust (hereafter in this subparagraph referred to as the "acquiring company") if--

(I)   the acquired company and the acquiring company are part of the same group of investment companies;

(II)   the securities of the acquired company, securities of other registered open-end investment companies and registered unit investment trusts that are part of the same group of investment companies, Government securities, and short-term paper are the only investments held by the acquiring company;

(III)   with respect to—

(aa)   securities of the acquired company, the acquiring company does not pay and is not assessed any charges or fees for distribution-related activities, unless the acquiring company does not charge a sales load or other fees or charges for distribution-related activities; or

(bb)   securities of the acquiring company, any sales loads and other distribution-related fees charged, when aggregated with any sales load and distribution-related fees paid by the acquiring company with respect to securities of the acquired fund, are not excessive under rules adopted pursuant to section 22(b) of this title or section 22(c) of this Act by a securities association registered under section 3 of this Act or the Commission;

(IV)   the acquired company has a policy that prohibits it from acquiring any securities of registered open-end investment companies or registered unit investment trusts in reliance on this subparagraph or subparagraph (F); and

      (V)   such acquisition is not in contravention of such rules and regulations as the Commission may from time to time prescribe with respect to acquisitions in accordance with this subparagraph, as necessary and appropriate for the protection of investors.

    (ii)   For purposes of this subparagraph, the term "group of investment companies" means any 2 or more registered investment companies that hold themselves out to investors as related companies for purposes of investment and investor services.

(H)   For the purposes of this paragraph, the value of an investment company's total assets shall be computed as of the time of a purchase or acquisition or as closely thereto as is reasonably possible.

(I)   In any action brought to enforce the provisions of this paragraph, the Commission may join as a party the issuer of any security purchased or otherwise acquired in violation of this paragraph, and the court may issue any order with respect to such issuer as may be necessary or appropriate for the enforcement of the provisions of this paragraph.

(J)   The Commission, by rule or regulation, upon its own motion or by order upon application, may conditionally or unconditionally exempt any person, security, or transaction, or any class or classes of persons, securities, or transactions from any provision of this subsection, if and to the extent that such exemption is consistent with the public interest and the protection of investors.

·(2)   It shall be unlawful for any registered investment company and any company or companies controlled by such registered investment company to purchase or otherwise acquire any security (except a security received as a dividend or as a result of a plan of reorganization of any company, other than a plan devised for the purpose of evading the provisions of this paragraph) issued by any insurance company of which such registered investment company and any company or companies controlled by such registered company do not, at the time of such purchase or acquisition, own in the aggregate at least 25 per centum of the total outstanding voting stock, if such registered company and any company or companies controlled by it own in the aggregate, or as a result of such purchase or acquisition will own in the aggregate, more than 10 per centum of the total outstanding voting stock of such insurance company.

(3)   It shall be unlawful for any registered investment company and any company or companies controlled by such registered investment company to purchase or otherwise acquire any security issued by or any other interest in the business of any person who is a broker, a dealer, is engaged in the business of underwriting, or is either an investment adviser of an investment company or an investment adviser registered under subchapter II of this chapter, unless (A) such person is a corporation all the outstanding securities of which (other than short-term paper, securities representing bank loans, and directors' qualifying shares) are, or after such acquisition will be, owned by one or more registered investment companies; and (B) such person is primarily engaged in the business of underwriting and distributing securities issued by other persons, selling securities to customers, or any one or more of such or related activities, and the gross income of such person normally is derived principally from such business or related activities.

(e)   Acquisition of securities issued by corporations in business of underwriting, furnishing capital to industry, etc.

Notwithstanding any provisions of this Act, any registered investment company may hereafter purchase or otherwise acquire any security issued by any one corporation engaged or proposing to engage in the business of underwriting, furnishing capital to industry, financing promotional enterprises, purchasing securities of issuers for which no ready market is in existence, and reorganizing companies or similar activities; provided—

(1)   That the securities issued by such corporation (other than short-term paper and securities representing bank loans) shall consist solely of one class of common stock and shall have been originally issued or sold for investment to registered investment companies only;

(2)   That the aggregate cost of the securities of such corporation purchased by such registered investment company does not exceed 5 per centum of the value of the total assets of such registered company at the time of any purchase or acquisition of such securities; and

(3)   That the aggregate paid-in capital and surplus of such corporation does not exceed $100,000,000.

For the purpose of paragraph (1) of section 5(b) of this Act any investment in any such corporation shall be deemed to be an investment in an investment company.

* * *

§ 13. Changes in Investment Policy

    (a)   No registered investment company shall, unless authorized by the vote of a majority of its outstanding voting securities--

        (1)   change its subclassification as defined in section 80a-5(a)(1) and (2) of this title or its subclassification from a diversified to a non-diversified company;

        (2)   borrow money, issue senior securities, underwrite securities issued by other persons, purchase or sell real estate or commodities or make loans to other persons, except in each case in accordance with the recitals of policy contained in its registration statement in respect thereto;

        (3)   deviate from its policy in respect of concentration of investments in any particular industry or group of industries as recited in its registration statement, deviate from any investment policy which is changeable only if authorized by shareholder vote, or deviate from any policy recited in its registration statement pursuant to section 8(b)(3) of this title; or

        (4)   change the nature of its business so as to cease to be an investment company.

    (b)   In the case of a common-law trust of the character described in section 80a-16(c) of this title, either written approval by holders of a majority of the outstanding shares of beneficial interest or the vote of a majority of such outstanding shares cast in person or by proxy at a meeting called for the purpose shall for the purposes of subsection (a) of this section be deemed the equivalent of the vote of a majority of the outstanding voting securities, and the provisions of paragraph (42) of section 80a-2(a) of this title as to a majority shall be applicable to the vote cast at such a meeting.

* * *

§ 14. Size of Investment Companies

(a) Public offerings

        No registered investment company organized after August 22, 1940, and no principal underwriter for such a company, shall make a public offering of securities of which such company is the issuer, unless--

    (1)   such company has a net worth of at least $100,000;

(2)   such company has previously made a public offering of its securities, and at the time of such offering had a net worth of at least $100,000; or

(3)   provision is made in connection with and as a condition of the registration of such securities under the Securities Act of 1933, which in the opinion of the Commission adequately insures (A) that after the effective date of such registration statement such company will not issue any security or receive any proceeds of any subscription for any security until firm agreements have been made with such company by not more than twenty-five responsible persons to purchase from it securities to be issued by it for an aggregate net amount which plus the then net worth of the company, if any, will equal at least $100,000; (B) that said aggregate net amount will be paid in to such company before any subscriptions for such securities will be accepted from any persons in excess of twenty- five; (C) that arrangements will be made whereby any proceeds so paid in, as well as any sales load, will be refunded to any subscriber on demand without any deduction, in the event that the net proceeds so received by the company do not result in the company having a net worth of at least $100,000 within ninety days after such registration statement becomes effective. At any time after the occurrence of the event specified in clause (C) of paragraph (3) of this subsection the Commission may issue a stop order suspending the effectiveness of the registration statement of such securities under the Securities Act of 1933 and may suspend or revoke the registration of such company under this Act.

(b)   Study on effects of size

The Commission is authorized, at such times as it deems that any substantial further increase in size of investment companies creates any problem involving the protection of investors or the public interest, to make a study and investigation of the effects of size on the investment policy of investment companies and on security markets, on concentration of control of wealth and industry, and on companies in which investment companies are interested, and from time to time to report the results of its studies and investigations and its recommendations to the Congress.

§ 15. Contracts of Advisers and Underwriters

(a) Written contract to serve or act as investment adviser; contents

It shall be unlawful for any person to serve or act as investment adviser of a registered investment company, except pursuant to a written contract, which contract, whether with such registered company or with an investment adviser of such registered company, has been approved by the vote of a majority of the outstanding voting securities of such registered company, and--

(1) precisely describes all compensation to be paid thereunder;

(2) shall continue in effect for a period more than two years from the date of its execution, only so long as such continuance is specifically approved at least annually by the board of directors or by vote of a majority of the outstanding voting securities of such company;

(3) provides, in substance, that it may be terminated at any time, without the payment of any penalty, by the board of directors of such registered company or by vote of a majority of the outstanding voting securities of such company on not more than sixty days' written notice to the investment adviser; and

(4) provides, in substance, for its automatic termination in the event of its assignment.

(b) Written contract with company for sale by principal underwriter of security of which company is issuer; contents

It shall be unlawful for any principal underwriter for a registered open-end company to offer for sale, sell, or deliver after sale any security of which such company is the issuer, except pursuant to a written contract with such company, which contract—

(1) shall continue in effect for a period more than two years from the date of its execution, only so long as such continuance is specifically approved at least annually by the board of directors or by vote of a majority of the outstanding voting securities of such company; and

(2) provides, in substance, for its automatic termination in the event of its assignment.

(c) Approval of contract to undertake service as investment adviser or principal underwriter by majority of noninterested directors

In addition to the requirements of subsections (a) and (b) of this section, it shall be unlawful for any registered investment company having a board of directors to enter into, renew, or perform any contract or agreement, written or oral, whereby a person undertakes regularly to serve

or act as investment adviser of or principal underwriter for such company, unless the terms of such contract or agreement and any renewal thereof have been approved by the vote of a majority of directors, who are not parties to such contract or agreement or interested persons of any such party, cast in person at a meeting called for the purpose of voting on such approval. It shall be the duty of the directors of a registered investment company to request and evaluate, and the duty of an investment adviser to such company to furnish, such information as may reasonably be necessary to evaluate the terms of any contract whereby a person undertakes regularly to serve or act as investment adviser of such company. It shall be unlawful for the directors of a registered investment company, in connection with their evaluation of the terms of any contract whereby a person undertakes regularly to serve or act as investment adviser of such company, to take into account the purchase price or other consideration any person may have paid in connection with a transaction of the type referred to in paragraph (1), (3), or (4) of subsection (f) of this section.

* * *

(f) Receipt of benefits by investment adviser from sale of securities or other interest in such investment adviser resulting in assignment of investment advisory contract

(1) An investment adviser, or a corporate trustee performing the functions of an investment adviser, of a registered investment company or an affiliated person of such investment adviser or corporate trustee may receive any amount or benefit in connection with a sale of securities of, or a sale of any other interest in, such investment adviser or corporate trustee which results in an assignment of an investment advisory contract with such company or the change in control of or identity of such corporate trustee, if—

(A) for a period of three years after the time of such action, at least 75 per centum of the members of the board of directors of such registered company or such corporate trustee (or successor thereto, by reorganization or otherwise) are not (i) interested persons of the investment adviser of such company or such corporate trustee, or (ii) interested persons of the predecessor investment adviser or such corporate trustee; and

(B) there is not imposed an unfair burden on such company as a result of such transaction or any express or implied terms, conditions, or understandings applicable thereto.

(2) (A) For the purpose of paragraph (1)(A) of this subsection, interested persons of a corporate trustee shall be determined in

accordance with section 2(a)(19)(B) of this Act: Provided, That no person shall be deemed to be an interested person of a corporate trustee solely by reason of (i) his being a member of its board of directors or advisory board or (ii) his membership in the immediate family of any person specified in clause (i) of this subparagraph.

(B)   For the purpose of paragraph (1)(B) of this subsection, an unfair burden on a registered investment company includes any arrangement, during the two- year period after the date on which any such transaction occurs, whereby the investment adviser or corporate trustee or predecessor or successor investment advisers or corporate trustee or any interested person of any such adviser or any such corporate trustee receives or is entitled to receive any compensation directly or indirectly (i) from any person in connection with the purchase or sale of securities or other property to, from, or on behalf of such company, other than bona fide ordinary compensation as principal underwriter for such company, or (ii) from such company or its security holders for other than bona fide investment advisory or other services.

(3) If—

(A)   an assignment of an investment advisory contract with a registered investment company results in a successor investment adviser to such company, or if there is a change in control of or identity of a corporate trustee of a registered investment company, and such adviser or trustee is then an investment adviser or corporate trustee with respect to other assets substantially greater in amount than the amount of assets of such company, or

(B)   as a result of a merger of, or a sale of substantially all the assets by, a registered investment company with or to another registered investment company with assets substantially greater in amount, a transaction occurs which would be subject to paragraph (1)(A) of this subsection, such discrepancy in size of assets shall be considered by the Commission in determining whether or to what extent an application under section 6(c) of this Act for exemption from the provisions of paragraph (1)(A) of this subsection should be granted.

(4) Paragraph (1)(A) of this subsection shall not apply to a transaction in which a controlling block of outstanding voting securities of an investment adviser to a registered investment company or of a corporate trustee performing the functions of an investment adviser to a registered investment company is—

(A) distributed to the public and in which there is, in fact, no change in the identity of the persons who control such investment adviser or corporate trustee, or

(B) transferred to the investment adviser or the corporate trustee, or an affiliated person or persons of such investment adviser or corporate trustee, or is transferred from the investment adviser or corporate trustee to an affiliated person or persons of the investment adviser or corporate trustee: Provided, That (i) each transferee (other than such adviser or trustee) is a natural person and (ii) the transferees (other than such adviser or trustee) owned in the aggregate more than 25 per centum of such voting securities for a period of at least six months prior to such transfer.

* * *

§ 17. Transactions of Certain Affiliated Persons and Underwriters

(a) Prohibited transactions

It shall be unlawful for any affiliated person or promoter of or principal underwriter for a registered investment company (other than a company of the character described in section-12(d)(3)(A) and (B) of this Act), or any affiliated person of such a person, promoter, or principal underwriter, acting as principal—

(1) knowingly to sell any security or other property to such registered company or to any company controlled by such registered company, unless such sale involves solely (A) securities of which the buyer is the issuer, (B) securities of which the seller is the issuer and which are part of a general offering to the holders of a class of its securities, or (C) securities deposited with the trustee of a unit investment trust or periodic payment plan by the depositor thereof;

(2) knowingly to purchase from such registered company, or from any company controlled by such registered company, any security or other property (except securities of which the seller is the issuer); or

(3)   to borrow money or other property from such registered company or from any company controlled by such registered company (unless the borrower is controlled by the lender) except as permitted in section 21(b) of this Act.

(b)   Application for exemption of proposed transaction from certain restrictions

Notwithstanding subsection (a) of this section, any person may file with the Commission an application for an order exempting a proposed transaction of the applicant from one or more provisions of said subsection. The Commission shall grant such application and issue such order of exemption if evidence establishes that--

(1)   the terms of the proposed transaction, including the consideration to be paid or received, are reasonable and fair and do not involve overreaching on the part of any person concerned;

(2)   the proposed transaction is consistent with the policy of each registered investment company concerned, as recited in its registration statement and reports filed under this Act; and

(3)   the proposed transaction is consistent with the general purposes of this Act.

(c)   Sale or purchase of merchandise from any company or furnishing of services incident to lessor-lessee relationship

Notwithstanding subsection (a) of this section, a person may, in the ordinary course of business, sell to or purchase from any company merchandise or may enter into a lessor-lessee relationship with any person and furnish the services incident thereto.

(d)   Joint or joint and several participation with company in transactions

It shall be unlawful for any affiliated person of or principal underwriter for a registered investment company (other than a company of the character described in section 12(d)(3)(A) and (B) of this Act), or any affiliated person of such a person or principal underwriter, acting as principal to effect any transaction in which such registered company, or a company controlled by such registered company, is a joint or a joint and several participant with such person, principal underwriter, or affiliated person, in contravention of such rules and regulations as the Commission may prescribe for the purpose of limiting or preventing participation by such registered or controlled company on a basis different from or less advantageous than that of such other participant. Nothing contained in this subsection shall be deemed to preclude any affiliated person from acting as manager of any underwriting syndicate or other group in which such

registered or controlled company is a participant and receiving compensation therefor.

(e)   Acceptance of compensation, commissions, fees, etc.

It shall be unlawful for any affiliated person of a registered investment company, or any affiliated person of such person--

(1)   acting as agent, to accept from any source any compensation (other than a regular salary or wages from such registered company) for the purchase or sale of any property to or for such registered company or any controlled company thereof, except in the course of such person's business as an underwriter or broker; or

(2)   acting as broker, in connection with the sale of securities to or by such registered company or any controlled company thereof, to receive from any source a commission, fee, or other remuneration for effecting such transaction which exceeds (A) the usual and customary broker's commission if the sale is effected on a securities exchange, or (B) 2 per centum of the sales price if the sale is effected in connection with a secondary distribution of such securities, or (C) 1 per centum of the purchase or sale price of such securities if the sale is otherwise effected unless the Commission shall, by rules and regulations or order in the public interest and consistent with the protection of investors, permit a larger commission.

(f)   Custody and maintenance of securities and investments

Every registered management company shall place and maintain its securities and similar investments in the custody of (1) a bank or banks having the qualifications prescribed in paragraph (1) of section 26(a) of this Act for the trustees of unit investment trusts; or (2) a company which is a member of a national securities exchange as defined in the Securities Exchange Act of 1934, subject to such rules and regulations as the Commission may from time to time prescribe for the protection of investors; or (3) such registered company, but only in accordance with such rules and regulations or orders as the Commission may from time to time prescribe for the protection of investors. Subject to such rules, regulations, and orders as the Commission may adopt as necessary or appropriate for the protection of investors, a registered management company or any such custodian, with the consent of the registered management company for which it acts as custodian, may deposit all or any part of the securities owned by such registered management company in a system for the central handling of securities established by a national securities exchange or national securities association registered with the Commission under the Securities Exchange Act of 1934, or such other

person as may be permitted by the Commission, pursuant to which system all securities of any particular class or series of any issuer deposited within the system are treated as fungible and may be transferred or pledged by bookkeeping entry without physical delivery of such securities. Rules, regulations, and orders of the Commission under this subsection, among other things, may make appropriate provision with respect to such matters as the earmarking, segregation, and hypothecation of such securities and investments, and may provide for or require periodic or other inspections by any or all of the following: Independent public accountants, employees and agents of the Commission, and such other persons as the Commission may designate. No such member which trades in securities for its own account may act as custodian except in accordance with rules and regulations prescribed by the Commission for the protection of investors. If a registered company maintains its securities and similar investments in the custody of a qualified bank or banks, the cash proceeds from the sale of such securities and similar investments and other cash assets of the company shall likewise be kept in the custody of such a bank or banks, or in accordance with such rules and regulations or orders as the Commission may from time to time prescribe for the protection of investors, except that such a registered company may maintain a checking account in a bank or banks having the qualifications prescribed in paragraph (1) of section 26(a) of this Act for the trustees of unit investment trusts with the balance of such account or the aggregate balances of such accounts at no time in excess of the amount of the fidelity bond, maintained pursuant to subsection (g) of this section covering the officers or employees authorized to draw on such account or accounts.

(g)   Bonding of officers and employees having access to securities or funds

The Commission is authorized to require by rules and regulations or orders for the protection of investors that any officer or employee of a registered management investment company who may singly, or jointly with others, have access to securities or funds of any registered company, either directly or through authority to draw upon such funds or to direct generally the disposition of such securities (unless the officer or employee has such access solely through his position as an officer or employee of a bank) be bonded by a reputable fidelity insurance company against larceny and embezzlement in such reasonable minimum amounts as the Commission may prescribe.

(h) Provisions in charter, by-laws, etc., protecting against liability for willful misfeasance, etc.

After one year from the effective date of this Act, neither the charter, certificate of incorporation, articles of association, indenture of trust, nor the by-laws of any registered investment company, nor any other instrument pursuant to which such a company is organized or administered, shall contain any provision which protects or purports to protect any director or officer of such company against any liability to the company or to its security holders to which he would otherwise be subject by reason of willful misfeasance, bad faith, gross negligence or reckless disregard of the duties involved in the conduct of his office.

(i) Provisions in contracts protecting against willful misfeasance, etc.

After one year from the effective date of this Act no contract or agreement under which any person undertakes to act as investment adviser of, or principal underwriter for, a registered investment company shall contain any provision which protects or purports to protect such person against any liability to such company or its security holders to which he would otherwise be subject by reason of willful misfeasance, bad faith, or gross negligence, in the performance of his duties, or by reason of his reckless disregard of his obligations and duties under such contract or agreement.

(j) Rules and regulations prohibiting fraudulent, deceptive or manipulative courses of conduct

It shall be unlawful for any affiliated person of or principal underwriter for a registered investment company or any affiliated person of an investment adviser of or principal underwriter for a registered investment company, to engage in any act, practice, or course of business in connection with the purchase or sale, directly or indirectly, by such person of any security held or to be acquired by such registered investment company in contravention of such rules and regulations as the Commission may adopt to define, and prescribe means reasonably necessary to prevent, such acts, practices, or courses of business as are fraudulent, deceptive or manipulative. Such rules and regulations may include requirements for the adoption of codes of ethics by registered investment companies and investment advisers of, and principal underwriters for, such investment companies establishing such standards as are reasonably necessary to prevent such acts, practices, or courses of business.

* * *

§ 18. Capital Structure of Investment Companies

(a)   Qualifications on issuance of senior securities

It shall be unlawful for any registered closed-end company to issue any class of senior security, or to sell any such security of which it is the issuer, unless—

(1)   if such class of senior security represents an indebtedness--

(A)   immediately after such issuance or sale, it will have an asset coverage of at least 300 per centum;

(B)   provision is made to prohibit the declaration of any dividend (except a dividend payable in stock of the issuer), or the declaration of any other distribution, upon any class of the capital stock of such investment company, or the purchase of any such capital stock, unless, in every such case, such class of senior securities has at the time of the declaration of any such dividend or distribution or at the time of any such purchase an asset coverage of at least 300 per centum after deducting the amount of such dividend, distribution, or purchase price, as the case may be, except that   dividends may be declared upon any preferred stock if such senior security representing indebtedness has an asset coverage of at least 200 per centum at the time of declaration thereof after deducting the amount of such dividend; and

(C)   provision is made either--

(i)   that, if on the last business day of each of twelve consecutive calendar months such class of senior securities shall have an asset coverage of less than 100 per centum, the holders of such securities voting as a class shall be entitled to elect at least a majority of the members of the board of directors of such registered company, such voting right to continue until such class of senior security shall have an asset coverage of 110 per centum or more on the last business day of each of three consecutive calendar months, or

(ii)   that, if on the last business day of each of twenty-four consecutive calendar months such class of senior securities shall have an asset coverage of less than 100 per centum, an event of default shall be deemed to have occurred;

(2) if such class of senior security is a stock--

   (A) immediately after such issuance or sale it will have an asset coverage of at least 200 per centum;

   (B) provision is made to prohibit the declaration of any dividend (except a dividend payable in common stock of the issuer), or the declaration of any other distribution, upon the common stock of such investment company, or the purchase of any such common stock, unless in every such case such class of senior security has at the time of the declaration of any such dividend or distribution or at the time of any such purchase an asset coverage of at least 200 per centum after deducting the amount of such dividend, distribution or purchase price, as the case may be;

   (C) provision is made to entitle the holders of such senior securities, voting as a class, to elect at least two directors at all times, and, subject to the prior rights, if any, of the holders of any other class of senior securities outstanding, to elect a majority of the directors if at any time dividends on such class of securities shall be unpaid in an amount equal to two full years' dividends on such securities, and to continue to be so represented until all dividends in arrears shall have been paid or otherwise provided for;

   (D) provision is made requiring approval by the vote of a majority of such securities, voting as a class, of any plan of reorganization adversely affecting such securities or of any action requiring a vote of security holders as in section 13(a) of this Act provided; and

   (E) such class of stock shall have complete priority over any other class as to distribution of assets and payment of dividends, which dividends shall be cumulative.

(b) Asset coverage in respect of senior securities

   The asset coverage in respect of a senior security provided for in subsection (a) of this section may be determined on the basis of values calculated as of a time within forty-eight hours (not including Sundays or holidays) next preceding the time of such determination. The time of issue or sale shall, in the case of an offering of such securities to existing stockholders of the issuer, be deemed to be the first date on which such offering is made, and in all other cases shall be deemed to be the time as of which a firm commitment to issue or sell and to take or purchase such securities shall be made.

* * *

(f)   Senior securities securing loans from bank; securities not included in "senior security"

(1)   It shall be unlawful for any registered open-end company to issue any class of senior security or to sell any senior security of which it is the issuer, except that any such registered company shall be permitted to borrow from any bank: Provided, That immediately after any such borrowing there is an asset coverage of at least 300 per centum for all borrowings of such registered company: And provided further, That in the event that such asset coverage shall at any time fall below 300 per centum such registered company shall, within three days thereafter (not including Sundays and holidays) or such longer period as the Commission may prescribe by rules and regulations, reduce the amount of its borrowings to an extent that the asset coverage of such borrowings shall be at least 300 per centum.

(2)   "Senior security" shall not, in the case of a registered open-end company, include aclass or classes or a number of series of preferred or special stock each of which is preferred over all other classes or series in respect of assets specifically allocated to that class or series: Provided, That (A) such company has outstanding no class or series of stock which is not so preferred over all other classes or series, or (B) the only other outstanding class of the issuer's stock consists of a common stock upon which no dividend (other than a liquidating dividend) is permitted to be paid and which in the aggregate represents not more than one-half of 1 per centum of the issuer's outstanding voting securities. For the purpose of insuring fair and equitable treatment of the holders of the outstanding voting securities of each class or series of stock of such company, the Commission may by rule, regulation, or order direct that any matter required to be submitted to the holders of the outstanding voting securities of such company shall not be deemed to have been effectively acted upon unless approved by the holders of such percentage (not exceeding a majority) of the outstanding voting securities of each class or series of stock affected by such matter as shall be prescribed in such rule, regulation, or order.

* * *

§ 20. Proxies; Voting Trusts; Circular Ownership

(a) Prohibition on use of means of interstate commerce for solicitation of proxies

It shall be unlawful for any person, by use of the mails or any means or instrumentality of interstate commerce or otherwise, to solicit or to permit the use of his name to solicit any proxy or consent or authorization in respect of any security of which a registered investment company is the issuer in contravention of such rules and regulations as the Commission may prescribe as necessary or appropriate in the public interest or for the protection of investors.

(b) Prohibition on use of means of interstate commerce for sale of voting-trust certificates

It shall be unlawful for any registered investment company or affiliated person thereof, any issuer of a voting-trust certificate relating to any security of a registered investment company, or any underwriter of such a certificate, by use of the mails or any means or instrumentality of interstate commerce, or otherwise, to offer for sale, sell, or deliver after sale, in connection with a public offering, any such voting-trust certificate.

(c) Prohibition on purchase of securities knowingly resulting in cross-ownership or circular ownership

No registered investment company shall purchase any voting security if, to the knowledge of such registered company, cross-ownership or circular ownership exists, or after such acquisition will exist, between such registered company and the issuer of such security. Cross-ownership shall be deemed to exist between two companies when each of such companies beneficially owns more than 3 per centum of the outstanding voting securities of the other company. Circular ownership shall be deemed to exist between two companies if such companies are included within a group of three or more companies, each of which—

(1) beneficially owns more than 3 per centum of the outstanding voting securities of one or more other companies of the group; and

(2) has more than 3 per centum of its own outstanding voting securities beneficially owned by another company, or by each of two or more other companies, of the group.

(d) Duty to eliminate existing cross-ownership or circular ownership

If cross-ownership or circular ownership between a registered investment company and any other company or companies comes into existence upon the purchase by a registered investment company of the securities of another company, it shall be the duty of such registered

company, within one year after it first knows of the existence of such cross-ownership or circular ownership, to eliminate the same.

* * *

§ 22. Distribution, Redemption, and Repurchase of Securities; Regulations by Securities Associations

(a)   Rules relating to Minimum and Maximum Prices for Purchase and Sale of Securities from Investment Company; Time for Resale and Redemption

A securities association registered under section 15A of the Securities Exchange Act of 1934 may prescribe, by rules adopted and in effect in accordance with said section and subject to all provisions of said section applicable to the rules of such an association—

(1)   a method or methods for computing the minimum price at which a member thereof may purchase from any investment company any redeemable security issued by such company and the maximum price at which a member may sell to such company any redeemable security issued by it or which he may receive for such security upon redemption, so that the price in each case will bear such relation to the current net asset value of such security computed as of such time as the rules may prescribe; and

(2)   a minimum period of time which must elapse after the sale or issue of such security before any resale to such company by a member or its redemption upon surrender by a member;

in each case for the purpose of eliminating or reducing so far as reasonably practicable any dilution of the value of other outstanding securities of such company or any other result of such purchase, redemption, or sale which is unfair to holders of such other outstanding securities; and said rules may prohibit the members of the association from purchasing, selling, or surrendering for redemption any such redeemable securities in contravention of said rules.

(b)   Rules relating to Purchase of Securities by Members from Issuer Investment Company

(1)   Such a securities association may also, by rules adopted and in effect in accordance with section 15A of the Securities Exchange Act of 1934, and notwithstanding the provisions of subsection (b)(6) thereof but subject to all other provisions of said section applicable to the rules of such an association, prohibit its members from purchasing, in connection with a primary distribution of redeemable securities of

which any registered investment company is the issuer, any such security from the issuer or from any principal underwriter except at a price equal to the price at which such security is then offered to the public less a commission, discount, or spread which is computed in conformity with a method or methods, and within such limitations as to the relation thereof to said public offering price, as such rules may prescribe in order that the price at which such security is offered or sold to the public shall not include an excessive sales load but shall allow for reasonable compensation for sales personnel, broker-dealers, and underwriters, and for reasonable sales loads to investors. The Commission shall on application or otherwise, if it appears that smaller companies are subject to relatively higher operating costs, make due allowance therefor by granting any such company or class of companies appropriate qualified exemptions from the provisions of this section.

(2) At any time after the expiration of eighteen months from December 14, 1970 (or, if earlier, after a securities association has adopted for purposes of paragraph (1) any rule respecting excessive sales loads), the Commission may alter or supplement the rules of any securities association as may be necessary to effectuate the purposes of this subsection in the manner provided by section 19(c) of the Securities Exchange Act of 1934.

(3) If any provision of this subsection is in conflict with any provision of any law of the United States in effect on December 14, 1970, the provisions of this subsection shall prevail.

(c) Conflicting rules of Commission and Associations

The Commission may make rules and regulations applicable to registered investment companies and to principal underwriters of, and dealers in, the redeemable securities of any registered investment company, whether or not members of any securities association, to the same extent, covering the same subject matter, and for the accomplishment of the same ends as are prescribed in subsection (a) of this section in respect of the rules which may be made by a registered securities association governing its members. Any rules and regulations so made by the Commission, to the extent that they may be inconsistent with the rules of any such association, shall so long as they remain in force supersede the rules of the association and be binding upon its members as well as all other underwriters and dealers to whom they may be applicable.

(d)   Sale of Securities Except to or Through Principal Underwriter; Price of Securities

No registered investment company shall sell any redeemable security issued by it to any person except either to or through a principal underwriter for distribution or at a current public offering price described in the prospectus, and, if such class of security is being currently offered to the public by or through an underwriter, no principal underwriter of such security and no dealer shall sell any such security to any person except a dealer, a principal underwriter, or the issuer, except at a current public offering price described in the prospectus. Nothing in this subsection shall prevent a sale made (i) pursuant to an offer of exchange permitted by section 11 of this title including any offer made pursuant to section 11(b) of this Act; (ii) pursuant to an offer made solely to all registered holders of the securities, or of a particular class or series of securities issued by the company proportionate to their holdings or proportionate to any cash distribution made to them by the company (subject to appropriate qualifications designed solely to avoid issuance of fractional securities); or (iii) in accordance with rules and regulations of the Commission made pursuant to subsection (b) of section 12 of this Act.

(e)   Suspension of Right of Redemption or Postponement of Date of Payment

No registered investment company shall suspend the right of redemption, or postpone the date of payment or satisfaction upon redemption of any redeemable security in accordance with its terms for more than seven days after the tender of such security to the company or its agent designated for that purpose for redemption, except--

(1)   for any period (A) during which the New York Stock Exchange is closed other than customary week-end and holiday closings or (B) during which trading on the New York Stock Exchange is restricted;

(2)   for any period during which an emergency exists as a result of which (A) disposal by the company of securities owned by it is not reasonably practicable or (B) it is not reasonably practicable for such company fairly to determine the value of its net assets; or

(3)   for such other periods as the Commission may by order permit for the protection of security holders of the company.

The Commission shall by rules and regulations determine the conditions under which (i) trading shall be deemed to be restricted and (ii) an emergency shall be deemed to exist within the meaning of this subsection.

(f) Restrictions on Transferability or Negotiability of Securities

No registered open-end company shall restrict the transferability or negotiability of any security of which it is the issuer except in conformity with the statements with respect thereto contained in its registration statement nor in contravention of such rules and regulations as the Commission may prescribe in the interests of the holders of all of the outstanding securities of such investment company.

(g) Issuance of Securities for Services or Property other than Cash

No registered open-end company shall issue any of its securities (1) for services; or (2) for property other than cash or securities (including securities of which such registered company is the issuer), except as a dividend or distribution to its security holders or in connection with a reorganization.

* * *

§ 30. Reports and Financial Statements of Investment Companies and Affiliated Persons

(a) Annual report by company

Every registered investment company shall file annually with the Commission such information, documents, and reports as investment companies having securities registered on a national securities exchange are required to file annually pursuant to section 13(a) of the Securities Exchange Act of 1934 and the rules and regulations issued thereunder.

(b) Semi-annual or quarterly filing of information; copies of periodic or interim reports sent to security holders

Every registered investment company shall file with the Commission--

(1) such information, documents, and reports (other than financial statements), as the Commission may require to keep reasonably current the information and documents contained in the registration statement of such company filed under this Act;

(2) copies of every periodic or interim report or similar communication containing financial statements and transmitted to any class of such company's security holders, such copies to be filed not later than ten days after such transmission.

Any information or documents contained in a report or other communication to security holders filed pursuant to paragraph (2) of this

subsection may be incorporated by reference in any report subsequently or concurrently filed pursuant to paragraph (1) of this subsection.

* * *

§ 34. Destruction and Falsification of Reports and Records

(a) Willful destruction

It shall be unlawful for any person, except as permitted by rule, regulation, or order of the Commission, willfully to destroy, mutilate, or alter any account, book, or other document the preservation of which has been required pursuant to section 31(a) or 80a-32(c) of this Act.

(b) Untrue statements or omissions

It shall be unlawful for any person to make any untrue statement of a material fact in any registration statement, application, report, account, record, or other document filed or transmitted pursuant to this Act or the keeping of which is required pursuant to section 31(a) of this Act. It shall be unlawful for any person so filing, transmitting, or keeping any such document to omit to state therein any fact necessary in order to prevent the statements made therein, in the light of the circumstances under which they were made, from being materially misleading. For the purposes of this subsection, any part of any such document which is signed or certified by an accountant or auditor in his capacity as such shall be deemed to be made, filed, transmitted, or kept by such accountant or auditor, as well as by the person filing, transmitting, or keeping the complete document.

§ 36. Breach of Fiduciary Duty

(a) Civil actions by Commission; jurisdiction; allegations; injunctive or other relief

The Commission is authorized to bring an action in the proper district court of the United States, or in the United States court of any territory or other place subject to the jurisdiction of the United States, alleging that a person serving or acting in one or more of the following capacities has engaged within five years of the commencement of the action or is about to engage in any act or practice constituting a breach of fiduciary duty involving personal misconduct in respect of any registered investment company for which such person so serves or acts--

(1)   as officer, director, member of any advisory board, investment adviser, or depositor; or

(2)   as principal underwriter, if such registered company is an open-end company, unit investment trust, or face-amount certificate company.

If such allegations are established, the court may enjoin such persons from acting in any or all such capacities either permanently or temporarily and award such injunctive or other relief against such person as may be reasonable and appropriate in the circumstances, having due regard to the protection of investors and to the effectuation of the policies declared in section 1(b) of this Act.

(b)   Compensation or payments as basis of fiduciary duty; civil actions by Commission or security holder; burden of proof; judicial consideration of director or shareholder approval; persons liable; extent of liability; exempted transactions; jurisdiction; finding restriction

For the purposes of this subsection, the investment adviser of a registered investment company shall be deemed to have a fiduciary duty with respect to the receipt of compensation for services, or of payments of a material nature, paid by such registered investment company, or by the security holders thereof, to such investment adviser or any affiliated person of such investment adviser. An action may be brought under this subsection by the Commission, or by a security holder of such registered investment company on behalf of such company, against such investment adviser, or any affiliated person of such investment adviser, or any other person enumerated in subsection (a) of this section who has a fiduciary duty concerning such compensation or payments, for breach of fiduciary duty in respect of such compensation or payments paid by such registered investment company or by the security holders thereof to such investment adviser or person. With respect to any such action the following provisions shall apply:

(1)   It shall not be necessary to allege or prove that any defendant engaged in personal misconduct, and the plaintiff shall have the burden of proving a breach of fiduciary duty.

(2)   In any such action approval by the board of directors of such investment company of such compensation or payments, or of contracts or other arrangements providing for such compensation or payments, and ratification or approval of such compensation or payments, or of contracts or other arrangements providing for such compensation or payments, by the shareholders of such investment company, shall be given such consideration by the court as is deemed appropriate under all the circumstances.

(3)   No such action shall be brought or maintained against any person other than the recipient of such compensation or payments, and no damages or other relief shall be granted against any person other than the recipient of such compensation or payments. No award of damages shall be recoverable for any period prior to one year before the action was instituted. Any award of damages against such recipient shall be limited to the actual damages resulting from the breach of fiduciary duty and shall in no event exceed the amount of compensation or payments received from such investment company, or the security holders thereof, by such recipient.

(4)   This subsection shall not apply to compensation or payments made in connection with transactions subject to section 17 of this Act, or rules, regulations, or orders thereunder, or to sales loads for the acquisition of any security issued by a registered investment company.

(5)   Any action pursuant to this subsection may be brought only in an appropriate district court of the United States.

(6)   No finding by a court with respect to a breach of fiduciary duty under this subsection shall be made a basis (A) for a finding of a violation of this subchapter for the purposes of sections 9 and 49 of this title, section 15 of the Securities Exchange Act of 1934, or section 203 of the Investment Advisers Act of 1940, or (B) for an injunction to prohibit any person from serving in any of the capacities enumerated in subsection (a) of this section.

(c)   Corporate or other trustees performing functions of investment advisers

For the purposes of subsections (a) and (b) of this section, the term "investment adviser" includes a corporate or other trustee performing the functions of an investment adviser.

SELECTED RULES AND REGULATIONS UNDER THE INVESTMENT COMPANY ACT OF 1940

(Codified at 17 C.F.R. § 270.___)

* * *

2a-4. Definition of "current net asset value" for use in computing periodically the current price of redeemable security.

(a) The current net asset value of any redeemable security issued by a registered investment company used in computing periodically the current price for the purpose of distribution, redemption, and repurchase means an amount which reflects calculations, whether or not recorded in the books of account, made substantially in accordance with the following, with estimates used where necessary or appropriate.

    (1) Portfolio securities with respect to which market quotations are readily available shall be valued at current market value, and other securities and assets shall be valued at fair value as determined in good faith by the board of directors of the registered company.

    (2) Changes in holdings of portfolio securities shall be reflected no later than in the first calculation on the first business day following the trade date.

    (3) Changes in the number of outstanding shares of the registered company resulting from distributions, redemptions, and repurchases shall be reflected no later than in the first calculation on the first business day following such change.

    (4) Expenses, including any investment advisory fees, shall be included to date of calculation. Appropriate provision shall be made for Federal income taxes if required. Investment companies which retain realized capital gains designated as a distribution to shareholders shall comply with paragraph (h) of S 210.6-03 of Regulation S-X.

    (5) Dividends receivable shall be included to date of calculation either at ex-dividend dates or record dates, as appropriate.

(6)   Interest income and other income shall be included to date of calculation.

(b)   The items which would otherwise be required to be reflected by paragraphs (a)(4) and (6) of this section need not be so reflected if cumulatively, when netted, they do not amount to as much as one cent per outstanding share.

(c)   Notwithstanding the requirements of paragraph (a) of this section, any interim determination of current net asset value between calculations made as of the close of the New York Stock Exchange on the preceding business day and the current business day may be estimated so as to reflect any change in current net asset value since the closing calculation on the preceding business day.

3a-2. Transient investment companies.

(a)   For purposes of section 3(a)(1) and section 3(a)(3) of the Act, an issuer is deemed not to be engaged in the business of investing, reinvesting, owning, holding or trading in securities during a period of time not to exceed one year; Provided, That the issuer has a bona fide intent to be engaged primarily, as soon as is reasonably possible (in any event by the termination of such period of time), in a business other than that of investing, reinvesting, owning, holding or trading in securities, such intent to be evidenced by:

(1)   The issuer's business activities; and

(2)   An appropriate resolution of the issuer's board of directors, or by an appropriate action of the person or persons performing similar functions for any issuer not having a board of directors, which resolution or action has been recorded contemporaneously in its minute books or comparable documents.

(b)   For purposes of this rule, the period of time described in paragraph (a) shall commence on the earlier of:

(1)   The date on which an issuer owns securities and/or cash having a value exceeding 50 percent of the value of such issuer's total assets on either a consolidated or unconsolidated basis; or

(2)   The date on which an issuer owns or proposes to acquire investment securities (as defined in section 3(a) of the Act) having a value exceeding 40 per centum of the value of such issuer's total assets (exclusive of Government securities and cash items) on an unconsolidated basis.

(c)   No issuer may rely on this section more frequently than once during any three-year period.

* * *

3c-4. Definition of "common trust fund" as used in section 3(c)(3) of the Act.

The term "common trust fund" as used in section 3(c)(3) of the Act (15 U.S.C. § 80a-3(c)(3)) shall include a common trust fund which is maintained by a bank which is a member of an affiliated group, as defined in section 1504(a) of the Internal Revenue Code of 1954 (26 U.S.C. § 1504(a)), and which is maintained exclusively for the collective investment and reinvestment of monies contributed thereto by one or more bank members of such affiliated group in the capacity of trustee, executor, administrator, or guardian; Provided, That:

(a)   The common trust fund is operated in compliance with the same State and Federal regulatory requirements as would apply if the bank maintaining such fund and any other contributing banks were the same entity; and

(b)   The rights of persons for whose benefit a contributing bank acts as trustee, executor, administrator, or guardian would not be diminished by reason of the maintenance of such common trust fund by another bank member of the affiliated group.

* * *

12b-1. Distribution of shares by registered open-end management investment company.

(a)   (1)   Except as provided in this section, it shall be unlawful for any registered open-end management investment company (other than a company complying with the provisions of section 10(d) of the Act (15 U.S.C. § 80a- 10(d))) to act as a distributor of securities of which it is the issuer, except through an underwriter.

(2)   For purposes of this section, such a company will be deemed to be acting as a distributor of securities of which it is the issuer, other than through an underwriter, if it engages directly or indirectly in financing any activity which is primarily intended to result in the sale of shares issued by such company, including, but not necessarily limited to, advertising, compensation of underwriters, dealers, and sales personnel, the printing and mailing of prospectuses to other than current shareholders, and the printing and mailing of sales literature.

(b) A registered, open-end management investment company ("Company") may act as a distributor of securities of which it is the issuer: Provided, That any payments made by such company in connection with such distribution are made pursuant to a written plan describing all material aspects of the proposed financing of distribution and that all agreements with any person relating to implementation of the plan are in writing: And further provided, That:

(1) Such plan has been approved by a vote of at least a majority of the outstanding voting securities of such company, if adopted after any public offering of the company's voting securities or the sale of such securities to persons who are not affiliated persons of the company, affiliated persons of such persons, promoters of the company, or affiliated persons of such promoters;

(2) Such plan, together with any related agreements, has been approved by a vote of the board of directors of such company, and of the directors who are not interested persons of the company and have no direct or indirect financial interest in the operation of the plan or in any agreements related to the plan, cast in person at a meeting called for the purpose of voting on such plan or agreements; and

(3) Such plan or agreement provides, in substance:

(i) That it shall continue in effect for a period of more than one year from the date of its execution or adoption only so long as such continuance is specifically approved at least annually in the manner described in paragraph (b)(2) of this section;

(ii) That any person authorized to direct the disposition of monies paid or payable by such company pursuant to the plan or any related agreement shall provide to the company's board of directors, and the directors shall review, at least quarterly, a written report of the amounts so expended and the purposes for which such expenditures were made; and

(iii) In the case of a plan, that it may be terminated at any time by vote of a majority of the members of the board of directors of the company who are not interested persons of the company and have no direct or indirect financial interest in the operation of the plan or in any agreements related to the plan or by vote of a majority of the outstanding voting securities of such company; and

(iv) In the case of an agreement related to a plan,

(A) That it may be terminated at any time, without the payment of any penalty, by vote of a majority of the members of the board of directors of such company who are not interested persons of the company and have no direct or indirect financial interest in the operation of the plan or in any agreements related to the plan or by vote of a majority of the outstanding voting securities of such company on not more than sixty days' written notice to any other party to the agreement, and

(B) For its automatic termination in the event of its assignment; and

(4) Such plan provides that it may not be amended to increase materially the amount to be spent for distribution without shareholder approval and that all material amendments of the plan must be approved in the manner described in paragraph (b)(2) of this section;

(5) Such plan is implemented and continued in a manner consistent with the provisions of paragraphs (c), (d), and (e) of this section;

(c) A registered open-end management investment company may rely on the provisions of paragraph (b) of this section only if selection and nomination of those directors who are not interested persons of such company are committed to the discretion of such disinterested directors;

(d) In considering whether a registered open-end management investment company should implement or continue a plan in reliance on paragraph (b) of this section, the directors of such company shall have a duty to request and evaluate, and any person who is a party to any agreement with such company relating to such plan shall have a duty to furnish, such information as may reasonably be necessary to an informed determination of whether such plan should be implemented or continued; in fulfilling their duties under this paragraph the directors should consider and give appropriate weight to all pertinent factors, and minutes describing the factors considered and the basis for the decision to use company assets for distribution must be made and preserved in accordance with paragraph (f) of this section;

(e) A registered open-end management investment company may implement or continue a plan pursuant to paragraph (b) of this section only if the directors who vote to approve such implementation or continuation conclude, in the exercise of reasonable business judgment and in light of their fiduciary duties under state law and under sections 36(a) and (b)(15

U.S.C. § 80a-35 (a) and (b)) of the Act, that there is a reasonable likelihood that the plan will benefit the company and its shareholders; and

(f)   A registered open-end management investment company must preserve copies of any plan, agreement or report made pursuant to this section for a period of not less than six years from the date of such plan, agreement or report, the first two years in an easily accessible place.

(g)   If a plan covers more than one series or class of shares, the provisions of the plan must be severable for each series or class, and whenever this section provides for any action to be taken with respect to a plan, that action must be taken separately for each series or class affected by the matter. Nothing in this paragraph (g) shall affect the rights of any purchase class under S 270.18f-3(e)(2)(iii).

* * *

17a-7.   Exemption of certain purchase or sale transactions between an investment company and certain affiliated persons thereof.

A purchase or sale transaction between registered investment companies or separate series of registered investment companies, which are affiliated persons, or affiliated persons of affiliated persons, of each other, between separate series of a registered investment company, or between a registered investment company or a separate series of a registered investment company and a person which is an affiliated person of such registered investment company (or affiliated person of such person) solely by reason of having a common investment adviser or investment advisers which are affiliated persons of each other, common directors, and/or common officers, is exempt from section 17(a) of the Act; Provided, That:

(a)   The transaction is a purchase or sale, for no consideration other than cash payment against prompt delivery of a security for which market quotations are readily available;

(b)   The transaction is effected at the independent current market price of the security. For purposes of this paragraph the "current market price" shall be:

(1)   If the security is a "reported security" as that term is defined in rule 11Aa3-1 under the Securities Exchange Act of 1934, the last sale price with respect to such security reported in the consolidated transaction reporting system ("consolidated system") or the average of the highest current independent bid and lowest current independent

offer for such security (reported pursuant to rule 11Ac1-1 under the Securities Exchange Act of 1934 if there are no reported transactions in the consolidated system that day; or

(2) If the security is not a reported security, and the principal market for such security is an exchange, then the last sale on such exchange or the average of the highest current independent bid and lowest current independent offer on such exchange if there are no reported transactions on such exchange that day; or

(3) If the security is not a reported security and is quoted in the NASDAQ System, then the average of the highest current independent bid and lowest current independent offer reported on Level 1 of NASDAQ; or

(4) For all other securities, the average of the highest current independent bid and lowest current independent offer determined on the basis of reasonable inquiry;

(c) The transaction is consistent with the policy of each registered investment company and separate series of a registered investment company participating in the transaction, as recited in its registration statement and reports filed under the Act;

(d) No brokerage commission, fee (except for customary transfer fees), or other remuneration is paid in connection with the transaction;

(e) The board of directors of the investment company, including a majority of the directors who are not interested persons of such investment company,

(1) Adopts procedures pursuant to which such purchase or sale transactions may be effected for the company, which are reasonably designed to provide that all of the conditions of this section in paragraphs (a) through (d) have been complied with,

(2) Makes and approves such changes as the board deems necessary, and

(3) Determines no less frequently than quarterly that all such purchases or sales made during the preceding quarter were effected in compliance with such procedures; and

(f) The investment company (1) maintains and preserves permanently in an easily accessible place a written copy of the procedures (and any modifications thereto) described in paragraph (e) of this section, and (2) maintains and preserves for a period not less than six years from the end of the fiscal year in which any transactions occurred, the first two years in an easily accessible place, a written record of each such transaction setting forth a description of the security purchased or sold, the identity of the

person on the other side of the transaction, the terms of the purchase or sale transaction, and the information or materials upon which the determinations described in paragraph (e)(3) of this section were made.

* * *

17e-1. Brokerage transactions on a securities exchange.

For purposes of section 17(e)(2)(A) of the Investment Company Act of 1940, a commission, fee or other remuneration shall be deemed as not exceeding the usual and customary broker's commission, if:

(a)   The commission, fee, or other remuneration received or to be received is reasonable and fair compared to the commission, fee or other remuneration received by other brokers in connection with comparable transactions involving similar securities being purchased or sold on a securities exchange during a comparable period of time;

(b)   The board of directors, including a majority of the directors of the investment company who are not interested persons thereof:

(1)   Has adopted procedures which are reasonably designed to provide that such commission, fee, or other remuneration is consistent with the standard described in paragraph (a) of this section;

(2)   Makes and approves such changes as the board deems necessary; and

(3)   Determines no less frequently than quarterly that all transactions effected pursuant to this section during the preceding quarter were effected in compliance with such procedures; and

(c)   The investment company (1) shall maintain and preserve permanently in an easily accessible place a written copy of the procedures (and any modification thereto) described in paragraph (b)(1) of this section, and (2) shall maintain and preserve for a period not less than six years from the end of the fiscal year in which any transactions occurred, the first two years in an easily accessible place, a written record of each such transaction setting forth the amount and source of the commission, fee or other remuneration received or to be received, the identity of the person acting as broker, the terms of the transaction, and the information or materials upon which the findings described in paragraph (b)(3) of this section were made.

* * *

17f-5. Custody of investment company assets outside the United States.

(a) Definitions. For purposes of this section:

    (1) Eligible Foreign Custodian means an entity that is incorporated or organized under the laws of a country other than the United States and that is:

        (i) A Qualified Foreign Bank or a majority-owned direct or indirect subsidiary of a U.S. Bank or bank-holding company;

        (ii) A securities depository or clearing agency that acts as a system for the central handling of securities or equivalent book-entries in the country that is regulated by a foreign financial regulatory authority as defined under section 2(a)(50) of the Investment Company Act of 1940; or

        (iii) A securities depository or clearing agency that acts as a transnational system for the central handling of securities or equivalent book-entries.

    (2) Foreign Custody Manager means a Fund's or a Registered Canadian Fund's board of directors or any person serving as the board's delegate under paragraphs (b) or (d) of this section.

    (3) Fund means a management investment company registered under the Act (15 U.S.C. § 80a) and incorporated or organized under the laws of the United States or of a state.

    (4) Qualified Foreign Bank means a banking institution or trust company, incorporated or organized under the laws of a country other than the United States, that is regulated as such by the country's government or an agency of the country's government.

    (5) Registered Canadian Fund means a management investment company incorporated or organized under the laws of Canada and registered under the Act pursuant to the conditions of Rule 7d-1.

    (6) Securities Depository means a system for the central handling of securities as defined in Rule 17f-4(a).

    (7) U.S. Bank means an entity that is:

        (i) A banking institution organized under the laws of the United States;

        (ii) A member bank of the Federal Reserve System;

      (iii) Any other banking institution or trust company organized under the laws of any state or of the United States, whether incorporated or not, doing business under the laws of any state or of the United States, a substantial portion of the business of which consists of receiving deposits or exercising fiduciary powers similar to those permitted to national banks under the authority of the Comptroller of the Currency and which is supervised and examined by State or Federal authority having supervision over banks, and which is not operated for the purpose of evading the provisions of this section, or

      (iv) A receiver, conservator, or other liquidating agent of any institution or firm included in paragraphs (a)(7)(i), (ii), or (iii) of this section.

(b) Delegation. A Fund's board of directors may delegate to the Fund's investment adviser or officers or to a U.S. Bank or to a Qualified Foreign Bank the responsibilities set forth in paragraphs (c)(1), (c)(2), or (c)(3) of this section, provided that:

    (1) The board determines that it is reasonable to rely on the delegate to perform the delegated responsibilities;

    (2) The board requires the delegate to provide written reports notifying the board of the placement of the Fund's assets with a particular custodian and of any material change in the Fund's arrangements, with the reports to be provided to the board at such times as the board deems reasonable and appropriate based on the circumstances of the Fund's foreign custody arrangements; and

    (3) The delegate agrees to exercise reasonable care, prudence and diligence such as a person having responsibility for the safekeeping of Fund assets would exercise, or to adhere to a higher standard of care, in performing the delegated responsibilities.

(c) Selecting an Eligible Foreign Custodian. A Fund may place and maintain in the care of an Eligible Foreign Custodian any investments (including foreign currencies) for which the primary market is outside the United States, and such cash and cash equivalents as are reasonably necessary to effect the Fund's transactions in such investments, provided that:

    (1) The Foreign Custody Manager determines that the Fund's assets will be subject to reasonable care, based on the standards applicable to custodians in the relevant market, if maintained with the custodian, after considering all factors relevant to the safekeeping of such assets, including, without limitation:

(i) The custodian's practices, procedures, and internal controls, including, but not limited to, the physical protections available for certificated securities (if applicable), the method of keeping custodial records, and the security and data protection practices;

(ii) Whether the custodian has the requisite financial strength to provide reasonable care for Fund assets;

(iii) The custodian's general reputation and standing and, in the case of a Securities Depository, the depository's operating history and number of participants; and

(iv) Whether the Fund will have jurisdiction over and be able to enforce judgments against the custodian, such as by virtue of the existence of any offices of the custodian in the United States or the custodian's consent to service of process in the United States.

(2) Contract. The Fund's foreign custody arrangements must be governed by a written contract (or, in the case of a Securities Depository, by such a contract, by the rules or established practices or procedures of the depository, or by any combination of the foregoing) that the Foreign Custody Manager has determined will provide reasonable care for Fund assets based on the standards specified in paragraph (c)(1) of this section.

(i) Such contract shall include provisions that provide:

(A) For indemnification or insurance arrangements (or any combination of the foregoing) such that the Fund will be adequately protected against the risk of loss of assets held in accordance with such contract;

(B) That the Fund's assets will not be subject to any right, charge, security interest, lien or claim of any kind in favor of the custodian or its creditors except a claim of payment for their safe custody or administration or, in the case of cash deposits, liens or rights in favor of creditors of the custodian arising under bankruptcy, insolvency, or similar laws;

(C) That beneficial ownership for the Fund's assets will be freely transferable without the payment of money or value other than for safe custody or administration;

(D)   That adequate records will be maintained identifying the assets as belonging to the Fund or as being held by a third party for the benefit of the Fund;

(E)   That the Fund's independent public accountants will be given access to those records or confirmation of the contents of those records; and

(F)   That the Fund will receive periodic reports with respect to the safekeeping of the Fund's assets, including, but not limited to, notification of any transfer to or from the Fund's account or a third party account containing assets held for the benefit of the Fund.

(ii)   Such contract may contain, in lieu of any or all of the provisions specified in paragraph (c)(2)(i) of this section, such other provisions that the Foreign Custody Manager determines will provide, in their entirety, the same or a greater level of care and protection for Fund assets as the specified provisions, in their entirety.

(3) (i)   Monitoring the Foreign Custody Arrangements. The Foreign Custody Manager must have established a system to monitor the appropriateness of maintaining the Fund's assets with a particular custodian under paragraph (c)(1) of this section, and the contract governing the Fund's arrangements under paragraph (c)(2) of this section.

(ii)   If an arrangement no longer meets the requirements of this section, the Fund must withdraw its assets from the custodian as soon as reasonably practicable.

(d)   Registered Canadian Funds. Any Registered Canadian Fund may place and maintain outside the United States any investments (including foreign currencies) for which the primary market is outside the United States, and such cash and cash equivalents as are reasonably necessary to effect the Fund's transactions in such investments, in accordance with the requirements of this section, provided that:

(1)   The assets are placed in the care of an overseas branch of a U.S. Bank that has aggregate capital, surplus, and undivided profits of a specified amount, which must not be less than $500,000; and

(2)   The Foreign Custody Manager is the Fund's board of directors, its investment adviser or officers, or a U.S. Bank.

* * *

17j-1. Certain unlawful acts, practices, or courses of business and requirements relating to codes of ethics with respect to registered investment companies.

(a)   It shall be unlawful for any affiliated person of or principal underwriter for a registered investment company, or any affiliated person of an investment adviser of or principal underwriter for a registered investment company in connection with the purchase or sale, directly or indirectly, by such person of a security held or to be acquired, as defined in this section, by such registered investment company:

   (1)   To employ any device, scheme or artifice to defraud such registered investment company;

   (2)   To make to such registered investment company any untrue statement of a material fact or omit to state to such registered investment company a material fact necessary in order to make the statements made, in light of the circumstances under which they are made, not misleading;

   (3)   To engage in any act, practice, or course of business which operates or would operate as a fraud or deceit upon any such registered investment company; or

   (4)   To engage in any manipulative practice with respect to such registered investment company.

(b)   (1)   Every registered investment company, and each investment adviser of or principal underwriter for such investment company, shall adopt a written code of ethics containing provisions reasonably necessary to prevent its access persons from engaging in any act, practice, or course of business prohibited by paragraph (a) of this section and shall use reasonable diligence, and institute procedures reasonably necessary, to prevent violations of such code.

   (2)   The requirements of paragraph (b)(1) shall not apply to any underwriter (i) which is not an affiliated person of the registered investment company or its investment adviser, and (ii) none of whose officers, directors or general partners serves as an officer, director or general partner of such registered investment company or investment adviser.

(c)   (1)   Every access person of a registered investment company or of an investment adviser of or principal underwriter for such investment company shall report to such investment company, investment adviser or principal underwriter of which he or she is an access person the

information described in paragraph (c)(2) with respect to transactions in any security in which such access person has, or by reason of such transaction acquires, any direct or indirect beneficial ownership in the security: Provided, however, That any such report may contain a statement that the report shall not be construed as an admission by the person making such report that he or she has any direct or indirect beneficial ownership in the security to which the report relates. For purposes of this section, beneficial ownership shall be interpreted in the same manner as it would be in determining whether a person is subject to the provisions of section 16 of the Securities Exchange Act of 1934 and the rules and regulations thereunder, except that the determination of direct or indirect beneficial ownership shall apply to all securities which the access person has or acquires.

(2)   Every report required to be made pursuant to paragraph (c)(1) shall be made not later than 10 days after the end of the calendar quarter in which the transaction to which the report relates was effected, and shall contain the following information:

(i)   The date of the transaction, the title and the number of shares, and the principal amount of each security involved;

(ii)   The nature of the transaction (i.e., purchase, sale or any other type of acquisition or disposition);

(iii) The price at which the transaction was effected; and

(iv)   The name of the broker, dealer or bank with or through whom the transaction was effected.

(3)   Notwithstanding the provision of paragraph (c)(1), no person shall be required to make a report:

(i)   With respect to transactions effected for any account over which such person does not have any direct or indirect influence or control;

(ii)   If such person is not an "interested person" of a registered investment company within the meaning of section 2(a)(19) of the Act, and would be required to make such a report solely by reason of being a director to make such a report solely by reason of being a director of such investment company, except where such director knew or, in the ordinary course of fulfilling his official duties as a director of the registered investment company, should have known that during the 15-day period immediately preceding or after the date of the transaction in a security by the director such security is or was purchased or sold

by such investment company or such purchase or sale by such investment company is or was considered by the investment company or its investment adviser;

(iii) Where the principal underwriter, as to which such person is an access person, (A) is not an affiliated person of the registered investment company or any investment adviser of such investment company, and (B) has no officers, directors, or general partners who serve as officers, directors or general partners of such investment company or any such investment adviser; or

(iv) Where a report made to an investment adviser would duplicate information recorded pursuant to Rules 204-2(a)(12) or 204-2(a)(13) under the Investment Advisers Act of 1940.

(4) Each registered investment company, investment adviser and principal underwriter to which reports are required to be made pursuant to this section shall identify all access persons who are under a duty to make such reports to it and shall inform such persons of such duty.

(d) Each registered investment company, investment adviser and principal underwriter which is required to adopt a code of ethics or to which reports are required to be made by access persons shall, at its principal place of business, maintain records in the manner and to the extent set forth below, and make such records available to the Commission or any representative thereof at any time and from time to time for reasonable periodic, special or other examination.

(1) A copy of each such code of ethics which is, or at any time within the past five years has been, in effect shall be preserved in an easily accessible place;

(2) A record of any violation of such code of ethics, and of any action taken as a result of such violation, shall be preserved in an easily accessible place for a period of not less than five years following the end of the fiscal year in which the violation occurs;

(3) A copy of each report made by an access person pursuant to this rule shall be preserved for a period of not less than five years from the end of the fiscal year in which it is made, the first two years in an easily accessible place; and

(4) A list of all persons who are, or within the past five years have been, required to make reports pursuant to this section shall be maintained in an easily accessible place.

(e)   As used in this rule

  (1)   "Access person" means:

   (i)   With respect to a registered investment company or an investment adviser thereof, any director, officer, general partner, or advisory person, as defined in this section, of such investment company or investment adviser;

   (ii)   With respect to a principal underwriter, any director, officer, or general partner of such principal underwriter who in the ordinary course of his business makes, participates in or obtains information regarding the purchase or sale of securities for the registered investment company for which the principal underwriter so acts or whose functions or duties as part of the ordinary course of his business relate to the making of any recommendation to such investment company regarding the purchase or sale of securities.

   (iii)   Notwithstanding the provisions of paragraph (e)(1)(i), where the investment adviser is primarily engaged in a business or businesses other than advising registered investment companies or other advisory clients, the term "access person" shall mean: any director, officer, general partner, or advisory person of the investment adviser who, with respect to any registered investment company, makes any recommendation, participates in the determination of which recommendation shall be made, or whose principal function or duties relate to the determination of which recommendation shall be made to any registered investment company; or who, in connection with his duties, obtains any information concerning securities recommendations being made by such investment adviser to any registered investment company.

   (iv)   An investment adviser is "primarily engaged in a business or businesses other than advising registered investment companies or other advisory clients" when, for each of its most recent three fiscal years or for the period of time since its organization, whichever is lesser, the investment adviser derived, on an unconsolidated basis, more than 50 percent of (A) its total sales and revenues, and (B) its income (or loss) before income taxes and extraordinary items from such other business or businesses.

  (2)   "Advisory person" of a registered investment company or an investment adviser thereof means:

(i)   Any employee of such company or investment adviser (or of any company in a control relationship to such investment company or investment adviser) who, in connection with his regular functions or duties, makes, participates in, or obtains information regarding the purchase or sale of a security by a registered investment company, or whose functions relate to the making of any recommendations with respect to such purchases or sales; and

(ii)   Any natural person in a control relationship to such company or investment adviser who obtains information concerning recommendations made to such company with regard to the purchase or sale of a security.

(3)   "Control" shall have the same meaning as that set forth in section 2(a)(9) of the Act.

(4)   "Purchase or sale of a security" includes, inter alia, the writing of an option to purchase or sell a security.

(5)   "Security" shall have the meaning set forth in section 2(a)(36) of the Act, except that it shall not include securities issued by the Government of the United States, bankers' acceptances, bank certificates of deposit, commercial paper and shares of registered open-end investment companies.

(6)   "Security held or to be acquired" by a registered investment company means any security as defined in this rule which, within the most recent 15 days, (i) is or has been held by such company, or (ii) is being or has been considered by such company or its investment adviser for purchase by such company.

* * *

22c-1. Pricing of redeemable securities for distribution, redemption and repurchase.

(a)   No registered investment company issuing any redeemable security, no person designated in such issuer's prospectus as authorized to consummate transactions in any such security, and no principal underwriter of, or dealer in, any such security shall sell, redeem, or repurchase any such security except at a price based on the current net asset value of such security which is next computed after receipt of a tender of such security for redemption or of an order to purchase or sell such security: Provided, That:

(1)   This paragraph shall not prevent a sponsor of a unit investment trust (hereinafter referred to as the "Trust") engaged exclusively in the business of investing in eligible trust securities (as defined in Rule 14a-3(b)) from selling or repurchasing Trust units in a secondary market at a price based on the offering side evaluation of the eligible trust securities in the Trust's portfolio, determined at any time on the last business day of each week, effective for all sales made during the following week, if on the days that such sales or repurchases are made the sponsor receives a letter from a qualified evaluator stating, in its opinion, that:

(i)   In the case of repurchases, the current bid price is not higher than the offering side evaluation, computed on the last business day of the previous week; and

(ii)   In the case of resales, the offering side evaluation, computed as of the last business day of the previous week, is not more than one-half of one percent ($5.00 on a unit representing $1,000 principal amount of eligible trust securities) greater than the current offering price.

(2)   This paragraph shall not prevent any registered investment company from adjusting the price of its redeemable securities sold pursuant to a merger, consolidation or purchase of substantially all of the assets of a company which meets the conditions specified in Rule 17a-8.

(b)   For the purposes of this section,

(1)   The current net asset value of any such security shall be computed no less frequently than once daily, Monday through Friday, at the specific time or times during the day that the board of directors of the investment company sets, in accordance with paragraph (e) of this section, except on:

(i)   Days on which changes in the value of the investment company's portfolio securities will not materially affect the current net asset value of the investment company's redeemable securities;

(ii)   Days during which no security is tendered for redemption and no order to purchase or sell such security is received by the investment company; or

(iii)   Customary national business holidays described or listed in the prospectus and local and regional business holidays listed in the prospectus; and

(2)   A "qualified evaluator" shall mean any evaluator which represents it is in a position to determine, on the basis of an informal evaluation of the eligible trust securities held in the Trust's portfolio, whether--

   (i)   The current bid price is higher than the offering side evaluation, computed on the last business day of the previous week, and

   (ii)   The offering side evaluation, computed as of the last business day of the previous week, is more than one-half of one percent ($5.00 on a unit representing $1,000 principal amount of eligible trust securities) greater than the current offering price.

(c)   Notwithstanding the provisions above, any registered separate account offering variable annuity contracts, any person designated in such account's prospectus as authorized to consummate transactions in such contracts, and any principal underwriter of or dealer in such contracts shall be permitted to apply the initial purchase payment for any such contract at a price based on the current net asset value of such contract which is next computed:

   (1)   Not later than two business days after receipt of the order to purchase by the insurance company sponsoring the separate account ("insurer"), if the contract application and other information necessary for processing the order to purchase (collectively, "application") are complete upon receipt; or

   (2)   Not later than two business days after an application which is incomplete upon receipt by the insurer is made complete, Provided, That, if an incomplete application is not made complete within five business days after receipt,

      (i)   The prospective purchaser shall be informed of the reasons for the delay, and

      (ii)   The initial purchase payment shall be returned immediately and in full, unless the prospective purchaser specifically consents to the insurer retaining the purchase payment until the application is made complete.

   (3)   As used in this section:

      (i)   "Prospective Purchaser" shall mean either an individual contract owner or an individual participant in a group contract.

      (ii)   "Initial Purchase Payment" shall refer to the first purchase payment submitted to the insurer by, or on behalf of, a prospective purchaser.

(d)   The board of directors shall initially set the time or times during the day that the current net asset value shall be computed, and shall make and approve such changes as the board deems necessary.

GLASS-STEAGALL ACT

(codified in scattered sections of 12 U.S.C.)

§ 16. Corporate powers of associations

[A national bank may have the power to] . . .

Seventh. To exercise by its board of directors or duly authorized officers or agents, subject to law, all such incidental powers as shall be necessary to carry on the business of banking; by discounting and negotiating promissory notes, drafts, bills of exchange, and other evidences of debt; by receiving deposits; by buying and selling exchange, coin, and bullion; by loaning money on personal security; and by obtaining, issuing, and circulating notes according to the provisions of title 62 of the Revised Statutes. The business of dealing in securities and stock by the association shall be limited to purchasing and selling such securities and stock without recourse, solely upon the order, and for the account of, customers, and in no case for its own account, and the association shall not underwrite any issue of securities or stock: Provided, That the association may purchase for its own account investment securities under such limitations and restrictions as the Comptroller of the Currency may by regulation prescribe. In no event shall the total amount of the investment securities of any one obligor or maker, held by the association for its own account, exceed at any time 10 per centum of its capital stock actually paid in and unimpaired and 10 per centum of its unimpaired surplus fund, except that this limitation shall not require any association to dispose of any securities lawfully held by it on August 23, 1935. As used in this section the term "investment securities" shall mean marketable obligations, evidencing indebtedness of any person, copartnership, association, or corporation in the form of bonds, notes and/or debentures commonly known as investment securities under such further definition of the term "investment securities" as may by regulation be prescribed by the Comptroller of the Currency. Except as herein after provided or otherwise permitted by law, nothing herein contained shall authorize the purchase by the association for its own account of any shares of stock of any corporation. The limitations and restrictions herein contained as to dealing in, underwriting and purchasing for its own account, investment securities shall not apply to obligations of the United States, or general obligations of any State or of any political subdivision thereof, or obligations of the Washington Metropolitan Area Transit Authority which are guaranteed by the Secretary of Transportation

under section 9 of the National Capital Transportation Act of 1969, or obligations issued under authority of the Federal Farm Loan Act, as amended, or issued by the thirteen banks for the cooperatives of any of them or the Federal Home Loan Banks, or obligations which are insured by the Secretary of Housing and Urban Development under title XI of the National Housing Act or obligations which are insured by the Secretary of Housing and Urban Development (hereafter in this sentence referred to as the "Secretary") pursuant to section 207 of the National Housing Act, if the debentures to be issued in payment of such insured obligations are guaranteed as to principal and interest by the United States, or obligations, participations, or other instruments of or issued by the Federal National Mortgage Association or the Government National Mortgage Association, or mortgages, obligations, or other securities which are or ever have been sold by the Federal Home Loan Mortgage Corporation pursuant to Section 305 or Section 306 of the Federal Home Loan Mortgage Corporation Act, or obligations of the Federal Financing Bank or obligations of the Environmental Financing Authority, or obligations or other instruments or securities of the Student Loan Marketing Association . . .

* * *

§ 20. Affiliation with organization dealing in securities; penalties

After one year from June 16, 1933, no member bank shall be affiliated in any manner described in subsection (b) of section 221a of this title with any corporation, association, business trust, or other similar organization engaged principally in the issue, flotation, underwriting, public sale, or distribution at wholesale or retail or through syndicate participation of stocks, bonds, debentures, notes, or other securities: Provided, That nothing in this paragraph shall apply to any such organization which shall have been placed in formal liquidation and which shall transact no business except such as may be incidental to the liquidation of its affairs.

For every violation of this section the member bank involved shall be subject to a penalty not exceeding $1,000 per day for each day during which such violation continues. Such penalty may be assessed by the Board of Governors of the Federal Reserve System, in its discretion, and, when so assessed, may be collected by the Federal reserve bank by suit or otherwise.

If any such violation shall continue for six calendar months after the member bank shall have been warned by the Board of Governors of the Federal Reserve System to discontinue the same, (a) in the case of a national bank, all the rights, privileges, and franchises granted to it under the National Bank Act, may be forfeited in the manner prescribed in sections 141, 222 to 225, 281 to

283, 285, 286, 501a, and 502 of this title, or, (b) in the case of a State member bank, all of its rights and privileges of membership in the Federal Reserve System may be forfeited in the manner prescribed in subchapter VIII of this chapter.

* * *

§ 21. Dealers in securities engaging in banking business; individuals or associations engaging in banking business; examinations and reports; penalties

(a)   After the expiration of one year after June 16, 1933, it shall be unlawful--

(1)   For any person, firm, corporation, association, business trust, or other similar organization, engaged in the business of issuing, underwriting, selling, or distributing, at wholesale or retail, or through syndicate participation, stocks, bonds, debentures, notes, or other securities, to engage at the same time to any extent whatever in the business of receiving deposits subject to check or to repayment upon presentation of a passbook, certificate of deposit, or other evidence of debt, or upon request of the depositor: Provided, That the provisions of this paragraph shall not prohibit national banks or State banks or trust companies (whether or not members of the Federal Reserve System) or other financial institutions or private bankers from dealing in, underwriting, purchasing, and selling investment securities, or issuing securities, to the extent permitted to national banking associations by the provisions of section 24 of this title: Provided further, That nothing in this paragraph shall be construed as affecting in any way such right as any bank, banking association, savings bank, trust company, or other banking institution, may otherwise possess to sell, without recourse or agreement to repurchase, obligations evidencing loans on real estate; or

(2)   For any person, firm, corporation, association, business trust, or other similar organization to engage, to any extent whatever with others than his or its officers, agents or employees, in the business of receiving deposits subject to check or to repayment upon presentation of a pass book, certificate of deposit, or other evidence of debt, or upon request of the depositor, unless such person, firm, corporation, association, business trust, or other similar organization (A) shall be incorporated under, and authorized to engage in such business by, the laws of the United States or of any State, Territory, or District, and

subjected, by the laws of the United States, or of the State, Territory, or District wherein located, to examination and regulation, or (B) shall be permitted by the United States, any State, territory, or district to engage in such business and shall be subjected by the laws of the United States, or such State, territory, or district to examination and regulations or, (C) shall submit to periodic examination by the banking authority of the State, Territory, or District where such business is carried on and shall make and publish periodic reports of its condition, exhibiting in detail its resources and liabilities, such examination and reports to be made and published at the same times and in the same manner and under the same conditions as required by the law of such State, Territory, or District in the case of incorporated banking institutions engaged in such business in the same locality.

(b)   Whoever shall willfully violate any of the provisions of this section shall upon conviction be fined not more than $5,000 or imprisoned not more than five years, or both, and any officer, director, employee, or agent of any person, firm, corporation, association, business trust, or other similar organization who knowingly participates in any such violation shall be punished by a like fine or imprisonment or both.

* * *

§ 32. Certain persons excluded from serving as officers, directors or employees of member banks

No officer, director, or employee of any corporation or unincorporated association, no partner or employee of any partnership, and no individual, primarily engaged in the issue, flotation, underwriting, public sale, or distribution, at wholesale or retail, or through syndicate participation, of stocks, bonds, or other similar securities, shall serve the same time as an officer, director, or employee of any member bank except in limited classes of cases in which the Board of Governors of the Federal Reserve System may allow such service by general regulations when in the judgment of the said Board it would not unduly influence the investment policies of such member bank or the advice it gives its customers regarding investments.

APPENDIX A

SAMPLE FORM N-1A PROSPECTUS

———————

(The sample prospectus reproduced in this Appendix is presented solely for illustrative purposes and not as an endorsement of the investments or investment advisers described therein.)

Dreyfus Large Company Value Fund

Investing in value stocks for
capital appreciation

PROSPECTUS June 1, 1998

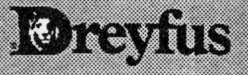

Contents

THE FUND

YOUR INVESTMENT

FOR MORE INFORMATION

Dreyfus Large Company Value Fund
Ticker Symbol: **DLCVX**

The Fund

GOAL/APPROACH

The fund seeks capital appreciation. To pursue this goal, it invests at least 65% of total assets in large-capitalization value companies (those whose total market value is more than $900 million). As of March 31, 1998, the fund's dollar-weighted average market capitalization was $33.4 billion. The fund's stock investments may include common stocks, preferred stocks and convertible securities of both U.S. and foreign issuers. The fund's economic sector weightings generally approximate those of the S&P 500® index.

Concepts to understand

Large companies: established companies that are considered "known quantities." Large companies often have the resources to weather economic shifts, though they can be slower to innovate than small companies.

Value companies: companies that appear underpriced according to certain financial measurements of their intrinsic worth or business prospects (such as price-to-earnings or price-to-book ratios). Because a stock can remain undervalued for years, value investors often look for factors that could trigger a rise in price.

In choosing stocks, the portfolio manager looks for value companies. The manager uses proprietary computer models to identify stocks that appear favorably priced and that may benefit from the current market and economic environment. The manager then reviews these stocks for factors that could signal a rise in price, such as:

- new products or markets
- opportunities for greater market share
- more effective management
- positive changes in corporate structure or market perception

The fund typically sells a stock when it is no longer considered a value company, appears less likely to benefit from the current market and economic environment, shows deteriorating fundamentals or falls short of the manager's expectations.

Information on the fund's recent strategies and holdings can be found in the current annual/semiannual report (see back cover).

MAIN RISKS

While stocks have historically been a leading choice of long-term investors, they do fluctuate in price. The value of your investment in the fund will go up and down, which means that you could lose money.

Because different types of stocks tend to shift in and out of favor depending on market and economic conditions, the fund's performance may sometimes be lower or higher than that of other types of funds (such as those emphasizing growth stocks). While there is the risk that a value stock may never reach what the manager believes is its full value, or may even go down in value, the fund's emphasis on large company value stocks could potentially limit the downside risk of the fund, because value stocks in theory are already underpriced and large company stocks tend to be less volatile than small company stocks. In the long run, the fund may produce more modest gains than riskier stock funds as a trade-off for this potentially lower risk.

In searching for attractive large company value stocks, the fund may invest a portion of its assets in foreign securities, which could carry additional risks such as changes in currency exchange rates, a lack of adequate company information and political instability.

Under adverse market conditions, the fund could invest some or all of its assets in money market securities. Although the fund would do this only in seeking to avoid losses, it could have the effect of reducing the benefit from any upswing in the market.

Other potential risks

The fund may invest some assets in options, futures and foreign currencies. It may also sell short. These practices are used primarily to hedge the fund's portfolio but may be used to increase returns; however such practices sometimes may reduce returns or increase volatility.

At times, the fund may engage in short-term trading, which could produce higher brokerage costs and taxable distributions.

The fund can buy securities with borrowed money (a form of leverage), which could have the effect of magnifying the fund's gains or losses.

PAST PERFORMANCE

The two tables below show the fund's annual returns and its long-term performance. The first table shows you how the fund's performance has varied from year to year. The second compares the fund's performance over time to that of the S&P 500®, a widely recognized unmanaged index of stock performance. Both tables assume reinvestment of dividends and distributions. As with all mutual funds, the past is not a prediction of the future.

What this fund is – and isn't

This fund is a mutual fund: a pooled investment that is professionally managed and gives you the opportunity to participate in financial markets. It strives to reach its stated goal, although as with all mutual funds, it cannot offer guaranteed results.

An investment in the fund is not a bank deposit. It is not FDIC-insured or government-endorsed. It is not a complete investment program. You could lose money in this fund, but you also have the potential to make money.

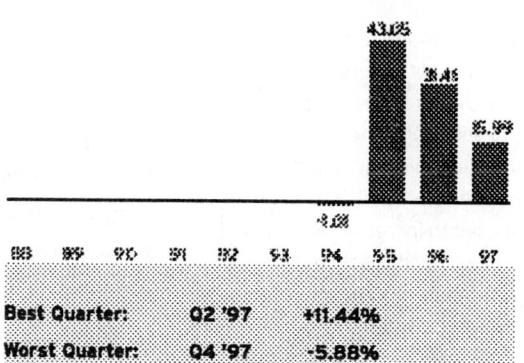

Year-by-year total return as of 12/31 each year (%)

Best Quarter:	Q2 '97	+11.44%
Worst Quarter:	Q4 '97	-5.88%

Average annual total return as of 12/31/97

	1 Year	3 Years	Inception (12/29/93)
Fund	15.99%	29.67%	20.96%
S&P 500® Index	33.35%	31.13%	22.94%*

* For comparative purposes, the value of the index on 12/31/93 is used as the beginning value on 12/29/93.

The fund's year-to-date total return as of 3/31/98 was 11.87%.

EXPENSES

As an investor, you pay certain fees and expenses in connection with the fund, which are described in the table below. Shareholder transaction fees are paid from your account. Annual fund operating expenses are paid out of fund assets, so their effect is included in the share price. The fund has no sales charge (load) or 12b-1 distribution fees.

Concepts to understand

Management fee: the fee paid to the investment adviser for supervising and assisting in the fund's management.

For the fiscal year ended October 31, 1997, Dreyfus waived a portion of its fee so that the effective management fee paid by the fund was 0.69%, reducing total expenses from 1.28% to 1.22%. This waiver was voluntary and is no longer in effect.

Service fee: a fee of 0.25% paid to the fund's distributor for shareholder account service and maintenance.

Other expenses: fees paid by the fund for miscellaneous items such as transfer agency, custody, professional and registration fees.

Fee table

Shareholder transaction fees
% of transaction amount

Maximum redemption fee	**1.00%**

charged only when selling shares you have owned for less than 15 days

Annual fund operating expenses
% of average daily net assets

Management fee	0.75%
Service fee	0.25%
Other expenses	0.28%
Total	**1.28%**

Expense example

1 Year	3 Years	5 Years	10 Years
$130	**$406**	**$702**	**$1,545**

This example shows what you could pay in expenses over time. It uses the same hypothetical conditions other funds use in their prospectuses: $10,000 initial investment, 5% total return each year and no changes in expenses. The figures shown would be the same whether you sold your shares at the end of a period or kept them. Because actual return and expenses will be different, the example is for comparison only.

MANAGEMENT

The fund's investment adviser is The Dreyfus Corporation, 200 Park Avenue, New York, NY 10166. Founded in 1947, Dreyfus manages one of the nation's leading mutual fund complexes, with more than $100 billion in more than 150 mutual fund portfolios. Dreyfus is the mutual fund business of Mellon Bank Corporation, a broad-based financial services company with a bank at its core. With more than $325 billion of assets under management and $1.6 trillion of assets under administration, Mellon provides a full range of banking, investment and trust products and services to individuals, businesses and institutions. Its mutual fund companies place Mellon as the leading bank manager of mutual funds. Mellon is headquartered in Pittsburgh, Pennsylvania.

The Dreyfus asset management philosophy is based on the belief that discipline and consistency are important to investment success. For each fund, the firm seeks to establish clear guidelines for portfolio management and to be systematic in making decisions. This approach is designed to provide each fund with a distinct, stable identity, and offers the potential for measuring performance and volatility in consistent ways.

Timothy M. Ghriskey, CFA, Senior Portfolio Manager and Head of Value Equities at Dreyfus, has managed the fund since September 1995. He joined Dreyfus in July 1995 after ten years as an analyst and money manager for Loomis Sayles & Co., and today manages several other funds at Dreyfus.

Concept to understand

Year 2000 issues: the fund could be adversely affected if the computer systems used by Dreyfus and the fund's other service providers do not properly process and calculate date-related information from and after January 1, 2000.

While year 2000-related computer problems could have a negative effect on the fund, Dreyfus is working to avoid such problems and to obtain assurances from service providers that they are taking similar steps.

FINANCIAL HIGHLIGHTS

This table describes the fund's performance for the fiscal periods indicated. "Total return" shows how much your investment in the fund would have increased (or decreased) during each period, assuming you had reinvested all dividends and distributions. These figures have been audited by Ernst & Young LLP, the fund's independent auditors.

	Year Ended October 31,			
	1997	1996	1995	1994[1]
Per-Share Data ($)				
Net asset value, beginning of period	18.05	15.46	12.63	12.50
Investment operations:				
Investment income – net	0.07	0.12	0.22	0.26
Net realized and unrealized gain (loss) on investments	4.33	4.68	2.93	(0.13)
Total from investment operations	4.40	4.80	3.15	0.13
Distributions:				
Dividends from investment income – net	(0.11)	(0.21)	(0.32)	–
Dividends from net realized gains on investments	(0.99)	(2.00)	–	–
Total Distributions:	(1.10)	(2.21)	(0.32)	–
Net asset value, end of period	21.35	18.05	15.46	12.63
Total return (%)	25.29	34.35	25.73	1.04[2]
Ratios/Supplemental Data				
Ratio of expenses to average net assets (%)	1.22	1.25	0.83	–
Ratio of net investment income to average net assets (%)	0.41	0.93	1.64	2.08[2]
Decrease reflected in above expense ratios due to actions by Dreyfus (%)	0.06	0.32	1.76	2.01[2]
Portfolio turnover rate (%)	110.14	186.39	143.61	48.35[2]
Net assets, end of period ($ x 1,000)	161,960	34,187	6,687	5,168

[1]From December 29, 1993 (commencement of operations) to October 31, 1994.

[2]Not annualized.

Your Investment

ACCOUNT POLICIES

Buying shares

You pay no sales charges to invest in this fund. Your price for fund shares is the fund's net asset value per share (NAV), which is generally calculated as of the close of trading on the New York Stock Exchange (usually 4:00 p.m. Eastern time) every day the exchange is open. Your order will be priced at the next NAV calculated after your order is accepted by the fund. The fund's investments are valued based on market value, or where market quotations are not readily available, based on fair value as determined in good faith by the fund's board.

Concepts to understand

Traditional IRA: an individual retirement account. Your contribution may or may not be deductible depending on your circumstances. Assets can grow tax-free; distributions are taxable as income.

Spousal IRA: an IRA funded by a working spouse in the name of a non-working spouse.

Roth IRA: an IRA with non-deductible contributions, tax-free growth of assets, and tax-free distributions to pay retirement expenses.

Education IRA: an IRA with nondeductible contributions, tax-free growth of assets, and tax-free distributions to pay educational expenses.

For more complete IRA information, consult Dreyfus or your tax professional.

Minimum investments

	initial	Additional
Regular accounts	$2,500	$100 $500 for Tele Transfer investments
Traditional IRAs	$750	no minimum
Spousal IRAs	$750	no minimum
Roth IRAs	$750	no minimum
Education IRAs	$500	N/A
Dreyfus automatic investment plans	$100	$100

All investments must be in U.S. dollars. Third-party checks cannot be accepted. You may be charged a fee for any check that does not clear. Maximum TeleTransfer purchase is $150,000 per day.

Selling shares

You may sell shares at any time. Your shares will be sold at the next NAV calculated after your order is accepted by the fund's transfer agent. Any certificates representing fund shares being sold must be returned with your redemption request. Your order will be processed promptly and you will generally receive the proceeds within a week.

Before selling recently purchased shares, please note that:

Written sell orders

Some circumstances require written sell orders, along with signature guarantees. These include:

- amounts of $100,000 or more
- amounts of $1,000 or more on accounts whose address has been changed within the last 30 days
- requests to send the proceeds to a different payee or address

A signature guarantee helps protect against fraud. You can obtain one from most banks or securities dealers, but not from a notary public. Please call us to ensure that your signature guarantee will be processed correctly.

- if the fund has not yet collected payment for the shares you are selling, it may delay sending the proceeds for up to eight business days
- if you are selling or exchanging shares you have owned for less than 15 days, the fund may deduct a 1% redemption fee (not charged on shares sold through the Automatic Withdrawal Plan or Dreyfus Auto-Exchange Privilege, or on shares acquired through reinvestment)

Limitations on selling shares by phone

	Minimum	Maximum
Check request	no minimum	$150,000 per day
Wire	$1,000	$250,000 for joint accounts every 30 days
TeleTransfer	$500	$250,000 for joint accounts every 30 days

There are no dollar limitations when selling shares by written request.

General policies

If your account falls below $500, the fund may ask you to increase your balance. If it is still below $500 after 45 days, the fund may close your account and send you the proceeds.

Unless you decline telephone privileges on your application, you may be responsible for any fraudulent telephone order as long as Dreyfus takes reasonable measures to verify the order.

Third-party investments

If you invest through a third party (rather than directly with Dreyfus), the policies and fees may be different than those described here. Banks, brokers, 401(k) plans, financial advisers and financial supermarkets may charge transaction fees and may set different minimum investments or limitations on buying or selling shares. Consult a representative of your plan or financial institution if in doubt.

The fund reserves the right to:

○ refuse any purchase or exchange request that could adversely affect the fund or its operations, including those from any individual or group who, in the fund's view, is likely to engage in excessive trading (usually defined as more than four exchanges out of the fund within a calender year)

○ refuse any purchase or exchange request in excess of 1% of the fund's total assets

○ change or discontinue its exchange privilege, or temporarily suspend this privilege during unusual market conditions

○ change its minimum investment amounts

○ delay sending out redemption proceeds for up to seven days (generally applies only in cases of very large redemptions, excessive trading or during unusual market conditions)

The fund also reserves the right to make a "redemption in kind" — payment in portfolio securities rather than cash — if the amount you are redeeming is large enough to affect fund operations (for example, if it represents more than 1% of the fund's assets).

DISTRIBUTIONS AND TAXES

The fund pays its shareholders dividends from its net investment income, and distributes any net capital gains that it has realized. Each of these distributions is generally paid once a year. Your distributions will be reinvested in the fund unless you instruct the fund otherwise. There are no fees or sales charges on reinvestments.

Fund dividends and distributions are taxable to most investors (unless your investment is in an IRA or other tax-advantaged account). The tax status of any distribution is the same regardless of how long you have been in the fund and whether you reinvest your distributions or take them as income. In general, distributions are taxable as follows:

Taxes on transactions

Except in tax-advantaged accounts, any sale or exchange of fund shares may generate a tax liability.

The table at right can provide a "rule of thumb" guide for your potential tax liability when selling or exchanging fund shares. The second row, "Short-term capital gains," applies to fund shares sold up to 12 months after buying them. The third row, "Medium-term capital gains," applies to shares held for more than 12 months but no more than 18. The last row, "Long-term capital gains," applies to shares held for more than 18 months.

Starting January 1, 2001, sales of securities held for more than five years will be taxed at special lower rates.

Taxability of distributions

Type of distribution	Tax rate for 15% bracket	Tax rate for 28% bracket or above
Income dividends	Ordinary income rate	Ordinary income rate
Short-term capital gains	Ordinary income rate	Ordinary income rate
Medium-term capital gains	15%	28%
Long-term capital gains	10%	20%

The tax status of the distributions for each calendar year will be detailed in your annual tax statement from the fund.

Because everyone's tax situation is unique, always consult your tax professional about federal, state and local tax consequences.

SERVICES FOR FUND INVESTORS

Automatic services

Buying or selling shares automatically is easy with the services described below. With each service, you select a schedule and amount, subject to certain restrictions. You can set up most of these services with your application or by calling 1-800-645-6561.

Dreyfus Financial Centers

Through a nationwide network of Dreyfus Financial Centers, Dreyfus offers a full array of investment services and products. This includes information on mutual funds, brokerage services, tax-advantaged products and retirement planning. Our experienced financial consultants can help you make informed choices and provide you with personalized attention in handling account transactions. The Financial Centers also offer informative seminars and events. To find the Financial Center nearest you, call **1-800-499-3327.**

For investing

Dreyfus Automatic Asset Builder®	For making automatic investments from a designated bank account.
Dreyfus Payroll Savings Plan	For making automatic investments through a payroll deduction.
Dreyfus Government Direct Deposit Privilege	For making automatic investments from your federal employment, Social Security or other regular federal government check.
Dreyfus Dividend Sweep	For automatically reinvesting the dividends and distributions from one Dreyfus fund into another (not available on IRAs).

For investing and for selling shares

Dreyfus Auto-Exchange Privilege	For making regular exchanges from one Dreyfus fund into another.

For selling shares

Dreyfus Automatic Withdrawal Plan	For making regular withdrawals from most Dreyfus funds.

Exchange privilege

You can exchange $500 or more from one Dreyfus fund into another (no minimum for retirement accounts). You can request your exchange in writing or by phone. Be sure to read the current prospectus for any fund into which you are exchanging. Any new account established through an exchange will have the same privileges as your original account (as long as they are available). There is currently no fee for exchanges, although you may be charged a sales load on any fund that has one.

Retirement plans

Dreyfus offers a variety of retirement plans, including traditional, Roth and Education IRAs. Here's where you call for information:

- for traditional, rollover, Roth and Education IRAs, call **1-800-645-6561**

- for SEP-IRAs, 401(k) and 403(b) accounts, call **1-800-322-7880**

- for Keogh accounts, call **1-800-358-5566**

Dreyfus TeleTransfer privilege

To move money between your bank account and your Dreyfus fund account with a phone call, use the Dreyfus TeleTransfer Privilege. You can set up TeleTransfer on your account by providing bank account information and following the instructions on your application.

Account statements

Every Dreyfus investor automatically receives regular account statements. You'll also be sent a yearly statement detailing the tax characteristics of any dividends and distributions you have received.

INSTRUCTIONS FOR REGULAR ACCOUNTS

TO OPEN AN ACCOUNT

TO ADD TO AN ACCOUNT

 — In Writing

TO OPEN AN ACCOUNT

Complete the application.

Mail your application and a check to:
The Dreyfus Family of Funds
P.O. Box 9387, Providence, RI 02940-9387

TO ADD TO AN ACCOUNT

Fill out an investment slip, and write your account number on your check.

Mail the slip and the check to:
The Dreyfus Family of Funds
P.O. Box 105, Newark, NJ 07101-0105

 — By Telephone

TO OPEN AN ACCOUNT

Wire Have your bank send your investment to The Bank of New York, with these instructions:
• DDA# 8900088133
• the fund name
• your Social Security or tax ID number
• name(s) of investor(s)

Call us to obtain an account number. Return your application.

TO ADD TO AN ACCOUNT

Wire Have your bank send your investment to The Bank of New York, with these instructions:
• DDA# 8900088133
• the fund name
• your account number
• name(s) of investor(s)

Electronic check Same as wire, but insert "1111" before your account number and add ABA# 021000018

TeleTransfer Request TeleTransfer on your application. Call us to request your transaction.

— Automatically

TO OPEN AN ACCOUNT

With an Initial Investment Indicate on your application which automatic service(s) you want. Return your application with your investment.

Without any Initial Investment Check the Dreyfus Step Program option on your application. Return your application, then complete the additional materials when they are sent to you.

TO ADD TO AN ACCOUNT

All services Call us to request a form to add any automatic investing service (see "Services for Fund Investors"). Complete and return the forms along with any other required materials.

— Via the Internet

Computer Visit the Dreyfus Web site, http://www.dreyfus.com and follow the instructions to download an account application.

TO SELL SHARES

Write a letter of instruction that includes:
• your name(s) and signature(s)
• your account number
• the fund name
• the dollar amount you want to sell
• how and where to send the proceeds

Obtain a signature guarantee or other documentation, if required (see "Account Policies – Selling Shares").

Mail your request to:
The Dreyfus Family of Funds
P.O. Box 9671, Providence, RI 02940-9671

Wire Be sure the fund has your bank account information on file. Call us to request your transaction. Proceeds will be wired to your bank.

TeleTransfer Be sure the fund has your bank account information on file. Call us to request your transaction. Proceeds will be sent to your bank by electronic check.

Check Call us to request your transaction. A check will be sent to the address of record.

Automatic Withdrawal Plan Call us to request a form to add the plan. Complete the form, specifying the amount and frequency of withdrawals you would like.

Be sure to maintain an account balance of $5,000 or more.

To reach Dreyfus, call toll free in the U.S.

1-800-645-6561

Outside the U.S. 516-794-5452

Make checks payable to:

The Dreyfus Family of Funds

You also can deliver requests to any Dreyfus Financial Center. Because processing time may vary, please ask the representative when your account will be credited or debited.

Concepts to understand

Wire transfer: for transferring money from one financial institution to another. Wiring is the fastest way to move money, although your bank may charge a fee to send or receive wire transfers.

Electronic check: for transferring money out of a bank account. Your transaction is entered electronically, but may take up to eight business days to clear. Electronic checks usually are available without a fee at all Automated Clearing House (ACH) banks.

TO SELL SHARES

Write a letter of instruction that includes:
• your name and signature
• your account number
• the fund name
• the dollar amount you want to sell
• how and where to send the proceeds
• whether the distribution is qualified or premature
• whether the 10% TEFRA should be withheld

Obtain a signature guarantee or other documentation, if required.

Mail in your request (see "Account Policies – Selling Shares").

Systematic Withdrawal Plan Call us to request instructions to establish the plan.

To reach Dreyfus, call toll free in the U.S.

1-800-645-6561

Outside the U.S. 516-794-5452

Make checks payable to:

Dreyfus Trust Co., Custodian

You also can deliver requests to any Dreyfus Financial Center. Because processing time may vary, please ask the representative when your account will be credited or debited.

Concepts to understand

Wire transfer: for transferring money from one financial institution to another. Wiring is the fastest way to move money, although your bank may charge a fee to send or receive wire transfers.

Electronic check: for transferring money out of a bank account. Your transaction is entered electronically, but may take up to eight business days to clear. Electronic checks usually are available without a fee at all Automated Clearing House (ACH) banks.

INSTRUCTIONS FOR IRAS

TO OPEN AN ACCOUNT	TO ADD TO AN ACCOUNT

 In Writing

Complete an IRA application, making sure to specify the fund name and to indicate the year the contribution is for.	Fill out an investment slip, and write your account number on your check. Indicate the year the contribution is for.
Mail your application and a check to: The Dreyfus Trust Company, Custodian P.O. Box 6427, Providence, RI 02940-6427	Mail in the slip and the check (see "To Open an Account").

By Telephone

————	**Wire** Have your bank send your investment to The Bank of New York, with these instructions: • DDA# 8900088133 • the fund name • your account number • name of investor • the contribution year
	Electronic check Same as wire, but insert "1111" before your account number and add ABA# 021000018
	Telephone Contribution Call to request us to move money from a regular Dreyfus account to an IRA (both accounts must have the same name).

 **Automatically**

Without any initial investment Call us to request a Dreyfus Step Program form. Complete and return the form along with your application.	**All services** Call us to request a form to add an automatic investing service (see "Services for Fund Investors"). Complete and return the form along with any other required materials.
	All contributions will count as current year.

Via the Internet

Computer Visit the Dreyfus Web site, http://www.dreyfus.com and follow the instructions to download an account application.	————

For More Information

Dreyfus Large Company Value Fund, a series of Dreyfus Growth and Value Funds, Inc.
SEC file number: 811-7123

More information on this fund is available free upon request, including the following:

Annual/Semiannual Report

Describes the fund's performance, lists portfolio holdings and contains a letter from the fund's manager discussing recent market conditions, economic trends and fund strategies.

Statement of Additional Information (SAI)

Provides more details about the fund and its policies. A current SAI is on file with the Securities and Exchange Commission (SEC) and is incorporated by reference (is legally considered part of this prospectus).

To obtain information:

By telephone
Call 1-800-645-6561

By mail Write to:
Dreyfus Family of Funds
144 Glenn Curtiss Boulevard
Uniondale, NY 11556-0144

By E-mail Send your request to info@dreyfus.com

On the Internet Text-only versions of fund documents can be viewed online or downloaded from:

SEC
http://www.sec.gov
Dreyfus
http://www.dreyfus.com

You can also obtain copies by visiting the SEC's Public Reference Room in Washington, DC (phone 1-800-SEC-0330) or by sending your request and a duplicating fee to the SEC's Public Reference Section, Washington, DC 20549-6009.

251P0698